D1573213

Resorts

Resorts

MANAGEMENT AND OPERATION

Robert Christie Mill, Ph.D.

School of Hotel, Restaurant, and Tourism Management
Daniels College of Business
University of Denver

John Wiley & Sons, Inc.
New York   Chichester   Weinheim   Brisbane   Singapore   Toronto

This book is printed on acid-free paper. ∞

Library of Congress Cataloging-in-Publication Data:

Mill, Robert Christie.
   Resorts : management and operation / by Robert Christie Mill.
      p. cm.
   ISBN 0-471-36188-7 (cloth : alk. paper)
      1. Resorts—Management. I. Title.
   TX911.3.M27 M538 2001
   647.94'068—dc21

                                                        00-043396

Printed in the United States of America.

10 9 8 7 6 5 4 3 2 1

To Patty

Contents

SECTION 3
Guest Activity Programming

Foreword

Perhaps no word in the English language evokes the immediate and electric response of the word *resort*. For an overworked, under-rested, and megastressed populace, a week at a resort is often seen as The Answer. It is salvation. It is the key to everything that ails, exhausts, and maddens us. The mantra of our time seems to be, "I don't have any problem that two weeks of sun and fun won't solve!" This visceral response to the word *resort* is the product of personal experience, lavish color photographs that leap from the pages of travel magazines and Web sites, and the gloating postvacation reports from coworkers who return from "ten days in heaven." Each of these sales, marketing, and public relations hits gives us a glimpse of the public face of the resort experience. And they make us yearn to be a part of it.

As current and future resort industry professionals, however, we can't be satisfied with the public facade. We have to dig deeper. To be successful, we have to be a little like Toto, who pulled back the curtain and unmasked the secret of the Wizard of Oz. We, too, need to look behind the scenes to get a clear understanding of what makes a resort a resort. We must study the sometimes overwhelming details, facts, figures, data, particulars, minutiae, fine points, and even the sweat that produces the awesome resort experiences that the world so eagerly anticipates.

It is no secret that, until now, this was not possible. There was no clear, comprehensive guide to understanding the myriad components of the modern resort. However, with the advent of Bob Mill's foundation textbook *Resorts: Management and Operation*, this void in the hotel, restaurant, and tourism management curriculum has been filled. As president and managing director of one of the world's most beloved resorts, I can only say, "Thank you, Bob! You have performed a great service for the entire resort management industry."

The fact is, having spent 13 years as general manager of commercial hotels and 17 years in resort management, I believe that hotel management and resort management are two entirely different industries. Ensuring that hotel operations run like clockwork, in a clean, carefree, and visually stunning environment, is just the beginning of resort responsibilities. As Bob's illuminating text clearly details, the modern resort is also responsible for meeting the needs of the widest variety of vacationing guest: golfers, boaters, skiers, snowboarders, adventure travelers, climbers, gamblers, backpackers, and cruise aficionados, at the least. Golf, in particular, is an absolute must for many resorts and, potentially, creates two seasons for the winter resort. Multiple sales and marketing programs must be developed that appeal to each of these market segments; retail shops must be built to provide merchandise specific to each group; guest activity programming must be developed to appeal to each sex separately, together, and with one eye keenly focused on age and cultural differences.

And don't forget children. Children must have their own planned activities each and every day. What about spas? In my experience, a true resort offers a complete spa—not just a hot tub, treadmills, and a weight rack. A spa offers, in gracious surroundings, a wide variety of treatments including exfoliation, spot and full-body treatments, water therapy, massage, aromatherapy, wet rooms, dry rooms, and combinations. The list of resort musts goes on and on and on. Clearly, a comprehensive book covering the facilities, operations, and activities of the resort is long overdue.

Thankfully, *Resorts* addresses each of these subjects in detail. If you are a developer considering the construction or purchase of a resort, this text gives you a road map for much of what your new facility will have to encompass. If you currently manage a resort, this book is a confirmation of the 1001 things you should be doing to ensure the growth and competitive position of your property. And, if you are in college—with your entire professional life ahead of you—this text is an excellent window onto the nuts-and-bolts, workaday world you may soon join.

Resort management, one of the great professions of the world, is often exhilarating. It is often rewarding. It is always a lot of hard work. But, frankly, even the hard work is pure enjoyment! In no other service industry can a group of like-minded individuals have such a profound impact on the physical and emotional well-being of their customers. We are guides through a world of fantasy—a world that soothes rattled nerves, calms pounding hearts, and envelops weary bodies in a delicious cocoon of heightened senses.

The challenge for our industry is to consistently deliver these experiences at a level beyond guest expectations. Our reward is obvious. It is the warm greeting from generations of the same family who return to our resorts year after year. It is the look of absolute contentment as a guest settles in to read a good book while surrounded by gardens of magnolias, begonias, and orchids—or a crystal blue ocean. Or both. And it is the wide-eyed excitement of a guest who regales an audience about a hole-in-one on #7 at Pebble Beach. Bob Mill's book is the first step in transforming each of these fantasies into breathtaking reality.

Ted J. Kleisner *(University of Denver 1967)*
President and Managing Director
The Greenbrier
White Sulphur Springs, West Virginia

Preface

Purpose

This book is the summary of over 20 years of thought, analysis, and research into the field of resort management. As I moved from teaching in a business-based hotel school into a department of park and recreation resources (both at Michigan State University), I developed the conviction that an academic program in resort management should be a blend of information from these two areas. Resorts are, in fact, a combination of three elements:

- ❖ recreational attractions that draw guests to the facility
- ❖ housing and food and beverage services that cater to people away from home
- ❖ activities to occupy guests during their stay

The traditional hotel school deals effectively with the second element. Departments of park and recreation resources traditionally address the topics of recreational facilities and guest activity programming, typically within the context of public rather than private recreation.

Development Process

Extensive secondary research unearthed few books on the subject of resort management. Whatever coverage there was focused on the hospitality angle. Much of the material was dated. I therefore developed new material using the few books on the topic and up-to-the-minute research material from trade and industry association groups.

Features

The text is written from a business viewpoint, yet takes into account the unique structure of resorts. Resort managers in ski areas, for example, should know something about the mountain on which their resort depends. They should know the process by which a virgin mountain is transformed into a viable ski area. They need to be aware of how to determine the capacity of the mountain. They are not—and this book will not turn them into—developers and planners. They do, however, need to know enough about planning and development to communicate effectively with these specialists.

Each section of the text has a philosophical basis for the principles and practices it describes. The first section focuses on the relationship between the natural resource base and the recreational facilities developed from that base. The belief is that it is both environmentally conscious and business-smart to develop facilities in such a way that the integrity of the natural base is maintained. This is, after all, the major reason guests visit. Management is doing nothing more than protecting its competitive differential advantage.

The second section describes how operating a resort is, indeed, different from operating a traditional hotel and explores the features that are unique. This section presumes a basic knowledge of hospitality operations.

The third section assumes that guest activity programming is crucial to producing satisfied guests. Good programming does not just happen; it is carefully planned for, thought about, and learned. It should be based on knowledge of the demographic, psychographic, and physical capabilities of each guest.

The sidebars are an important feature throughout the book. Titled Quick Getaways, they bring the text to life with practical examples of the principles it espouses. Provocative questions are intended to prompt readers to insert their own points of view into the book. To reinforce the book's theme of environmentally conscious development, each chapter has at least one sidebar devoted to issues surrounding the environment or sustainable tourism.

To assist instructors, an Instructor's Manual (ISBN: 0-471-40732-1) is available to qualified adopters. In addition, PowerPoint slides may be downloaded at www.wiley.com/college.

Acknowledgments

I am grateful to the faculty of the Department of Park and Recreation Resources at Michigan State University for exposing me to the specialized knowledge that goes into managing resorts that depend on the natural resource base for their success. In addition, they provided the foundation of the material on guest activity programming.

The administration at the University of Denver's Daniels College of Business in general and the School of Hotel, Restaurant, and Tourism Management in particular has always been supportive of my research and writing activities.

Design Workshop—in particular, Becky Zimmerman and Sara Fontaine— contributed the final chapter, numerous photographs of their many resort projects, and important material for many of the Quick Getaways.

Thanks to Wiley and JoAnna Turtletaub, who saw potential in this effort and provided guidance and encouragement throughout the process. Jennifer Mazurkie at Wiley, who oversaw production, is a very thorough and professional editor. The initial proposal would not have gone forward but for the detailed, helpful, and insightful reviews. The following people generously took the time to provide thoughtful comments and suggestions, the vast majority of which are incorporated into the book to make it an improved text:

Percival Darby, Florida International University
Donald Getz, University of Calgary
Thomas Jones, University of Nevada–Las Vegas

Michael R. Rogers and Jill Lamoureaux were especially helpful with developing Quick Getaways and Powerpoint slides. Terra J. Pugh, my research assistant, was tireless in her efforts on the instructor's manual. I, of course, take full responsibility for any errors.

Section 1
RECREATIONAL FACILITIES

Chapter 1
RESORTS: AN INTRODUCTION

INTRODUCTION

To understand where the resort industry is today, it is important to consider how resorts have evolved through the ages. A historical perspective leads to a picture of the modern types of resorts.[1] The differences between managing a traditional hotel and a resort are highlighted to complete this introduction.

HISTORY OF RESORTS

The sole purpose of a resort, in the classic sense, is to afford its users a place for escape or restoration from the world of work and daily care.

—CHUCK Y. GEE
Resort Development and Marketing

ROMAN EMPIRE Prior to the eighteenth century, pleasure travel was not available for the masses. Lack of time and money combined with poor transportation and a general lack of facilities to make travel something that one had to rather than wanted to do.

However, the roots of the resort concept can be traced to the Romans. Extending from the public baths, resorts were initially built in and around Rome before being developed for the pleasure of Roman legionnaires and consuls throughout the empire—from the coast of North Africa to Greece and Turkey, from southern Germany to St. Moritz in Switzerland, and on through England. In fact, Bath in England still has relics dating to A.D. 54, when it was known as Aquae Sulis (Waters of the Sun).

The first baths, introduced in the second century B.C., were small and modestly furnished. Men were separated from women. Later, the baths became integrated, larger, and more ornate. They served both health and social purposes. The public bath allowed for relaxation, while the sale of food and drink on the premises encouraged social interaction. A typical structure consisted of an atrium surrounded by recreational and sporting amenities, restaurants, rooms, and shops.

Outside the major centers of population, baths were located by mineral springs, which were known for their restorative powers. The Greeks had earlier associated mineral springs with the gods and had built holy wells and altars on the sites. Roman legions appropriated these sites for the construction of baths.

❖ Taking the waters at Bath, England. [Source: Author.]

The Roman Empire began to decline at the beginning of the fifth century A.D. Social life at the English resorts languished until the seventeenth century, when it was refueled by improvements in roads and the introduction of the stagecoach.

EUROPE In A.D. 1326, Colin le Loup, a Belgian ironmaster, was cured of a long-term illness by the iron-rich waters of a spring near Liège. As thanks, he developed a shelter there to welcome others. The popularity of the area grew so much it was renamed Spa, meaning fountain.

Back in England, King Charles II restored the monarchy in 1660 after years of Puritan rule. He spent time at the popular resorts of the day—Bath, Tunbridge Wells, and Harrogate. Thus began a long history of attractions being popularized by the rich and famous, a tradition that continues today. In other parts of the world, royalty continues to be the trendsetters, while in North America, stars of the popular culture determine the "in" places. There is an old saying in tourism that mass follows class. Destinations are initially made popular by a small band of influential people. This

❖ Historic European village. [Source: Design Workshop, Inc.]

puts the place on the map. Seeking to emulate this group, others are attracted to the location.

A second factor leading to the popularity of the spas was the endorsement of the medical profession. The waters of Tunbridge Wells, for example, were promoted as an aphrodisiac. Likewise, bathing in and even drinking saltwater was regarded as a cure for numerous diseases and helped promote seaside resorts. Popular activities at the baths included gambling, dancing, and other forms of entertainment, including concerts, grand parades, and the pump room, where health-seekers "took the waters."

The rise in popularity of the spas created a demand on the part of the affluent for more private facilities. This led directly to the development of the Swiss resort industry. Before railroads were built, guests traveled long distances over poor roads to arrive at their destination. Having spent so much time and effort in reaching the spa, they wanted to spend a long time—up to two months—to get their money's worth. This led to the development of facilities more extensive than those offered by a modest inn. In Zurich, the most famous resort was the Hotel Baur au Lac, opened by Johannes Baur in 1838. After several expansions, the hotel was completely rebuilt with an innovative design that still is used today. While all other hotels faced the town, Baur built the new resort facing Lake Lucerne. He became the first developer to recognize the benefit of a scenic view.

In the early 1800s, Switzerland was known as a summer resort. However, in 1860, several English visitors were convinced to stay on for the winter. Skating was already a favorite activity. In Switzerland, the guests were introduced to skiing and tobogganing. While the initial attraction was the promise of health cures, the popularity of the resorts was due more to the social activities organized by management. One example was the Bains de Monaco, renamed Le Mont Charles (Monte Carlo) in 1863. Operating in the winter months when traditional summer resorts were closed, it offered guests year-round gambling. While the health spa was the overt attraction, the real source of the resort's success was the gambling.

NORTH AMERICA The earliest resorts in the United States were developed in the East and, as in Europe, were established around spas. Resort hotels were opened in Virginia, New York, and West Virginia in the eighteenth century. At approximately the same time, the seaside resort became popular. Examples include Long Branch, New Jersey, and Newport, Rhode Island. The latter was a commercial port where molasses was distilled into rum, which was then traded for slaves from Africa. When the slave trade was abolished at the end of the eighteenth century, the town turned to tourism for its economic future. Wealthy southerners ventured north to escape the heat and malaria of South Carolina in the summer.

Amenities Early hotels were rather barren in terms of amenities. The forerunner of many upgraded facilities to be later found in resort hotels was not a resort hotel itself. The Tremont Hotel in Boston, built in 1829, is credited with introducing a number of innovations in service, including:

- ❖ elegant marble
- ❖ carved walnut furniture in private rooms
- ❖ a pitcher and bowl and free cake of soap in each guestroom
- ❖ gaslight instead of candles
- ❖ French cuisine and silver table service that included forks
- ❖ bellboys to handle guest luggage
- ❖ an "annunciator"—the forerunner of the room telephone

Civil War   The American Civil War changed the nature of many eastern resorts. Saratoga Springs, New York, had long catered to southern gentlemen who brought their horses (and their slaves) with them to race while they took the waters. As the popularity of the springs declined, the resort focused on its social activities. A new racetrack was built, but ultimately it could not compete with the higher purses at Newport and Monmouth Park in Long Branch, New Jersey. The resort turned to gambling and drew some interesting and some notorious characters until the early twentieth century, when reformists took their toll.

White Sulphur Springs, West Virginia, changed too after the war. A shortage of eligible men and a surplus of eligible women led the resort to position itself as a place to find a worthy husband. The addition of a railroad line through the town in 1868 gave it a leg up on the competition. Not until 1891 a spur was extended into Hot Springs, enabling The Homestead to compete successfully with the Greenbrier of White Sulphur Springs, as it does to this day.

Resort Cities   America's first resort city was Atlantic City. Developed in the late 1800s, it attracted the middle as well as the upper classes. It built the first boardwalk to accommodate those seeking the health benefits of sunshine and fresh air, the first amusement pier that extended over the Atlantic, and the Observation Roundabout—later renamed the Ferris wheel. The railroad

❖ Traditional resort, The Greenbrier, White Sulphur Springs, West Virginia. [Source: Design Workshop, Inc.]

brought day trippers; other guests stayed for the season in boarding-houses and resort hotels. Today, buses bring day gamblers from New York City and other metropolitan areas.

The Twentieth Century

The typical resort hotel in North America at the beginning of the twentieth century was a summer operation. Improvements in transportation changed the structure of resorts. The railroads were instrumental in opening up areas of the country that were previously inaccessible. Both railroads and resorts targeted the relatively few, very wealthy individuals who, before the enactment of a federal income tax law, had a great deal of disposable income.

Winter resorts did not become popular until the development of the automobile, which provided access to areas of the country suitable for winter vacations. California, in contrast, was the first area to develop as a warm winter resort, appealing to those looking to escape the winter cold. Florida, as a warm winter resort, was developed later and more slowly. There, Henry Flagler saw the importance of transportation in opening up new destinations and was instrumental in laying railroad tracks to the south of the state. By 1920, Florida had surpassed California in popularity as a winter retreat for North Americans.

The economy had barely climbed back from the stock market crash of 1929 when the Second World War erupted. Resort development was put on hold. The end of rationing after the war precipitated a period of economic prosperity. Leisure travel was available to a much broader segment of the population. The development of the interstate highway system in the 1950s gave the average American great mobility. The development of Disneyland in California in 1955 was followed by numerous other theme parks in the 1960s and 1970s. Disney World opened in 1971 in Florida and has set the standard for destination family resorts.

In the mid-1950s, the development of jet travel opened up, for North Americans, areas of Europe and the Pacific that were previously inaccessible. Air travel was still costly, however, and relatively few could afford it.

The early 1960s saw the development of the four-season resort. Realizing the risk involved in relying for business on one season of the year, hotels sought to develop year-round attractions. The Homestead added skiing in 1959, while resorts in Colorado extended their season by developing golf and tennis packages and summer music festivals. Others went after group business by constructing convention centers.

In Eastern Europe, Japan, and some parts of Western Europe, social tourism contributed to resort development. Social tourism involves

History of Resorts: Skiing

Skis were not widely used for recreational purposes until the mid-1800s. The first technological innovation that stimulated demand was the stiff toe-and-heel binding developed by Sondre Norheim of Telemark, Norway. The binding allowed the skier to perform long, gliding turns. By the end of the nineteenth century, skiing was growing in popularity in the United States. The Austrians, during the first three decades of the twentieth century, were responsible for developing the basic techniques of Alpine or downhill skiing. By 1930, the downhill and the slalom were recognized by the International Ski Federation, the sport's ruling body. The 1932 Olympics at Lake Placid, New York, resulted in even more American interest in the activity. By some accounts, as few as four U.S. ski areas were in operation in the early 1930s.

In 1934, at Gilbert's Hill in Vermont, the first ski lift was unveiled. A rope and a Model T engine dragged people up the slope for a dollar a day. Since then, innovations in technology, equipment, clothing, and instruction have resulted in skiing's increased popularity by making it easier and more comfortable for average skiers to enjoy the sport. For example, the 1930s and 1940s brought modern bindings with steel edges, which, by giving the skiers more control, led to easier turns.

The first chairlift was installed at Sun Valley in Idaho. The relative remoteness of this location led to the development of housing at the resort, thus beginning the marriage of skiing and real estate development.

While development was halted during World War II, two major events occurred as a result of the war that had a tremendous impact on the future of the industry. First, the Tenth Mountain Division, the most decorated American division of the war, developed a significant reputation for its skiing activities. After the war, many of its members migrated into the industry, including the founding members of the Aspen Skiing Corporation. Second, many of Europe's best skiers and instructors came to the United States, bringing their talent and European style.

Innovations in the 1950s, such as easier-turning metal skis, buckled ski boots, step-in bindings, slope-grooming machines, stretch pants, and the inauguration of the interstate highway system, all helped popularize the sport. Television coverage of the 1960 Winter Olympic Games, held in Squaw Valley, California, continued the momentum.

The condominium form of ownership was formally recognized in 1962 and helped cement the relationship between skiing and real estate development. Condos could be constructed at higher densities than single-family housing. Scarce area at the base of the mountain was used efficiently. In addition, condos were easy to rent for short periods during the ski season. These movements led to the development of Vail, Colorado, in 1962, as the first planned destination ski resort.

Great growth occurred in the next decades as the number of ski areas increased to 90 by 1947, over 200 by the late 1950s, and over 600 by the late 1960s. The 1970s, however, added only an additional hundred areas to the inventory.

In 1960, half of all ski sites were located in the West, with slightly less than 40 percent in the East. At the end of the growth decade of the 1960s, ski sites were more numerous in the East than in the West—50 percent in the East and approximately 33 percent in the West. Over the same period, the share of the Midwest and the South remained steady at 20 percent. Western areas, however, tend to be larger than those elsewhere and, as a consequence, account for more skier visits.

Though innovations in the 1970s continued to make skiing more accessible to more people with less ability, the development of ski areas was slowed by high land prices, significant interest rates, and the time and money required to obtain development approval due to an increased concern for the environmental impact of large-scale developments.

The growing popularity of cross-country skiing, which benefited from the development of waxless skis and increased concern for and appreciation of the environment, offered an opportunity to cultivate another market segment.

Skiing is heavily influenced by demographics. While many skiers participate in the activity well into their golden years, the rate of participation is a function of age. If people do not take up the sport early in life, chances are they will not later. Demand, then, is a direct function of population numbers. The number of teenagers declined significantly in the 1980s, causing concern throughout the industry. Children of the baby boomers, however, returned to the slopes not only as downhill skiers but also as snowboarders.

While concern over the flattening of the skier growth curve has been felt in most regions of the country, the rapid increase in snowboarding is cause for optimism. Overcoming initial problems when skiers and snowboarders came into contact, a growing number of resorts are developing runs specifically for snowboarders. As the sport becomes more mainstream, it is attracting people who have money to spend.

Source: Patrick L. Phillips, *Developing with Recreational Amenities: Golf, Tennis, Skiing, Marinas* (Washington, D.C.: The Urban Land Institute, 1986).

Questions: What factors were instrumental in the development of skiing as a recreational activity? To what extent are they still relevant today?

offering employees vacations that are wholly or partially subsidized. While government and unions subsidize much of the social tourism in Eastern Europe, the equivalent in Japan is the corporate resort that is owned and operated by a major company to provide vacations for white-collar workers. A common alternative in Western Europe is the holiday fund. Equal contributions are made by the employee, the company, and the government to provide funds that employees use for vacation travel.

LESSONS   Four things can be learned from a brief review of the history of resorts:

1. The history of transportation has, to a large extent, determined where, when, and what types of resorts have evolved.
2. The desire for pleasure travel is deep-rooted.
3. Resorts began as seasonal operations. To minimize the risk of relying on one season of the year, resorts developed year-round attractions and appealed to the group market.
4. Resorts develop through life cycles. To be successful, resorts have had to adapt to changes in transportation, consumer tastes, demographics, and competition.

TYPES OF RESORTS

[R]esort communities work best when they are not 100 percent resort but have a mix of full- and part-time residents. Full-time residents provide customers for the doctors, the lawyers, and the restaurants year round. [This] enables the community to provide a myriad of services that would not be possible with just seasonal residents.
—CHARLES E. FRASER
Founder and Chair, Sea Pines Company

Resorts can be characterized in terms of:

❖ proximity to primary market
❖ setting and primary amenities
❖ mix of residential and lodging properties[2]

PROXIMITY TO   Resorts are either destination resorts or nondestination resorts. The dif-
PRIMARY MARKET   ference depends on how far the resort is from its primary market; how visitors reach the resort; and the patterns of stay—how many times a guest

quick getaways 1.2

Resorts of the Catskills

The social history of the Catskills as a resort community is a function of the history of eastern cities in general and New York City in particular. The closeness of the mountains to the city meant that access was easy and travel costs were low. Resorts were developed to appeal to a growing urban middle class. The upward mobility of New York's ethnic groups, particularly its Jewish population, provided the market. Increases in leisure time and an improved standard of living resulted in increasing numbers of people with the time and money to enjoy this resort experience.

Guests who will live with strangers for a week or even a summer need to be reassured that they will find mutual respect and understanding. The homeyness of the Catskill resorts guaranteed that. They offered the sociability, conveniences, and amusements of the city in the mountains.

Two images come to mind when people think of the Catskills today—the mountains and the resorts. The natural beauty of the region was the primary attraction. As access to the mountains improved, resorts were developed to take care of visitor needs. In addition to fresh air and a relaxed vacation pace, many places offered pleasurable excitement to their guests. Balls, hayrides, county fairs, and baseball were all popular activities.

In addition to the growth of the cities, two other factors contributed to the character of Catskill resorts: family proprietorship and guest loyalty. Many of the resorts can trace their ownership roots through five generations. Over the years, they have survived changes in the economy with the help of family and friends—and loyal guests. At Sugar Maples, for example, guests can inscribe their names in concrete after 25 years of attendance.

The development of new programs to appeal to new market segments takes into account past traditions. Built on such a rich history, the resorts of the Catskills will need to continue to adjust to changing market and economic conditions.

Source: Betsy Blackmar, "Going to the Mountains: A Social History," in *Resorts of the Catskills* (New York: St. Martin's Press, 1979), 71–99.

Question: Identify the factors that contributed to the development of resorts in the Catskills. What changes will be necessary in these resorts to take advantages of changes in the market and economic environment?

visits, how long the stay is, and the quality of the setting. Destination resorts tend to be at least several hundred miles from the market. Visitors tend to fly rather than drive there and visit once a year for one to two weeks. Further, the resorts are located at places attractive enough to entice people to travel large distances to get there.

Nondestination resorts tend to be within a two- to three-hour drive of the primary market. Guests arrive by car, visit more frequently, and stay three to four days each time. As a result, destination resorts have a higher ratio of hotel rooms to second homes, than do regional resorts. Within these generalities, it should be mentioned that a resort may fit into both categories. Colorado resorts, for example, draw visitors from Denver several times over the season while also attracting people from Europe for a once-a-season experience.

SETTING AND PRIMARY AMENITIES

Visitors categorize resorts by their location and amenities. Defined thus, resorts can be either ocean resorts, lake/river resorts, mountain/ski resorts, and golf resorts.[3] Ocean resorts depend on the quality and extent of their beaches, views, climate, and water sports activities. Lake/river resorts obviously rely on water but rely even more on the recreational activities that are water-oriented than do ocean resorts. They are more likely to be located several hours by auto from the resident's home and marketed as second-home communities. Mountain/ski resorts have, in recent years, moved away from their traditional reliance on the winter season to become four-season resorts. Capitalizing on their spa heritage, many are using health as their theme. Mountain resorts in the West tend to be destination resorts, while those in the Midwest and Northeast, because of their proximity to large population bases, tend to be regional in scope.

The increased popularity of golf has helped spawn an increase in the number of resort properties themed around this activity. Growth is also a function of supply. As the number of waterfront locations expanded, fewer sites associated with water were available. As a result, golf course resort developments have sprung up in Florida, North Carolina, and southern California. They are also popular in desert settings, which, lacking water, rely on scenery, climate, and golf to attract visitors. Other resorts rely on specialized amenities, including tennis, equestrian facilities, ranches, health, natural attractions, sporting expeditions, and entertainment.

RESIDENTIAL AND LODGING PROPERTIES

Real estate people like to categorize resorts based on the type and mix of residential lodging facilities. This makes sense for the developer, as lodging is the major revenue source for the resort, accommodation planning takes a great deal of time, and housing plays a major part in defining the character of the resort.

Three types of real estate product are found in resorts:

1. hotels, which require a relatively modest financial investment
2. timeshares and other vacation ownership requiring a one-time investment of $5,000 to $100,000 and a weekly maintenance fee
3. second homes ranging from $50,000 to more than $500,000[4]

A resort can, in fact, contain all three types of facilities, thus forming a multiuse resort community (Table 1.1).

Resort Hotels The resort hotel is the most common form of resort development. The guest at a traditional hotel selects the property on the basis of convenience. For the business traveler, convenience might mean the hotel is close to the highway or to the businesses to be visited. For the leisure traveler, convenience translates into proximity to the beach or other tourist attractions. The resort hotel guest, on the other hand, visits the development simply for relaxation. A growing number of resort hotels, however, are seeking to attract the businessperson, usually as part of a conference or meeting. The company holding a business meeting in a self-contained resort setting keeps the outside distractions of a city to a minimum while utilizing the recuperative effects of recreation to improve business productivity.

Resort hotels differ from their commercial counterparts in other ways. They are located in areas that take advantage of attractive natural features, and they offer more amenities, either on site or with easy access to off-site facilities. They can range from as few as five rooms to as many

❖ TABLE 1.1 Resort Types by Residential/Lodging Types

Resort Hotels	Timeshare/Vacation Ownership	Second-Home Developments	Multiuse Resort Community
25 rooms or less	Timeshare	Resort condo	Resort hotels
25–125 rooms	Vacation ownership	Low-density	Timeshare/vacation ownership
125–400 rooms	Club ownership	Single-family	
400+ rooms	Interval ownership	Large planned community	Second-home development
	Fractional ownership		
	Vacation clubs		

Adapted from Dean Schwanke et al., *Resort Development Handbook* (Washington, D.C.: Urban Land Institute, 1997), 7–18.

as 1500 or more. Facilities under 25 rooms are independently owned and managed guesthouses, bed-and-breakfasts, inns, cabins, or motel-type properties. They tend to be located in rural areas and cater to short-stay guests.

Facilities in the 25- to 125-room range can include properties from the above group as well as small specialty resorts. Many are called lodges and cater to hikers, hunters, and skiers. Part of this category is the growing number of boutique resort hotels that cater to a small, upscale segment of the market. These are often located in beautiful and delicate settings that are not appropriate for larger-scale development.

Resort hotels ranging in size from 125 to 400 rooms tend to be affiliated with a chain and located in major resort areas. They can be either low-rise or high-rise, though they are usually more horizontal than vertical in design. They have large balconies and larger rooms than comparable commercial hotels, and offer more amenities as well. Hotels with more than 400 rooms are located in prime resort locations offering major attractions such as beach frontage (Florida, the Caribbean, and Hawaii), ski facilities (Colorado, Utah), large theme parks (Orlando), gaming (Las Vegas), and golf (Arizona, Palm Springs).

Timeshare and Vacation Ownership Resorts

Timesharing began in France in the late 1960s and was first seen in the United States in the 1970s.[5] Over 4100 timeshare resorts owned by over 3 million households are located in more than 80 countries.[6] The terms *vacation ownership* and *vacation club* are also used to mean *timeshare*. Timesharing is defined as "the right to accommodations at a vacation development for a specified period each year, for a specified number of years or for perpetuity."[7] Owners pay a lump sum up front, either in full or financed over a seven- to ten-year period, in addition to an annual maintenance, management, and operations fee. In 1999, weighted average prices of an interval week, low to high season, encompassed these ranges:

❖ studio: $7,000–$11,000
❖ one bedroom: $7,000–$11,000
❖ two bedrooms: $8,500–$14,500
❖ three bedrooms: $11,000–$15,500[8]

After the purchase, the owner pays an annual maintenance fee that, in 1998, averaged $344. The fee covers the cost of management and maintenance of the resort. Timeshare owners can exchange weeks through membership in exchange companies like Interval International and Resort Condominium International.

Entry into the field by such companies as Marriott, Hyatt, Hilton, Thomas Cook, and Disney has helped improve the image of the industry while blurring the distinction between timeshare and hotel. Expansion by these established companies also has an effect on the popularity of the concept. Forty percent of those interested in purchasing a timeshare prefer a branded product, while 21 percent rate it as very or extremely unimportant in their decision making.[9]

Timeshare Options. Several timeshare options are possible.[10] The *fixed week option* allows consumers to buy a specific week—for example, the first week in August. Under the *floating week option,* consumers buy a week within a given period. Consumers may buy one week within weeks 6 through 12. A *combination option* allows weeks in high-demand periods to be fixed and those in low-demand periods to float. School holidays, for example, might be fixed at a specific week, while, for the rest of the year, people buy the right to use the resort for a nonspecific week during the off-season. Four Season Resort Club operates by selling a fee-simple deed for both floating and fixed weeks.

Recently, resorts have introduced *points-based memberships,* which give members points that can be used to "buy" resort stays. Marriott Vacation Club International and Hilton Grand Vacations are both point-based programs. Times of high demand require more points than times of low demand. Guests can bank, borrow, or split up how and when they use their points. Many properties are finding that they can cut back on marketing expenses because they sell the points program to a captive audience. It is, however, initially confusing for the guest and, as such, more complex for the operating company to run.

Points programs make particular sense for a company with multiple sites. To work effectively, choices must be available for the customer, and multiple sites allow for this. The keys to successful implementation of a points system are:

- ❖ setting the dollar-per-point ratio and sending the corresponding message to the community
- ❖ having a staff sophisticated enough to track point values and inventory
- ❖ effective communication between the marketing staff and the operator
- ❖ implementing the technology and a central reservation system with sufficient capital to back it up[11]

Finally, the *club concept* does not involve any ownership of real estate. Instead, consumers buy shares or points in the club; these are exchanged for accommodation or travel. Hyatt's Hyatt Vacation Club and the Sunterra Corporation brand (Embassy Vacation Resorts, Westin Vacation Club Resorts, and Sunterra Resorts) are examples of the club-based concept.

Timeshare options have evolved in recent years. They started with traditional fixed units in a set week, then added a floating week option and, most recently, the flexible points option.[12]

Mixed-Use Developments. Increased numbers of resorts are utilizing mixed-use developments, which feature a timeshare component.[13] In the past, developers built a property, then created demand for it. Nowadays, the demand for timeshare products dictates production. Preferred configurations are:

- ❖ two-bedroom suite (55 percent)
- ❖ one-bedroom suite (27 percent)
- ❖ three-bedroom suite (16 percent)
- ❖ studio (2 percent)[14]

A major reason for mixed-use developments is the high cost of amenities. Because high-quality amenities cost a great deal of money, being able to spread out the use and cost of these facilities makes it cheaper for everyone. In addition to the cross-utilization of amenities, hotel guests are exposed to timeshare products and may well be induced to buy. In this way, timeshare operators can reduce their marketing costs. The timeshare component brings a steady stream of revenue into the resort; everyone benefits. It does, however, take an experienced staff to meet the differing needs of timeshare owners and hotel guests.

Financing. Because of the unique nature of timeshare financing, specialized timeshare lenders have emerged. The financing of a timeshare property is different from that of a traditional hotel. Most hotel mortgages are long-term deals wherein the payback comes from the hotel's cash flow, which is generated from daily operations. Timeshare loans, on the other hand, are shorter-term loans based on the developer's ability to market and sell interest in the timeshare.[15] In addition, the lending process is more complex because of the regulatory issues involved in timeshare.

However, in many respects, timeshare financing is simpler and more predictable than hotel financing. Both revenue and expenses are more foreseeable for timeshares. Once the timeshare unit is sold, revenue is accounted for. The hotel room has to be resold each and every night, with no guarantee that it will produce revenue. Hotels incur many costs whether they are full or empty, while timeshare costs are easier to predict. High customer satisfaction with and solid growth of timeshares, together with the financial characteristics noted above, means fewer timeshare defaults compared to hotels.

Industry Trends. The most significant trends in the timeshare industry are:

- ❖ *Hotel brand involvement*—Hotel companies are combining timeshare facilities with adjacent hotels to offer more vacation options to guests. The hotel industry is in the mature stage of its life cycle and sees the high-growth timeshare industry as a way of increasing occupancy. This, in turn, has added credibility to the timeshare industry.
- ❖ *Wall Street recognition*—The number of public companies in the industry has increased in recent years. Between 1995 and 1997, the total market capitalization increased from $282 million to over $1 billion. As more and more analysts and investors get involved in timeshares, the need for information about vacation ownership increases.
- ❖ *Consolidation*—As the industry develops, vacation ownership will be in the hands of fewer and better-capitalized companies. Large companies enjoy economies of scale in operations, sales and marketing, and facilities.
- ❖ *Flexibility*—As more and more people look for more frequent vacations for shorter periods of time at destinations located close to home, demand for flexibility from the guest will increase. In 1985, almost 85 percent of U.S. interval owners purchased fixed-time intervals. Ten years later, fixed-time intervals accounted for less than 30 percent of all intervals sold. Most intervals sold now offer some type of flexible time use system that does not tie owners to a specific time each year.[16]

Second-Home Developments

A second-home development consists of a project that consists primarily of second homes and does not include a resort hotel. A second home is "a home that is owned fee simple by an individual or family that also owns or rents another home as a primary residence."[17] While second homes are not necessarily found in resort areas, second-home *developments* are. They consist of a variety of types of properties—detached, attached, multifamily—and can be combined with other uses. The Miami region of Florida, the Phoenix region of Arizona, and the Palm Springs region of California are examples of combination retirement, primary-, and second-home developments.

Developments are one of four types:

1. *Resort condominiums* are usually high-rises located on oceanfronts.
2. *Small, low-density residential communities* are typically located close to a beach or lake.
3. *Single-family developments* incorporate a golf course or clubhouse.
4. *Large planned communities* include a variety of housing types as well as a number of amenities.[18]

Compared to primary homes, second homes place more emphasis on outdoor areas, they are developed at lower densities, and their design is less formal. They are managed under a long-term arrangement by a community association rather than by a developer or resort operator. However, the latter may be involved in the management of a principal amenity, such as a golf course.

Multiuse Resort Communities

A multiuse resort community combines two or more of the above categories of facilities. As such, they tend to be larger than the other types. By offering more than one type of ownership and use pattern, they can appeal to a larger variety of markets. Their amenity package is more extensive and usually consists of at least two major amenities, such as a beach and a golf course, or ski slopes and a golf course in a four-season format. As the needs of the resort user change, the development offers appropriate units for rent or purchase. A resort guest may end up buying a second home for eventual retirement. The diversity of property types requires more sophisticated management.

Cruise Ships

Cruise ships represent a specialized type of resort—for cruise ships are nothing more than floating resorts!

History. The steamship era had its beginnings in the 1840s, when Sir Samuel Cunard pioneered the first transatlantic scheduled liner trips. In 1957, transatlantic ship traffic reached a post–World War II high as some 1,036,000 passengers were transported on ocean liners. However, just as the automobile led to the demise of the train, the introduction of intercontinental commercial airline service precipitated the rapid decline in the use of ships as a scheduled passenger transportation mode. Although travel by ship remained strong for several years thereafter, air travel had, by 1958, eclipsed it in terms of volume of transatlantic passengers.

The decline was rapid. Passenger departures from New York fell from approximately 500,000 in 1960 to 50,000 in 1975. So great has been the decline in scheduled liner passenger transport volume that it has almost completely disappeared.

Cruising has taken the place of scheduled liner service. Ships originally built for ocean crossings do not make the best cruise ships. Ocean liners were large and heavy—built to withstand the rigors of the Atlantic Ocean. As a result, the fuel costs were great. As cruising took off, the lines built ships specifically for cruising. These ships were smaller—800 to 850 passengers and 20,000 tons—and lighter, with smaller cabins, larger deck space and public areas, and a lower ratio of staff to passengers. Fuel costs were also reduced by spending time in more ports, a move that satisfied passengers.

Market. About two-thirds of the passengers who cruise each year are from the United States. Cruise Lines International Association (CLIA) identifies two major segments as potential first-time cruisers:

1. The "want-it-alls" (11 million people, or 17 percent of the total vacation market) are the most likely to cruise. With an average age of 42 and average annual income of $53,000, they are workaholics and value what is fashionable and trendy. They enjoy shopping, fine dining, and nightlife. They need to be convinced that cruise vacations can meet their high vacation expectations. Thirty-seven percent of this segment—some 4 million people—are considered hot prospects—that is, likely to cruise within the next two years.
2. Comfortable spenders (16 million people, or 25 percent of the total vacation market) are the second most-likely group to buy a cruise vacation. With an average age of 44 and an annual income of $64,000, they are physically active and enjoy nightlife, fine dining, and gambling. They are most likely to presently vacation at resorts, especially beach resorts. Thirty percent (4.8 million people) are considered likely to cruise within the next two years.[19]

Some observers expect a few years of consolidation followed by steady growth.

Perceptions. The size of the cruise market is limited by a number of negative perceptions. First, ships are associated with isolation, storms, and seasickness. While the number of outbreaks of illness has declined in recent years, ships are vulnerable because of the close quarters and because many passenger are elderly. The Centers for Disease Control (CDC) runs a vessel sanitation program that performs unannounced inspections of ships docked in U.S. ports and publishes sanitation ratings in a document sent to travel agents. However, the agency's mission is more advisory than regulatory. It relies on voluntary compliance, as many ships are of foreign registry and sail in international waters. The CDC also helps in designing ships' galleys and sanitation systems, and trains kitchen crews in food handling and hygiene.[20]

It does not appear that the age or passenger-carrying capacity of the ship affects its vessel sanitation score. There is a weak indication that larger cruise ships and a moderate indication that higher per-diem prices produce better sanitation scores.[21] Modern equipment has been installed on older ships to help ensure sanitary conditions. Higher prices might mean that more money is available for training and the production of higher-quality food. The key is management.

A second negative perception is that ships are slow, cramped, and boring, with regimented activities. Cruises offer high levels of satisfaction, with the industry reporting an 85 percent repeat business ratio. However, the repeat factor is not very good. Of the 19 million Americans who have cruised, only 2.25 million (12 percent) repeat.[22]

The dominance of Americans in the cruise market has meant that strict standards have been imposed on all foreign flag carriers operating out of U.S. ports. Strict standards are expected in the areas of hygiene, safety, and financial protection for passengers in case of the collapse of the carrier.

Locations. The most important areas for cruises from the United States are the Caribbean, the Mexican Riviera, and Alaska. Seventy percent of all passengers leaving the United States cruise in these areas. The popularity of the Caribbean has been built on warm winter weather, good sailing conditions, the ability to visit a number of ports in a relatively short time, and the capacity of Miami International Airport to bring in passengers.

Approximately 15 percent of the total number of cruises sail out of San Diego and Los Angeles, mostly to the Mexican Riviera. Cruises to Alaska originate in San Francisco, Seattle, and Vancouver. Because of the Passenger Service Act of 1886, passengers on foreign vessels sailing from a U.S. port must visit a foreign port before docking at a second U.S. port. Thus, passengers leaving from Seattle may not disembark in Alaska unless they first visit a foreign port. The intent of the law is that foreign vessels (and most vessels operating out of the U.S. are foreign) will not carry U.S. passengers from one U.S. city to another. This, obviously, is a problem for Seattle. A popular package to Alaska is the seven-day fly-and-cruise package, which involves a one-way trip by ship and an air or land return. This type of tourism must originate in neighboring Vancouver, Canada. Restrictions on the number of cruise ships into Glacier Bay have placed limits on the growth of this market.

One reason for the growth of the U.S. market to the Caribbean was the deregulation of the airlines in 1978, which allowed cruise operators to offer cheap fly-cruise packages. Flights from northern cities were heavily subsidized. By flying to Florida, the time spent in warm weather was maximized. In theory, deregulation in Europe could offer the same boost to Mediterranean cruising. However, this deregulation must take into account the diversity of national markets and cannot benefit from economies of scale enjoyed in the United States. Growth in the Mediterranean occurred in the late 1960s and early 1970s as a result of lines expanding their fleets. The extra capacity generated additional interest from operators in the former West Germany and the United Kingdom. This interest coincided with significant growth in the overseas inclusive vacation market—the practice of packaging and selling all elements of the vacation as a single entity.

While Germany and the United Kingdom make up the largest market segments for Mediterranean cruises, the development of the market differs greatly in the two countries. In the United Kingdom, tour operators set up their own cruise divisions, negotiating charter deals with cruise lines. The initial effect was to increase the size of the market. However, lack of expertise in operating a cruise ship meant that the narrow profit margins that were a result of concentrating on volume and market share put companies at risk. Tour operators now have no operating responsibility for the cruise and tend to feature cruises in their vacation brochures on an open-sale basis with no charter commitments. A major problem for cruise operators in the United Kingdom is the difficulty of selling a rather sophisticated travel product through retail travel agents. By some estimates, fewer than one in ten travel agents is productive in terms of cruise sales because agents lack the skill to sell cruises.

In Germany, tour operators dominate the cruise booking market. In part, this is because a flight must be packaged in to get the vacationer from Germany to the Mediterranean. About 75 percent of the Mediterranean cruise market travels on tour-operated chartered ships.

Incentive travel accounts for 15 percent of all cruise berths; this rate may be higher in the United States. Yet, because cruise lines tend to be registered in foreign countries, they have been unable to penetrate the business or convention markets to a larger extent. Legal restrictions prevent the tax deductibility of convention-oriented expenses if they are incurred on a non–U.S. flag cruise vessel.

Marketing. Most cruise-line marketing has been oriented to capturing market share from other lines rather than to increasing the size of the total market. In the United States, travel agents sell about 95 percent of all sea vacations. Some lines have successfully found themselves a market niche. One Line has developed a unique package by combining three days in Disney World with four days of cruising. In addition to appealing to families who want a balanced vacation, the competition will find the product difficult to duplicate. Another niche has been developed by Windstar Sail Cruises. Aiming at affluent, active vacationers who normally would not cruise, Windstar markets cruises on a sail-cruising ship, which offers a wide variety of water sports activities and visits to remote, small islands that ships do not traditionally visit.

In terms of the size of ships, there are two trends. First, excess capacity in the industry has meant that operators are looking to larger ships to spread overhead and to capitalize on economies of scale. The cruise ships now being built are mainly in the 40,000-ton range. The commercial life of a cruise ship is about twenty years, but pressure is great to make a profit by the third year of operation. This has resulted in a selling orientation on the part of the operators to fill their berths through heavy price discounting. The corresponding battle for market share has done little to expand the size of the market for cruises. Ships are also becoming smaller, with the development of a number of vessels with a capacity of 150 passengers or fewer to cruise the more remote waters of the world.

Cruises share a kinship with other distinctive transportation offerings, such as traveling on the Orient Express train, in that they offer more a vacation experience than a transportation mode. The romance of cruising has been heavily promoted, and this was helped along by a popular television program known as *The Love Boat.* Today, cruise ships are like portable resort hotels that ply the waters of the Caribbean, Mediterranean, and other regions.

Special-interest or hobby-type cruises have grown, packaging such elements as theater, gourmet dining, bridge, flower arranging, water sports, jazz, country and western music, and many other themes and activities. This ties in closely with the trend toward vacation travel for the purpose of learning or improving on a leisure or recreation activity.

As with its correlate in history, the train, the ship also has considerable importance in tourism as an attraction. Examples of short-duration sightseeing cruise-ship attractions are abundant in North America and elsewhere. Characteristically, these cruises are for a day or less. Viewing scenic surroundings is the major focus of many of these operations, including those featuring the Thousand Islands (New York, Ontario), the Mississippi River, Muskoka Lakes (Ontario), Niagara Falls (New York, Ontario), and many others. Other cruises combine nostalgia with scenic viewing. Steamer and riverboat cruises are examples of these. One study of a restored steamer sightseeing cruise operation indicated that its appeals were in learning about the history of steamships and of the surrounding area, seeing the scenery, watching the visible operation of steam engines, and using the ship's dining/bar service.

RESORT MANAGEMENT

In addition to daily operations, a general manager's major duties and responsibilities can be divided into four broad categories: budgeting, on-site rental program responsibilities, board relations, and owner relations.
—ROBERT A. GENTRY, PEDRO MANDOKI, AND JACK RUSH
Resort Condominium and Vacation Ownership Management

Managing a resort is different from managing a commercial hotel in the following ways:[23]

- ❖ *Visitor market*—No matter how different resorts are from each other, they all seek to satisfy guests who have three fundamental needs:
  1. desire for a change of pace, getting away from the familiar
  2. desire to satisfy recreational interests while being entertained and stimulated
  3. desire to travel to interesting and attractive places[24]

  Resorts certainly attract conventions and group business. However, the scheduling of business meetings must be coordinated with recreational activities.
- ❖ *Facilities*—Because the average length of stay at a resort is longer than at a hotel, the facilities are different. Rooms, in general, are larger. More closet space is needed. Large amounts of land are

quick getaways 1.3

Resort Management: Developing a Service Culture

The Cornerstone Program at The Boulders, a resort in Carefree, Arizona, consists of ten principles by which employees provide excellent guest service:

1. the Zone (when anyone is within 5 feet of you, make eye contact, speak first, smile, use the guest's name)
2. ownership of the request
3. fiscal responsibility
4. ambassadorial attitude
5. adherence to image
6. phone etiquette
7. cleanliness
8. respect for priorities
9. personalization of the experience
10. having fun

The vision statement, "Seek opportunities to create memories," was developed to differentiate the resort from its competition. Once owners and management determined the vision statement and cornerstones, they identified 15 managers from all departments to become Cornerstone Coaches. These managers teach, promote the program, and remind staff of the cornerstones. The cornerstones are introduced

required for recreational facilities. Guests are looking to participate in a variety of activities as part of their total resort experience.

❖ *Location*—Guests are attracted to many resorts because of their remote location. Many guests travel considerable distances to "get away from it all" or to enjoy an area of natural beauty. This means that these properties must be self-contained. Support services, such as laundry and maintenance, must be provided. Transportation

once every two weeks in fifteen-minute training sessions. Some employees felt that they already knew the concepts. Some managers thought the program was silly. However, management support for the program was ensured by making such support part of the managers' evaluation.

Coaches must spend a great deal of time in preparing for and implementing the program—as many as six hours a week each. Despite the heavy time investment (and subsequent cost), the coaches' position is a coveted one and tryouts are needed to select new coaches.

Cornerstones are covered during new employee orientation. One month after starting, employees go to Cornerstone College, an interactive half-day session. Cornerstone Awareness Training is a refresher program that employees participate in after 90 days on the job.

Employees who do a good job of carrying out the cornerstones can be nominated for the Brag program and mentioned in the resort's monthly newsletter. Special employees are rewarded with specially struck coins that relate to a specific cornerstone. These coins can be redeemed for prizes and trips. A Memory Maker of the Month program has replaced the usual Employee of the Month practice. Each month, an employee is selected from the front and the back of the house and given a special lunch and prize.

This program has helped The Boulders retain employees in a tight labor market. Morale has improved.

In retrospect, management would have put more time and effort into planning the program and in examining each step prior to rollout. All managers would have been involved in the beginning to ensure their support. All would have gone through the training first before rolling out the program for the employees.

Source: Laurette Dube, Cathy A. Enz, Leo M. Renaghan, and Judy A. Siguaw, *The Key to Best Practices in the U.S. Lodging Industry* (Ithaca, N.Y.: Cornell University, 1999), 49–50.

Questions: What do you think of the cornerstones? Would you make any additions? deletions? What lessons can be learned about the development and implementation of such programs?

may need to be provided for employees. Similarly, shuttle service to and from the airport may have to be provided for guests.

❖ *Recreation*—A resort, by definition, is a place where people go for recreation. Most resorts specialize in one recreational type, such as beach activities, skiing, or tennis. However, it is economic folly to rely on one season of the year. One bad snow season, for example, can ruin the entire year. To combat this, resorts have attempted to become year-round attractions. In the Colorado mountains, for example, ski lifts are used to bring mountain bikes up the mountain in summer.

❖ *Seasonality*—Commercial hotels operate year-round. However, some resorts, by virtue of their location, are precluded from doing so. Seasonality produces particular problems. Each season, a new group of employees must be hired, trained, and motivated. Inventory management, particularly perishables, becomes a problem as the season comes to an end. When the resort is closed, security and maintenance are constant headaches. A season of 90 to 120 days places tremendous pressure on management to cover fixed costs for the year, variable costs for the season, and still make a profit.

❖ *Personnel attitude*—Resort guests have extremely high expectations of service. They expect to be pampered. In vacation ownership resorts, where units are actually bought, the guests are owners who like to be treated as such. This places great pressure on employees to perform at a high level.

❖ *Managers*—While all managers need to know about rooms, food and beverage, marketing, human resources management, and so on, resort managers must have additional knowledge in two areas: (1) the natural resource on which the resort is based, and (2) guest activity programming. A manager of a ski resort has to know something about the mountain. A resort specializing in golf must be managed by someone who knows the relationship between golf course layout and profitability.

Resort guests expect to participate in a number of activities. When a guest is on property for several days or weeks, a well-designed guest activity program is required to satisfy them. This means much more than offering a sleigh ride next Tuesday. Implementing a guest activity program involves specialized knowledge regarding leisure, recreation, and play. Programs must take into account the demographic, psychographic, and physical backgrounds of guests.

❖ *Corporate/employer responsibility*—Because many resorts are large and located in remote areas, they constitute a major, if not *the* major, piece of the local economy. As such, management takes on a certain responsibility to the community that goes beyond the responsibility of a hotel in a metropolitan area. The community may be totally dependent on the resort for its economic future. Management has to take this into account when making decisions to lay off employees during the off-season.

❖ *Employee housing*—The remote location of certain properties means that the resort may have to provide housing for its employees. This raises issues of employee privacy and access to services.

❖ *Labor skills*—Employees at resorts tend to rotate into different jobs both during the season and in the off-season. If there is no snow at a ski area, employees may find themselves working in maintenance. This is especially true in the off season, when being employed means being flexible and having multiple skills. Commercial hotel jobs tend to be more specialized and static throughout the year.

❖ *Sources of revenue*—Commercial hotels derive most of their revenue from rooms, food and beverage, and various minor operating departments. At a resort, retail sales are more important, as is revenue from recreational activities. Some properties derive a great deal of revenue from land sales.

❖ *Activity control*—Accounting statements are more complex in a resort than in a commercial hotel. Every recreational activity and retail outlet is a potential profit center, with separate profit and loss statements.

❖ *Balance sheet*—Land and fixed asset investment is greater in a resort than in a conventional hotel, which changes the look of the balance sheet. The large amount of land means the resort has few alternate commercial uses. The payback period—the number of years needed to repay the original investment—is longer for resorts because of the large investment in land and other fixed assets.

❖ *Resorts and traditions*—Traditions are more important for resorts than for other types of hotels. Many resorts cater to repeat guests who are attracted by annual festivals and theme weekends. They come back to enjoy the experience year after year.

SUMMARY

A brief history of resorts demonstrates that transportation has, to a large extent, determined where, when, and the type of resorts that have evolved; that the desire for pleasure travel is deep-rooted; that resorts developed year-round operations to minimize the risk of relying on one season of the year; and that resorts move through life cycles. Today, resorts can be characterized in terms of their proximity to primary markets, the setting and primary amenities, and the mix of residential and lodging properties. Managing a resort is different from managing a traditional hotel in a number of significant ways that will be explored in detail in the remaining chapters.

quick getaways 1.4

What Is Ecotourism?

The Ecotourism Society, in its *Definition and Ecotourism Statistical Fact Sheet,* defines ecotourism as "purposeful travel to natural areas to understand the cultural and natural history of the environment, taking care not to alter the integrity of the ecosystem, while producing economic opportunities that make the conservation of natural resources financially beneficial to local citizens."

- Ecotourism areas should be respected as the abode of local residents with their own traditions and customs.

- Ecotourism use should minimize negative effects on the local and natural environment as well as on local inhabitants.

- Ecotourism should contribute to the management of protected areas and improve the links between local communities and managers of protected areas.

- Ecotourism should procure economic as well as other social benefits for local inhabitants and maximize their participation in deciding what type of tourism and how much tourism should develop.

- Ecotourism should promote genuine interaction between hosts and guests as well as a real interest in the sustainable development and protection of natural areas.

- Ecotourism should supplement and complement traditional activities of the area without marginalizing them or attempting to replace them.

Source: National Ecotourism Strategy, Mexican Secretariat of Tourism in cooperation with the World Conservation Union, 1994.

ENDNOTES

1. Chuck Y. Gee, *Resort Development and Management*, 2nd ed. (East Lansing, Mich.: Educational Institute of the American Hotel and Motel Association, 1988), 26-50.

2. Dean Schwanke et al., Urban Land Institute, *Resort Development Handbook* (Washington, D.C.: Urban Land Institute, 1997), 4.

3. Ibid., 5.

4. Ibid., 7.

5. *The United States Timeshare Industry: Overview and Economic Impact Analysis* (Washington, D.C.: American Resort Development Association, 1997), 5.

6. *The Nevada Timeshare Industry: An Industry Overview and Economic Impact Analysis* (Washington, D.C.: American Resort Development Association, 1997), 1.

7. *The United States Timeshare Industry*, 5.

8. M.A. Baumann, "Segmentation Creates More Niches, Price Points," *Hotel and Motel Management*, 16 October 1999, p. 26.

9. M.A. Baumann, "Study Indicates Timeshare Buyers Have Carolinas on Their Minds," *Hotel and Motel Management*, 5 July 1999, p. 31.

10. Beverly Sparks and Jo Anne Smith, "Development of Timeshare Resort Management: Educational Opportunities," *Journal of Hospitality and Tourism Education* 11, no. 2/3 (1999): 54-59.

11. M.A. Baumann, "New Points System Points Industry in Right Direction," *Hotel and Motel Management*, 17 May 1999, p. 22.

12. Ibid.

13. M.A. Baumann, "Mixed-Use Projects Possess Right Ingredients," *Hotel and Motel Management*, 20 September 1999, p. 10.

14. M.A. Baumann, "Exchange Companies Provide Flexibility and Expertise," *Hotel and Motel Management*, 19 July 1999, p. 22.

15. M.A. Baumann, "Specialized Lenders Cater to Timeshares," *Hotel and Motel Management*, 3 June 1999, p. 20.

16. *United States Timeshare Industry*, 5-6.

17. Schwanke et al., *Resort Development Handbook*, 11.

18. Ibid., 12.

19. "CLIA Survey Aims to Help Agents Identify 'Likely' Cruisers," *Travel Weekly*, 7 October 1996, pp. 1, 4.

20. Marilyn Chase, "Avoid Rough Sailing on Vacation Cruises by Cautious Planning," *Wall Street Journal*, 1 July 1996, p. B1.

21. Bruce E. Martin, "The Cruise Ship Sanitation Program," *Journal of Travel Research* 33, no. 4 (Spring 1995): 29-38.

22. "Holland America Line President Pulls No Punches," *Tour and Travel News*, 25 September 1995, pp. 25, 29.

23. Gee, *Resort Development and Management*, 16-22.

24. Schwanke et al., *Resort Development Handbook*, 3.

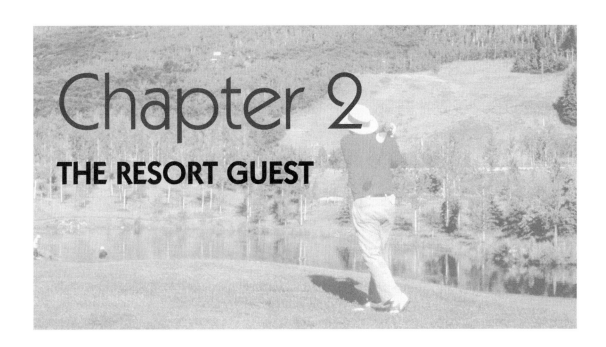

Chapter 2
THE RESORT GUEST

INTRODUCTION

Segments of the market for a resort vacation are outlined in terms of both their motivation and behavior and trends in the luxury market are noted. A detailed profile of important segments is given so readers have a clear picture of the characteristics of each.

SEGMENTS OF THE MARKET

In the post-1945 world, the tourist market became segmented; in the American West, nearly every resort and most national parks had options to suit almost every budget, especially in the places where an off-season remained.
—HAL K. ROTHMAN
Devil's Bargains

MOTIVATION Early attempts to define the U.S. travel market used the stated motivation as the basis for the segmentation. One national probability sample divided the U.S. market into six segments using benefits/motivations. The segments are:

❖ *Friends and Relatives: Nonactive Visitors*—Representing 29 percent of the market, these travelers look for familiar surroundings where they visit friends and relatives. They tend not to participate in activities.

❖ *Friends and Relatives: Active City Visitors*—An additional 12 percent of the population seeks out the familiar when they visit friends and relatives. However, this group is more inclined to see the sights, shop, and engage in cultural activities.

❖ *Family Sightseers*—Six percent of the market looks for new vacation places that would entertain and enrich their children.

❖ *Outdoor Vacationers*—The 19 percent who fall into this category want clean air, rest and quiet, and beautiful scenery. Recreation facilities are important for the numerous campers who are part of this segment. Children are also important.

❖ *Resort Vacationers*—Nineteen percent fall into this category. They are primarily interested in water sports and good weather. Popular places with a big-city atmosphere are preferred.

❖ *Foreign Vacationers*—Over a quarter of the market—26 percent—consists of people who seek destinations they have never been to before. A foreign atmosphere offering an exciting and enriching atmosphere with beautiful scenery is important. Good accommodations and service are more important than the cost.[1]

❖ Interactive public art, Aspen, Colorado. [Source: Design Workshop, Inc.]

BEHAVIOR   More recently, it has been suggested that segmentation on the basis of actual behavior is a better reflection of the market. It has been found that what people *say* they want is not necessarily what they actually *do*. A recent study of the U.S. population identifies three major market segments.[2]

1. *Getaway/Family Travelers* represents almost 38 percent of the total and is similar to the Nonactive Friends and Relatives, Family Sightseers, and Outdoor Vacationers noted above. They tend to visit places that are:
   ❖ a good place for children
   ❖ where friends and family live
   ❖ scenic
   ❖ places they can rest and relax
   ❖ full of friendly residents

❖ Proposed new
village, Sunday
River, Maine.
[Source: Design
Workshop, Inc.]

- ❖ within driving distance
- ❖ places where they can learn new things
- ❖ safe
- ❖ good mountain areas
- ❖ congestion-free

On the other hand, it is unimportant to them that the vacation destination is popular, that inclusive packages are available, or that variously priced accommodations are available.

2. *Adventurous/Educational Travelers* make up 31 percent of the market. This segment is similar to the Foreign Vacationers noted above. Adventurous Travelers tend to engage in cultural activities such as visiting museums, galleries, opera and theater. More than two-thirds visit places that:

- ❖ someone else they know had been to
- ❖ offer a number of things to see and do
- ❖ are famous cities or places
- ❖ have elegant dining
- ❖ offer a full range of hotel accommodations

They are less concerned with rest and relaxation, friendly locals, crime, congestion, clean air, and cost.

3. *Gamblers/Fun Travelers* represent just under 30 percent of the market and are linked to the Resort Vacationers in the previously mentioned study. They want a highly popular place where they can gamble, participate in recreation or sport, and enjoy a good night-life and fine dining. They are also concerned about price, the avail-ability of good beaches, sunbathing, and good weather. On the other hand, they are less concerned about cultural activities, being close to friends and relatives (while on vacation), and the presence of amusement parks.

TravelScope, a national survey, estimates that 9 percent of trav-elers gamble. In 1994, American households made 125 million visits to casinos, spending $16.5 billion.[3]

TRENDS IN THE LUXURY MARKET Recent research on the affluent market indicates various trends in upscale travel that have implications for resorts.[4] The LuxeReport is a compilation of more than 3500 survey responses from travel consultants serving afflu-ent clients who spend an average of $6,000 per person per trip. In this market in general, and among clients age 34 to 52, the following trends are on the rise:

	All	*34–52-year-olds*
❖ adventure travel	35%	22%
❖ traveling with children	24%	11%
❖ educational travel	10%	
❖ more frequent, shorter trips	9%	7%
❖ spa vacations	7%	
❖ cruises (especially top luxury and expedition)	31%	
❖ biking and walking trips abroad	7%	

TIMESHARE OWNERS

Colorado is best known for the breathtaking beauty of the Rocky Mountains, which are still visible in some areas peeking out from under a dense protective layer of condominium units.
—DAVE BARRY
Dave Barry's Only Travel Guide You'll Ever Need

There has been dramatic growth in the resort timeshare industry over the past two decades. The growth can be seen in the following numbers:

quick getaways 2.1

Segments of the Market: Convention, Meeting, and Leisure Guests

Abbey Group Resorts, which has three resorts in Wisconsin, has developed the Return Special Value Program (RSVP) to provide incentives to meeting planners and convention-goers to return to the resorts as leisure guests. Meeting attendees are given a future leisure stay at the lower group rate given by the resort that hosted the group. The group rate is good for one year but excludes certain holiday weekends.

The program was developed because the Abbey Group is a seasonal resort operator with shoulder seasons from April to the first two weeks in May and from late September through October. Even during the high season, space is available early in the week. The overall objective, then, is to increase year-round occupancy. A room that sells for $60 to $65 in the winter can go for three times as much during the summer. Thus, the meeting attendee has a strong financial incentive to book the space-available summer rate at the winter price.

The concept was developed in the spring and summer of 1998 by the director of sales and marketing, presented to the president and general managers, and implemented that same summer. The RSVP program is now included in sales presentations to meeting planners. The sales department finds that the program attracts the attention of the meeting planners and may actually result in more conventions being booked. The meeting planners can use the incentive for themselves at a later date, and they can (and do) use it as an incentive to increase attendance at the conference.

Source: "Abbey Group Resorts: Increasing Leisure Stays from Convention and Meeting Guests," *The Key to Best Practices in the U.S. Lodging Industry* (Ithaca, N.Y.: Cornell University, 1999), 33.

***Question:* What factors have to be taken into account in deciding whether or not to implement this program and others like it?**

	1978	1998
U.S. annual sales volume	$300 million	$3 billion
Number of timeshare resorts in the U.S.	240	1,200
Number of U.S. households owning timeshares	100,000	1.9 million[5]

As of 1998, 5 million timeshare owners worldwide held intervals in 5156 projects. Worldwide sales in 1998 were $6.1 billion, up 20 percent from 1994. The United States dominates the timeshare market with just under 40 percent of new intervals sold and half of the annual dollar sales. Europe is the second-largest area for timeshares, followed by South America. In Europe, the major countries with projects are Spain, Italy, France, and Portugal. Over 90 percent of those who own timeshares in Spain live outside the country. Significant percentages are also found for those with timeshares in Austria (91 percent), Portugal (75 percent), Greece (34 percent), and France (32 percent). The top six countries, in terms of number of timeshare projects, are:

Country	World Share
USA	33.2%
Spain	9.2%
Mexico	6.1%
Italy	3.6%
South Africa	3.5%
France	3.2%[6]

The average U.S. vacation ownership package includes two bedrooms and costs about $10,000. Over 89,000 timeshare units are offered at 1200 resorts in the United States, which dominates the world market, accounting for 37 percent of worldwide sales. Seven states account for approximately 60 percent of all units. Almost one-quarter of the U.S. timeshare industry is located in Florida, with Orlando having the greatest concentration. Significant development is also found in California, South Carolina, Hawaii, Colorado, North Carolina, and Texas.

TIMESHARE OWNERS Baby boomers, those presently in the 35 to 55 age group, make up 59 percent of the buyer market. The typical buyer is married, 50 years old, and has an average household income of $71,000. Over half have at least a bachelor's or associate's degree, and over a quarter have a graduate degree.

Residence Most timeshare owners live in the Northeast. Table 2.1 shows the residence of owners by location of resort. Florida attracts buyers from central and northeastern states, although one in eight buyers lives in Florida itself. The overwhelming number of timeshare owners in the Northeast live in that region. Most owners of southeastern units also live in that region, although significant percentages live in the Northeast and Central regions. Three-quarters of timeshare owners in the Central region have their primary residence there as well, while one in ten lives in the Southeast. Over 40 percent of Mountain timeshare owners live in that region too, while 25 percent and over 20 percent respectively live in the Central and Pacific regions. While over 70 percent of Pacific owners live in that region, one in eight resides in the Central region.

Purchase Motivation Eight out of ten owners state they are satisfied with their purchase. In fact, three-quarters of all owners recommend timeshares to friends. Why do people purchase timeshares? Four reasons are given:[7]

1. *Flexibility* over when, where, and how they vacation—The exchange opportunity has increased in importance over the past two decades and is the item noted most by buyers.[8]
2. *Economics*—Owners report they save money over the long term. This is the second most noted consumer motivation.[9]
3. *Certainty* about the availability and quality of popular resorts.
4. *Safety* and secure environments for family vacations.

❖ TABLE 2.1 Residence of Timeshare Owners by Resort Location

Residence Region	Location of Timeshares					
	Florida	Northeast	Southeast	Central	Mountain	Pacific
Florida	3					
Northeast	1	1	2			
Southeast			1	2		
Central	2		3	1	2	2
Mountain					1	
Pacific					3	1

Adapted from *The United States Timeshare Industry: Overview and Economic Impact Analysis* (Washington, D.C.: American Resort Development Association, 1997), 41.

Motivation varies by where the timeshare is located. Owners in Florida weigh the following factors more heavily than do owners in other regions:

❖ wanting to own in that resort area
❖ location of the resort in the area
❖ liking the timeshare unit, resort amenities, or resort features
❖ confidence in the timeshare company
❖ being treated well during the sales presentation
❖ leaving property to heirs
❖ chance to profit on rental or resale[10]

In contrast, owners in the Central and Northeast regions place less emphasis on the factors Florida owners consider important. Their major motivations involve the opportunity to take advantage of exchanges and the diversity of locations in the region. In the Pacific, the desire to return to the same resort each year scores much higher compared to other regions.

Hesitation About Buying When timeshare owners are asked about why they hesitated before buying, three reasons are prevalent. The primary concern is financial and concerns the initial purchase and the annual maintenance fee. Note that one of the motivations for purchasing was economic—the feeling that they would save money in the long run. To purchase, the potential owner must feel that the long-term savings will outweigh the initial and continuing costs. This factor is of particular importance to owners of Florida timeshares. Hawaiian owners note the high cost of travel to the resort as a negative factor.

Second, owners are concerned about using the timeshare enough to justify the expense of the purchase. This may reflect the increasing demands on people's time at home and in the workplace. This factor is of less importance to owners in the Northeast and Southeast and of highest importance to those in the Central region.

Third, owners worry that the resort experience will not meet the expectations created during the sales presentation. In fact, almost 20 percent indicated that high-pressure sales techniques caused them to hesitate before buying. The reputation of the timeshare industry has improved since the years when abuses occurred regularly. The poor image may remain in the minds of potential purchasers.[11]

Dissatisfaction Most owners are not interested in buying more time at any resort, either inside or outside of the United States. On the other hand, just under half are either very interested (22 percent) or somewhat interested in selling one or more of their U.S. timeshares.[12] The most common reasons given

quick getaways 2.2

Timeshare Owners

	1978	1982	1989	1993	1995	1998
❖ **Most Important Motivators for Purchasing Timeshares—Percentage Agreeing**						
Exchange opportunity	75	79	81	81	82	84
Save money on future vacation costs	63	65	59	65	61	60
Like resort, amenities, and/or unit	69	52	58	49	54	52
Certainty of quality accommodations	31	23	32	33	36	41
Opportunity to own at affordable price	27	19	21	22	20	20
Investment or resale potential	38	37	27	18	15	12
❖ **Reasons for Hesitating Before Purchase—Percentage Agreeing**						
Disliked idea of annual maintenance fee	NA	32	34	40	40	44
Concept was new or unfamiliar	32	37	39	38	38	36
Read or heard something negative about timeshare	NA	11	30	34	34	32
Was not sure would use it enough	24	36	33	35	32	40
Wondered if too good to be true	37	40	28	28	28	21
Cost too much	11	21	29	29	26	27
Sales presentation too high-pressured	NA	21	22	27	26	27
Did not want to be tied to fixed annual use period	17	24	16	16	15	NA
Travel to unit too expensive or inconvenient	4	12	10	13	14	12
Did not want to be tied to one resort location	12	16	11	11	11	NA
Concept was complicated to understand	6	9	6	8	7	8
Having to share with others	4	5	5	3	3	3

Source: Richard L. Ragatz and John C. Crotts, "U.S. Timeshare Purchasers: Who Are They and Why Do They Buy?" *Journal of Hospitality and Tourism Research* 24, no. 1 (February 2000): 55.

Questions: How have the motivations for purchasing and customer concerns changed over the years? Why do you think these changes have occurred? In what ways would a sales presentation have to be changed to take these factors into account?

are a change in lifestyle or personal situation and not using the timeshare enough to justify ownership. However, over half of all owners report they are very satisfied and another 30 percent are somewhat satisfied with their purchases. The two areas of concern to owners are the actions of their homeowners' association and their annual maintenance fees. These concerns are often due to a lack of communication between the association and the owners.

Use Patterns   Over 40 percent of timeshare owners report that, on average, they exchange their timeshare, while just under 40 percent report household use of the timeshare. Nine percent say their timeshare is not used at all, while smaller percentages give theirs away or rent it out. Florida owners report the highest household use, while those in the Northeast indicate the highest percentage of renting out their units. Few owners in the Southeast rent out their units. They also, relatively speaking, do not exchange their interest for time elsewhere. Less than one-third of Central owners actually use the timeshare they own themselves. In the Mountain region, slightly less than half, the highest percentage of all regions, exchange the timeshare for time elsewhere. Owners in the Pacific report the highest overall use and the second-highest use by the household.[13]

Party Composition   Approximately 40 percent of all U.S. timeshare vacation groups include children. Over half of all parties include two adults, while an additional fourth include four adults.[14] This explains the increased popularity of two- and three-bedroom purchases in many areas. The average length of stay in the timeshare is seven days. People spend an average of $36 per person per night, or $137 per night per party, in the local resort area.

TIMESHARE PLAN CHARACTERISTICS   Resorts offer timeshares in a variety of formats. Over 90 percent sell interval interests in increments of one week of use each year or as points offerings. Under a points-based system, consumers obtain a number of points that are redeemable each year for a number of accommodation nights that vary depending upon the season, day of week, size of unit, and resort location chosen. Biennial offerings show recent growth, particularly in Hawaii; these give the buyer one week of use every two years. Fewer than 10 percent of all resorts, primarily in the Mountain and Southeast regions, sell fractional interests offering several weeks of annual use. An even smaller market overall exists for undivided interests, whereby shares are sold on a ratio of multiple members per unit. While only one in 15 resorts nationwide offers this option, it is available for sale in one in five timeshare properties in the Mountain region.

Ownership   The standard type of ownership is the deeded week, offered by almost 90 percent of resorts. Customers feel more secure in their title than with other ownership options. The right-to-use form of ownership has, however, been increasing. Found mostly in Hawaii, due to the operation of many Hawaiian resorts on leased land, this form of ownership offers more flexibility to the customer. Overall, however, it is available at only one resort in ten.

Use   Timeshares can be used in a variety of ways. Most feature a fixed-week system that offers the customer the same one-week period each year. This was the industry norm until the mid-1980s, when a variety of more flexible options became available. Floating times within seasons allow customers to book any time, subject to availability, within a particular season. This type of plan is most commonly found in the Mountain and Pacific regions. One in five resorts overall, and more in Hawaii, allows a floating time year-round without seasonal restrictions. This type of plan is suitable only in areas that do not experience variability of seasonal demand. Finally, some resorts offer a points plan whereby the customer gets a vacation credit, expressed as a number of points, that can be redeemed for a varying number of nights based on season, day of week, unit size, and resort location. The number of resorts offering this flexible arrangement has increased in the past five years to the point where it is available in over 20 percent of facilities nationwide. The plan allows customers to split their total time into smaller intervals of less than one week. The so-called split-week option is most prevalent in the Mountain and Pacific regions. It is particularly useful to those who live in the same region as the resort and who can travel there often and at minimal cost.

Exchange   The vast majority of timeshare resorts are affiliated with companies that expedite exchanges to other properties. The reason is that exchange is the most important motivation that customers give for buying timeshares. The major organization of this sort is Resort Condominiums International (RCI), with which over 80 percent of properties are affiliated. Forty percent of resorts are affiliated with Interval International (II), the second-largest exchange organization. Over one-quarter of all resorts also run clubs or networks that offer owners the flexibility to vacation in other locations at different times of the year.

Bonus Time   Bonus time refers to nights that are not being used, as when the time was not sold or was not reserved by a member under a floating-time or points-based system. Bonus time is rented at a greatly reduced rate, with the net proceeds usually going to the property owners association.

Public Rentals   Units that are unsold or that are made available by owners can be rented by the public through the resort. Over half of all resorts rent unsold inventory to the public.[15]

SNOWSPORTS

Skiing offered a way to personally achieve the strong sense of individual control over raw nature that American travelers craved.

—HAL K. ROTHMAN
Devil's Bargains

DEMOGRAPHICS   By some estimates, alpine skiing accounts for almost 80 percent of the snowsport equipment market, while snowboarding, after a dramatic rise in participation in recent years, has 20 percent of the total market. Telemark skiing and snowskates are used by 1 percent each of winter-sports enthusiasts. About 75 percent of those who ski have never snowboarded. One in eight snowboarders has never skied, while a similar number has done both.[16] More snowboarders have skied than skiers have snowboarded.

More males than females participate in all snowsports. Snowboarders, alpine skiers, and telemark skiers are 69, 58, and 53 percent male respectively. Most alpine skiers and snowboarders call themselves intermediate participants, while telemark skiers are more likely to think of themselves as advanced or expert. A higher proportion of snowboarders than other snowsporters classify themselves as beginners.

Families with children make up over 40 percent of snowsport participants; singles without children account for an additional 35 percent. Families with children are more heavily represented among alpine skiers, while snowboarders are mainly single. Most snowboarders are in the 10- to 23-year-old age group, while most alpine skiers are between 40 and 54 years old. Telemark skiers are most likely to be between 25 and 35.

U.S. snowsporters are likely to be from California, Colorado, New York, Michigan, Massachusetts, and Ohio. Canadian skiers visiting the United States are more likely to ski at East Coast and Midwest resorts, while international skiers are more likely to visit resorts in the Rocky

quick getaways 2.3

Demographics at Some Top Ski Resorts

	Male	Female	Under Age 35
Aspen/Snowmass Ski Resorts Aspen, Colorado	57%	43%	18%
Breckenridge Ski Resort Breckenridge, Colorado	63%	37%	51%
Keystone Mountain Keystone, Colorado	69%	31%	34%
Killington Resort Sherburne, Vermont	57%	43%	49%
Mammoth Mountain Ski Area Mammoth Lakes, California	59%	41%	30%
Vail Resort Vail, Colorado	70%	30%	30%
Winterpark/Mary Jane Winterpark, Colorado	58%	42%	50%

Source: Stefan Fatsis and Daniel Costello, "Down a Slippery Slope," *Wall Street Journal*, 8 January 1999, pp. W1, W6.

Question: **What are the operational implications of the demographics of the various resorts profiled above?**

Mountains. Snowboarders are more likely to be from California, Washington, and Colorado, while telemark skiers are much more likely to be from Colorado and, to a lesser extent, from the Pacific Northwest.

Peak active skiing, as measured by the number of days skiers say they will ski, occurs between the ages of 15 and 26 and above the age of 60.[17] The younger segment is dominated by snowboarders. The latter group has much more free time. The lowest frequency of skiing is found among people constrained by time, job, family, and budget. These data point out the importance of introducing people to the sport early in their lives and seeking to retain skiers in their mid-50s, when the tendency to drop out is great. Because the younger segment has shown an interest in snowboarding, promotion of this activity is instrumental in expanding the market for snowsports.

SNOWBOARDERS Recent years have seen a dramatic increase in the number of snowboarders hitting the ski slopes. In many cases, considerable friction initially ensued between skiers and snowboarders, as they were different in many respects, from clothes to attitudes. However, as the number of snowboarders increased and the number of skiers leveled off, ski areas have become more accommodating of this new segment of the market. More than 90 percent of U.S. ski areas allow unrestricted access to snowboarders, while over three-quarters of all resorts indicate that snowboarding is important to their profitability. Teens new to skiing and snowboarding represent the major growth factor for the latter sport. Growth also results from teens and, to a lesser extent, skiers older than 20 crossing over from skiing.[18]

Nationally, over 20 percent of all resort visits are by snowboarders. Regionally, the Pacific West represents the highest participation, with one-third of all visits attributable to snowboarders. In the Northeast and the Rocky Mountains, the percentage of all visits attributable to snowboarders is lower than the national average. Smaller resorts, being closer to urban areas, more moderately priced, and attracting a younger crowd, are more popular among snowboarders than are larger resorts. It is expected that visits by snowboarders will increase at just under 10 percent a year through 2003.[19]

Less than half of all resorts actually track snowboarder visits. The larger the resort, the more likely it is that visits are tracked. Visits are tracked through on-slope surveys (the most popular method), lift counts, and ticket office surveys.[20]

Demographics Females account for 30 percent of all snowboarding visits, a figure expected to increase to 38 percent by 2003.[21] This latter figure is approximately the gender mix for skiing and is an indication that snowboarding is becoming more mainstream. Increased participation from females is expected in the larger resorts and those in the Rocky Mountains and the Pacific West.

Attitudes   While snowboarders and skiers are integrated at most resorts, friction still
exists. Acceptance is better at smaller resorts than at larger resorts. Most
snowboarders feel that relations between the two segments are getting
better. Improvements have come about because snowboarders have
gotten older, more skiers have tried snowboarding or have a snowboarder
in the household, skiers realize that snowboarding will not go away, and
resorts have shown a commitment to snowboarding through the construction of specialized facilities.

In addition, resorts have developed policies in an attempt to reduce
friction. Examples include:

❖ treating all guests alike

❖ accepting and showing respect for snowboarders

❖ strictly enforcing rule violations from skiers and riders alike

❖ educating snowboarders about rules and safety on the mountain

❖ maintaining an active on-slope ski patrol presence

❖ determining whether it is better to separate snowboarders from
   skiers or to let them mix (both have worked well at different
   resorts)[22]

Programs and   Virtually all resorts offer separate snowboard lessons and lessons for chil-
Facilities   dren. The average minimum age for the latter is six, with a range from two
to ten years. Almost all resorts rent snowboards, and over 90 percent offer
specialized repair services. While between 70 and 80 percent of resorts
have special racks, tools, and benches for snowboarders, less than 60 percent have retail shops selling snowboard equipment and less than a third
offer a separate snowboard shop. Resorts that do not have separate facilities give as reasons a lack of space, insufficient demand, or that they do
not wish to antagonize local ski shops.

Two-thirds of all resorts have special halfpipes for snowboarders.
These are more commonly found at larger rather than at smaller properties, as they require expensive grooming equipment and high maintenance. By comparison, more than 80 percent of resorts offer terrain parks.

Almost 90 percent of resorts run special snowboarding events to stimulate visits. It is anticipated that more resorts will schedule more events in
the future. Additionally, resorts are seeking to attract more snowboarders
by upgrading mountains, improving customer relations, offering special
beginner packages, designing snowboard-specific ads, and promoting fre-
quent-rider programs and product giveaway promotions.[23]

BOATERS

*There is **nothing**—absolutely nothing—half so much worth*
doing as simply messing about in boats.
                                            —KENNETH GRAHAME

INDUSTRY Marinas—the term is adapted from the Italian word for small harbor—
PROFILE have come to include any collection of slips for pleasure boats. Marinas
have developed from facilities "long on boatyard ambience and short on
creature comforts" to attractive, bustling waterfronts that often serve as
the key recreational attraction in a variety of types of development. They
have changed from being outgrowths of a boatyard or commercial harbor
to being more like fishing villages in appearance. The close relationship
between real estate, boats, and water has resulted in increased property
values. The International Marina Institute divides marinas into five business types:

❖ port authority
❖ private marina
❖ municipal marina
❖ boatyard
❖ destination resort

They define a destination marina as "accessible both by land and
water [and including] wet slips for visitors, hotel accommodations, restaurant facilities, swimming pool and other recreational amenities that creates a resort atmosphere."

The increased interest in boating is a function of a growing economy
that features increases in disposable income, leisure time, and individual
mobility. Technological advances also help. Polyester resins and fiberglass boats make boats essentially maintenance-free. Their development
led directly to the introduction of small sailboats and outboard-powered
runabouts.[24]

The National Marine Manufacturers Association (NMMA) estimates
that 74.5 million people participated in recreational boating in 1998 in
10.3 million boats. NMMA also estimates that there were 10,320 marinas,
boatyards, yacht clubs, dockominiums, and boat parks in 1998. The top
five states account for almost one-third of all the boat registrations in the
United States. In order, the top five states for boating registration in 1998
were:

quick getaways 2.4

Sea Shares

It may be that the next trend in timeshare is waterborne vacation ownership or "yachtsharing" in an urban marina setting. San Diego Yacht & Breakfast doing business as the Harbor Vacations Club, offers a flexible right-to-use program that is sold on the basis of a ten-year dock lease with the San Diego Port Authority. Watercraft are either permanently moored houseboat-style vacation villas or ocean-going luxury yachts as long as 50 feet.

Secure arrangements for docking facilities must be made through either a dock purchase or lease program. Typically, docks are leased from a harbor or port authority. The term of the lease determines the term of the sea shares. Likewise, yachts must be bought or leased. If leased, the terms should extend beyond the term of the sea share. Craft are insured for their replacement value, and any encumbrances against them are removed or subordinated to the interest of the sea share owner.

A decision has to be made as to whether the sea share interest will be an ownership interest or a right-to-use interest. If the latter is selected, what will the actual use rights be? Will owners have fixed-use periods in a specific craft, or will they have floating interests that allow reservations during specific seasons? A points-based reservation system is another possibility. This involves assigning a number of points to each sea share based on the equivalent to a one-week reservation in a single watercraft. Points are used to reserve as many nights as the owners have at their disposal, varying by the size and luxury of the craft and the desirability of the season.

Source: Arthur O. Spaulding Jr., "Selling Sea Shares by the Sea Shore," *Urban Land* (August 1998) vol. 57: 16–17.

***Question*: What are the advantages and disadvantages to potential boaters of the various options noted above?**

1. Michigan, with 8 percent of the total
2. California, with 7 percent
3. Florida, with 6 percent
4. Minnesota, with 6 percent
5. Texas, with 5 percent[25]

In the northern half of both U.S. coastlines, sailing is favored over power boating.

GOLFERS

Golf is a good walk spoiled.
—MARK TWAIN

PARTICIPATION According to the National Golf Foundation (NGF), close to 12 million golf travelers aged 18 or older were on the move in the United States in 1998. A golf traveler is defined as a golfer who plays golf at least once while traveling on business, vacation, or a golf-only trip. They played 72 million rounds of golf, 14 percent of all rounds played in the country in 1998. The number of golf travelers grew almost 50 percent from 1989 to 1998. Within the same period, the total number of golfers increased just over 6 percent. In the late 1980s, one-third of all golfers took at least one golf-related trip a year. Ten years later, nearly one-half of all golfers took at least one golf-related trip annually. The number of women making such trips has increased significantly in recent years; they now constitute over 20 percent of all golf travelers. It is estimated that each U.S. golfer spends over $2,000 on travel that includes golf.[26]

GOLF TRAVELER PROFILES Over half of all golf travelers are between the ages of 30 and 49. Two-thirds have a household income of more than $50,000. Nearly half of all golfers have golf-related travel in any year. The three types of golf traveler are business, vacation, or golf-only. A business golf traveler plays golf at least once while on a business trip. A vacation golf traveler plays golf at least once while on a vacation trip, while a golf-only golf traveler plays golf at least once while traveling on a golf-only trip. Vacation golf travelers represent 37 percent of all golfers, while golf-only travelers and business golf travelers represent almost 20 percent and 12 percent of all golfers respectively. (The sum of the three categories exceeds the total of nearly half of the entire golfing population because golfers may make a trip in more than one category.) Business travelers tend to be between 30 and 59 years

❖ Golfer, Aspen, Colorado. [Source: Design Workshop, Inc.]

of age and have higher incomes than other golf travelers, who are spread more evenly over the age categories.

Each golf traveler took an average of 6.6 trips in 1998, with business travelers taking twice as many as those in other categories. On average, just under three of these trips are golf-related. As might be expected, golf-only travelers play more rounds of golf when traveling than do those in the other categories (nine compared to seven and six for business and vacation golf travel respectively). The bottom line is that one in five business trips and nearly half of vacation trips taken by golfers include golf. Golfers, on average, play between 20 and 25 percent of the rounds played each year while traveling.

Golfers can be characterized as avid, moderate, or occasional based on the number of rounds they play annually. Avid golfers play 25 or more rounds a year, moderate golfers play 8 to 24 rounds a year, while occasional golfers play between 1 and 7 rounds a year. They represent 35 percent, 33 percent, and 32 percent of golf travelers respectively. Avid golfers are more likely to travel to play golf than are occasional golfers.[27]

PLANNING THE TRIP The most common source of information for planning a trip is friends, used by 60 percent of travelers. Golf-related magazines and books are used by 15 percent and travel guides by 12 percent. One in ten golf travelers uses the Internet.

The most important characteristics for golfers in selecting a destination are the overall price of the trip and the weather or climate at the destination. Golfers are least concerned with the presence of golf schools or the availability of lessons, spas, shopping in the area, and other family-type activities.

Six out of ten golfers plan their vacation themselves, while 15 percent rely on travel agents. Business travelers are less likely than others to plan the trip themselves and are more likely to use a travel agent. The automobile is the overwhelmingly preferred method of transportation, used in over 70 percent of trips. Commercial airlines are used in slightly less than half of all trips. As might be expected, business travelers are more likely than others to use commercial airlines and rental cars. The most popular U.S. destination for golf travel is Florida, which accounts for 30 percent of all golf travel. South Carolina, California, and Texas each get about 15 percent of all travel, followed in popularity by North Carolina, Arizona, and Nevada. Less than one in ten golf travelers visits international destinations. Their top choices are Mexico, Canada, England, Jamaica, the Bahamas, and the Cayman Islands.[28]

SPENDING Those who play golf while traveling spend over $24 billion on all travel-related expenses, an average of just over $2,000 per golf traveler. One-third is spent on lodging, just over half on transportation, and over 20 percent on food. Entertainment accounts for 10 percent of the total. Travel-related greens fees and golf car fees bring in an additional $1.8 billion. Business travelers spend more on transportation (commercial airline) and less on accommodation (trips are shorter) than do other golfers.

LATENT DEMAND A latent demand of 41 million people who are highly interested in golf and expect to play or play more frequently in the future is estimated. This group comprises four segments:

❖ *Current players*—Current players are some 14 million strong, who presently play less than 25 rounds per year.

❖ *Former golfers*—Twelve million former golfers (out of a total of 42 million adult former golfers) indicate that they have a high interest in becoming committed golfers. These people, though, have specific barriers inhibiting their return to the game (e.g., intimidating environment, cost of play, difficulty learning the game, and no one to play with).

❖ *Nongolfers*—Only about 7 million (representing about 5 percent) of the 130 million nongolfers are highly interested in the game. Golf is doing a good job of offering opportunities for those interested in trying the game. Many of the triers, though, quickly exit the game, having had an early experience insufficient to justify the time and expense involved. Interestingly, 60 percent of the nongolfer opportunity group is women (who comprise only 20 percent of the overall golf population). For golf to become a more satisfying experience for a wider range of people, particularly women, triers' early experiences must be enhanced and strengthened.

❖ *Junior golf opportunity*—Juniors represent another opportunity for the industry. There are 51 million juniors (ages 5 to 17) in the United States. Of these, 15 to 18 percent would like to play more. Less than 10 percent presently play golf. Juniors who presently play golf really enjoy the game, which is encouraging for the industry. Juniors who play golf like it nearly as much as team sports and more than other individual sports.

TAPPING LATENT DEMAND

The barriers inhibiting the 41 million high-potential golfers from playing or playing more often are all addressable at the course level. Course operators, for the most part, currently focus their attention on creating the best possible experience for the avid player. Services must be created to address the needs of a wider range of existing and potential players.

For instance, the NGF/McKinsey team suggests five actions facility owners and operators might consider in an effort to enhance the golf experience:

1. *Targeted programs*—Create a wider variety of programs designed to ease the entry and development of high-potential target groups (e.g., programs designed for women, mixed singles, parents/children, couples, etc.).
2. *Tailored products*—Develop products that appeal to a broader spectrum of golfers and that ease the transition from ranges to courses (e.g., better utilization and marketing of existing par-3, executive, and 9-hole courses; and more and better practice facilities).
3. *Dynamic pricing*—Provide special pricing in much the same way as airlines do. The golf product can be priced in many ways (e.g., by

time of day, day of week, group discounts, and frequent-player programs) to create value for both customer and owner.

4. *Skills training*—Make learning the game more fun and inviting. Golfers want to learn in a user-friendly and unintimidating environment. Golf instruction must become more than just swing mechanics; it should encompass strategy, course management, short game, and other important aspects of playing that a golfer must learn to become a genuinely committed player.

5. *Enriched understanding of golf*—Provide a stronger connection to golf's traditions and values. A valuable part of the golfing experience involves the history, traditions, etiquette, and other nuances of the game about which committed players are so passionate. Teaching these values enriches the golf experience and helps increase commitment among new players.[29]

Developing facility-level marketing plans that attract high-potential candidates will also be an important key to success. Each facility must develop a successful marketing strategy given their target customer and their available skills and assets.

It is important to remember that every industry stakeholder benefits from more players, more rounds, and more spending. Facilities alone cannot achieve this goal without industry help and cooperative effort. Creating a better experience for more people more often will require golf facilities and golf companies to work together more effectively than ever before via the formation of strategic partnerships and advertising cooperatives and the sharing of information.

The golf industry is at a crossroads. It may continue to grow at a slow but steady rate, or we may take advantage of a large and addressable opportunity to increase participation. Over 40 million people say they want to play or play more. Awareness and trial are at an all-time high. Most macrotrends are favorable. Now is an excellent time to take advantage of golf's growth opportunities.

A more successful future requires that industry stakeholders make concerted efforts to cultivate the ranks of committed golfers by eliminating barriers to play and improving the golfing experience for occasional and new players.

Action must take place primarily at the facility level, but facility owners and operators cannot be expected to do all this on their own. The brightness of the future depends on how well industry stakeholders can work individually and collectively for the growth of golf.

quick getaways 2.5

Golfers: What Do They Want to See?

Visual Preference Theory (VPT) indicates that people prefer:

- parklike views of manicured meadows with distinctive groups of large trees
- views that provide visual access
- inviting views
- wayfinding views
- views with an aura of mystery
- views of special cultural elements
- views with elevation changes
- views that include water

Source: David Jensen, "Points of View," *Urban Land* (August 1998) vol. 57: 66–69.

Question: Can you give examples of, or take pictures of, views illustrating the above points?

ADVENTURE TRAVELERS

Trails need to be reconstructed. Please avoid building trails that go uphill.

—Actual comment on a comment card
at a Forest Service trailhead

According to the Travel Industry Association of America (TIA), one-half of U.S. adults—98 million people—took an adventure vacation during the last five years of the twentieth century. Adventure travel can consist of either hard or soft activities. Hard adventure includes:

- ❖ backpacking across rugged terrain
- ❖ whitewater rafting, kayaking
- ❖ hot-air ballooning
- ❖ rock climbing or mountain climbing
- ❖ off-road biking, mountain biking
- ❖ hang gliding, parasailing, windsurfing
- ❖ parachuting or skydiving
- ❖ skateboarding, snowboarding
- ❖ roller hockey
- ❖ bungee jumping
- ❖ spelunking, cave exploring
- ❖ snorkeling, scuba diving
- ❖ survival games (e.g., paintball)[30]

Soft adventure encompasses:

- ❖ camping
- ❖ biking
- ❖ "gentle" hiking
- ❖ bird-watching
- ❖ animal-watching
- ❖ sailing
- ❖ horseback riding
- ❖ snow skiing
- ❖ water skiing
- ❖ canoeing
- ❖ visiting a cattle/dude ranch
- ❖ photo safari
- ❖ wilderness tours[31]

Of the 98 million people who take adventure vacation trips, 67 million, or two-thirds, take soft-adventure trips exclusively, 6 million take hard adventure trips only, and the remaining 25 million, or one-quarter, take both soft- and hard-adventure vacations. One-quarter of those who have not taken an adventure trip in recent years indicate that they are very or somewhat likely to do so in the next five years.

The most popular soft-adventure activities are camping, hiking on gradually changing terrain, and biking; for hard-adventure trips, the most popular choices are whitewater rafting/kayaking, snorkeling/scuba diving, and mountain biking. While men and women are equally likely to participate in adventure travel, men are more likely than women to participate in hard adventure. Participation is also related to age. Two-thirds of Generation Xers (ages 18–34), half of all Boomers (ages 35–54), and a quarter of those 55 or over have taken a recent adventure vacation. While the South, because of the large population base, generates the largest number of adventure travelers, the greatest proportion of residents who take such trips are found in the Western states. Over two-thirds of adventure travelers enjoy it periodically, while 10 percent describe themselves as fanatic. Another 10 percent did not enjoy the experience.[32]

HARD ADVENTURERS

The average hard-adventure traveler is 35 years old, has some college education, and is employed full time. Hard adventurers are more likely to be men, single, belong to Generation X, and work in a professional or managerial job. Seventy percent of soft adventurers have attended some college; two-thirds are married.[33]

Both soft- and hard-adventure travelers take an average of three adventure trips every five years. The former are likely to participate in several types of activities, while the latter are likely to engage in one activity only. Compared to hard adventurers, soft adventurers are more likely to take along a spouse, child, or grandchild, and less likely to take a friend with them on a trip. Hard-adventure travelers tend to spend more on trips than soft adventurers.

SOFT ADVENTURERS

As noted above, the most popular soft-adventure activities are camping, hiking on gradually changing terrain, and biking. Other popular pursuits are bird- and animal-watching, horseback riding, canoeing, and water skiing. Boomers are more likely to go hiking, while older adults are more likely to go bird- and animal-watching or on a photo safari. This latter segment is less likely to go biking, canoeing, horseback riding, snow skiing, and sailing. Generation Xers are most likely to go water skiing. Compared to men, women are more likely to go horseback riding or sailing. Boomers are most likely to bring a spouse and children on a trip, while Generation Xers typically travel with friends or parents/grandparents.[34]

The popularity of various activities is linked to regional geography. The Northeast is popular for biking, sailing, and photo safaris, the South for horseback riding, and the West for skiing. Westerners are most likely to list adventure as the primary motivator for a trip. Participation in high-cost activities such as sailing and skiing is proportional to household income.

quick getaways 2.6

Ecotourism for Tourists

The Tourism Industry Association of Canada has developed the following Code of Ethics for Tourists:

➤ Enjoy our diverse natural and cultural heritage, and help us to protect and preserve it.

➤ Assist us in our conservation efforts through the efficient use of resources, including energy and water.

➤ Experience the friendliness of our people and the welcoming spirit of our communities. Help us preserve these attributes by respecting our traditions, customs, and local regulations.

➤ Avoid activities that threaten wildlife or plant populations, or that may be potentially damaging to our natural environment.

➤ Select tourism products and services that demonstrate social, cultural, and environmental sensitivity.

ACTIVITIES

Camping

This section offers a profile of the participants in various recreational facilities. One in four of those who camp also participate in hard-adventure activities.[35] The most popular of these are rafting, snorkeling/scuba, and off-road biking. Campers tend to be married with children at home and have attended some college. Campers make up the lowest percentage of college attendance and are also the lowest income group. About one-half also hikes, while a third each also bike and canoe.[36]

Hiking

About 30 percent of all hikers participate in hard-adventure activities also. The favorites are rafting, snorkeling/scuba, and backpacking. Members of this group are most likely to be married. Three-quarters of hikers also take camping trips, while 40 percent each participate in biking and bird-watching.[37]

Biking   About 40 percent of those who take a biking vacation also participate in hard-adventure activities. The favored activities are off-road biking or mountain biking, snorkeling or scuba diving, and whitewater rafting or kayaking. This segment of the market is young and relatively prosperous. Approximately one-half are Generation Xers, the same percentage are professionals or managers, and one-third, second only to snow skiers, are single. Over 80 percent of bikers also camp, 70 percent also hike, and almost 40 percent also canoe.

Watching Birds and Animals   One-quarter of those who watch birds or animals also take hard-adventure vacations. The top activities are whitewater rafting or kayaking, snorkeling or scuba diving, and backpacking across rugged terrain. This segment of the market has the highest proportion of all soft-adventure vacationers (20 percent) aged 55 or older as well as the highest percentage (23) with postgraduate college education. Bird- and animal-watchers also participate in soft-adventure travel. Three-quarters of them also camp, 70 percent hike, and almost 40 percent also bike.

Horseback Riding   Thirty-three percent of those who ride horses also take hard-adventure vacations. Preferred activities are rafting, snorkeling/scuba, and off-road biking. This segment has the highest percentage of women (57). This is a young group that tends to have children at home. Equestrians also camp (74 percent), hike (64 percent), and bike (40 percent).

Canoeing   Those who canoe also participate in rafting, backpacking, and off-road biking. Almost 40 percent of canoers also participate in other hard-adventure vacations. They tend to be young and have attended, though not necessarily graduated from, college. Mostly, the segment consists of households with a single wage earner. Canoeists also camp (83 percent), hike (64 percent), and bike (48 percent).

Water Skiing   Water skiers have a high participation rate (44 percent) in other hard-adventure activities. They tend also to snorkel/scuba, raft, and bike off-road. They are young and affluent. Fifty-six percent are male. They also camp (83 percent), hike (59 percent), and bike (47 percent).

Snow Skiing   Snow skiers have the highest participation rate in other hard-adventure activities. Forty-five percent undertake other activities, notably rafting, off-road biking, and snorkeling/scuba. Snow skiers are young and affluent. Fifty-four percent are male. Over half have completed college, making snow skiers the best-educated group of hard-adventure vacationers. Like water skiers, they also camp (82 percent), hike (72 percent), and bike (57 percent).

THE GAMING MARKET

*If you aim to leave Las Vegas with a small fortune, go there
with a large one.*
                                        —AMERICAN SAYING

In 1931, gaming was legalized in Nevada, and for 45 years, this was the
only legal location for gaming in the United States.[38] Nevada was joined by
Atlantic City in the mid-1970s. By the mid-1990s, the number of states
allowing some type of land-based, riverboat, dockside, or small-stakes
gaming, video lottery machines, or casinos run by Native American tribes
increased to 25.

In the 1996 election, voters in Ohio, influenced by strong opposition
from the governor of the state and the mayor of Cincinnati, rejected a con-
stitutional amendment to allow riverboat casinos in Cleveland, Cincinnati,
Youngstown, and Lorain. However, a number of other initiatives were sup-
ported by voters elsewhere. Michigan approved a plan allowing casinos to
be constructed in Detroit; Arizona approved more Native American casinos in the state; Arkansas residents authorized casinos in Hot Springs,
subject to local voter approval; six Louisiana parishes voted to keep legalized gambling, while 23 others voted to approve floating casinos; Colorado voters approved expansion of gambling to Trinidad, subject to local
voter approval.

Gambling is a $19 billion business, with Nevada accounting for 37 per-
cent (Las Vegas itself takes in over $4 billion in revenues). Riverboats
(operating in five states) are responsible for almost 25 percent of the
market, Atlantic City accounts for 19 percent, and Native American
gaming brings in about 18 percent. New Orleans, with revenues of $140
million, has 1 percent of the market.

Clearly, casino gambling is accepted as a form of entertainment, which
means more than gaming, more than slot machines. In Las Vegas, for example, it means fake volcanoes, jousting machines, and pirate battles.

There are two types of casino locations:

❖ *Transient*—Serving the day tripper market, people travel to the site by
   car or bus and use little lodging or off-premise food facilities. Most
   Native American casinos and many riverboats fall into this category.
❖ *Destination*—The premiere example continues to be Las Vegas. Over
   40 percent of visitors arrive by air, while slightly less than that
   number drive to the destination. People stay an average of four
   days, 90 percent staying in hotels. On average they spend, *per day:*

$ 52 on accommodation
$120 on gambling
$ 75 on shopping
$ 53 on shows
$ 4 on sightseeing
$ 24 on food

quick getaways 2.7

Mirage Resorts

The philosophy of Mirage Resorts, as stated by its chairman Steve Wynn, is as follows:

> When an artist paints a picture, the intent is to provoke a reaction in the viewer. . . .
> A great painting draws the observer into being a participant, to interact with the art
> and to realize the emotions it is creating. Great hotels are similar to great pieces of
> art. They stimulate, provoke and entertain the guest. They draw the guests into the
> experience and enhance their lives, making the world a better place.

Perhaps as a result, chainwide occupancy is 98.7 percent, and the average daily
rate (ADR) is the highest in Las Vegas. Of all the comments received from the casino
guests, 90 percent are complimentary about employees and 10 percent deal with
issues needing resolution.

The purchase decision was driven by friendliness and overall service quality followed, at some distance, by convenient location, familiarity with the brand image,
and reputation. During the stay itself, food and beverage service was the strongest
factor in creating value for the customers. Service was ranked next, followed by the
aesthetics of the property and security.

The key benefit that drives guests to the Mirage is an "enjoyable" experience, comfort, and relaxation.

Source: "Mirage Resorts," The Key to Best Practices in the U.S. Lodging Industry *(Ithaca, N.Y.: Cornell University, 1999), 309–311.*

**Question: Based on this article, what criteria should a casino general man-
ager focus in on to attract and keep guests?**

THE CRUISE MARKET

My experience of ships is that on them one makes an interesting discovery about the world. One finds one can do without it completely.
                                                                —MALCOLM BRADBURY

Only 8 percent of the U.S. population has ever taken a cruise.[39] The growth potential appears to be excellent, as cruise lines have begun to look at less traditional demographic groups. For example, the Cruise Lines International Association (CLIA) reports that only 36 percent of people who cruise are 60 years of age or older. Those under 40 make up one in five cruisers, while over a third are between 40 and 59 years old. In fact, among first-time cruisers, slightly less than half are under 40 years of age.

CLIA identifies six market segments:

1. *Enthusiastic baby boomers*—Excited about cruising, they live intense, stressful lives and want to escape and relax when on vacation. This segment accounts for 20 percent of cruisers and 15 percent of all cruising days. Forty-six percent of this group are first-time cruisers.
2. *Restless baby boomers*—The newest cruisers, they like to try new vacation experiences and, while they enjoy the cruise experience, cost may be an inhibiting factor. Making up one-third of all cruisers and 17 percent of all cruising days, almost 60 percent are first-timers.
3. *Luxury seekers*—They want to be pampered in deluxe accommodations and are willing and able to pay for it. Thirty percent of these cruisers are first-timers. They comprise 14 percent of the market and account for 18 percent of all cruising days.
4. *Consummate shoppers*—Committed to cruising, they seek the best value (though not necessarily the cheapest price). Accounting for 16 percent of the market and one-fifth of all cruising days, 20 percent of them are first-time cruisers.
5. *Explorers*—Well-educated and well-traveled, they are interested in unusual and exotic destinations. Twenty percent are first-timers. Explorers comprise 11 percent of the market and account for 18 percent of all cruising days.
6. *Ship buffs*—The most senior segment, ship buffs cruise extensively and will continue because of the pleasure and comfort it brings them. Only 6 percent of the market, this segment accounts for 11 percent of cruising days. Thirteen percent are first-timers.

Several attitudes are common to all six segments. Sixty percent like to experiment with new and different things. In choosing a cruise, over 70 percent say the destination is the most important factor, followed by cost and time of year (each 60 percent) and cruise line or ship (57 percent).

The top three benefits of cruising are the ease of visiting several destinations (91 percent), the many activities (83 percent), and the reasonable price in relation to value (83 percent).[40]

SUMMARY

Any development must be based on market demand. Early attempts to define the U.S. travel market used stated motivation as the basis for segmentation. More recently, it has been suggested that segmentation on the basis of actual behavior is a better reflection of the market. Because it is necessary to understand the market characteristics of potential guests prior to examining development strategy, a detailed profile of important segments of the market is given.

ENDNOTES

1. Shirley Young, Leland Ott, and Barbara Feigin, "Some Practical Considerations in Market Segmentation," *Journal of Marketing Research* 15 (1978): 405-442.
2. Stowe Shoemaker, "Segmenting the U.S. Travel Market According to Benefits Realized," *Journal of Travel Research* 32, no. 3 (Winter 1994): 8-21.
3. TravelScope special report on gambling (Washington, D.C.: Travel Industry Association of America, 1995).
4. "What's Hot—and What's Not—in the Luxury Market," *Travel Weekly,* 29 April 1999, p. 56.
5. Richard L. Ragatz and John C. Crotts, "U.S. Timeshare Purchasers: Who Are They and Why Do They Buy?" *Journal of Hospitality and Tourism Research* 24, no. 1 (February 2000): 49-66.
6. "Our World at a Glance," *Developments* (June 1999) vol. VI: 34-35.
7. *Phenomenal Growth in the U.S. Timeshare Industry* (Washington, D.C.: American Resort Development Association, Spring 1999), 5.
8. Ragatz and Crotts, "U.S. Timeshare Purchasers," 55.
9. Ibid.
10. *The United States Timeshare Industry: Overview and Economic Impact Analysis* (Washington, D.C.: American Resort Development Association, 1997), 43.
11. Ibid., 44-45.
12. Ibid., 53.
13. Ibid., 47.
14. Ibid., 48.

15. Ibid., 23–27.
16. *National Ski Areas Association National Demographic Study: Final Report 1997–1998* (Lakewood, Colo.: National Ski Areas Association, 1998), 6–7.
17. Ibid., 10.
18. *Transworld SNOWboarding Business/National Ski Areas Association: 1997–1998 Ski Resort Snowboarding Survey* (Englewood, Colo.: National Ski Areas Association, 1998), 8.
19. Ibid., 1–4.
20. Ibid., 6.
21. *National Ski Areas Association National Demographic Study: Final Report 1997–1998*, 7.
22. Ibid., 10–11.
23. Ibid., 12–15.
24. International Marina Institute, *1998 Financial and Operational Benchmark Study for Marina Operators* (Nokomis, Fla.: 1998), 5.
25. Ibid., 7.
26. *The U.S. Golf Travel Market* (Jupiter, Fla.: National Golf Foundation, 1999), 7.
27. Ibid., 4–19.
28. Ibid., 24–29.
29. Ibid., 29.
30. *Adventure Travel: Special Report* (Washington, D.C.: Travel Industry Association of America, 1998), 1.
31. Ibid.
32. Ibid., 4–11.
33. Ibid., 31, 34.
34. Ibid., 41.
35. Ibid., 55–72.
36. Ibid., 58–59.
37. Ibid., 59–60.
38. John J. Rohs, "1996 Outlook for Gaming," *1996 Outlook for Travel and Tourism*, Proceedings of the Twenty-First Annual Outlook Forum at the Travel Industry National Conference (Washington, D.C.: Travel Industry Association of America, 1985), 114–119.
39. James E. Godsman, "1996 Outlook for the Cruise Industry," *1996 Outlook for Travel and Tourism*, Proceedings of the Twenty-First Annual Outlook Forum at the Travel Industry National Conference (Washington, D.C.: Travel Industry Association of America, 1985), 165–166.
40. Ernest Blum, "CLIA-Sponsored Survey Draws Profiles of Those Who Cruise," *Travel Weekly*, 13 November 1995, pp. 32, 36.

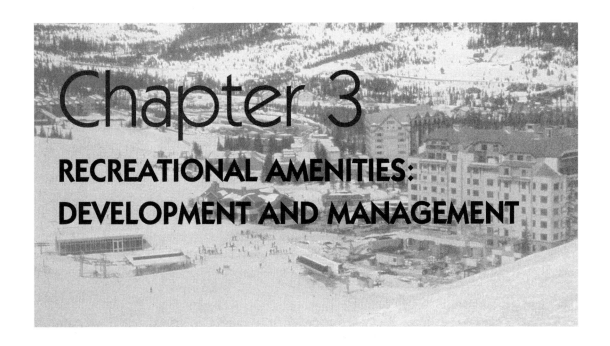

Chapter 3

RECREATIONAL AMENITIES:
DEVELOPMENT AND MANAGEMENT

INTRODUCTION

*Staying power is the first requirement for success; without it,
projects that might have been successful fail.*
—WILLIAM BONE
Chair of the Board, Sunrise Company

The recreational amenities are a significant part of the character of any
planned community. According to the Urban Land Institute, the decision
to include or exclude a specific recreational amenity should be based on
six factors:

1. what is being offered in similar local projects
2. the residents/users for whom these amenities are being planned
3. how much money is available for amenities and whether the costs
   are justified
4. how the amenity fits in with the total project physically, economically, and as part of its image
5. what quantity of the amenity should be provided and what the climate will allow
6. what the marketing benefits will be[1]

In this chapter, the place of the amenity program within the overall
development process is identified and principles for developing an amenity strategy are laid out. Options are explored for effectively structuring
the management of the community and its amenities.

THE DEVELOPMENT PROCESS

*Avoid personal guarantees on land acquisition and develop-
ment loans. The failure to heed this advice has broken more
developers than anything else. If more equity is needed to
avoid the need for a guarantee, then by all means put it in
or find a partner.*
—WILLIAM BONE
Chair of the Board, Sunrise Company

The process for developing a resort is complex, time-consuming, and
involves many related activities. The developer, who may also be the
resort manager, must assemble a team of people who have expertise in
various areas.[2] The team, overseen by a project manager, brings together
people with a background in:

❖ *Law*—attorneys and legal advisers

❖ *Finance*—financial and technical analysts, financiers

❖ *Management*—construction and project managers

❖ *Marketing*—market analysts, marketing and public relations advisers, sales managers, and real estate agents

❖ *Planning and design*—site planners, architects, landscape architects, engineers, and environmental scientists

STAGES IN THE DEVELOPMENT PROCESS A resort development goes through three stages: (1) feasibility analysis and planning, (2) construction, and (3) operations/management.[3]

Feasibility Analysis and Planning A project is usually initiated based on potential market demand. A preliminary estimate is made of the likely demand, alternative sites are investigated, one is chosen for in-depth analysis, and a development team is assembled.

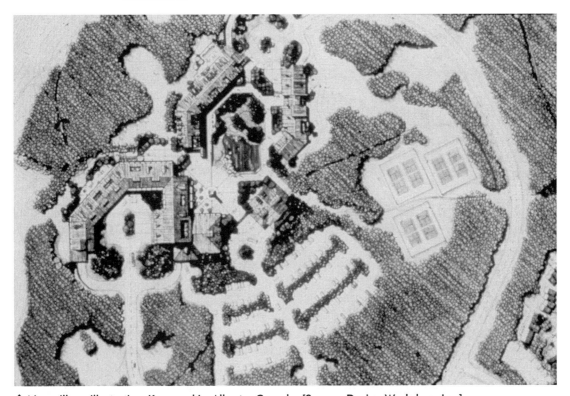

❖ New village illustrative, Kananaskis, Alberta, Canada. [Source: Design Workshop, Inc.]

quick getaways 3.1

Ecotourism and Development in Scotland

In Scotland, it has been shown that high-quality tourism can occur when:

- The infrastructure is locally controlled.
- The infrastructure is underdeveloped.
- The natural environment is moderately hostile and thus attracts specialists rather than mass tourists.
- Resorts are in the early stages of the life cycle.
- Tourism is one of several sectors of a regional economy.
- Development can be conditional rather than a critical priority.
- Numbers can be controlled.
- The market for Visitors of Friends and Relatives is significant.

Source: A.V. Seaton, "Quality Tourism Sustained: A Small Island Case from the Shetlands," in *Quality Tourism: Concept of a Sustainable Tourism Development, Harmonizing Economical, Social, and Ecological Interests,* Proceedings of the 1991 Congress of the International Association of Scientific Experts on Tourism, Seychelles, 17–23 November 1991, 209–236.

The development concept is then agreed upon. This means considering the buildable area, development capacity, access, and options for community governance. This is followed by a detailed feasibility analysis comprising an in-depth market and regulatory analysis, an examination of the characteristics of the site, and a determination of the financial feasibility of the project.

At this point, the concept may have to be refined or, if the financial feasibility is unfavorable, an alternative site may have to be selected and the process begun again. Next, product programming is put into place. The type and mix of residential, timeshare, and hotel products are determined, an association structure and amenity program agreed on, and the phasing of the development set up.

Preliminary planning and design is followed by approvals from necessary agencies and citizen groups, and the plan finalized in detail. Financing is then secured and marketing begun.

Construction Planning, construction, and marketing activities overlap with the plan (and the corresponding construction) being adjusted to changes in the marketplace. Large amounts of money and manpower are being spent at this stage of the development.

Operations/ Management When the first part of the resort is ready for use, the project moves into the operations stage. The various stages of development may overlap, as it can take years or even decades for a resort to be completed. A resort may consist of resident owners, periodic renters, and hotel guests who stay a few days. Specialized management services may be required. At this point, developers may provide for the transfer of community management to associations of owners or members. Finally, planning has to consider renovation and repositioning of the resort.

DEVELOPING AN AMENITY STRATEGY

The most common mistake is not having a superior land plan, including the appropriate recreational and other amenities. The objective is to maximize the residential lot values by creating the maximum lot premium potential.
—WILLIAM BONE
Chair of the Board, Sunrise Company

An amenity is "a rather broad concept that can encompass virtually any feature that is attractive to a given market and thus adds value to land."[4] The first of two basic reasons for including amenities in a recreational development is that they increase the value of the real estate. The up-front cost of adding a golf course to a development, for example, can be recovered through the sale of premium lots that front the fairways. Amenities may be developed with the idea that they will form the basis for a profitable operation. This latter is the motivation behind resort developments, while the former is more true of primary- and second-home communities.

The second reason for the inclusion of amenities within a development is to get marketing leverage. A well-designed recreational attraction adds credibility to the development and the developer and can aid in attracting guests to a property or customers to a development.[5]

❖ New village master plan, Winter Park, Colorado. [Source: Design Workshop, Inc.]

The downside is that substantial costs are involved in providing what is often a seasonal attraction. The key is to achieve a balance between the cost of providing the amenity with the sales generated by its presence. Timing is of the essence. Plans must also be made to transfer ownership and management of the amenity to an appropriate group or body after it has achieved its purpose of bringing in guests or customers.

AN AMENITY STRATEGY

An amenity strategy is a "clear understanding of the role of recreational facilities within an overall project." While every project is unique, certain principles are accepted as appropriate for any recreational development.

- ❖ Provide what the market wants.
- ❖ Provide for the changing role of the amenity package over the life cycle of the development.
- ❖ Balance the cost of the amenities with the revenue they generate.
- ❖ Guarantee developer control in the early steps of the project.
- ❖ Provide for an orderly transfer of control from the developer to residents.[6]

Importance of the Customer For a recreational development to be successful, it is critical that it be developed, designed, and managed to meet the needs of the customer. This means, first, that the package of amenities should be a function of the overall project. As a project progresses from single-family home to multifamily units to a resort hotel, more and better amenities become appropriate. Next, preference should be given to natural over built features. Early golf courses in Scotland, for example, relied on the natural features of the coastline. Development was less costly, impact on the environment was minimized, and the course was more difficult for competitors to copy because it was truly unique to the area. These advantages—lower costs, unique design, and less intrusion on the environment—will occur wherever natural resources can be used as the basis for amenities.[7]

Recognizing the risk of dependence on one season of the year, resorts have sought to reduce their investment risk by converting amenities to off-season use. Many golf courses rope off their greens and promote cross-country skiing in winter. Ski areas market mountain biking down their ski runs during the summer.

A final principle is that facilities should be sufficient to meet the needs of the number of people expected to be attracted to the development.

Changing Role The developer and the users can be in conflict with respect to the type and amount of amenities developed. Developers build certain facilities because of their marketing appeal—they will help sell real estate—or because they will be heavily used, thereby becoming valuable in themselves. A championship golf course may help sell real estate, but it may be costly to maintain and difficult for retired residents to play. Meeting the needs of the residents by providing an easier course might not attract the publicity necessary to sell the project. An operational plan is needed that identifies "who will develop, own, and operate the facilities and for how long; who will use the facilities and on what terms; and precisely what the expected relationship will be between real estate and recreational amenities, in both the short term and over the long run."[8]

Timing Development must be timed such that the cost of constructing the amenities is balanced by the revenue generated by their presence. The rule of thumb is that recreational amenities should be developed up front and used to draw guests or stimulate real estate sales. Because of the heavy cost involved, this strategy increases the developer's risk and produces an initial low rate of return on the project.

Developing an Amenity Strategy: Timeshares and Clubs

Ski resorts are in competition not only with each other but also with beach resorts, golf clubs, cruises, and other vacation options. Timeshares, despite being more affordable than owning a condominium or second home, lost their attractiveness because the destinations for which people were trading were not of the same quality as their own. That has changed as hotel brands like Marriott and Hyatt have entered the field. Both appeal and quality have gone up. For example, the Marriott Mountain Valley Lodge at Breckenridge, Colorado, a 78-unit timeshare project, offers full kitchens, indoor and outdoor Jacuzzis, exercise and game rooms, and storage for skis and mountain bikes. An affiliation with Interval International allows owners to trade time in their units for time at other Marriott properties worldwide.

Private ownership and residence clubs allow owners to forgo the hassles of condo or second-home ownership. Typically, clubs are luxury projects with common exercise facilities. Owners buy fee simple interest in a development and reserve the use of a unit for two weeks in the winter, two in the summer, and another week of their choice. Some allow owners to trade time in other resorts. The Franz Klammer Lodge in Mountain Village, Telluride, Colorado, pioneered the concept in 1996. Its 29 residences belong to 290 owners. Membership begins at $165,000 for a two-bedroom unit and guarantees five weeks residence a year. Additional stays are possible at no extra cost, subject to availability.

The River Club, also in Telluride, combines the club concept with a sports theme. It offers members ski equipment and access to hang gliding, fly fishing, and four-wheeling. Prices range from the mid-$30,000s to the mid-$100,000s.

Source: Jill Jamieson-Nichols, "Beyond Skiing: New Trends in Colorado Mountain Resort Development," *Urban Land* (April 1998): 82–85.

Question: What are the relative advantages of second-home ownership, timeshares, and clubs?

There are several ways to reduce this risk. If recreational developments already exist in an area, it may be possible to negotiate cooperative agreements whereby residents of the newer project can use the facilities of the existing project. In this way, the recreational facilities at the newer project can be phased in gradually and their development cost spread over a number of years.

Another strategy is to open amenities for use by nonresidents. Revenue is generated while prospective buyers are exposed to the project. This requires careful management. Residents may resent having outsiders use "their" facilities, and it may be difficult to phase out the outside members when the project is more fully developed.[9]

Developer Control

It is generally accepted that the developer should continue to control construction, operation, and maintenance of the amenity package as the development is being built out. If the amenities are not under the control of the developer, they may be poorly managed and maintained. This, in turn, could adversely affect future real estate sales. The developer, of course, assumes the operational burden and must have, or hire, the expertise necessary. The rule of thumb is that the developer retains control until at least 50 percent of the project is completed. Residents will probably want a role in the management of the facilities prior to this point. An advisory committee of residents can provide useful input and pave the way toward eventual transfer of control.

Orderly Transfer

If recreational areas are making money, there is no need for the developer to transfer their management to a third party. This is true of resort hotels and ski areas, for example. However, in residential developments, once the recreational amenity has served its primary purpose of selling real estate, its value to the developer declines while the carrying costs increase. The amenity is then either given away or sold to the residents of the project, who are usually represented by a property owner's association. The developer has already received a return on the investment by charging premium prices on certain real estate units based on their proximity to the amenity.

Developers have little or no leverage at the end of the build-out phase. They are incurring the costs involved in running the amenity. All the real estate has been sold. It is, therefore, a good idea for the developers to negotiate at the beginning of the project how and when the recreational amenities will be transferred to a resident group.

COMMUNITY MANAGEMENT STRUCTURES

*The pitfall facing the developer revolves around the crucial
point of obtaining long-range approval to develop future
properties that will meet the resort's needs years after the initial development proposal is approved.*
                                        —DEAN SCHWANKE ET AL.
                                        Resort Development Handbook

The management structure of an amenity package is vital to its successful
implementation. Properly designed, a community management structure
helps develop a process for:

- ❖ preserving common areas
- ❖ developing a long-term strategy for owning, maintaining, and operating the development's amenities
- ❖ fulfilling the obligations taken by the developer in order to get
  approval for development
- ❖ establishing and enforcing community maintenance and design
  standards

No one structure is appropriate in all cases. A detailed analysis of the
factors unique to each development must be completed before determining
what will work best. Three types of organizational structures can be mixed
and matched to provide maximum flexibility for the developer while maximizing the marketability of the community: government bodies, nonprofit
tax-exempt organizations, and community associations.[10]

GOVERNMENT BODIES Communities can be managed through municipal corporations and community improvement districts. However, because of the disadvantages
discussed below, they are best used in combination with other options.

Municipalities have the power to tax and have the power of emi-
nent domain—the right of the state to take private property for public use.
They have access to public funds in addition to the ability to issue debt.
This latter consideration can open funds for development purposes at a
lower cost than the more traditional tax revenue–based options. However,
government bodies must follow both state and federal laws that can
increase the costs for property owners. For example, they cannot restrict
public access to parks and roads. This means that they do not have the
flexibility to develop private amenities for the exclusive use of the owners,
tenants, and guests of a resort.

❖ Squaw Valley, California. [Source: Design Workshop, Inc.]

From the developer's viewpoint, he/she has no control. The residents of the municipality elect the governing body, which makes most operating decisions. The developer cannot be assured that the body will accept responsibility for maintenance of the amenities that are developed. The developer may or may not have initial influence or control over the election of the governing body. A municipality may decide to limit votes to those who are registered to vote. A developer who does not live in the community would have no vote. Even if he did reside in the community, he would have one vote only.

NONPROFIT TAX-EXEMPT ORGANIZATIONS

Like the municipality noted above, a tax-exempt organization must allow public access to the facilities. However, unlike the municipality, it can be managed by a board of directors rather than by elected members. To get tax-exempt status, the nonprofit must serve "the common good and general welfare of a community."[11] A developer could, in essence, select and control the board indefinitely. A nonprofit organization can get involved in maintenance of public areas, architectural control, and expense assessment without losing its tax-exempt status. Because it cannot get involved in the maintenance of private property, however, a tax-exempt organization does not have the authority to enforce covenants. Covenants are usually desirable in a master-planned development. As a result, this type of organization is best used in conjunction with other types.

quick getaways 3.3

Community Management: Gore Creek Valley

Prior to 1961, Gore Creek Valley consisted of undeveloped agricultural land. In that year, Vail Associates, Inc. (VAI), began to develop the first major planned ski-oriented resort community in North America. Initially, VAI delivered such services as road maintenance, utility infrastructure, and fire protection. Later, these services were transferred to the town of Vail, which incorporated in 1966. The town additionally became responsible for zoning and land use ordinances. Collaboration between VAI and the town of Vail has allowed the original village to develop in a way consistent with the original design. VAI continues to stay involved through the Vail Valley Foundation. This nonprofit organization is dedicated to enhancing the local quality of life. In addition to marketing summer programs, the foundation has been involved in the World Alpine Ski Championships, the Gerald Ford Amphitheater, and the Bolshoi Ballet Academy at Vail. Vail Village has over 2000 residential units and more than 300,000 square feet of retail space.

Source: Dean Schwanke et al., *Resort Development Handbook* (Washington, D.C.: Urban Land Institute, 1977), 241.

***Questions:* How else could VIA have organized its community management? Was the way they chose the best option? Explain.**

COMMUNITY ASSOCIATIONS   A community association is a "mandatory membership association responsible for performing various functions within a planned real estate development."[12] The association, with or without one of the options discussed above, gives most flexibility for a resort community. All property owners are members. However, various classes of membership can be designed so as to allow the developer to control the community until it can be transferred to the owners later. Voting rights and dues assessment are usually based on the benefits received rather than on property value alone. Unlike the first two types of organization discussed above, an association can own and maintain property not open to the public.

In deciding on the way the association is to be structured, consideration must be given to the balance between the interests of residents and hotel and other resort operators; how absentee owners will affect the management of the development; what private services, if any, will be offered to owners; what control will be taken of public areas such as beaches; and what services will be provided to the community and how they will be paid for. The next major decision involves whether residential and nonresidential uses should be under the control of one association or whether they should be dealt with separately.

A community association is set up to do two things. It acts as a business that maintains and manages private property and as a government entity in delivering services while enforcing covenants and rules.[13] It can be structured in various ways,[14] as discussed below.

Single Community Associations
A single community association is simple and reduces the administrative burden of dealing with two associations while providing a body to keep community standards. However, some owners may believe they would have more autonomy if they had a separately incorporated subassociation. This is especially true if different owners have the need for varying levels of service. In addition, a single association leaves residential and nonresidential owners subject to control of one group by the other.

Single Residential Associations
A second alternative is to design an association with a neighborhood structure together with a covenant to share costs on nonresidential units. Nonresidential owners are protected from involvement in matters that primarily affect the residential community. However, residential owners are provided with no protection with respect to the use and appearance of nonresidential properties. In addition, the structure can be difficult when residential and nonresidential properties are intertwined.

Dual Associations with Joint Committee
Dual associations—one for the residential community and the other for nonresidents—is another possibility. Communitywide standards can be maintained while both resident and nonresident owners each have an appropriate level of autonomy. Joint committees comprising representatives of each group ensure communication and mediation between both sets of owners. Developers maintain long-term control over community standards while allowing for the transition of control of service provision to the owners. Limiting membership and the scope of the committee's powers can control any perception that the joint committee is more administration than is needed.

Dual Associations with Covenant — Having two associations to represent resident and nonresident owners with a covenant obligating nonresident owners to share certain costs offers several advantages. Each group of owners is provided a certain level of autonomy while the number of entities involved in governing the community is minimized. No single group can establish and enforce communitywide standards. Second, owners are given little or no input into the use and appearance of the other types of properties. This may become a problem where the standards for one type of residential unit differ significantly from the other and are detrimental to the appearance and standards of the entire development.

MANAGEMENT AND OPERATIONS

A resort operating company is in the fantasy fulfillment business.

—WILLIAM BONE
Chair of the Board, Sunrise Company

The management of recreational amenities has become more sophisticated over the years. A variety of organizational structures are possible.

ORGANIZATIONAL STRUCTURES — When resort operators, particularly of ski areas, choose to own and operate amenities themselves, one of four structures is typically selected: equity club, right-to-use club, convertible club, or association membership.[15]

Equity Club — Developers can transfer ownership of the recreational facilities to a separate nonprofit corporation while retaining the right to operate the facilities until most of the residential property is sold. This protects the developer by ensuring that the amenities will not be operated in a way that adversely affects sale of the remaining real estate units. The developer contributes the recreational amenities in return for the right to sell equity memberships to real estate owners. Once all the real estate is sold, the club is owned and controlled by the members and run by a duly elected board of directors. Club members pay annual dues for the right to use the facilities. They also benefit from any increase in the value of the amenities. It may be possible for property purchasers to inherit the equity membership of owners. This, obviously, increases the value of the equity membership. If all memberships are sold, new owners must wait for one to become available before they can participate in the amenity program.

Right-to-Use Club In a right-to-use club, the developer retains ownership and control of the facilities. Members buy the right to use the amenities rather than acquire an ownership interest, as above. An initial payment plus annual dues is common. The developer decides whether the initial payment is a fee or a deposit. Under a fee program, a member who resigns from the club may receive all, some, or none of the deposit back. How much, if any, is returned depends on whether or not the membership is reissued to a new member. The initial fee is treated as taxable income to the developer and as a deductible business expense when refunded to a member who resigns.

Under a deposit program, members receive the full deposit when they resign, but not until 20 to 30 years after their acceptance into the program. The deposit might, thus, be characterized as a loan to the recreational amenities that is not taxable income.

Convertible Club When a developer feels that a market exists for an equity club but is
Program unsure when the club can be turned over to members, a convertible club is a viable option. The program begins as a right-to-use club, but members are made aware up front of the intention to turn it into an equity club. The one-time fee or deposit is refundable. When members pay this fee, they are told the likely timing of the switch to an equity club together with the purchase price to be paid by members for the facilities, as well as any likely additional costs to be incurred in the transition. The fee or deposit may be applied to the equity club membership.

Association The developer may turn over the recreational facilities to a homeowners'
Ownership association set up to represent the surrounding property units. Association members do not buy memberships but can pay off the debt through assessments and user fees. Memberships may be sold to owners who want preferential treatment.

The developer recovers the cost of building the recreational amenities through means other than the sale of real estate. In this way, the return on investment for the project may increase because the profit on real estate sales does not have to take into account the construction costs of the recreational amenities. It is crucial that an association pay off the debt and maintain the facilities while keeping assessments reasonable.

COMPARISON OF The four options discussed above can be compared on a number of crite-
BASIC OPTIONS ria.[16] The choice should be based on the criteria most important to the developer and the development. The up-front cost is highest for the

equity club; however, on conversion, the membership price on an initial right-to-use club is even higher. The cost, however, is reduced by the original initiation fee. There is no up-front cost for the association ownership unless annual memberships are sold. Even then, the annual cost is relatively low.

Gross proceeds from the membership program are greatest with the right-to-use club, although the income is dependent on the selling of memberships. While the income is less in an equity club, the guarantee that the money will be realized is greater. The convertible program produces less gross income, while association management produces none at all unless annual memberships are sold.

The initial operational cash flow is low with both association management and an equity club and moderate with the other two options. On the other hand, the sell-out operational cash flow is greatest in an equity club, slightly less in a right-to-use club, and lower in the other two options.

Because association members own and operate the recreational facilities, a greater sense of community exists among them. It remains good in an equity club, less so in a right-to-use club because of the loss of owner control and uncertainty over the amenities, and even less in a convertible club program because owners have no control over the facilities.

The developer has the greatest flexibility under a convertible club program and none with association ownership. In the other two cases, the degree of flexibility is dependent on terms of the membership plan. Litigation risk to the developer is low in both an equity club and association membership, moderate to low in a right-to-use club, and greatest when a developer sells the amenities in a convertible club program.

The convertible club program is the best option where nonowner access to club facilities is important. In an equity club, access is limited to available memberships until a cap is reached. In a right-to-use club, access is good until conversion takes place. It varies in association ownership depending on the regulations set by the members themselves.

MEMBERSHIP STRUCTURES

Memberships can be structured differently within each of the structures noted above. The type of membership structure depends on the development concept and the type of owner or guest. For example, in a resort consisting of primary residences, long-term membership options that do not expire until the member sells are made available to owners. In communities where second-home owners stay for shorter periods, they are given the option of making changes to the service package they have.

Tiered Membership A tiered membership structure offers a variety of options to members: the more services, access, and flexibility given, the greater the price charged. For example, full golf membership might allow an owner to make a tee reservation up to 30 days in advance, while a less expensive membership category might restrict reservations to 5 days in advance.

When the number of memberships in each category is limited, owners are enticed into purchasing the more expensive options. This makes their property more valuable in the event they wish to sell. This may, in turn, create a greater demand for higher-priced memberships than would occur under a different membership structure. If owners buy the membership as an investment, golf memberships may sell out but the golf course remain underutilized because owners are not using their privileges fully. This system works best in residential communities where the number of memberships available is approximately equal to the number of units. A rule of thumb, for example, is 350 golf members per 18-hole course.[17] Another structure may become necessary when the number of residential units surpasses the capacity of the amenity.

Unitary Membership Under a unitary membership structure, all members pay a membership price and receive the same interest in the amenities. Each year, members select the membership category they wish. In one year, a member may purchase the social category, which allows access to the dining facilities, and then, in the following year, select a category—at a greater expense—that allows access to all the amenities. The member is assured that, if she sells, the next owner will also have an annual choice of category.

A unitary membership works when the recreational amenities are insufficient to meet the demands of the residents. Unlike the tiered membership described above, artificial demand is not created for a particular level of membership. Members annually select the program that meets their needs. Imbalances in demand for specific categories of membership can be handled by adjusting the type and price of memberships available.

Add-on Membership Convertible or add-on memberships are a combination of the above two categories. All members purchase a social membership, then are free to buy add-ons depending on the additional access they want. This type of structure works best when the developer is unsure about the level of demand for the recreational amenities.

GENERAL APPROACHES Developers tend to mix and match organizational and membership structures to accommodate both their needs and those of the members. An equity club may be organized that offers full golf membership to equity members as well as social memberships to others. In settings that have both residents and resort hotels, a club may be developed for residents but also offer access to hotel guests. Several advantages accrue to both resident and hotel guests:

❖ Both receive higher-quality services than if two lesser-quality facilities were built for each.

❖ Club members get access to hotel services, such as concierge and room service.

❖ Hotel guests add life to the facility in the early stages of real estate development.[18]

However, residents tend to favor exclusivity, while hotel guests desire access at will. Conflicts can be minimized by a reservation system that protects the rights of use for each group. As an example, a members-only lounge can be created. In resorts with several golf courses, a different course each day can be designated for the exclusive use of members. Members can be given a longer lead time than guests in signing up for tee times.

SUMMARY

Recreational amenities are a significant part of the character of any planned community. This chapter identified the place of the amenity program within the overall development process and laid out the principles for developing an amenity strategy. Finally, the options for effectively structuring the management of the community and its amenities were explored.

ENDNOTES

1. Patrick L. Phillips, *Developing with Recreational Amenities: Golf, Tennis, Skiing, Marinas* (Washington, D.C.: Urban Land Institute, 1986), 1.
2. Dean Schwanke et al., *Resort Development Handbook* (Washington, D.C.: Urban Land Institute, 1977), 30.
3. Ibid.
4. Phillips, *Developing with Recreational Amenities*, 4.
5. Ibid., 2.
6. Ibid., 15-21.
7. Ibid., 15.

8. Ibid., 16.

9. Ibid., 17.

10. Schwanke et al., *Resort Development Handbook*, 239.

11. Ibid., 240.

12. Ibid., 244.

13. Ibid.

14. Ibid., 242.

15. Ibid., 247-250.

16. Ibid., 248-249.

17. Phillips, *Developing with Recreational Amenities*, 23.

18. Schwanke et al., *Resort Development Handbook*, 253.

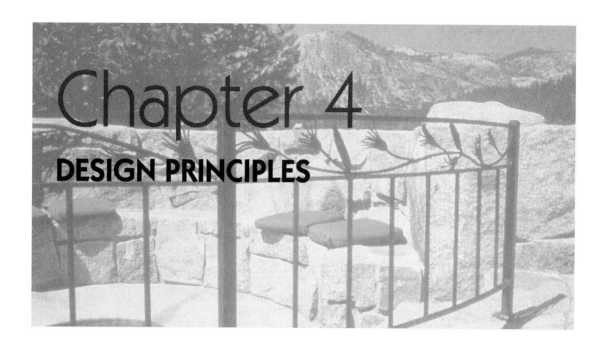

Chapter 4

DESIGN PRINCIPLES

INTRODUCTION

All too often, the development and design of a facility is thought of as a process divorced from its management and maintenance. However, decisions made in the concept's design can have significant impact on maintenance and management costs. The idea of site design is to "anticipate problems of land usage and provide a physical form solution to ensure that the problems never arise."[1] Through the application of the following principles, resort management can develop recreational attractions and facilities that will respect the natural resources base while minimizing management and maintenance problems.

DESIGN PRINCIPLES AND PRACTICES

Too many trees. Couldn't see the scenery.
—Actual comment written on comment card
at Forest Service trailhead

Rutledge has identified eight overriding principles to which all design projects should adhere:

1. Be sure that everything has a purpose.
2. Design for people.
3. Satisfy both function and aesthetics.
4. Establish a substantial experience.
5. Establish an appropriate experience.
6. Satisfy technical requirements.
7. Meet needs for the lowest possible cost.
8. Provide for supervision ease.[2]

BE SURE THAT EVERYTHING HAS A PURPOSE The natural resource base is a precious thing; as Will Rogers once said, "The good Lord is makin' more people, but he ain't makin' no more land." All development should be thought out ahead of time, and attractions and facilities that are built should be there for some reason. Consider, for example, the provision of play areas in a resort setting. Play may be the primary purpose of the area, in which case certain design principles should be applied. Just as play areas are used by fast-food restaurants to bring people in to eat, however, play might be the secondary purpose of the area. In this case, other design principles take precedence. First, establish the purpose, then determine the most important design criteria.

Typically, every outdoor recreational site has six parts:

1. *natural elements,* such as land, water, and plants
2. *use areas,* such as parking lots, roads, and recreational areas
3. *major structures,* such as buildings
4. *minor structures,* such as utility lines, signs, and drinking fountains
5. *people* and *animals*
6. *forces of nature,* such as wind, sunlight, and rain, that affect all of the other elements

It is vital to understand the relationship between each of these six parts and that no one part can exist in isolation from the others. Consider, for example, Figure 4.1. Before deciding where to build the amphitheater,

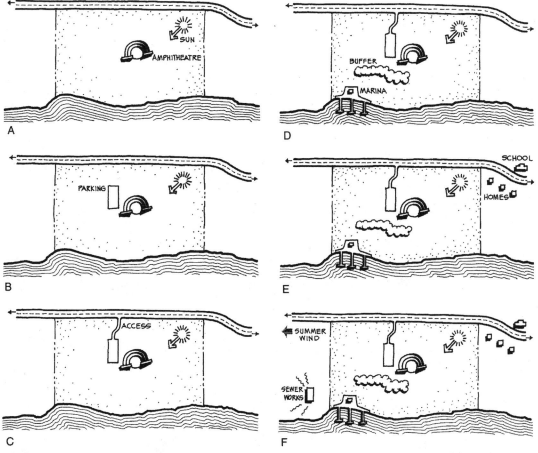

❖ FIGURE 4.1 The location of every element influences the effectiveness of all the other elements. [Source: Albert J. Rutledge, *Anatomy of a Park: The Essentials of Recreation Area Planning and Design* (New York: McGraw-Hill, 1971), 15.]

the orientation of the sun must be taken into account (A). After all, people do not want the sun shining into their eyes while they watch a performance. The location of the amphitheater determines the location of the parking lot (B). The lot should be between the structure and the road so that the noise of latecomers and early departers does not disturb the audience. The parking lot, in turn, suggests the location of the access route to the main road (C). A proposal to build a marina necessitates construction of a buffer zone to minimize noise between a relatively noisy activity and a relatively quiet one (D). Taking the surrounding school and homes into account suggests the placement of the access road as far away from the housing as possible for reasons of safety and noise (E). Finally, the neighboring sewer works and the direction of the prevailing winds must be considered to ensure that the enjoyment of boaters and theatergoers is not lessened by obnoxious smells (F).

quick getaways 4.1

The Development Process

Oz Architecture has developed the following general rules for construction of public facilities in the Rocky Mountain region.

- *cultural influences*—rustic, ranching, Native American, Spanish territorial, farming, railroads, mining
- *natural forces*—sparse rainfall, dramatic freeze–thaw cycles, high winds, lack of diverse vegetation
- *buildings*—adequate sun for heat and light, simple designs, outdoor plazas and porches
- *colors*—earthy rose, pale greens, rusty brown, warm gray
- *making the building last longer*—indigenous building materials, natural, non-toxic building materials, passive solar design

Source: "Forest Service Guidelines," *Denver Post*, 16 July 1999, p. C1.

Question: Can you develop similar guidelines for your region of the country?

Surroundings   The recreational site cannot be viewed in isolation from its surroundings.
The impact of the development on its neighbors must be considered. Will
the development obscure views or cause traffic problems or water short-
ages? When the conference center at Keystone Resort in Colorado was
designed, care was taken to make it virtually invisible to passing motorists.
Because snowmaking equipment requires heavy use of water, snowmaking
operations must stop when the water level in surrounding rivers reaches a
certain point.

Use Areas   Within the site itself, the location of various activities must be developed
in areas compatible with each use. To cite obvious examples, tennis courts
require flat surfaces and ski runs require relatively steep slopes, while
extremely steep inclines can serve as a buffer between incompatible activities. The activities to take place in an area can be characterized relative to
their need for:

- *Slope* (flat, degree of pitch)
- *Type of soil* (stability, fertility, permeability)—Soil can be characterized as clay, sand, or silt.[3] Clay absorbs and holds moisture; sand
  does not; the term *silt* covers everything that is not clay or sand. Certain types of activities are not compatible with certain types of soil.
  Roads built over clay are subject to cracking.
- *Need for vegetative cover*—Vegetation presents one of two problems:
  too much of it or not enough.[4] In some situations, it is better to remove
  vegetation. For example, a surfaced parking lot will cut off the air and
  moisture needed by the root systems of adjacent trees and other vegetation. Uprooting most of the trees during the construction phase will
  be less costly than having to do it a few years later.[5]

Many recreation areas suffer from overshading—having too many
trees providing cover. Far from providing a satisfying experience, too
much vegetation can almost intimidate visitors. Some types of trees are
hardier than others. Young hardwoods, such as the deep-rooted hickory,
are compatible with recreational use. Other shallow-rooted trees, such as
scarlet oak, American beech, Douglas fir, white pine, and aspen are candidates for damage.[6]

It can be appropriate to cut vegetation to provide vistas along road-
ways. Selective cutting can significantly enhance viewing. Safety can be
another factor; it may be prudent to provide parking areas or turnouts
that allow visitors to safely enjoy the views. Within any resort, a hierarchy
of preferred locations depends on the view and accessibility to major

amenities.[7] The prime location in a beach resort is next to the waterfront; in a ski resort, it is next to the ski run. The next preferred location is frontage on or a view of an amenity such as a lake, open space, or golf course. Next is what is termed an overview, which allows a view of an amenity from a distance and over other properties. Locations are ranked depending on the quality of the nearer amenities.

Examples of how vegetation and slope can affect how units are placed on a site are shown in Figure 4.2 on pages 94 and 95. To understand the figure, first identify the appropriate vegetation type. Four possibilities are given:

1. tree crown dominant at 50% +
2. significant tree crown from 10% to 50%
3. small tree cover
4. ground cover with bushes and shrubs

Next, find the terrain that most closely resembles the topography of the site in question. These possibilities include:

❖ flat land
❖ gentle slope
❖ gently rolling land
❖ ravine—steep slope
❖ stream valley

Finally, where the two axes intersect, the figure offers suggestions for the appropriate positioning of built units relative to the site conditions.

When the tree crown is dominant on flat land, clearings can be exploited and platform structures used to reduce ground coverage. On a gentle slope, the building structure must take the grade change into account. On a gently rolling terrain, tree house structures offer a distinctive solution. Building should be avoided in ravines and on steep slopes because of the sensitivity of the vegetation. Finally, in a stream valley, the units could be sited in a clearing between the forest and stream.

When the tree crown is between 10% and 50%, different possibilities exist. On flat land, buildings constructed at the edge of the clearing create a large open space and give a choice of views. On a gentle slope, the change in grade allows porches to face the clearing and the forest. On gently rolling hills, stacked units may be built in compact clearings. Terraced units on a steep slope give privacy while supporting views of the landscape. The larger clearing in a stream valley makes the stream a feature in an area between the units.

Small tree cover on flat land provides focal points of interest for groups of units. On a gentle slope, the openness of the site allows a view from several sides. This is important because views are an attraction that people are willing to pay for. On gently rolling hills, various views are available to and over landscape elements. A single tree on a steep slope is an invitation to stop and relax; in a stream valley, a row of trees along a stream forms a promenade between units.

Where there is little cover, buildings on flat land become dominant forms in the landscape, with vertical elements particularly strong in terms of the identity of the structure. On a gentle slope, the roof profile on an open site can be counterform to the slope. Gently rolling hills allow the possibility of using buildings to create shade and shelter. On a steep slope, a strong stepped form allows many units to have open views. Finally, in a stream valley, units can be grouped to form a dense cluster with the stream as the focus.

Proximity to Water. Because water flows downhill, erosion can result. To cope with this potential problem, a ditch and berm—a narrow ledge at the top of a slope—can be placed above a recreational area to channel runoff water away from the recreational area. Erosion is also checked by reducing the distance over which the water descends. The greater the distance before the water comes to rest, the more momentum it builds, the faster it travels, and the greater the erosion.

Pollution is another problem potentially caused by runoff. Vehicles emit pollutants. When the parking lot is uphill from the recreational area, the pollutants can be carried by rainwater to the area below. This can be prevented by constructing the parking areas at a slight grade *away from* the recreational area below. If the lot and recreational areas are already built, a filter strip consisting of a ditch filled with rock and crushed stone can be used to stop the polluted runoff.

Because water collects at the lowest point in an area, facilities built on flat ground should be crowned in the middle. Raising the center point slightly higher than the edges drains water off the facility.

Utilities. Because they are often located in remote regions, a common challenge facing resorts is providing basic utilities in areas where municipal water and wastewater systems do not exist. Provision of water is usually the responsibility of a municipality or special district. Especially in the West, water provision can be a political football. Even if ground- or surface water is available, getting the right to use it can be difficult. Developers can minimize long-term water needs by incorporating water conservation into their plans.

Vegetation ▷

Tree crown dominant 50%+   Significant tree crown 10-50%

Site topography

Flat land

Reduce ground coverage — exploit clearings, platform structure could be used

Buildings at edge of clearing create large open space & give choice of view

Gentle slope

 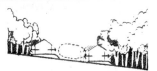

Building structure articulates grade change while performing above functions

Grade change forms porches facing clearing and into forest

Gently rolling

Tree-house type structures with catwalks can be a unique solution

Possibility for stacked units in compact clearing with easy access

Ravine — steep slope

 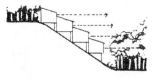

Generally an area to be avoided because of vegetation sensitivity

Terraced units on slope give privacy and views out to landscape

Stream valley

 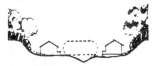

Units could be sited in clearing between forest and stream

A larger clearing makes the stream a feature in an area between units

Vegetation ▷

Small tree cover   Ground cover with bushes and shrubs

Site topography
▽

Flat land

Trees provide focal point for groups of units

Buildings are dominant forms on landscape, with vertical elements for identity

Gentle slope

Openness of site continues under building; allows a view from several sides

Roof profile on open site can be counterform to slope

Gently rolling

Various views available out to and over elements in landscape

Possibility of using building to create shade and shelter

Ravine — steep slope

Single tree on a slope is identified as a place to stop and relax

This strong stepped form can be appropriate on an open site

Stream valley

A row of trees along stream forms a promenade between units

Units are grouped to form a dense cluster with stream as focus

❖ FIGURE 4.2 Impact of vegetation and slope on development. *Planning Seasonal Tourist Accommodation* (Toronto, Ontario: Tourism Ontario, n.d.).

Waterborne wastes can be disposed of either by piping the wastes off site to a municipal sewage treatment system or by disposing of the wastes on site. The former is preferable but not always available. If the waste has to be disposed of on site, a small-scale community system is preferable to individual on-lot disposal. This latter may be the most cost-effective, however, if building density is low and the soil is appropriate. A large piece of land is required as a disposal field. It should slope away from the dwelling and be kept free of trees and shrubs to allow sunlight action.

Transportation. How people get to and from the resort as well as move around when they are there is important to the success of the project. The basic element in any resort transportation plan is the internal road and street system. The way the streets are laid out, their width, and the types of transportation allowed are often different from those of primary home communities. In some cases, the roads are left unpaved, while in others, utility lines are buried underground. In Sun City, Las Vegas, golf carts are allowed as a primary mode of transportation for the residents. The Grand Cypress Resort in Orlando has developed an electric trolley system, while Beaver Creek in Colorado is one of many winter resorts that uses horse-drawn sleighs for transporting guests.

Trails are an effective way of transporting people and their machines around recreational areas. Parks Canada classifies trails as follows:

❖ *Class 1: Primitive Trails*—marked but unimproved except for clearing and some work on dangerous areas.
❖ *Class 2: Minor Trails*—signed and improved to accommodate foot, horse traffic, or both.
❖ *Class 3: Major Trails*—as for class 2 but, in addition, reaches many of the main visitor attractions and serves as a terminus for minor and primitive trails.
❖ *Class 4: Walks*—including boardwalks and bituminous trails that connect developed areas or serve as short scenic walks.
❖ *Class 5: Special-Purpose Trails*—including bicycle, cross-country ski, and accessible trails for people with disabilities.[8]

Design standards have been developed for each of these trail types.

Three elements are important in the development of a trail:

1. function of the trail
2. relation of the trail to others in the area
3. relation of the trail to other facilities[9]

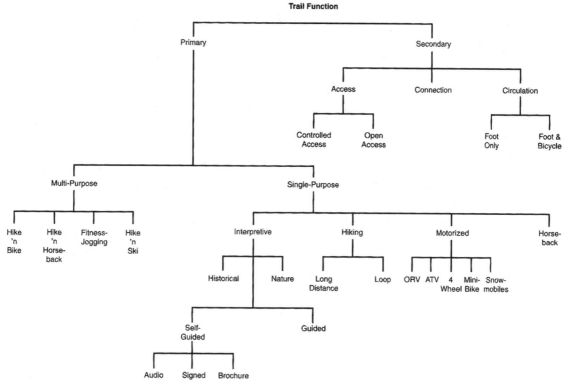

❖ FIGURE 4.3 Trail function tree diagram. [Source: John Hultsman, Richard L. Cottrell, and Wendy Z. Hultsman, *Planning Parks for People*, 2nd ed. (State College, Penna.: Venture Publishing, 1998), 49.]

Figure 4.3 shows a tree diagram to assist in determining the appropriate trail function. Note that the primary function of the trail can be single-purpose or multipurpose. A single-purpose trail might be used for interpretation, hiking, motorized, or horseback riding. Examples of multipurpose uses are hiking and biking, hiking and horseback, fitness/jogging, and hiking and skiing. Secondary uses include access, connection, and circulation. The important point is that the primary function of the trail should be identified and every subsequent design decision should be tied to that function. A trail designed to serve too many or conflicting purposes will disappoint users.

Once the function is determined, the relation of this trail to others must be determined. Some trails conflict with each other, while others complement their neighbors. Hiking and interpretation do not mix, as do not horseback and off-highway vehicles. On the other hand, dirt bike and four-wheel trails can be complementary. The final consideration is the relationship of the trail to other facilities. Again, compatibility is the issue. Motorized trails should be separated from such quiet venues as campsites.

Several important design considerations pertain to trails:

- ❖ A circular loop is preferable to a linear design. A loop eliminates backtracking and seeing the same views twice. A linear trail means traffic moves two ways on the trail. The result is more congestion.
- ❖ Use a single entry/exit point. Administration and control is easier, and visitors have less chance of being disoriented by exiting the trail and not knowing where they are.
- ❖ The trail entrance is particularly important. The entrance should be designed to funnel people into the trail in an inviting manner. The trail should be rather wide initially and gradually get narrower. This allows participants to get used to the trail.
- ❖ Trails that begin by going uphill represent an unfriendly barrier to many people. Trails that go downhill at first are much more user-friendly. Preferably, the trail should be designed so that, after the entrance, the first half of the trail has a gradual upward incline (when participants are more energized) and the latter half slopes downward (when people are more tired).
- ❖ The natural tendency for people is to move to the right. This tendency can be reinforced through proper design. A barrier to the left discourages movement that way, while a gentle curve to the right reinforces that natural movement (most people are more comfortable moving to the right).
- ❖ The need for variety is particularly important if the primary function of the trail is as a foot trail. Because people move rather slowly over such trails, a great deal of visual variety is necessary to guard against boredom. The use of curves and different kinds of scenery can enhance the experience.
- ❖ Consider orientation to sun, wind, etc.[10]

The site can be defined in terms of its positives and negatives. A picnic area is inappropriate where there are no trees for shelter; stable soil bases are necessary for the construction of buildings; roads should not be constructed where snow loads are heaviest.

Additionally, use areas should be examined relative to their compatibility with each other. For example, nature walks, canoeing, and areas for contemplation demand a certain level of peace and quiet. Tennis courts, basketball courts, and other physically active sports areas create noise as part of the enjoyment of the activity. The quiet activities and the loud activities should each be clustered together and buffered from the other. Similar activities usually require similar maintenance—another reason for the clustering.

Another consideration is the grouping of areas into zones by type of user. Day-use activities may be zoned together, away from overnight-use activities. Hultsman et al. suggest the development of "neutral zones," where primary attractions such as shorelines, scenic vistas, and overlooks are designed such that all visitors have equal access to them.[11] Thus, for example, individual-use areas such as picnic and camp units would be kept a minimum of 75 feet away from such attractions.

Structures Structures, be they major (a building) or minor (a trash can), affect the design of a facility. The relationship of the various parts of the structure to the outdoor activity areas is particularly important. Is the entrance to the building easily accessible? When swimmers leave the changing rooms, do they have immediate access to the pool or must they cross public areas used by nonswimmers? Are trash cans located in such a way that litter disposal is encouraged?

DESIGN FOR PEOPLE A major thesis of this work is that development, to be considered worthy, must take into account the physical strengths and weaknesses of the site. However, the designer has a responsibility to the final user—the guest of the operation. This raises an interesting question. Do we develop what the guest wants, what the guest needs, or what we think the guest needs—that is, what we think is best for the guest? This topic is explored in great detail in the chapters dealing with guest activity programming. Several preliminary points can, however, be made at this time. People often do not know what they do or do not want. Research studies typically show a difference between intention and participation. When asked whether or not they would engage in a particular activity, more people reply in the affirmative than actually participate when the activity is available to them. On the other hand, individuals may indicate an unwillingness to try an activity because they are unfamiliar with it. In the first instance, demand for an activity may be overstated; in the latter case, it may be understated.

Designers must be careful about putting their views ahead of the guests'. Some professionals, for example, believe that recreational activities that encourage cooperation rather than competition have positive effects on society as a whole. When this personal philosophy intrudes into the design process, the result can be politically correct play areas that users hate.

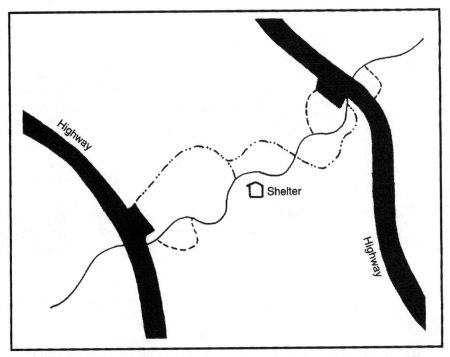

❖ FIGURE 4.4 Trail design for people. [Source: John Hultsman, Richard L. Cottrell, and Wendy Z. Hultsman, *Planning Parks for People*, 2nd ed. (State College, Penna.: Venture Publishing, 1998), 60.]

Figure 4.4 shows how a trail can be well designed for people. This example of a linear corridor trail indicates approximately 20 to 25 miles between access points. The trail is designed for the serious hiker who would leave a car at one access point, hike to the shelter for an overnight, then hike to the second access point. It illustrates several problems. Hikers can bring two vehicles, leaving one at each access point, or they can hike back the way they came. Neither is a particularly attractive option. This configuration also does not encourage the less serious hiker. The alternative is to design a series of loops of varying distances to encourage more hikers of varying degrees of stamina. A short loop of one-quarter to one-third of a mile suits the casual walker. A longer loop of one to two miles on the other side of the main trail suits the more serious walker. Mix-and-match possibilities mean that hikers can cover varying distances. For serious hikers without a second vehicle, long circular loops can bring them back to their starting point. Instead of being limited by one length of trail, planners can provide options to visitors, encouraging use by more people.

Balance
Impersonal and
Personal Needs

In seeking to address both the personal and the universal needs of the guest, the designer has to consider the purpose of various elements within the site. At certain times, all guests require information. Where is the entrance? the exit? Which slope is the steepest? When does the facility open? close? For people seeking information, repetition creates familiarity. A distinctive look to signage makes it easier and faster for the guest to pick up important information. Standardization becomes acceptable.

On the other hand, each guest has personal needs that also can be met through good design. Consider the placement of seats in airport terminals. Locked in place and built in rows, they do not encourage eye contact. Some people have even suggested that their design is part of a plan to encourage people to sit in bars and restaurants, which have seating areas more conducive to conversation and personal contact. This also encourages people to spend money, which is good for the airport authorities. Consider the differences between the two seating arrangements in Figure 4.5. One encourages interaction while the other definitely does not.

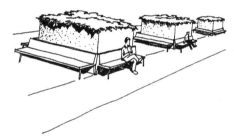

❖ FIGURE 4.5 Encouraging (and discouraging) personal interaction. [Source: Albert J. Rutledge, *Anatomy of a Park: The Essentials of Recreation Area Planning and Design* (New York: McGraw-Hill, 1971), 27.]

A variety of needs must be taken into account. Design should offer spaces for companionship as well as solitude, safety and challenge, standardization and creativity. Each guest brings a specific frame of mind to the resort associated with the recreational activity she or he intends to engage in. Snowboarders want a wild and crazy experience; conference attendees seek information. It is important to identify the characteristics of these frames of mind and design the site such that the expectations brought to the resort and its activities are met.

Play areas, especially those for children, should encourage creativity. If pieces of equipment are designed such that they relate to each other, they offer more opportunities for integrated and creative play. Individual pieces of equipment, in contrast, tend to encourage static play. Nevertheless, the need for safety must be balanced against the desire for creativity. While it is a good idea to get input from the users of the play area, children will focus on the fun part of the design while being ambivalent about safety issues.

Three types of play equipment can be used to satisfy the needs of the user: stationary, manipulated, and motion. Stationary play equipment consists of climbers, horizontal ladders, balance beams, and tunnels. The design should encourage movement *between* the various pieces. A tunnel might connect a horizontal ladder with a hill. Because the equipment itself is static, flow in the play area comes from the movement of the users. The primary safety consideration is how users move through the play area.

Manipulated equipment covers wagons, bicycles, balls, and toys. To overcome the possibility of theft of equipment, it is wise to have a designated space for manipulated equipment. Supervision is easier and creativity can be encouraged.

Motion equipment consists of equipment on which the user moves or rides. Slides, swings, and merry-go-rounds are examples. Because user and equipment may be in motion at the same time, safety is a primary concern. Additionally, it is possible for the equipment in motion to hit a bystander. The answer is to have a neutral zone to segregate areas that have motion equipment.

SATISFY BOTH FUNCTION AND AESTHETICS   In balancing function and aesthetics, it is important to balance both dollar and human values. The lower cost of doing something must be balanced with what Rutledge calls "adding to or deducting from a person's well-being."[12] The balance is between function, to which a dollar value can be attributed, and aesthetics, which is a measure of pleasurable human response. J.C. Penney said, in this regard, "If you satisfy the customer but

❖ Western icon, Jackson Hole, Wyoming. [Source: Design Workshop, Inc.]

fail to get the profit, you'll soon be out of business; if you get the profit but fail to satisfy the customer, you'll soon be out of customers." Guest satisfaction and functional profitability must go hand in hand. This means providing a satisfying experience as efficiently as possible.

For example, the path between a parking lot and a scenic overlook can be cut straight or as a curving, meandering line. While the former is functional (the shortest line between two points is a straight line), the latter is more aesthetically pleasing, builds anticipation, and helps create a pleasing recreational experience.

ESTABLISH A SUBSTANTIAL EXPERIENCE

For participants to understand what they are seeing, it is important that a label be placed on the site—that is, the site should be substantial enough so that visitors can immediately relate one or more adjectives to it, such as *peaceful*, *exciting*, or *awesome*. The key is to establish a theme—a vision of what should be.[13] Resorts might build on the unique culture or archaeology of a region in establishing the style of a resort.

Lines, Forms, Textures, Colors

A site designer uses four elements to create a substantial experience by placing a label on the site (Figure 4.6):

quick getaways 4.2

General Design Principles: Sea Pines

Sea Pines, located on Hilton Head Island, South Carolina, pioneered a number of design features that have been followed by other resorts. Among them are:

- The main access road is located in the interior and parallel to the ocean, with feeder roads connecting homesites, located on cul-de-sacs, leading toward the sea.

- Fifty-foot walkways are placed on both sides of each subdivision to allow residents to walk to the beach without crossing a street. At the same time, views are enhanced and the design both allows for breezes throughout the area and protects underground and power easements.

- Approval is required to cut down any tree more than 6 inches in diameter.

- One-quarter of the development is set aside as a nature preserve.

- The roads have no curbs or gutters, which gives them a rural feel.

- Many architectural restrictions are in place to maintain design standards.

- Wood is used for signage to blend with the natural surroundings.

Source: Adapted from David Pearson, "It Started at Sea Pines," *Urban Land* (August 1994): 22. Quoted in Dean Schwanke et al., *Resort Development Handbook* (Washington, D.C.: Urban Land Institute, 1977) vol. 53, 15.

Question: In what ways are these practices indicative of the principles outlined in the chapter?

- ❖ *Lines*—single edges indicating directional movement
- ❖ *Forms*—external appearance of objects defined by lines making closed circuits
- ❖ *Textures*—distribution of lights and darks over surfaces caused by inconsistencies in illumination
- ❖ *Colors*—qualities of light reflected off surfaces as refracted by the eye's prism[14]

❖ FIGURE 4.6 The raw materials of design.
[Source: Albert J. Rutledge, *Anatomy of a Park:
The Essentials of Recreation Area Planning and
Design* (New York: McGraw-Hill, 1971), 38.]

Lines, for example, can be used in several ways. Straight lines create a dominating effect as they move the eye forward. Horizontal lines are peaceful and create a feeling of calm, lying as they do on the ground. Ninety-degree vertical lines move the eye upward, giving an uplifting feeling. Diagonal, zigzagging lines suggest activity, while curved lines suggest tranquility.

Textures can be rough at one extreme, fine at the other. The former is bulkier, the latter more casual. Colors can be lively or mellow. Neutral colors blend into the background and can be used to separate tones that clash.

Hultsman et al. cite the — Trace, a ribbon park traversing northern Mississippi, northwest Alabama, and southern Tennessee, as a prime example of the effective use of these elements for visual variety:

The tree canopy over the parkway alternatively opens and closes to produce a sensation of changing environments. Plantings of pines have been
employed to create contrasts in color. Variations in topography and
sweeping curves are used to prevent long line-of-sight visuals along the
right-of-way and to avoid monotonous views. Grass-mowing crews,
instead of cutting on straight lines along the edge of the road, create natu-
rally shaped patterns on the side of the Trace.[15]

Dominance The various elements of a landscape are not viewed in isolation; they are
seen in relation to one another. Once a theme or label is determined, every
element in the landscape should be designed to support rather than
detract from that theme.

Enclosure Enclosing a space helps emphasize the dominant effect while having a psychological impact on the viewer. Two elements influence this feeling: the
volume of emptiness surrounding us and the type or form of the enclosure.
Compare the different feelings of being shut in a closet to being alone in an
empty Houston Astrodome. Both situations probably feel somewhat
uncomfortable. In the former instance, we feel too confined, while in the
latter, the amount of empty space around us causes discomfort.

There are three types of enclosure: static or complete, linear, and
free.[16] Static enclosure is usually square or rectangular and is suited to
functions that require isolation or attention to the center. Static enclosures

❖ Attention to
detail, Resort at
Squaw Creek,
California. [Source:
Design Workshop,
Inc.]

say "stop." They are suitable for passive forms of recreation or suggest the spot for meeting or congregating. Linear enclosures move in a definite direction and are open at both ends. They are well suited to and are used to promote movement or circulation. Linear spaces say "go." Free enclosures are suitable for unregimented activities, as they allow for movement of the eyes in a variety of directions. Free enclosures say "wander."

The point is that outdoor landscapes are three-dimensional. Various methods are used to create spaces. A major purpose is to "create three-dimensional volumes so that aesthetics and functional advantages of enclosure might be gained."[17] It was previously mentioned that no landscape element exists in isolation. The same is true of enclosures; a journey through spaces must consider their relationship. The designer asks, "What do I want visitors to feel first as they move from one space or enclosure to another?" Considered as a series of interconnected parts, the various enclosures that make up a site have more impact on the visitors than if treated as unrelated wholes.

ESTABLISH AN APPROPRIATE EXPERIENCE

Establishing a substantial experience means answering the question *what is there?* and establishing an appropriate experience means answering the question *why is it there?* The key for the designer is to extend the aesthetics of what nature has already provided into man-made structures that are added to the site. To find this key, the designer examines the physical characteristics of the site, the personality of the users, and the ambience that is usually part of the activity being undertaken on the site.

Personality of the Place

Physical places have personalities. It is "easier to provide a substantial experience through an intensification of what already exists than to first water down a pervasive mood and then begin all over again with the insertion of a feeling from scratch."[18] There are two ways to do this: as physical extension and through an awareness of factors that give a place its personality. New features can be developed as if they are extensions of the natural site. A structure might appear to "grow" out of the top of a rise. By repeating colors, textures, materials, or dominant forms in man-made structures that appear in the natural landscape, designers show their awareness of and appreciation for the natural elements that express the personality of the site.

Personality of the User

The people attracted to a particular location—the target market—might be somewhat homogeneous in their personality type. If this is the case, it is appropriate to account for this in the final plan. The key is to surround

quick getaways 4.3

Ecotourism Design

Here are some ecotourism design practices:

- Use local construction techniques, materials, and cultural images.
- Provide building forms and images in harmony with the natural environment.
- Use canopies to cover high-use trails between structures to minimize erosion.
- Avoid energy-intensive products and hazardous materials.
- Use low-tech design solutions.
- Prominently post an environmental code of conduct for visitors and staff.
- Select interior furnishings and equipment to represent local resources.
- Design trail systems to respect travel patterns and wildlife habitats.
- Minimize trail crossing points at rivers and streams.
- Space buildings to allow for wildlife travel patterns and forest growth.
- Discreetly label plant/tree types around the immediate lodging facilities to acquaint visitors with species they may encounter.
- Limit and control site lighting to avoid disruption of wildlife diurnal cycles.

Source: Kreg Lindberg and Donald E. Hawkins (eds.), *Ecotourism: A Guide for Planners and Managers* (North Bennington, Vt.: Ecotourism Society, 1993), 124–129.

users with the familiar. Some people are more conservative in taste than others, some more flamboyant. Conservatives prefer clean, no-nonsense design, while the more extroverted appreciate more flash.

Personality of Function Just as individuals have personalities, so, too, do the various activities that will take place on a specific site. Meditation requires a peaceful setting, while a child's playground needs bright colors and action-oriented spaces.

❖ Specialty signage, River Run Village, Colorado. [Source: Design Workshop, Inc.]

Space The need for scale has two aspects: human scale and speed scale. To feel comfortable in a space, individuals need to be able to relate it to things they are familiar with—mainly themselves. Photographers of landscapes are taught to put something in the foreground that gives the viewer a feeling of scale. How large is this tree *compared to the size of the average individual?* It is the same for designers. Providing elements that can be mentally measured gives the visitor a feeling of security.

The speed at which elements will be viewed must also be considered. When traveling at speed in a car, the driver can comprehend only large shapes, great blotches of color, and contrasting textures. Areas meant for walking, however, demand greater attention to detail—smaller shapes, subtler colors, and finer textures. This need is intensified for areas in which people are meant to sit still.

SATISFY TECHNICAL REQUIREMENTS To be usable, each site has certain technical requirements.

Sizes The size of a recreational site must be large enough to ensure a high-quality experience. This is a relative concept. Expert skiers on a steep run are less tolerant of sharing the slope with other skiers than are beginner skiers on an easier slope. Apart from the perception of crowding, there is a safety factor. The density of expert slopes must be less than that of beginner slopes because the experts travel at higher speeds. Some people prefer beaches where there is a lot of action and people-watching is a major attraction; others prefer solitude. The standards available for recreational sites should be taken as general guidelines to be adapted to the needs of the market.

In balancing quality with cost, it is important to locate facilities where a minimum remodeling of topography is necessary. Wherever possible, dual use of facilities allows for the provision of more facilities at a reasonable cost. The idea of dual use is to utilize the same piece of ground for different purposes at different times. In some parts of the country, for example, after roping off the greens, golf courses are used in winter for cross-country skiing.

Quantities Good planning means providing not only for existing demand but anticipating possible future expansion and, wherever possible, having a contingency plan for that expansion.

Orientation to Natural Forces Sun, wind, rain, and snow must all be taken into account when developing recreational facilities. The effect of the sun on participants can detract from enjoyment of the activity being undertaken. For example, tennis courts should be laid out at a 90-degree angle to the course of the sun to prevent it from shining directly into the eyes of the players. The sun should remain at the backs of spectators during peak viewing hours. Beaches, obviously, should get maximum exposure to the sun, while an eastern exposure is preferred for campsites. In this way, the early-morning rays help get rid of morning dampness, yet shade is provided in the heat of the afternoon.

Wind can help or hinder certain activities. A breeze is effective in helping remove cooking smells from picnic areas. However, heavier winds have a negative impact on sporting activities. This is as true for playing tennis as it is for docking boats. The key is to orient the area activities to the path of prevailing winds.

The amount and frequency of rain will affect the timing of events. That the lee side of a hill and its north-facing slopes are where snowfall is heaviest has implications for recreation. These slopes are preferred for ski and toboggan runs—and not for the placement of roads.

Operating Needs A variety of specific restrictions need to be adhered to. For example:

❖ The minimum turning radius of a car is 20 feet.
❖ The maximum grade for a boat launching ramp is 15 percent.
❖ The maximum slope negotiable by power mowers is 33 percent.[19]

Similarly, from an administrative viewpoint, if maintenance is to occur during times when the facility is closed to the public, public roads and walkways can be used. When maintenance is to occur when the public is around, a secondary service circulation system is required.

Last, but by no means least, the comfort of the user must be taken into account. This might mean ensuring the correct pitch on a bench, setting easily negotiable proportions for outdoor steps, and otherwise considering the user's physical ease (Figure 4.7).

MEET NEEDS FOR LOWEST POSSIBLE COST

Balance Needs and Budget

Communication between developer and designer is necessary to ensure that facilities meet the needs of the visitor at a cost that allows the developer to make a profit. This means considering development as well as maintenance costs. Too often, the cost of building a facility is considered apart from the cost of maintaining it. Savings made at the time of building can result in unnecessarily high maintenance costs. A lower grade of insulation might reduce construction costs but result in higher utility bills during the life of the facility. Another example concerns the building of trails. Where frost is not a concern—frost tends to cause roads and trails to heave—hot-mix asphalt is a popular treatment for trails that need to be reinforced because of heavy use. The problem with asphalt is that, especially in hot weather, it crumbles along the edges when people step on it. From a maintenance viewpoint, this means that the edges must be patched periodically. However, if, during the construction phase, the planner considered the management and maintenance of the trail, a border of

❖ FIGURE 4.7 Consider the comfort of the user. [Source: Albert J. Rutledge, *Anatomy of a Park: The Essentials of Recreation Area Planning and Design* (New York: McGraw-Hill, 1971), 60.]

Management and Operation of Swimming Pools

According to some experts, an attractive pool is one of the most visible and cost-effective resort amenities. Keeping the pool attractive requires constant maintenance.

➤ *Know your chemistry*—The single most important factor in extending the life of the pool and reducing repairs is keeping the water chemistry in balance. An automated water chemistry control system measures chlorine and pH levels every three seconds and automatically dispenses the right amount of chemicals into the pool. These systems cost between $3,000 and $5,000 but pay for themselves after two years due to savings on chemicals and manpower.

➤ *Renovations*—Exposed-aggregate pool finishes, such as Diamond Bright and Krystal Krete, cost 15 percent more than regular finishes but last longer and are easier to maintain. Decks can be spruced up with emulsions or concrete pavers in different shapes, textures, and colors. Adding lighting for evening ambience completes the effect.

➤ *Starting over*—There comes a time when it is cheaper to tear out the pool and start over rather than to repair it. If your pool is over 30 years old, this be may the better strategy. During pool replacement is a good time to integrate changes in construction such as larger multipurpose decks, dramatic architectural elements such as waterfalls, shallow wet decks for kids, and access for seniors and people in wheelchairs.

Source: Delores Wright, "In the Swim," *RCI International* (January/February 2000): 24.

Question: What factors are important to you in determining the attractiveness of a swimming pool?

crushed rock could be placed along the edge of the trail and tapered to ground level. The weight of the gravel would prevent crumbling along the side. Any additional cost during development pays off in reduced maintenance expenditures later.

Use Existing Site Resources Using the strengths and being aware of the limitations of the site can help reduce costs. Campsite construction is much lower if building occurs on soil that drains well and does not require underdraining. Pine trees die quickly when subject to heavy foot traffic, while hardwoods survive longer. The key is to place activities on parts of the site that, in their undeveloped form, approximate the desired finish grade. The cost of earth removal is reduced while the task of integrating the new with the old is made easier. Can existing buildings be renovated rather than torn down? Can we design around trees rather than chopping them down?

Provide Appropriate Structural Materials Materials used in construction should be selected based on these qualities:

- *Durability*—Will it stand up to wear and tear?
- *Appearance*—Does it blend with its surroundings?
- *Availability*—Can it be found locally?
- *Tactile qualities*—How does it feel to the touch?
- *Climatic adaptability*—Will it remain stable in this environment?
- *Drainability*—Is it usable after storms?[20]

Provide Appropriate Plant Materials As noted throughout, plants can be used to enhance any design. They work best when the selection takes into account the surrounding activity as well as the specific needs of the plants. Plant needs are described in terms of:

- *Soil*—heavy, light, acid, alkaline
- *Moisture*—heavy or light
- *Hardiness*—ability to handle extreme temperatures
- *Life span*—longevity
- *Susceptibility to disease*

As a rule, select, as new growth, plant varieties with characteristics similar to existing vegetation. Another factor is the effect of the plant on visitors. For example, oleander, in many ways, is effective around campsites. It is dense for screening, attractive for aesthetics, and can provide lots of sticks suitable for roasting hot dogs. Unfortunately, it is also poisonous!

PROVIDE FOR SUPERVISION EASE

Proper design can encourage "good" behavior while discouraging "bad." Traffic flows can be anticipated and obstacles eliminated. For example, a parking lot might be used by two use areas—a picnic area and a lake used for swimming. Placing the parking area between these two use areas will encourage foot traffic from one to the other through the parking area. The result is a safety hazard. Placing the parking area peripheral to both use areas allows foot traffic from one to the other that bypasses the lot. Consider, for example, the difference in design between Figures 4.8 and 4.9. In Figure 4.8, a proposal for an Indiana State Park campground, over 20 intersections are planned—each a potential safety hazard. By developing primary and secondary routes, as in Figure 4.9, circulation and safety are improved.

Activities can be made safer by locating like activities together and using buffer zones to separate incompatible activities. Cushioning surfaces can help prevent injuries in fall zones. Slides can be built into natural slopes. Play equipment involving motion should be built into the corners of play areas.

People intent on vandalizing natural features on a trail tend to do so within 500 feet of the trail entrance.[21] Placing expensive facilities such as benches well into the trail helps minimize this problem. Another tendency

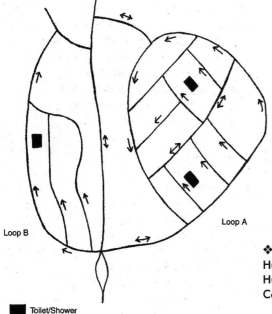

Loop B

Loop A

Toilet/Shower

❖ FIGURE 4.8 Unsafe circulation. [Source: John Hultsman, Richard L. Cottrell, and Wendy Z. Hultsman, *Planning Parks for People*, 2nd ed. (State College, Penna.: Venture Publishing, 1998), 7.]

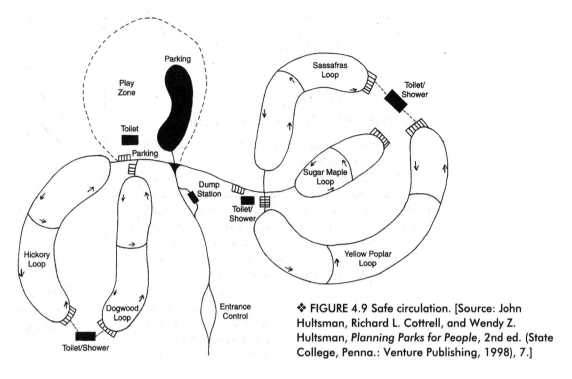

❖ FIGURE 4.9 Safe circulation. [Source: John Hultsman, Richard L. Cottrell, and Wendy Z. Hultsman, *Planning Parks for People*, 2nd ed. (State College, Penna.: Venture Publishing, 1998), 7.]

is for vandals to carve names in smooth-barked trees, such as aspen in the West and American beech in the East. The solution is to build the trail at least 10 feet from such vegetation.

SUMMARY

It is important to avoid thinking of the development and design of a facility as a process divorced from its management and maintenance. The reason is that decisions made in the concept's design can significantly affect maintenance and management costs. Various principles of design were suggested, the application of which encourages the development of recreational attractions and facilities that respect the natural resources base while minimizing management and maintenance problems.

ENDNOTES

1. Albert J. Rutledge, *Anatomy of a Park* (New York: McGraw-Hill, 1971), viii.
2. Ibid., 23–79.

3. John Hultsman, Richard L. Cottrell, and Wendy Z. Hultsman, *Planning Parks for People*, 2nd ed. (State College, Penna.: Venture, 1998), 16.
4. Ibid., 17.
5. Rutledge, *Anatomy of a Park*, 17.
6. Hultsman, Cottrell, and Hultsman, *Planning Parks for People*, 18.
7. Dean Schwanke et al., *Resort Development Handbook* (Washington, D.C.: Urban Land Institute, 1977), 114.
8. Data from the Parks Canada website (http://parkscanada.pch.gc.ca/library/trails/english/trailce.html), obtained June 1999.
9. Hultsman, Cottrell, and Hultsman, *Planning Parks for People*, 49-52.
10. Ibid., 52-55.
11. Ibid., 24.
12. Rutledge, *Anatomy of a Park*, 31.
13. Schwanke et al., *Resort Development Handbook*, 111.
14. Rutledge, *Anatomy of a Park*, 37-38.
15. Hultsman, Cottrell, and Hultsman, *Planning Parks for People*, 35.
16. Rutledge, *Anatomy of a Park*, 41-42.
17. Ibid., 42.
18. Ibid.
19. Ibid., 58-59.
20. Ibid., 64.
21. Hultsman, Cottrell, and Hultsman, *Planning Parks for People*, 57.

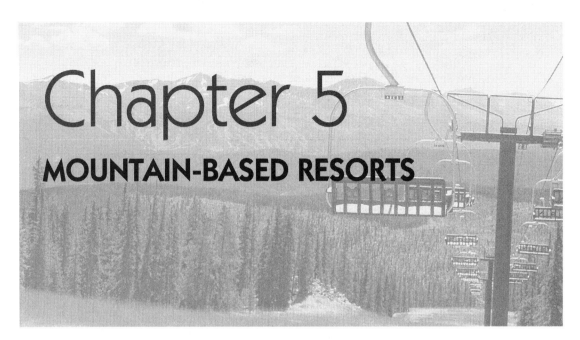

Chapter 5
MOUNTAIN-BASED RESORTS

Introduction

The Development Process
    Balance   Planning Process   Permits

Desirable Sites
    Site Feasibility

General Design Guidelines

Capacity
    Potential Capacity

Ski Runs
    Site Design

Ski Lift Network
    Types of Lifts

Base Area
    Parking   Access Roads   Food Service   Accommodation
    Maintenance   Emergency Care

Other Winter Sports Activities
    Cross-Country Skiing   Snowmobiling   Tobogganing   Ice Skating

Summer in the Mountains

Summary

Endnotes

INTRODUCTION

Compared to other major amenities, ski areas are much like-
lier to be profitable business ventures that may, as a logical
adjunct, also engage in real estate development.
—URBAN LAND INSTITUTE
Planning Considerations for Winter Sports Resort Development

The physical facilities of a ski area figure prominently in skiers' evaluation of the overall quality of the resort complex. In one study, skiers at four Vermont resorts rated the most meaningful potential indicators of quality as:

1. daily lift ticket price
2. maximum waiting time in lift lines
3. type of food service
4. walking time from parking lot to base lodge
5. percentage of terrain covered by snowmaking
6. attitudes of ski area employees[1]

Three of these items—2, 4, and 5—are design issues, while item 3 deals with the provision of specific services.

In this chapter, the process of developing a ski resort is outlined. Care must be taken to strike a balance between the physical capacity of the site to accommodate skiers and the economic need of the developer to make a profit. Characteristics of desirable sites and general design principles are noted. The all-important order in which decisions are made is defined.

THE DEVELOPMENT PROCESS

Although private land values are affected by the location of
resort areas, maximizing the value of individual tracts of pri-
vate land must be a secondary consideration of the Forest
Service.
—U.S. FOREST SERVICE

BALANCE   The conceptual design philosophy involves a balance—a physical balance, first, between the ski area and the market, and, second, an economic balance between investment and earning power.[2]

Physical Balance   *Physical balance* means that the size of the ski area must be sufficient to meet the needs of the market without being so large that the area is underutilized. Within the resort area itself, balance is also required. The

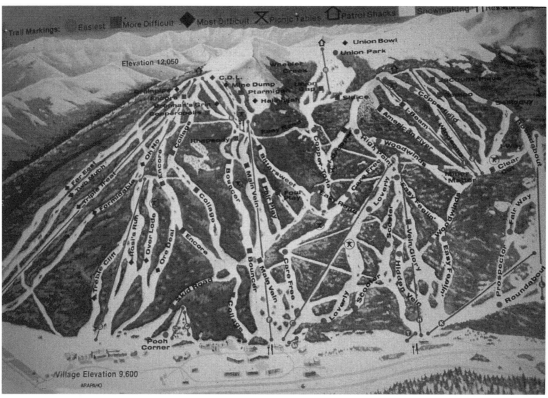

❖ Balancing the
physical elements.

capacity of the mountain dictates the number of skiers that can be accommodated, both from a safety angle and from the viewpoint of skier enjoyment. The capacity of the mountain to handle skiers, in turn, dictates the ski lift network capacity required. In other words, the capacity of the lifts to bring people up the mountain must be in balance with the trail capacity to bring them down the mountain. Capacity, in turn, indicates the support facilities needed at the base and surrounding areas.

Economic Balance

The second area of balance suggested by Farwell brings together the amount of money invested in the project and its earning capacity. Investors put money into developing infrastructure and buildings—physical plant—which is then used to generate revenue. The quantity and quality of physical plant must be sufficient to generate enough revenue for investors to get a decent return on their investment. Revenue generation is a function of number of skiers, revenue per skier visit, and the length of the season. At the same time, to ensure a return, management must keep costs in line.

PLANNING   The general process for developing a ski area is outlined in Figure 5.1.
PROCESS

Concept and   An initial concept is created. Ski areas, because of their high cost of devel-
Objectives   opment, are more likely than other recreational facilities to be developed
as for-profit recreational developments first and real estate opportunities
second. However, the trend is toward ski areas using land development as
a way of increasing the profits of the operation.

Ski areas can be designated as:

❖ *Type I resorts*—These international destinations feature excellent
   mountains and a wide variety of lodging and real estate.
❖ *Type II resorts*—These resorts are not as well known in the marketplace as Type I resorts; they offer fewer activities and appeal to a
   more limited market, such as ski clubs and groups.
❖ *Type III resorts*—These resorts offer high-quality skiing but little
   real estate development. Many operate only on weekends.[3]
❖ *Small, often marginal developments*—These resorts operate only on
   weekends. For example, the typical club hill in Ontario has no
   snowmaking, is less than a 300-foot drop, and has a T-bar lift and a
   chalet without a liquor license.[4]

Real estate buyers at Type I resorts tend to be older, more loyal to the
area, more family-oriented, and less likely to rent out their units. Those at
Type II resorts are younger, ski more often and at more areas, and are
more interested in their real estate as an investment rather than its use
potential. The smaller weekend areas cater to families, children, and
beginning skiers. Important to local residents, they do not attract out-of-
towners. They can, however, help develop a pool of skiers eager for bigger
challenges.

The specific objectives for the development are then established. A
survey of the potential market and a comparison of sites, together with an
examination of the likelihood of financing, produce a determination of the
most desirable site. This site becomes the subject of a detailed analysis.

General design guidelines are then established and the ski and base
area capacities are determined. Detailed design guidelines can then be for-
mulated and the ski runs laid out. As noted above, the ski runs determine
the layout and size of the ski lift network, which will, in turn, influence the
layout of the base area. At each step, the ski area capacity might have to be
revised and the layouts revised.

Next, the access route is laid out and a final check made to ensure that
the ski runs, the ski lifts, the base area, and the access route are balanced.

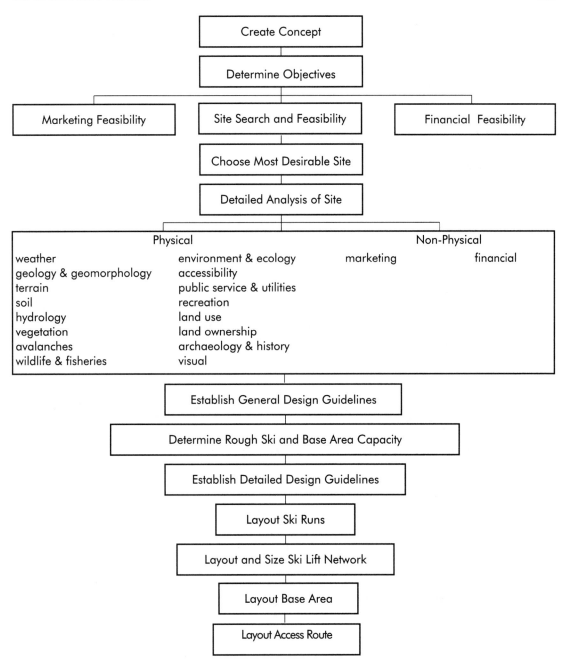

❖ FIGURE 5.1 The development process for ski areas.

quick getaways 5.1

The Development Process: Doing More with Less

Resort master planning used to be, and in many cases still is, a long, drawn-out process that could take upwards of 20 years. As ownership of ski resorts falls into the hands of large, publicly traded companies, there is increased pressure from shareholders for resorts to produce shorter-term returns. According to Becky Zimmerman, principal of Design Workshop, "Real estate products are becoming the driving force for these areas because you don't make a lot of money in operating a mountain." Skiers are getting older, they have discretionary income, and are potential real estate customers. Developments are being created at a variety of price points. A few years ago, Vancouver-based Intrawest began building smaller condominium units to appeal to those unable to afford expensive second homes. At Keystone's Buffalo Lodge, the condominiums average 900 square feet, well below the 1200 to 1400 square feet at other Colorado resorts. Even at this size, they are priced at $327,000.

Source: Jill Jamieson-Nichols, "Beyond Skiing: New Trends in Colorado Mountain Resort Development," *Urban Land* (April 1998) vol. 57: 82–85.

Question: **What impacts have the entry of publicly traded companies into the marketplace had on ski resort development?**

If necessary, the design can be revised, development phased in, and a master base area, construction, and operating plan developed. An environmental statement is then drafted, a profitability or pro-forma analysis made, and final design approval sought.

PERMITS Most of the largest and most visible ski areas in the United States are built, at least partially, on land managed by the U.S. Forest Service (USFS). Over 90 percent of ski areas in the Rocky Mountain and Pacific West operate under USFS permits. This compares to 35 percent of areas in the Northeast, 8 percent in the Midwest, and none in the Southeast.[5] The 1960 Multiple Use Sustained Yield Act allows private ski areas on national forest land. This policy was codified by various memoranda of understanding between U.S. Skiing, the National Ski Areas Association (NSAA), and the U.S. Forest Service. U.S. Skiing is the governing body for the sports and snowboarding in the United States. The NSAA is the trade association for U.S. ski areas and represents most of the ski areas permitted to operate on lands administered by the United States Forest Service. The USFS is responsible for managing multiple activities in national forests in a way that is environmentally sustainable. Together they seek to emphasize:

❖ public/private partnerships in developing recreational facilities
❖ multiple use public land management
❖ sustainable communities
❖ viable local economies
❖ ecosystem health

Because development requires a permit from the USFS, developers are expected to show that the resort development will provide a public benefit in addition to a profit benefit to the developer. The permit process has six steps:

1. identification of a potential site by both a developer and the USFS
2. issuance of a study permit by USFS to allow close physical examination of the site by the developer
3. issuance of a development prospectus by USFS giving the developer (and others) the opportunity to bid for development rights
4. awarding of development rights by USFS to a developer
5. preparation of master plan and environmental assessment by the selected developer
6. issuance of a special use permit by USFS. This is the legal contract and operating agreement between the USFS and the concessionaire. A term permit, usually 20 to 30 years, is issued for areas at the base of the mountain, while annual permits cover the rest of the development.[6]

Future development is subject to negotiation. The concessionaire is charged an annual fee for the right to use public land. The fee is based on the amount of physical improvement and on revenue generated.

Three points can be made relative to operations on USFS land:

1. The USFS permit process for initial development and/or expansion can be extremely time-consuming and costly.
2. Changes in USFS policies relative to fees, long-term land ownership, and so on directly affect resort operations.
3. Resorts operating under USFS permits may be required to shut down late in the season even if late spring snow conditions are such that operations could continue.[7]

The point is that resorts operating under USFS jurisdiction do not have the flexibility that areas operating on private lands enjoy.

In France, since the Environmental Protection Act of 1976, an impact study must be conducted for any project whose cost exceeds 6 million francs. In Germany, the political acceptability of the project is a major factor in determining whether or not it will be approved. In contrast to the United States, no ski area in France has been stopped because of environmental concerns. Skiing is not viewed as detrimental to the mountain.[8]

In Australia, the state of Victoria created the Victoria Alpine Commission, an agency totally independent from the Parks Service. Recognizing that skiing is very different from other activities taking place in the parks, this agency handles all of the skiable terrain in addition to a few potential sites.

DESIRABLE SITES

The guiding principle is clear: wherever conflicts occur
between resource protection and increased use and develop-
ment, protection will take precedence.
                                —Banff National Park Management Plan, 1988

SITE FEASIBILITY   The development of mountain sites is a particularly challenging endeavor. The USFS has developed an inventory form for evaluating the development potential of a site (Figure 5.2, pages 126–127). The overall physical feasibility of the site is a function of four factors:

❖ scope and attractiveness of the site
❖ access and proximity to markets
❖ environmental limitations
❖ unusual site-specific costs[9]

Attractiveness   The attractiveness of the site is determined by various factors. First, in terms of the environment, people look for a desirable mix of climate, snow conditions, exposure and snow retention, and forest cover.[10]

Extreme temperatures should be avoided and wind problems should be infrequent. The best snow is dry. A minimum of 250 inches of snow is the standard for a modern ski area.[11] Machine snowmaking, in recent years, has allowed previously marginal ski areas to operate profitably. In New England and other eastern states, the wide temperature variations followed by periods of rain and freezing weather mean that the length of the season depends on the quality of man-made snow.[12] Increasingly, natural snow is being supplemented by artificial snow.

Similar to the irrigation system of a golf course, a snowmaking system requires a water reservoir, a distribution network of piping and pumps, and numerous nozzles or guns to spread the snow over the slopes.[13] The system works because, at certain temperature and humidity levels, water can be broken into small droplets and forced into the atmosphere under pressure provided by compressed air or large fans; the water returns to the ground as snow. It is denser and contains more water and less air than natural snow. Compressorless systems are less expensive to operate and, because they are quieter, are attractive around base areas. Compressed air systems require less maintenance and last longer. They also operate effectively under a greater range of temperatures. Compressorless systems perform best under colder temperatures, ideally 0°F.

Snowmaking equipment requires a dependable, high-quality water supply together with easy access to utilities. Machine snowmaking, for example, requires 180,000 gallons per acre-foot of snow.[14] This translates into usage of between 500 and 10,000 gallons of water per minute. Once the water is converted to snow, 78 percent of it returns to the watershed during spring melting and runoff.

GROUP DELTA, a major ski resort consultant, has pioneered a method of combining low snowmaking cost and maximum attractiveness to skiers. One or more trails, 300 to 400 feet in width, are built with islands in the middle to enhance the aesthetics by breaking up the monotony of empty trail. A single set of snowmaking pipeline is buried up the center of the trail, where strategically placed hydrants, 140 feet apart, can service both sides of the run.

Fully automated snowmaking systems have been available since the mid-1980s. These systems mean few people are needed to handle hoses and nozzles. This is particularly helpful in countries like France, where labor laws are strict and scheduling flexibility is restricted.[15]

In North America, a north and northeast exposure helps protect the terrain from the effects of sun and wind. Steep slopes and those at lower levels increase the problem of exposure. This also depends on location. At

Criterion	As measured by					
Snow Cover (Period Adequate)	Number of months	4 or more	3	2	1	1 or less
Snow Texture	Dry snow, fraction of season	2/3 or more	1/2	1/3	1/4	Less than 1 month
Snow Depth	Feet of snow—average	4 or more	3 to 4	2 to 3	1 to 2	Less than 1
Artificial snow if natural is inadequate	Weather and economics of snow making	Well suited	Marginal	Inappropriate		
Snowfall (as adverse factor)	Occurrence of major problems	None to negligible	Occasional	Frequent	Continuous	
Ice (consider for ice skating only)	Satisfactory (period of days)	90 or more	60 to 90	30 to 60	Less than 30	Rate only if ice skating involved
Slopes (vertical rise)	Skiable feet of rise	More than 3000	2000–3000	1000–2000	500–1000	
Slope steepness and range of challenge	For Novice: Intermediate: Advanced:	All All All	Majority Majority Majority	Adequate Adequate Adequate	Inadequate Inadequate Inadequate	None None None
Slopes—aspect	General aspect of	North	Northeast	East	West	Northwest South
Slopes—continuity	Single-class skier trails	Can be easily developed	Developed at moderate cost	Substantial modification required	Major terrain changes required	Cannot reasonably be developed
Slope clearing cost	Cost	Low	Moderate	High		
Ground surface conditions	Cost of slope modification and revegetation	None	Low	Moderate	High	Modification desirable but not allowed
Slope protection	Natural protection from wind and sun	Adequate for all slopes	Adequate for most slopes	Inadequate for all slopes		
Winds	Typical of season	Slight	Occasional with drifting	Occasional high winds	Frequent high winds	
Temperature (air)	Daytime temperature	Above 0°F most days	Max is above 0°F most days	Max is below 0°F most days		
Avalanche (potential and control)	Avalanche potential Avalanche hazard Control level	None None None	Occasional Slight Nominal	Frequent Moderate Moderate	Sustained Acceptable most of season Intensive	 Unacceptable most of season
Electrical Power	Availability and cost	At site; cost nominal	Available at moderate cost	Available at high cost	Unavailable or cost prohibitive	

Criterion (cont'd)	As measured by (cont'd)					
Parking and base area size	Availability of space needed for base facility development	Adequate for extensive development	Adequate for essential services	Adequate but with complex land-ownership	Inadequate (surface transportation needed)	Inadequate
Season potential	Compare winter and summer operations	Summer better than winter	Winter better than summer	Winter season only		
Landownership status	Private vs. USFS ownership of base area	Unimportant for success	Desirable but not essential	Necessary—private land in large blocks	Necessary—private land in small blocks	
Optimum size of development	Size of area	National importance	Regional importance	Local importance		
Aesthetic Impact	Visibility from main roads or nearby community	None to slight	Moderate	Obvious	Report visibility, not if it is objectionable	
Access	Adequacy of transportation from population centers	Excellent to site	Good, but some roads needed	Good, but much road needed	Poor, but acceptable	Inaccessible
APPRAISER'S RATING: JUDGMENTAL:		Outstanding	Good	Marginal	Unacceptable	Unacceptable

❖ FIGURE 5.2 Inventory form—potential winter sports development sites. [Source: H. Peter Wingle, *Planning Considerations for Winter Sports Resort Development* (Washington, D.C.: USDA Forest Service, 1994), 3.]

Mount Hood, Oregon, there is so much snow that even the south-facing slopes above timberline are ideal for skiing late in the season.

Forest cover adds to the aesthetics of the experience while providing protection from the wind to both the skier and the slope. It adds contrast when the light is flat and challenge to experienced skiers.

Terrain is the second factor affecting the attractiveness of a site. The grade of the terrain should match the ability level of the market to be served. A variety of grades and views make for an aesthetically pleasant experience. Developers must be especially aware of the following:

❖ steep and unstable slopes and rockfall zones
❖ heavy snowfall
❖ avalanches
❖ microclimate conditions, such as wind hazards
❖ watersheds and wetlands

❖ flooding and unstable water flows
❖ air quality problems due to inversion (the brown cloud effect caused by cold air trapping warm air close to the ground)
❖ vistas
❖ sun orientation and shadows
❖ impact of seasonal changes on the resort's activity patterns[16]

The skier carrying capacity is noted in skier density per acre of terrain and takes into account that just under half of the skiers are on the ski runs at any one time. The others are riding the lifts, resting in the lodges, or waiting in lift lines. Acceptable density depends on the market being served. Vacation destination areas average 10 to 15 skiers per acre. This is a question of economics in addition to safety and attractiveness. The higher the development cost and/or the shorter the season, the higher the density needed to operate economically. New England ski areas average 20 skiers per acre while, in the Midwest, the average increases up to 100 per acre.

Density is also related to snow cover, slope and trail design, and slope maintenance.[17] Higher densities are acceptable when snowfall and snow retention is greater, where snow maintenance is practiced, and where the design of the slope keeps skiers on the fall line.

A major constraint for ski areas, and the third factor affecting the attractiveness of a site, is lack of space at the base. This is especially true for parking facilities. The most effective way for a mountain to operate is by way of a lift system that disperses skiers across the resort. The lifts radiate from one or two points. The staging area at the base must be large enough to permit this.

The density of housing units lessens the farther away they are from the base area. High-density, expensive units—typically hotels—surround the base area to meet the needs of skiers who stay a relatively short time. Farther away are medium-density condominium or timeshare units. Farther away still are single-family homes where premiums are paid for attractive views. Direct access to the ski slopes increases the room rate or real estate prices.

Retail development is structured similarly, with restaurants, ski shops, and specialty stores located close to the slopes, convenience services farther out, and services and larger stores even farther out.[18]

The fourth and final factor affecting the attractiveness of a site is the potential length of the season. The typical ski season of 130 days runs from Thanksgiving to Easter, with variations depending on climate. For example, northern Ontario and northern Michigan have a season of 131

quick getaways 5.2

Sno-Engineering

Sno-Engineering is a consulting company that specializes in developing new ski resorts as well as helping existing resorts improve their trails and services. When it is working on a new site, the company, founded in 1958, examines every aspect of the venture. What may look at first like a good mountain for skiing may have several flaws as a resort.

Trails must face the right direction to hold enough snow cover. The terrain should be varied enough so that skiers of all skill levels have the opportunity to enjoy the mountain. Environmental constraints have to be considered.

There have been times when Sno-Engineering has told prospective resort makers that their mountains were unsuitable. Sno-Engineering's solid reputation in the industry is based partly on its refusal to represent any particular product. Basically, it modifies equipment to fit the specific mountain. In addition to offering mountain planning and design, the company will place a construction manager on site to supervise any building that needs to be done.

Source: Michael Kirkpatrick, "Jack Frost, Inc.," New England Business 13, no. 2 (February 1991): 52–53.

Question: How do the Sno-Engineering philosophy and trail criteria compare to those identified in the text?

days, while in southern Quebec the season is 10 days shorter. Central and southern Michigan have a season of 100 days, from the middle of December until the third week in March. In southern Ontario, the 70-day season starts just before Christmas and lasts until the end of February.[19]

By adding night skiing, resorts can significantly increase the number of skiers who can be accommodated, thus making the resort area more economically viable.

Access to Markets   The more attractive the site, the farther people will travel to get there. The flip side is that, as distance from major markets increases, the scope and attractiveness of the area must increase. Skiers are willing to travel one to two hours at most to ski at a day area aiming for a local market. Weekend ski areas targeting a regional market can expect skiers to travel up to half a day to enjoy the slopes, while the national or international market seeking a vacation destination will travel more than a half day for this option.

Environmental Limitations   In large part, skiers are attracted to a winter resort because of the opportunity to experience nature. Balancing the economics of skier numbers with the aesthetics of the outdoor experience is important for the long-

❖ Beautiful places, Big Sky, Montana.
[Source: Design Workshop, Inc.]

term profitability of the resort. Resorts may face such environmental limitations as the presence of wildlife habitats that are home to endangered species, the existence of special cultural or archaeological sites deemed worthy of preservation, and a scarcity of natural resources. Ski areas have to be particularly sensitive to:

- ❖ minimizing impact during construction
- ❖ preserving wildlife patterns
- ❖ using storage ponds or reservoirs to minimize the impact of snowmaking on streams and rivers
- ❖ providing employees with public transportation and guests with shuttle service to help improve air quality
- ❖ developing recycling and waste management programs
- ❖ conserving energy[20]

Site Costs The cost of the land must be balanced against the revenue an area can generate. In the West, where over three-quarters of all ski areas are on public land, an annual lease payment is made. In other regions, land cost is a major item in determining the economic viability of an area. Anything more than $1000 per acre makes the area too expensive, unless other favorable factors are present that would offset the high cost.

Increasing numbers of areas have added snowmaking as a way of increasing capacity. Careful analysis must be made, as snowmaking requires a capital investment of $25,000 to $70,000 per acre. In addition, it costs $2.00 per hour per acre to operate the equipment. The costs of power and water must be carefully considered against the potential extra revenue.

GENERAL DESIGN GUIDELINES

Good design evolves as a process that articulates goals and values, identifies design-determining forces, targets strategic priorities and concepts and facilitates change over time without the loss of community identity.
—ELDON BECK AND SHERRY DORWARD
Resort Development Handbook

Mountain resort communities must have goals intended to meet the expectations of guests while emphasizing what is special about the local area. This link between people and the natural environment should aim at creating livable year-round communities of people who have strong emotional bonds to the area.

Physical, aesthetic, and social forces help determine the design of a community. Concepts that must be taken into account include:

❖ subordination of the automobile
❖ human scale
❖ pedestrian amenities
❖ physical and visual links between the community and its natural resource base
❖ provision for the needs of a permanent population[21]

Certain design principles provide an umbrella for the specifics of site planning.

1. To avoid land use conflicts, it is important that the design of the ski area conform to the existing physical site. This makes for an environmentally sound project. In addition, by minimizing changes to the terrain, costs are significantly reduced.

2. The ability of skiers approximates a bell curve, with 5 percent to 15 percent on either end of the curve and approximately 70 percent in the middle. Participation at resorts tends to follow these proportions. The ideal ski area matches the difficulty of its slopes to this bell curve.

3. Newly groomed slopes attract skiers one or two classes below the design difficulty of the slope. On the other hand, slopes with many moguls or icy conditions increase the slope difficulty.

4. A given ski area supports fewer and fewer skiers as their ability level increases. More experienced skiers are more expensive to take care of than beginners as they demand more vertical feet of skiing per day. Because of their slope demands, they ride the lifts more often and prefer to ski at the top of the mountain where development, construction, and maintenance costs are greater. Because they ski faster than less experienced skiers, fewer can be accommodated on a trail.

5. Novices and intermediate skiers bring in more money than do advanced skiers.

6. Access road design should be based on expected peak traffic where weather is not a factor. Generally speaking, skiers arrive at an area over a two-hour period in the morning. This principle means that traffic can be handled approximately 60 percent of the time. Weather can be expected to be poor 20 percent of the time during the peak season, requiring more than two hours to access the area. Additionally, another 20 percent of the time, more than two hours will be needed when crowds over capacity want to ski.[22]

CAPACITY

*Think about how to separate skiers that have different skiing
abilities. They should not interfere with each other; a mixture of
difficulty on a single trail may either make the entire trail too
difficult for the less able, or sections that are too easy for some
skiers may render the entire trail unpopular for that group.*
                                                    —U.S. FOREST SERVICE
                        Planning Considerations for Winter Sports Resort Development

The general process of identifying capacity is to use the amount of skiable
area for each skier classification to determine ski area capacity, which is
used, in turn, to determine the ski lift and base area facilities necessary.

**POTENTIAL
CAPACITY**
The capacity of the ski area is determined by carefully following these
seven steps.

1. *Legal boundaries*—First, identify the legal boundaries of the area
   and delineate them on an area map.
2. *Total skiable acres*—Next, determine the total skiable acreage that
   is available. Terrain can be classified as unskiable, marginal, or
   attractive.[23] Terrain may be unskiable because it is too steep, too
   flat, has an excess of rocks, is subject to avalanches, or is in an
   extremely windy area. Base and cliff areas as well as areas of excessive soil instability should be excluded.

   Marginal terrain is skiable but is not attractive. It might consist
   of narrow, flat ridges. This type of terrain can be used for access
   and egress to base areas or for linking attractive ski runs. It is not
   included as skiable acreage.
3. *Skier classification*—The total skiable acreage is made up of slopes
   of various gradients. The steeper the slope, the more advanced the
   skier has to be. Advanced skiers prefer less crowded conditions
   than are tolerated by novice skiers. Additionally, the safety factor
   dictates that steeper slopes have fewer skiers per acre on them.
   Thus, the next step is to break down the total skiable acreage by
   type of skier.

   The U.S. Forest Service suggests that beginners have a 15-25%
   slope gradient, intermediate skiers a 25-40% slope gradient, and
   advanced skiers a slope gradient greater than 40%. The guidelines
   suggested by noted industry consultant Ted Farwell are shown in
   Table 5.1.

❖ TABLE 5.1 Ski Area Planning

Skill Class	Terrain Gradients	Terrain Capacity			Vertical Feet[a]	Vertical Meters[a]
		Skier Market	Skiers/Acre			
			Slopes	Total		
Beginner	10–15%	5%	22–44	50–100	421	128
Novice	15–25%	10%	18–26	40–60	946	288
Low Intermediate	25–35%	20%	13–22	30–50	1262	385
Intermediate	30–40%	30%	9–15	20–35	1683	513
High Intermediate	35–45%	20%	7–9	15–20	2322	577
Advanced	45–60%	10%	4–7	10–15	2709	673
Expert	60%+	5%	4–7	10–15	3871	962
Average			10–17	23–38	2000	497
Daily Average[b]					9299	2834

[a] Vertical feet of skiing demand per hour.

[b] Based on 5 hours of skiing for beginners through intermediates and 6 hours of skiing for high intermediates through experts.

Source: Ted Farwell, *The Concept of Balance, Ski Area Design Analysis, and the Mountain Design Process* (Boulder, Colo.: Ted Farwell & Associates, Inc. n.d.), 26ff.

4. *Ideal ratios*—Next, compare the actual number of acres in each gradient category to ideal ratios. The ideal takes into account that about 20 percent of skiers are beginners and advanced skiers, while approximately 60 percent are intermediate. The actual average distribution of terrain by skier ability is actually 24 percent beginner, 45 percent intermediate, and 31 percent advanced/expert. The tendency is toward more beginner terrain in the Southeast and Midwest and more expert terrain in the Rocky Mountains.[24] Refer again to Table 5.1 for a more detailed breakdown. Additionally, note that advanced skiers spend significant time on intermediate slopes.

The development ratio for any particular resort depends on the characteristics of the target market, the unique characteristics of the site, the continuity of the total ski run and lift network, and the overall concept of the ski resort.

5. *Developed acres*—Determine the number of acres to be developed in each category. The result should be the most desirable ski run mix rather than a maximum potential number of skiers who can fit onto the mountain.

6. *Acres cleared*—Next, determine the total number of acres to be cleared. Typically, ski areas leave from half to two-thirds of the mountain in its natural state.[25] The goal is an approximately equal amount of trails and buffer zones. This arrangement provides shelter from winds for both the trails and the skiers while serving as a visual reference in foggy conditions. Aesthetically, the effect is pleasing, while good forest management is practiced by taking soil stability, water runoff, and environmental preservation into account. The result is the number of net skiable acres.

7. *Number of skiers*—Calculate the total number of skiers, which is equal to the number of net skiable acres times the appropriate skier density factor. This latter figure depends on:

   ❖ *type of ski area*—Day areas have a greater density factor than do weekend areas and both have a density factor greater than vacation resorts.
   ❖ *planned snow grooming*—The degree of slope difficulty varies with snow conditions. However, grooming the slopes accommodates more skiers per acre with, up to a point, no loss of skier experience. Grooming the run takes the terrain down to another skier level.
   ❖ *skier preference for different types of runs*
   ❖ *extent of ski schools*
   ❖ *extent of snowmaking*—Between 80 and 85 percent of U.S. ski areas require snowmaking. Making this capital investment increases the skier density factor.
   ❖ *width of run*—The wider the run, the greater the skier density.
   ❖ *ground configuration*
   ❖ *lift network capacity*

Various estimates of skier density per acre are contained in Table 5.2. Vacation resorts prefer variety and lower densities, while higher densities are acceptable to areas in the Midwest, day-night places, and resorts that rely on snowmaking equipment for much of their snow cover. The wide range of figures means that the above criteria must be carefully adapted to each unique situation.

Skiers at One Time (SAOT) Within a ski resort, not all of the skiers will be on the slope at the same time. The USFS standard is that 50 percent of all skiers are on the slope at any one time. Using this guideline, the mountain can accommodate twice as many skiers as are on the runs. The skier density per acre indexes in

❖ TABLE 5.2 Density per Acre Estimates

	Ted Farwell	Aspen Corp.	Pacific NW Area	USFS	Various Ski Consultants
Beginner	50–100	15	35	25	50–100
Novice	40–60				
Low Intermediate	30–50	10	15	15	20–35
Intermediate	25–35				
Advanced Intermediate	15–20				
Advanced	10–15	5	5	10	10–15
Expert	10–15				

Source: Ted Farwell, *The Concept of Balance, Ski Area Design Analysis, and the Mountain Design Process* (Boulder, Colo: Ted Farwell & Associates, Inc. n.d.), 5.

Table 5.2 do, in fact, include this assumption. When this is the case, the skier capacity should not be adjusted.

Persons at One Time (PAOT)   The number of persons at one time (PAOT) takes into account that nonskiers also visit the resort. Perhaps a parent takes the children skiing but remains in the lodge. The extent to which resort capacity must be adjusted depends on the type and extent of the facilities. USFS uses a multiplier of 1.15.

$$PAOT = SAOT \times 1.15$$

The resultant figure is the number of people who can be accommodated at the ski area.

Night Skiing   For a relatively small increase in cost, adding illumination can increase capacity as much as 60 percent. About 45 percent of U.S. ski areas offer night skiing. The distribution is higher in the Northeast, Southeast, and Midwest (44 percent, 89 percent, and 92 percent respectively) and lower in the Pacific West and Rocky Mountains (36 percent and 20 percent respectively).[26] Because of the increased illusion of speed, slopes offer more challenge at night than during the day. Thus, even a gentle slope can be challenging to an intermediate skier.

SKI RUNS

Isolated base areas should be connected to public parking or
public transportation centers with ski trails when possible.
—U.S. FOREST SERVICE
Planning Considerations for Winter Sports Resort Development

SITE DESIGN Slopes that face predominantly north or northeast have less sun exposure and retain their snowfall. Wind, however, can be more destructive than snow, stripping slopes of needed powder. While snowmaking equipment has allowed ski resorts to develop in regions that would otherwise be uneconomic, certain requirements remain in effect. A combination of artificial and natural snow that allows 80 to 100 days of skiing a year is necessary. For areas that rely on snowmaking equipment, this means 800 to 1000 hours of temperatures below 28°F.[27] This kind of information can be obtained from local offices of the weather service.

The following guidelines are useful in laying out the ski runs at a resort.

❖ Locate the runs parallel to the fall line. The fall line is the path of natural descent between two points on the mountain and is perpendicular to the contour. Following the fall line as much as possible produces efficient, high-quality trails. Using natural hollows and depressions reduces costly cutting and filling on the mountain.

❖ Offer a variation in gradient for a more interesting experience. At the top of the trail, skiers should be able to see enough to determine generally how difficult the run is, but they should discover some surprises as they go downhill.

❖ Widen the steeper portion of runs from a minimum of 80 feet up to 250 feet.[28] Trail widths can vary from 50 to 400 feet. Mostly, they range from 100 feet to 200 feet.[29] They should also be wider at the top and bottom to avoid congestion.

❖ Separate runs and lifts for purposes of safety.

❖ Increase shade and wind control to help keep snow on the slopes.

❖ Keep the cutting boundary feathered and uneven and retain trees at varying heights and at varying distances from the trail's center line to help control wind while maintaining a pleasing aesthetic. Use tress islands to channel skiers, separate skiers of different abilities, and add visually to the experience. Avoid clearing vegetation that protects weak or shallow-rooted trees to wind, which can cause them major damage. This is especially true for conifers.

❖ Groom all ski runs.

❖ Add moguls to make the slopes more interesting for the more advanced skier, but be aware that they also reduce density and safety.

quick getaways 5.3

Northstar-at-Tahoe

California ski resort Northstar-at-Tahoe competes with a dozen ski areas, all within an hour's drive. When making technology decisions, Northstar likes to be on the cutting edge while making only practical choices.

In addition to having state-of-the-art high-speed lifts, grooming vehicles, and snowmaking equipment, Northstar is the first mountain in the United States to use an electronic trail map. Northstar also has a frequent-skier program, Club Vertical. Club members wear personalized, programmed microchip wristbands that give them access to member's-only, electronically gated lines at each lift. The microchip scans and records the number of vertical feet the member has skied to date, and the resort awards prizes and discounts based on that number. Members can charge lift tickets, food, ski lessons, and even child care with their wristbands, and can also receive electronic messages while skiing.

It is estimated that Club Vertical has brought Northstar $2 million in incremental business since its 1992 launch, with members accounting for 14 percent of the 500,000 skier visits. Northstar definitely got the return on investment they were looking for.

Source: Allessandra Bianchi, "The Ultimate Frequent Flier," *Inc.* 18, no. 6 (May 1996): 125.

Question: What management tools has Northstar-at-Tahoe instituted to improve the skier experience in regards to the ski lift network?

SKI LIFT NETWORK

Helicopters used for ski lift construction eliminate the need for roads to individual tower sites.
—U.S. FOREST SERVICE
Planning Considerations for Winter Sports Resort Development

The capacity of the lifts to bring skiers up the mountain must be balanced against the capacity of the trails to take them down. The goal is to spread skiers over the mountain while ensuring that the time spent in line is no greater than that spent riding the lift.[30]

The ideal ski lift system covers 1000 to 2000 vertical feet over a slope length of 4000 to 5000 feet.[31] These figures take into account skier characteristics as well as ski area economics. For skiers who live at sea level, the physical exertion of skiing at high altitude means that periods of skiing have to be balanced by resting in line or in the lodge. Many skiers feel more comfortable when they can see both ends of the lift and everything in between. Because most skiers prefer consistent conditions, they prefer a vertical standard of less than 2000 feet. Above 2500 feet, snow conditions tend to vary. Finally, long ski lifts that are open to the elements can be cold and unattractive.

From an economic viewpoint, the earning potential of the lift increases as the length increases while cost per foot decreases. Because longer lifts increase potential capacity, more skiers can be accommodated at a lower cost. Each lift requires a minimum of three operators. With longer lifts, more skiers can be accommodated while labor costs remain fixed.

The hourly capacity required to service a mountain, or part thereof, is determined as follows:

1. Identify the number of skiers by ability level.
2. Multiply by the appropriate vertical transport feet (VTF) per feet requirement (see Figure 5.3).
3. Add to get the total VTF/hour to service the mountain or part thereof.
4. Divide by the vertical rise of the mountain.[32]

The total is the hourly capacity required to service the mountain. By comparing this number to the hourly capacity of various lifts, the number of lifts required can be determined.

There is an aesthetic as well as a capacity aspect to the ski lift network. To attract people in all seasons of the year, ski areas, including the ski lift network, must be visually attractive. It may be possible to screen lifts in critical areas. The color and reflectivity of lifts has been a concern. The international practice of galvanizing towers has helped in this regard. Light-colored anticorrosion towers installed at Copper Mountain, Colorado, were approved after it was shown that, after three to five years, they would darken adequately to blend into the surroundings.

TYPES OF LIFTS   Four types of lifts are in general use today: tows, surface cable lifts, chairlifts, and gondolas or tramways.

Tows   The early rope tows dragged people up the mountain. Cheap and simple to operate, they were also uncomfortable and potentially dangerous over

❖ Ski lift network.

long distances and up even moderately steep hills. A modified version exists today, with handles fixed to a moving cable set a short distance above the ground. These so-called handle tows or cable tows are effective for distances up to 1000 feet.

Cable Lifts   Cable lifts also use moving cables, but the cable stretches overhead while the skier remains on the surface of the ground. They go by various names— T-bars, J-bars, platter lifts, Poma lifts. Like tows, these lifts restrict skier circulation because traffic is unable to cross the path of the lift.

Chairlifts   Chairlifts—the workhorse of the industry—allow skiers to rest as they ascend the mountain. Unlike the first two categories, they do not interrupt skier traffic across the path of the lift. Chairs are either single, double, triple, or quadruple. As the size of the chairs increases, significant capacity is added at a relatively low capital cost.

quick getaways 5.4

Poma Detachable Grip Chairlifts

Skiers love speed, and resort owners and operators demand maximum reliability and minimum maintenance costs. Poma has consistently been the leader in high-speed aerial lifts. Consider that when the Green Mountain Express was installed in 1990 at Sugarbush, Vermont, it was the first chairlift anywhere to operate at 1100 feet per minute and has now logged over 8000 hours. The Stowe eight-passenger gondola, installed in 1991, was the first gondola anywhere to operate at 1200 feet per minute, and it has now logged more than 10,000 hours.

Poma now has 18 chairlifts in North America that move 1100 feet per minute, six gondolas and eight detachable chair modifications (DMCs) that move 1200 feet per minute, and chairlifts at Mount Hood Meadows and Angel Fire (both in Washington) that move 1200 feet per minute. Poma's detachable grip chairlift allows the line to slow down when skiers are getting on and off the lift, and to increase speed when skiers are moving up the mountain.

Poma continues to design lifts that are designed for speed and comfort. Currently, the rubber-mounted sheave trains designed by Poma soften the ride, decrease overall vibration, and decrease maintenance costs—all while providing skiers with a faster and noticeably smoother ride.

Source: The Poma Group website (http://www.pomagroup.com/detach.htr) in August, 2000.

Questions: From a marketing and image perspective, do you have any concerns about getting on a detachable grip chairlift? Could/should these have been named something else? If so, what?

The development of high-speed detachable quad chairlifts has increased capacity safely. The system runs on a high-speed continuously moving cable. Thus, the chairs travel quickly up and down the mountain. When it comes to loading and unloading, however, the chair unit detaches from the cable and essentially comes to a halt. The increased speed allows the lifts to cover greater distances than tows and cable lifts. They need not travel in a straight line up the hill but can be angled up the mountain, thereby moving people over difficult terrain. Crowd problems may develop at the top of the mountain due to the ability of the lifts to move large numbers of people quickly up the hill.

Gondolas or Tramways   Where weather conditions make riding in a chairlift uncomfortable, gondolas offer an expensive and slower alternative.

BASE AREA

Building imitation Swiss chalets next to real miners' cottages makes both look out of place.
—JOHN COTTLE
Hagman Yaw Architects

The size and number of elements in the base area is determined by the number and type of skiers on the slopes. At a minimum, base areas should offer equipment rental, a ski shop, a first aid station, a ski patrol office, a ski school with sufficient space for people to gather outside, and food and beverage services.[33]

PARKING   The major problem in base area design is reducing potential conflicts between vehicles, pedestrians, and skiers. Underground parking, while expensive, helps the separation while freeing valuable space for retail and cultural developments. Skiers arrive at the base in one of three ways: private auto and/or charter bus, public transportation and/or shuttle bus, and on foot or skis from resort accommodations.[34]

Locating accommodations within easy walking or skiing distance of the slopes reduces the need for parking, loading, and unloading at the base. The proportion of skiers arriving by each of these three methods must be estimated to determine the acreage required for parking and access.

ACCESS ROADS   The capacity of access roads is determined by the speed of and the safe distance between vehicles. This, in turn, depends on the number and width of driving lanes, the extent and width of the shoulder, how the road surface is constructed, highway gradients, and weather conditions.[35] The patterns of arrival and departure must also be considered. Most people arrive between 8:00 a.m. and 10:00 a.m. and leave between 3:30 p.m. and 4:30 p.m. At Keystone, Colorado, ski patrols install fences on the moun-

❖ Lionshead Village, Vail, Colorado.
[Source: Design Workshop, Inc.]

tain at the end of the day to slow down skiers hurrying to get off the
mountain. This improves safety and helps control skier egress from the
resort. In addition, congestion is reduced by selling a combination
day/night ticket. Of course, relatively few ski areas have night skiing to
spread out demand in this manner.

A final factor is the average number of persons per vehicle. This can
vary from a low of 2.5 in commuter areas to a high of four per car at destination resorts.

The importance of access is crucial to getting people to the resort. In
California, for example, it takes a minimum of six hours to drive from San
Diego to Squaw Valley. In Europe and Japan, where population densities
are greater, public transportation is used. The travel time from Tokyo to a
Gala resort terminal is 1¼ hours. Bullet trains travel at up to 150 miles per
hour to a modern terminal, where skiers can board a high-speed gondola
to the top of a mountain and connect with three resorts.

FOOD SERVICE Food service areas should be balanced against number of skiers to allow skiers to refuel quickly and get back on the slopes. Thus, a balance of restaurants and snack bars on the mountain as well as at the base gives options to the skiers and helps even demand. Cafeteria seating capacity ranges from 20 percent of design capacity in the West, where sunshine keeps skiers on the slopes for longer periods, to 35 percent of design capacity elsewhere. Seating capacity is a measure of customer turnover, which, in turn, is heavily influenced by the weather. Cold, windy weather brings people indoors more often.

ACCOMMODATION A variety of housing and retail opportunities exists at ski resorts. The types of housing found in many areas range from resort hotels and second homes to condominiums and timeshares. While whole-unit condominiums were the prevalent form of housing in the late 1960s and early 1970s, segmented ownership, such as one-week timeshares and quartershares, have become increasingly attractive to guests. That easy access to the slopes is important means that higher-density housing is increasingly common, as this allows more people to be housed closer to the ski runs.[36]

A common pattern of lodging development is that the closer to the slope, the higher the density of accommodation. The base area tends to be surrounded by high-density, expensive lodging units whose users stay a short time. Farther away are medium-density housing and timeshares. A premium is paid for direct access to the slopes. Single-family homes tend to be farther from the activity core and located on slopes with premium views.

Demand Model Midmountain lodges are difficult to build and operate but offer attractive get-away-from-it-all environments. Table 5.3 shows a model developed by the USFS for determining the percentage of visitors needing overnight accommodation. This percentage increases as:

- ❖ The vertical rise increases.
- ❖ The skiable area increases.
- ❖ The variety of terrain approaches the ideal ratio.
- ❖ Travel time increases.
- ❖ Access roads are poorer.
- ❖ Surrounding population density is greater.
- ❖ The resort draws from a larger geographic area.
- ❖ The attractiveness of the site increases.
- ❖ The climate gets better.
- ❖ The length of the season increases.
- ❖ The snow conditions get drier.

❖ TABLE 5.3 Determining the Percentage of Visitors Needing Overnight Accommodation

Method: Sum the ratings for each of the following categories to yield a numerical score to be applied to the scale at right.

A. Vertical rise	1. 500–1500 feet
	2. 1501–2500 feet
	3. 2501–3500+ feet
B. Skiable area	1. 0–200 acres
	2. 201–600 acres
	3. 600+ acres
C. Variety of terrain	1. over 35% of area either advanced or novice
	2. 25–35% of area either advanced or novice
	3. ideal slope ratio: 20% beginner, 60% intermediate, 20% advanced
D. Travel time	1. 0–1½ hours
	2. 1½–3 hours
	3. 3+ hours
E. Accessibility	1. easy access
	2. average access (some storm closures)
	3. poor access (frequent road closures)
F. Population within 150 miles	1. 0–30,000
	2. 30,001–100,000
	3. 100,000+
G. Unique qualities other than skiing	0. nothing unusual
	1. regional attraction
	2. national attraction
H. Climate	1. cloudy, unpredictable temperatures, windy
	2. partly sunny, variable temperatures, windy
	3. sunny, predictably cold, little wind
I. Length of season	1. less than 115 days
	2. 115–130 days
	3. 130+ days
J. Snow conditions	1. dry less than 30% of the season
	2. dry 30–50% of the season
	3. dry over 50% of the season

Need for overnight accommodation:

Rating from sum of categories	Percentage of site capacity
14	1
15	2
16	3
17	4
18	5
19	10
20	15
21	20
22	25
23	30
24	35
25	40
26	45
27	50

Source: *Winter Sports Base Area Study*, USDA Forest Service, Region 6, Portland, Oregon, n.d.

quick getaways 5.5

Sunday River Village

Sunday River Resort, located in Newry, Maine, has continually expanded its on-mountain facilities since 1981 and now wants to expand and enhance its mountain village with residential and retail space. The proposed village, designed by the Design Workshop in Denver, Colorado, calls for 1369 residential units, including the existing Jordan Grand Hotel, 153,375 square feet of retail/commercial space, and 67,000 square feet of resort support space.

The master development plan for Sunday River Village delineates the location and form of buildings, roads, plazas, walks, parking, trails, and landscape elements. The plan was prepared in detail to understand the capacity of the property, assess marketability, quantify development costs, identify the potential effects of development activity, and clarify opportunities for construction projects.

The underlying principles and key components that establish the foundation of the Sunday River Village neighborhood include:

- an enhanced and choreographed arrival experience
- carefully located and identifiable real estate clusters that create a diverse new residential neighborhood at the resort and provide a variety of product options for the potential purchaser
- a clearly defined village core that includes optimal hotel and mixed-use residential buildings for a critical mass of visitor and activities during the course of each day
- a wide variety of shopping, dining, and entertainment experiences that engage visitors and encourage guests to spend more time in the village
- a series of recognizable and usable public spaces
- a year-round system of walkways and trails that offers uninterrupted pedestrian circulation throughout the resort

Source: Design Workshop, *Master Development Plan: Sunday River Resort* (Denver, Colo.: Design Workshop, 1999).

Question: How do the principles noted above compare to base area recommendations in the text?

❖ Developing resort, Big Sky, Montana. [Source: Design Workshop, Inc.]

MAINTENANCE   Maintenance facilities should be located near the base area. They are often combined with the area's snowmaking facilities. Grooming vehicles are the most useful and expensive maintenance tools a ski area possesses. The standard is for one vehicle per 25 acres of skiable terrain in the East and per 50 to 75 acres in the West.[37]

EMERGENCY CARE   Ski patrol and emergency care facilities must be provided at all ski areas. Some areas can rely on local clinics for emergency care once the ski patrol has provided basic first aid. Members of the volunteer National Ski Patrol System (NSPS) are often used on weekends to supplement resort employees. Insurance companies may require qualified emergency medical technician (EMT) skills for members of the NSPS. In addition to sophisticated communications systems, heliports suitable for flight-for-life helicopter services may be needed.[38]

quick getaways 5.6

How Safe Is Your Schuss?

The *Wall Street Journal* lists these safety barometers for top ski resorts:

	Lift Capacity (per hour)	Medical Facilities			Groomed Trails	Rating*
		First Aid Rooms	Clinics	Patrollers		
Aspen/Snowmass, CO	48,545	6	1	97	39 of 159	2
Breckenridge, CO	30,625	4	1	45	40 of 139	3
Keystone Mountain, CO	27,873	4	1	80	20 of 116	1
Killington Resort, VT	53,288	6	1	50	130 of 205	5
Mammoth Mountain, CA	56,600	3	0	90	130 of 150	4
Vail Resort, CO	46,781	6	0	59	16 of 174	5
Winterpark/Mary Jane, CO	34,910	3	1	65	69 of 134	3

* 1 = lowest risk, 5 = highest risk

Source: Stefan Fatsis and Daniel Costello, "Down a Slippery Slope," *Wall Street Journal*, 8 January 1999, pp. W1, W6.

OTHER WINTER SPORTS ACTIVITIES

Cross-country ski tour centers and associated activities are an important part of a resort that wants to provide full service winter recreation to its guests.

—U.S. FOREST SERVICE
Planning Considerations for Winter Sports Resort Development

CROSS-COUNTRY SKIING Fewer constraints pertain to cross-country or Nordic facilities than to downhill. For example, a greater range of terrain is suitable for cross-country skiing. Therefore, areas can be located closer to the market. Development and maintenance costs are less, lifts are not needed, and trails are narrower. Fewer regulatory permits are needed, as Nordic skiing is more compatible with the environment than is downhill skiing. Because of lower costs, cross-country facilities can break even with a season of 40 to 80 days.

Site Selection   The most important factors for cross-country trails are the suitability of the landscape and the development of appropriate facilities.[39] Technical information about the suitability of a site can be obtained from aerial photographs, topographic maps, master plans from earlier studies, and zoning maps. While aerial photos are useful for determining the location of trails, paths, roads, rivers, and vegetation masses, topographic maps are used more because they give more detailed information. Of particular interest are the contour lines, which give information on slope percentages, drainage patterns, and high and low points.

Water location is critical when planning a trail system. Only frozen water is safe for skiing over. Running water, because it does not freeze completely, must be avoided. Season length can be calculated via thawing temperatures.

Vegetation is important because it adds to the enjoyment of the experience. Heavy groupings of conifers reduce the snow depth and add contrast to the snow and deciduous trees.

Design Criteria   The width of a trail depends on the volume of traffic, type of trail (one-way or two-way), and steepness of the grade. Trail width can vary from 1.5 to 6 meters, depending on the above criteria. Grooming increases the speed of the trail. Skiers will pick up speed on a gradient of 10 percent or more, so trails should be wider under this condition. Run-outs at the bottom of the trail add to the safety of those coming down the hill. Wider trails are also needed on turns, especially at the end of a long downhill stretch. Finally, passing areas should be provided on long, flat areas, tight corners, and steep slopes.

Where trees are part of the trail system, care must be taken to ensure sufficient clearance between the snow line and the lowest branches. Depending on the amount of snow the trail receives, the snow line can be significantly higher than the ground line. This safety factor should not be overlooked when trail planning occurs when the ground is bare of snow.

Standardized signs throughout the trail are a basic requirement. A variety of signs is common:

❖ *Caution signs* alert the skier to difficult areas or obstacles.
❖ *Trail Closed signs* should be placed at all points of access to the trail.

- ❖ *Trail markers* should be visible in a snowstorm and close enough to the trail to prevent straying.
- ❖ *Informational signs* are usually found at the trailhead and include the routing map, the trail length in distance and average time, locations of rest areas and warming shelters, trail difficulty, location of hazards, and rules and regulations.
- ❖ Additional *distance and time signs* can be strategically placed along the trails.

Wind, sun, and vegetation must all be considered when planning the trail. North slopes are exposed to cold winds and drifting snow. The latter makes tracking more difficult and time-consuming. Steep, open south-facing slopes lose the snow early because of exposure to the sun. Open or running water must be avoided unless a bridge across it is planned. This is because, as noted earlier, it does not freeze completely.

Variability of terrain adds to the enjoyment of the experience. A convenient rule of thumb is that one-third of the trail should be uphill, one-third downhill, and one-third flat. Downhill slopes can be categorized as easy, intermediate, or difficult. Easy slopes have a maximum drop of 10 percent and consist of short climb and descent areas. Intermediate slopes consist of a maximum drop of 20 percent, with climb areas that are short but steeper and longer down slopes with run-outs at the bottom. Difficult slopes have a maximum drop of 40 percent, with up to one-half of the trail having an uphill grade.

Certain activities are incompatible with cross-country skiing. Snow-mobiling is one of them. While snowmobiles can be used for grooming and track setting, the two sports should be kept separate for several reasons:

- ❖ Snowmobiles pack the snow and cause icing. This causes side slippage of the skis.
- ❖ Snowmobiles cause bumps and moguls.
- ❖ Snowmobiles require different turning radii and wider trails.
- ❖ Snowmobiles cause ridges that makes skiing difficult.
- ❖ Snowmobiles are noisy.[40]

Snowshoes also compact the snow and create ice spots. Sledding and tobogganing both create icy runs that make skiing more difficult.

Maintenance is necessary in both the off and the on season. The off season is a good time to clear all rocks and woody material to the ground. Areas where erosion has taken place can be fixed, overhead branches trimmed, facilities repaired, and snow fences installed to help control drifting snow. During the season, trails should be periodically inspected for fallen branches and areas of erosion. In addition, the trails should be groomed as often as necessary—at least after every 4 to 6 inches of new snowfall. Grooming does three things: packs the snow, prepares the surface, and sets the tracks. As noted earlier, a snowmobile can be used for this purpose; however, a snow tractor is preferable. The snow tractor rakes the snow to the center of the trail and then spreads the loose snow evenly. Tracks are then set in the snow and allowed to set. Temperatures need to be cold enough to allow the tracks to set. Wet snow should be allowed to dry before grooming.

The distance covered depends on the experience level of the skier. Beginners travel about 2 kilometers or 1¼ miles per hour; intermediate skiers are capable of 5 kilometers or 3⅜ miles per hour; advanced skiers can cover up to 10 kilometers or 6¼ miles per hour.

The three basic types of trails are point to point, out and back, and looped. Point-to-point trails connect villages, touring centers, and/or overnight shelters. Skiers should be able to easily cover the distance in one day. The trail should be double tracked to allow two-way movement, accommodate the skier ability level being targeted, and have sufficient trail markings to prevent wrong turns in a snowstorm.

Out-and-back trails are two-way trails that use the same route for the return. They require adequate passing areas, marked distances to and from the starting point, and trail markers that can be seen from both directions. Looped trails can be stacked or satellite. Both are one-way trails that consist of a major or primary loop aimed at the beginner and additional loops meant for more advanced skiers.

SNOWMOBILING While snowmobiling includes both trail and no-trail experiences, the latter is difficult to plan for and manage except where a vast amount of land is available. Warm-up areas are used to check whether or not the machine is operating effectively. The maze is used for beginners or as an instructional trail. It is high-density and does not cross other trails.

Many of the same criteria noted above for cross-country trails are also important to snowmobile trails. Vistas and scenic overlooks add to the enjoyment of the experience. Marking and periodic packing of trails is important for safety reasons. Trail gradient should not exceed 10 percent for long distances and 25 percent for short distances.

Where trails exceed 25 miles, a series of trailheads should be developed to disperse snowmobilers over the various trails, which can be targeted toward specific groups (families, organizations) or uses (racing, rec-

quick getaways 5.7

The Adventure Ridge at Eagle's Nest

Skiers are demanding more choices in how they spend their nonskiing hours. The Adventure Ridge at Eagle's Nest, an activity center on top of Vail Mountain in Colorado, offers a variety of family activities for those who do not ski, including ice skating, tubing, snowmobile tours, a snowboarding half-pipe, and snow biking. A popular attraction for kids is a round of Laser Challenge on Sled Dogs (snow skates). In addition, food from pizza to five-star dining is available.

On top of the mountain, people can check voice mail and e-mail and read the *Wall Street Journal* online before heading back to the slopes. Research indicates that, if people can work during their vacation, they will stay longer.

Resorts are finding that a village is a necessary part of attracting visitors in both winter and summer. Winter Park, Colorado, is planning a $350 million development that includes a base area village with ski-in, ski-out lodging in an attempt to increase length of stay.

Source: Jill Jamieson-Nichols, "Beyond Skiing: New Trends in Colorado Mountain Resort Development," *Urban Land* (April 1998) vol. 57: 82–85.

Question: To what extent does the provision of business services enhance or detract from the vacation experience?

reational). Care should be taken to avoid lake and stream crossings, avalanche hazard areas, cliffs and other steep terrain, road crossings on maintained roads, and zones for cross-country ski areas.

TOBOGGANING Guidelines for a typical toboggan run are shown in Table 5.4. A minimum of 5 acres is needed for even a small hill. Beginner and intermediate runs should be straight, a minimum of 150 feet wide, and well groomed. Expert runs can be narrower and longer, with longer areas for run-out at the bottom. All runs should be steeper at the top and shallower at the bottom. Return chutes allow participants to return up the hill. One chute per two runs, separated by strips of vegetation, should suffice.

❖ TABLE 5.4 Toboggan Hill Classification

Type of Slope	Minimum Length of Run (feet)	Slope Area (%)	Gradient (%)
Tot	50–75	10	<15
Beginner	150	40	15–25
Intermediate	300	40	25–40
Expert	300	10	>40

Source: *Winter Sports Base Area Study*, USDA Forest Service, Region 6, Portland, Oregon, n.d., 259

On a small hill, the north, east, and west gradients can be used for separate skill levels, with the south side being used as a return chute, as exposure to the sun is less important when moving up the hill. The top of the hill should be flat, with enough space to allow people to congregate.

ICE SKATING A pond or small lake can be used for ice skating if enough extended periods of cold weather maintain the ice. Shading the pond from direct sunlight will help. Guidelines call for a minimum ice depth of 8 inches, although others indicate that less depth is acceptable where there is low visitor density and the ice conditions are uniform.

Areas can also be flooded in stages, with sideboards used to hold the water. The sideboards should be twice the thickness of the ice to prevent surface rippling and screened to help minimize direct solar radiation to both the ice and the skaters. Lightly watering the surface in the early morning helps maintain the rink during the season.

SUMMER IN THE MOUNTAINS

Environmental education and interpretation of the natural resources and developments at a ski area can improve the public's understanding about the relationship between ski areas and the environment. Programs can attract summer visitors who might otherwise not visit ski areas. Favorable summer experiences might dispel concerns by visitors that ski area development is detrimental to the environment and wildlife.

—U.S. FOREST SERVICE
Planning Considerations for Winter Sports Resort Development

❖ Summer use of an ice rink, Aspen, Colorado. [Source: Design Workshop, Inc.]

Mountain resorts offer a variety of recreational activities, from downhill and cross-country skiing to snowmobiling and dogsled rides. Increasing numbers of resorts are taking advantage of natural springs to emphasize spas as part of the package, appealing to the public's growing interest in health and beauty. Realizing that the large investment in a ski resort is especially risky when a year's operation is dependent on a good winter season, resorts have become four-season attractions. Winter's cross-country ski trails become summer's hiking trails. Mountain bikes replace skis on ski lifts after the snow melts. Winter Park in Colorado, for example, has converted old logging trails, mining trails, and railroad rights-of-way into 500 miles of mountain bike trails at little expense. Care must be taken to separate bikers and hikers. Additional summer activities include:

❖ summer slide
❖ miniature golf
❖ interpretation of skiing history
❖ competitive and recreational mountain biking
❖ sightseeing from ski lifts
❖ food services
❖ changing events[41]

quick getaways 5.8

Summer in the Mountains at the Keystone Resort

At one time, resorts at skiing destinations routinely shut down during the warmer months, but operators started to realize two limitations of that approach. First, infrastructure isn't cheap to erect, and, second, many ski towns happen to have delightfully mild summer weather. Since then, many resorts have developed activities to fill rooms in the off-season and to attract the nonskier.

During the summer months, Keystone Resort in Colorado markets itself as a family destination, with activities that include swimming in a dozen pools, paddle boating, golf, biking, horseback riding, and barn dances. Keystone also sponsors a handful of signature events, including the July 4th festival, a Celtic music festival, and a culinary celebration.

In Breckenridge, Colorado, year-round group traffic is driving local businesses to stay open all year, a practice somewhat new to the local entrepreneurs. Today, Breckenridge has an active nightlife, with a number of bars, eateries, and shops. Local businesses celebrate summer by planting a carpet of flowers, and activities such as golf, river rafting, horseback riding, and off-road four-wheeling attract many tourists. The spectacular setting and flowers of Breckenridge have also made it a popular wedding site, especially for Coloradans.

Source: Megan Rowe, "No Snow? No Problem!" *Lodging Hospitality* 55, no. 6 (15 May 1999): 49–52.

Question: **What additional summer activities are appropriate for a ski resort?**

SUMMARY

In developing a ski resort, care must be taken to strike a balance between the physical capacity of the site to accommodate skiers and the economic needs of the developer to make a profit. Desirable sites have specific characteristics that reduce construction and maintenance costs. General design principles, when adhered to, make for a better ski area. Development decisions must be made in a certain order. The capacity of the mountain is determined by its natural characteristics and the market to be served. This, in turn, indicates the number and type of ski runs, which dictates the ski lift network, which indicates the number and type of base area facilities needed.

ENDNOTES

1. D. Ormiston, A. Gilbert, and R.E. Manning, "Indicators and Standards of Quality for Ski Area Management," *Journal of Travel Research* 3, no. 3 (1998): 35–41.
2. Ted Farwell, *The Concept of Balance, Ski Area Design Analysis, and the Mountain Design Process* (Boulder, Colo.: Ted Farwell and Associates, n.d.), 2.
3. Dean Schwanke et al. *Resort Development Handbook* (Washington, D.C.: Urban Land Institute, 1977), 147.
4. Anthony Blackbourn, "Restructuring and Growth in the Northern Ontario Ski Industry," in Alison Gill and Rudi Hartmann, *Mountain Resort Development: Proceedings of the Vail Conference* (Burnaby, British Columbia: Centre for Tourism Policy and Research, Simon Fraser University, 1991), 95.
5. RRC Associates, *Economic Analysis of United States Ski Areas* (Lakewood, Colo.: National Ski Areas Association, 1999), 7.
6. Patrick L. Phillips, *Developing with Recreational Amenities: Golf, Tennis, Skiing, Marinas* (Washington, D.C.: Urban Land Institute, 1986), 137.
7. RRC Associates, *Economic Analysis*, 7.
8. Alain J. Lazard, "Expanding Recreation and Conserving Beauty—Finding Solutions: European Examples and Practices," in Alison Gill and Rudi Hartmann, *Mountain Resort Development: Proceedings of the Vail Conference* (Burnaby, British Columbia: Centre for Tourism Policy and Research, Simon Fraser University, 1991), 221.
9. Farwell, *Concept of Balance*, 5.
10. Ibid.
11. Ibid., 26.
12. H. Peter Wingle, *Planning Considerations for Winter Sports Resort Development* (Washington, D.C.: USDA Forest Service, 1994).
13. Phillips, *Developing with Recreational Amenities*, 133.
14. Farwell, *Concept of Balance*, 18.
15. Wingle, *Planning Considerations*, 66.

16. Schwanke et al., *Resort Development Handbook*, 117-118.
17. Farwell, *Concept of Balance*, 28.
18. Phillips, *Developing with Recreational Amenities*, 23.
19. Alison Gill and Rudi Hartmann, *Mountain Resort Development: Proceedings of the Vail Conference* (Burnaby, British Columbia: Centre for Tourism Policy and Research, Simon Fraser University, 1991), 83.
20. Michael Berry, "Corridor of Last Resorts: Sprawling Ski Areas, Wilderness Duel Along I-70," *Denver Post*, 20 December 1998, p. 1.
21. Gill and Hartmann, *Mountain Resort Development*, 65.
22. Farwell, *Concept of Balance*, 13-14, 18; Schwanke et al., *Resort Development Handbook*, 149.
23. Farwell, *Concept of Balance*, 15-16.
24. RRC Associates, *Economic Analysis*, 8.
25. Farwell, *Concept of Balance*, 15.
26. RRC Associates, *Economic Analysis*, 7.
27. Schwanke et al., *Resort Development Handbook*, 150.
28. Ibid., 152.
29. Farwell, *Concept of Balance*, 15-16.
30. Ibid., 7.
31. Ibid., 34.
32. Ibid., 19-20.
33. Phillips, *Developing with Recreational Amenities*, 131.
34. Farwell, *Concept of Balance*, 23.
35. Ibid., 16-17.
36. Schwanke et al., *Resort Development Handbook*, 147.
37. Phillips, *Developing with Recreational Amenities*, 132.
38. Wingle, *Planning Considerations*, 32.
39. Gaylan Rasmussen, *Cross-Country Trail Design* (East Lansing: Michigan State University Cooperative Extension Service, n.d.), 3.
40. Ibid., 4-7.
41. Wingle, *Planning Considerations*, 88.

Chapter 6
WATER-BASED RESORTS

INTRODUCTION

George III, suffering from severe abdominal spasms, came to drink the waters there [Cheltenham] in 1788 and made it fashionable as a summer resort.

—PHYLLIS HEMBRY
The English Spa, 1560–1815: A Social History

A variety of recreational activities utilize water as the major attraction:

❖ *Natural beaches*, which can be used for sunbathing, swimming, and beachcombing. Very popular, they may require little development, though maintenance costs can be high. Beaches allow for a variety of complementary activities, including snorkeling and scuba diving.
❖ *Open space and trails*, typically found around lakes and wetlands. They can be used as sites for fishing or camping or for observing wildlife, and fit well into the ecotourism movement.
❖ *Golf courses*, developed in Scotland, the reputed home of golf, on the coast to give participants the benefit of the invigorating sea air. Many U.S. resorts exploit oceanfront settings to highlight their golf facilities.
❖ *Marinas* servicing sailboats and motorized crafts as well as wind-surfing and other water sports. Depending on the type of craft catered to, the amount of development can range from little to extensive.
❖ *Residential development*, as home sites on the waterfront generate premium prices. Care must be taken to balance preservation of the often sensitive ecology and obtaining an economic return on the investment.
❖ *Commercial development*, such as hotels, retails stores, and restaurants. This most intense type of waterfront development must be approached carefully because of environmental concerns.
❖ *Cruise ships*, which, after all, are nothing more than floating resorts.
❖ *Spas*, as noted in the above quote.[1]

Certain water-based activities are compatible with others, while some do not mix. Figure 6.1 indicates the types of activities that can and cannot take place in close proximity to each other. This chapter focuses on beach resorts and marinas. The development process for both is outlined. The characteristics important for an economically successful and environmentally sensitive water-based resort are explored.

Compatible Activities	Angling	Canoeing	Rowing	Sailing	Sub Aqua	Waterskiing	Hydroplane/ motorboat racing	Motorboat cruising	Wildlife
Angling	●	✔	✔	✔	✔			✔	✔
Canoeing	✔	●	✔		✔			✔	
Rowing	✔	✔	●		✔				
Sailing	✔			●	✔				✔
Sub Aqua	✔	✔	✔	✔	●				
Waterskiing						●			
Hydroplane/ motorboat racing							●		
Motorboat cruising	✔	✔						●	
Wildlife	✔			✔					●

❖ FIGURE 6.1 Compatibility of water sports. [Source: Donald W. Adie, *Marinas: A Working Guide to Their Development*, 3rd ed. (New York: Nichols, 1984). Reprinted by permission of Butterworth-Heinemann Publishers, a division of Reed Educational & Professional Publishing, Ltd.]

THE DEVELOPMENT PROCESS

Geologically, the Hawaiian island chain was formed when volcanoes on the floor of the Pacific Ocean spewed out molten lava, which eventually cooled off and formed large resort hotel complexes.

—DAVE BARRY
Dave Barry's Only Travel Guide You'll Ever Need

The designer should begin by considering the reasons people go to beaches. While, indeed, many people go to swim, others are primarily interested in sunbathing, socializing, people-watching, relaxing, or engaging in recreational activities. Ideally, the beach design should permit a

quick getaways 6.1

Indoor Water Parks

Indoor water parks are increasingly being installed at northern resorts as a way to increase revenue during the off-season and to attract families. Parks can range from a simple swimming pool to an elaborate facility with tube slides and an aquatic game center that might include tree houses and water games. Indoor water parks can range in size from 10,000 square feet to upwards of 65,000 square feet. They are most commonly found in resorts in the Wisconsin Dells. Developers feel the construction cost of $5 million to $10 million is justified by increased occupancy and increased daily rate. It is common for the resort to include water park admission in the average daily rate (ADR) while, for a nonguest, admission can range from $10 to $20 when it is allowed. During peak season, resorts with water parks charge from $20 to $50 more than comparable properties without water parks. In the winter (low) season, water park resorts can charge up to $100 more a night compared to those without these facilities. Occupancy rates are higher year-round, as families are attracted during spring break and weekends. Water parks make economic sense for resorts that have strong occupancy during the season and that are looking to attract business from people seeking a short getaway who are unable to fly south to a warmer climate.

Source: David J. Sangree, "Northern Operators Test Waters for Indoor Recreation Areas," *Hotel and Motel Management*, 7 February 2000, p. 10.

Question: Given the above figures, determine the financial feasibility of installing an indoor water park. What additional information is needed to make an informed decision?

range of uses. This means designing the facility for the different types of people who go to a beach. Some go to play in the water. Others go to play on the beach. A third group goes because their friends want to play in the water or on the beach. Providing tables, chairs, and shade for this third group makes their visit more enjoyable.

BEACH DEVELOPMENT Six important aspects warrant consideration with respect to beach development: the sea, seashore, beach, back beach, coastal stretch, and surrounding countryside.[2]

Sea A variety of factors related to the sea affect the attractiveness of the site:

❖ *Air temperature*—There is a high correlation between swimming and maximum air temperature and a fairly high correlation between beach use and maximum air temperature.[3]

❖ *Amount and intensity of the wind and sun*—There is a weak inverse relationship between both swimming and beach use and wind. There is a straight-line correlation between sunshine hours and both swimming and beach use. The correlation is higher than that of maximum air temperature for beach use and lower for swimming.

❖ *Water temperatures*, including the temperature range

❖ *Currents, tides, and waves*, including their direction, strength, and seasonality. Wave action, and the corresponding erosion, is greater when beaches are exposed to the main channel of a lake. On the other hand, beaches developed on lakes are subject to less erosion when placed on the side of a bay or inlet.

❖ *Ecology*, including seaweed and fish.

❖ *Pollution*—In Jersey, the largest of the English Channel Islands, state-of-the-art sewage treatment plants use ultraviolet light radiation to destroy bacteria and microorganisms before they pass into the surrounding waters.

❖ *Clarity of water*—Of the 496 coastal resorts around bathing destinations on the northwest coast of England, 89 percent passed germ tests and only 146 met standards that are above average for bathing waters.[4]

❖ *Possible attractions*, such as islands, coral, and conditions for water recreation. At the 1992 Coral Reef Symposium, it was announced that only 30 percent of the world's coral would remain a generation from now. Dying coral can be helped by limiting the number of people who scuba dive, improving sewage treatment and drainage in the islands, and monitoring dumping and draining into the surrounding waters.[5]

Seashore The seashore consists of the surface under the water, extending out to a depth of six feet. A gentle, uniform slope of 7 percent to this depth is ideal.[6] The makeup and stability of the bottom is important to bathers. It should consist of coarse sand or sand and pea gravel to a depth of 12 inches. Mud bottoms have to be stabilized with crushed rock as a base and a coarse sand overlay. Bathers should be able to walk into the water a sufficient distance to allow them to engage in play activities without risk of danger from tidal movement.

Beach The slope of the beach should be between 2 and 10 percent, with 5 percent being the ideal.[7] Both purity and color of the material—a minimum of 12 inches of sand or a mixture of sand and pea gravel—and the stability of the beach are important. Beach erosion can result in heavy annual maintenance costs. Often, sand must be dredged from the swimming area back to the beach because the grade of the beach is too steep. This raises the point made in Chapter 3 about considering development and maintenance costs together. While annual dredging takes care of the symptom, it does nothing to alleviate the cause of the problem. Perhaps the original slope to the water's edge can be cut down to a grade of 2 to 3 percent, with a retaining wall behind the beach to help retard erosion.

The size of the beach is a function of its depth and length. People do not want to walk too far to get to the water, neither do they want to feel too crowded (although people-watching on a busy beach is a major motivation for many). A good rule of thumb is for square feet of beach per swimmer day. The density varies depending on the market being sought. Some estimates are given in Table 6.1.

Beaches themselves are zoned for best use. The 20 to 30 feet nearest the edge of the water should be designated as a circulation area to allow swimmers to move in and out of the water and walkers to move laterally along the beach. Lifeguard platforms are the only service facility in this zone. The next 50 to 150 feet is the general-use area for sunbathing, play, and sightseeing. Finally, a western exposure takes advantage of the afternoon sun.[8]

❖ TABLE 6.1 Beach Capacity

	Square Feet/Person	Persons/Feet of Coast Depth of Beach		
		65.5 ft.	110 ft.	165 ft.
Overdensity	35	6.5	11	16.5
Public beach	55	4	6.5	10
Resort (Low standard)	110	2	3.5	5
Resort (Medium standard)	160	1.5	2	3.5
Resort (High standard)	215	1	0.5	2.5
Resort (Deluxe)	320	0.7	1	1.5

Source: Manuel Baud-Bovy and Fred Lawson, *Tourism and Recreation Development* (London: Architectural Press; Boston: CBI, 1977), 74. Reprinted by permission of Butterworth-Heinemann, Oxford.

❖ Developing the beach site.

Back Beach   The back beach offers views to both the sea and inland. The geomorphology—cliffs, dunes, and flatlands—can dramatically add to the setting. Vegetation and the effect of the microclimate must be considered because of the fragile nature of the resource. Protection against degradation is a major concern as developers consider future improvements.

Coastal Stretch   The coastal stretch consists of the beach environment between 0.5 and 3 miles from the back beach. This is where service facilities and access roads are placed. Parking facilities, bathhouses for changing, comfort stations, and concessions are located here. Large beaches may require several parking areas, each capable of accommodating from 50 to 100 vehicles, in order to disperse traffic and beachgoers.

    Two schools of thought exist with respect to the placement of access roads (Figure 6.2). One philosophy is to place the access road between the beach and the surrounding hotels. People who drive by can view the sea, and everyone has access to the beach. However, hotel residents, to reach the beach, have to cross the road, creating safety problems. The other philosophy is to have the access road behind the hotels. Access to the beach is direct from the hotels—which, in some cases, limit access to their own guests. The drivers' view is of the fronts of hotels. Access to locals is restricted.

quick getaways 6.2

Good, Clean Fun?

Every year, Americans take 1.8 billion trips to beaches, rivers, and lakes. However, also each year, 2000 beaches are closed due to sewage overflows, urban and agricultural runoff, and direct contamination caused by human waste.

Robert Haile of the University of Southern California found that people swimming near storm drains were 50 percent more likely to develop fevers, vomiting, respiratory infections, or earaches compared to people who stayed 400 yards away. Here's what people can do to ensure a clean swimming spot:

- Don't swim near storm drains.
- Don't swim after a big rainfall (it flushes contaminants off city streets into the sea).
- Ensure the water is checked weekly during the swimming season and reports are made public.
- Ensure that beaches provide adequate toilets, sinks for handwashing, and diaper changing facilities.
- Check the annual survey of U.S. beaches conducted by the Natural Resources Defense Council at http://www.nrdc.org.

Source: Marilyn Chase, "Swimmers May Find Beaches Are Not All Good, Clean Fun," *Wall Street Journal,* 17 June 1966, p. B1.

Surrounding Country The country surrounding the beach development provides the setting for the attraction. Many people wish to combine relaxing days at the beach with more active pursuits. Natural attractions, the extent of development, surrounding infrastructure, and the opportunity for excursions all need to be considered.

DESIRABLE SITES In selecting a site for beach development, these elements warrant particular attention:

- ❖ access to a permanent or transient seasonal population
- ❖ access to major roads

❖ FIGURE 6.2 Access to beaches.   *A*   *B*

❖ Climate—Minimum water temperatures should be in the upper 60s during the swimming season. Warm, sunny conditions are required before and during the season to warm the water and attract swimmers and sunbathers. Seasonal storms negatively affect usage.

❖ Water quality needs to be analyzed before and after development. Keep in mind that swimmers will add to the existing bacterial count. This is of greater concern in bodies of standing water than in flowing streams and rivers. Each year, 2000 beaches are closed due to sewage overflows, urban and agricultural runoff, and direct contamination by human waste. Restricting diaper-age children to toddler wading pools and having adult pools on separate filtration systems help prevent the spread of disease. Particular care needs to be taken to prevent runoff into the sea, as heavy rainfall flushes contaminants from city streets into the surrounding waters.[9]

Coastal Sites The biggest problem facing developers of coastal resorts is shoreline and beach erosion. As a result of problems caused by development along the coastline, regulations tend to restrict building to 200 feet or so from the beach. In addition, building density is usually low, and laws tend to require dune preservation to help control erosion. The planting of sea grasses helps produce more stable beaches while encouraging a diverse wildlife.

EVOLUTION One model of beach resort evolution describes the following stages. At first, no tourism is present. Some kind of settlement, however, is connected by a road to the rest of the area. Phase two—explorative tourism—begins with the visit of adventurous tourists with independent itineraries and an interest in the local culture. Contact between visitors and locals is high.

Major changes begin with the development of the first hotel. Strip development along the beach occurs, with each additional property bringing in more visitors, thus creating the need for additional facilities to serve their needs. As beachfront property increases in value, residents sell or are forced out because of higher taxes. They move to new residential communities at some distance from the beach.

Land next to the beach becomes built out and more hotel development takes place away from the recreational resource that attracted visitors in the first place. A second road parallel to and some distance away from the beach is built, improving access to businesses farther inland. Further development in this new area is encouraged. In the final stage of development, the resort becomes a city with a recreation business district and a commercial business district.[10]

quick getaways 6.3

Ecosystem Indicators for Coastal Zones

- *Degradation:* percentage of beach degraded, eroded
- *Use intensity:* persons per foot of accessible beach
- *Shore/marine fauna:* number of key species sightings
- *Water quality:* fecal coliform bacteria and heavy metals count

Source: Edward W. Manning, "What Tourism Managers Need to Know," *WTO News* no. 2 (May/June 1996), 12.

MARINAS

One advantage of developing marinas is that they generate water frontage where beach use is limited, which may then lead to the development of residential units.
—BILL WHITNEY
Arthur Andersen

THE DEVELOPMENT PROCESS

The process for developing a marina consists of five steps:

1. Analyze the market.
2. Develop a market strategy and marina concept.
3. Identify the site.
4. Perform feasibility analyses and preliminary design.
5. Design and develop the marina.

The first step involves an analysis of the market. Taking into account the area's economy, analyze both demand and competitive supply to give a preliminary assessment of current market conditions.

❖ Marina development.

Next, develop a market strategy and a concept for the marina. Determine the services to be offered, define the size and mix of boats, specify the number of wet slips and dry storage areas, identify funding sources, calculate fees, and estimate cash flow.

At this point, begin to identify a preferred site by compiling and mapping data, scrutinizing development factors, and selecting several alternative sites. Note state and federal policies controlling proposed uses of the sites and select the superior site. Take an option on the land.

The next step is to perform a feasibility analysis and approve a preliminary design. This involves conducting an in-depth financial feasibility study, including an analysis of cash flow. Determine the preliminary design and technical feasibility of the site and address local zoning and building permits.

Develop the final design next. Create detailed construction photos, file for and obtain permits, secure local approvals, obtain construction bids and loans, and exercise the option on the land.[11]

ONSHORE/ OFFSHORE

Marinas can be sited onshore or offshore. The major concern regarding onshore facilities is ensuring enough space. The guideline is that the land space should be equal to water space. An acre of water can handle anywhere from 25 to 65 boats, depending on the size of the boats and the layout of the facility. The land on which onshore facilities will be built should be above the floodplain and have enough bearing capacity to support construction of necessary facilities.

Two especially important aspects of offshore development are water depth and water level fluctuations. The minimum depth for a marina is 8 feet below the low-water datum.[12] Anything less than 8 feet limits the number and type of craft that can be accommodated. Dredging to increase depth is a possibility, but it is very expensive. On the other hand, if the basin is too deep, it may not offer sufficient protection for moored boats. In addition, deep basins limit the pier designs that can be accommodated.

Marinas require a stable level of water throughout the year. Differences in water levels due to tides, storms, rain, and ice flows must be noted and their impact determined. Water stagnation and pollution from fueling operations will result in water quality problems if water flow is insufficient.

BASIS FOR MARINA DEVELOPMENT

A marina can be a private, public, or joint venture. It might serve as the base for hotels and concessions; profits in such arrangements are dependent on income from concessionaires, who often manage both lodging and food and beverage facilities. Pier 66 in Florida is one such example. In Chi-

quick getaways 6.4

Slips Ahoy

Marina construction does not lend itself to simple supply-and-demand theories. While the need for slips is demonstrated, the financial benefits no longer justify the costs. Sophisticated modeling techniques and government-sponsored research are producing better and more cost-effective methods of protecting harbors and shorelines. Public awareness of the environmental impact of marina construction is lengthening the planning and design time needed before permits are secured and construction can begin.

There is a trend toward combining the benefits of civic leadership and public funding available to municipal and state governments with the financial strength and flexibility of the private sector to create first-rate, large-scale projects with a positive impact on communities. A mixed-use, interactive waterfront development can mean fully occupied marinas, housing complexes, and retail centers. If the implementation strategy is structured properly, the objectives of both the public and private sectors can be achieved.

Source: Fred A. Klancnik, "Slips Ahoy," *Civil Engineering* 60, no. 5 (May 1990): 59–61.

Question: What implications does this article have for marina developers?

cago, Marina City is the basis for a residential development. A multistory apartment complex has a marina in the basement. Boats are launched from forklifts into the Chicago River in less than ten minutes. Mystic Seaport, Connecticut, is one of many areas using marina development for both urban renewal and historic preservation. Marinas are also developed to stimulate boat sales, as part of a boatbuilding operation, or as the headquarters of a club or boating organization.

An example of a private/public development is Marina Del Rey in Los Angeles County, California. Launched with federal assistance in the 1950s, the project opened in 1965 with 5600 boat slips on 780 acres. On a more ambitious scale, in the Languedoc-Roussillon region of France, an $800 million private/public investment involves 20 new harbors capable of berthing 40,000 boats along 120 miles of the Mediterranean.

Even if a marina is developed privately, issues relative to access to public waters complicate the process. Developers may have to permit public access, or the project may be required to offer public benefit before permissions are given to build. Restrictions may be placed on the number of slips that can be developed and the maximum price that can be charged.

In the United States, federal programs regulating marina development are the purview of the U.S. Army Corps of Engineers. Most fill activities, including wetlands, come under their authority. Approval is contingent on both state and local approval. However, the jurisdiction of the Corps supersedes that of state and local authorities. It can take as little as six months to obtain a federal permit, although two years is a more likely estimate.

At both the state and local levels, two goals affect marina development: the provision of recreational opportunities for residents and protection of sensitive or scarce environmental resources.[13] The degree to which development is favored over conservation, or vice versa, can be determined from an examination of community master plans.

At the state level, 28 states, under provisions of the Coastal Zone Management Act, have coastal management plans that try to balance coastal development and resource conservation. State permits, required by most marinas, reflect the particular bias of each governing body. Local governments charged with the implementation of state requirements may impose even stricter guidelines for marina development.

The environmental movement has resulted in marina projects taking longer to get approval, with additional costs to institute environmentally friendly facilities. The major environmental considerations involved in the siting and design of marinas come from the loss of habitat from dredging and the construction of shoreline structures, the impact of stormwater runoff and discharge from boats on water quality, and the effects on coastal aesthetic values.[14] Calm, sheltered areas are ideal spots for marinas. Because such locations usually support wetlands and submerged seagrass beds, the potential for habitat loss is great unless the marina is excavated from an upland area.

The following checklist will help identify issues regarding permit approval. The more *yes* answers to these questions, the more problems are likely to crop up in getting a permit.

❖ Will dredging be required for the access basin and/or the boat basin?
❖ Will filling be required on wetlands and/or in open water?
❖ Will dredged material be disposed of at locations other than currently permitted public disposal areas?

❖ Will structures such as bulkheads and revetments (sheathing that protects riverbanks) be required?

❖ Will the water body at the site be characterized by low flushing rates?

❖ Does the water body presently fail to meet state water quality standards?

❖ Is the site located within 1 mile (1.6 km) of a designated wildlife refuge or wilderness area?

❖ Are any rare, threatened, or endangered aquatic or terrestrial species or their habitats present at the site?

❖ Do shellfish beds occur within 2000 feet (600 m) of the site or within 1000 feet (300 m) of access channels?

❖ Are grassbeds located within 1000 feet (300 m) of the marina or access channels?

❖ Is the site in an area of historic, archaeological, or scenic value?

❖ Will the proposed activity be inconsistent with state or local coastal zone management plans or zoning requirements?

❖ Will the project obstruct public land access to navigable waters?

❖ Will the project require structures that extend into or obstruct existing channels?[15]

Because of issues like these, potential marina sites are fewer than they used to be, which has resulted in dramatic increases in the cost of waterfront land suitable for recreational purposes. Increased costs, together with the popularity of fiberglass, has resulted in the increased popularity of stack storage marinas, where boats are housed three high in warehouse-type buildings. The 1980s saw a dramatic increase (which has since leveled off) of facilities being developed as condominiums or dockominiums, with individual ownership of a slip space and common ownership of the rest of the facilities.

In an attempt to encourage environmentally sensitive development, the National Marine Manufacturers Association (NMMA) sponsors an annual environmental award. Previous winners have instituted such practices as:

❖ constructing wide openings between the breakwaters, docks, and shorelines to allow easy access to young salmon migrating out of Puget Sound in addition to allowing for tidal circulation

❖ using more expensive concrete pillars and floats to help sustain algae, mussels, and barnacles

❖ creating rock beaches at the ends of the marina to serve as feeding grounds for young salmon[16]

Carrying Capacity   In environmental terms, a site's boat-carrying capacity depends on three factors:

- ❖ The volume of water available at the site to dilute waste = Q
- ❖ The amount of pollution generated by each boat = L
- ❖ Area water quality requirements = C

Hence, the number of boats a site can carry = QC/L[17]

DEVELOPMENT   Marinas were originally developed as an alternative to berthing in open
CRITERIA   waters for three reasons: convenience, safety, security.[18]

Any new marina must ensure that these criteria are met. For example, roads can improve access; breakwater can increase safety; better management can improve security. To meet these criteria, it is important that a marina offers:

- ❖ proximity to a population base
- ❖ accessibility by a main road artery
- ❖ sufficient water in the marina basin for development
- ❖ sufficient water depth and surface for the proposed activities—A minimum of 8 feet below low-water depth is ideal. Shallow sites can be dredged at a high cost. Of greater concern are deep basins, as these do not provide adequate protection from wave action and limit pier designs.
- ❖ natural protection from winds, storms, and flooding
- ❖ a stable shoreline
- ❖ good southerly exposure
- ❖ good water quality—A healthy flow of water through the marina helps wash pollutants away, while too strong a flow may make the marina unstable for boat storage.
- ❖ aesthetically pleasing quality surroundings
- ❖ reasonable fluctuation in water levels—High water levels constitute a safety threat.
- ❖ freedom from ice—In northern climates, boats have to be removed from the water in winter, or expensive aeration systems must be installed to keep the water moving, which prevents ice from forming.[19]

The water requirements vary depending on the activities to be undertaken. The water access requirements for typical boat uses are outlined in Figure 6.3.

The development of a marina is complicated by the requirement that both land and water uses be suitable for the finished product. Usually the

Deep-Sea Fishing (includes fishing on the Great Lakes and similar bodies of water)
- ❖ access to open water within no more than 15 miles and access to the fishing waters within 15 to 50 miles
- ❖ no restrictions on speed or wake, except within the immediate vicinity of the marina
- ❖ safe access to a port of refuge at all times
- ❖ easy navigation to and from the marina, with many aids
- ❖ minimum channel depths of 5 feet

Estuaries and Freshwater Fishing (includes typical inland lake fishing)
- ❖ access to suitable fishing waters within no more than 5 miles
- ❖ easy navigation, with readily identifiable landmarks and many aids
- ❖ minimum channel depths of 4 feet

Waterskiing and Similar Aquatic Sports
- ❖ access to suitable open water within 10 to 15 minutes
- ❖ few or no restrictions on speed or boat utilization except in the immediate vicinity of the marina
- ❖ minimum channel depths of 4 feet

Casual Cruising—Powerboats
- ❖ access within 30 miles to interesting waters containing many inlets, islands, small beaches, and safe and quiet anchorages
- ❖ minimum channel depths of 5 feet
- ❖ easy navigation to and from the marina, especially at night

Casual Cruising—Sailboats
- ❖ access within 15 miles to interesting waters containing many inlets, islands, small beaches, and safe and quiet anchorages
- ❖ location such that the course to and from the interesting waters is essentially at right angles to prevailing winds
- ❖ minimum channel depths of 5 feet
- ❖ easy navigation to and from the marina, especially at night

Long-Distance Cruising
- ❖ easy access to the ocean or major lake on a course compatible with prevailing winds, easy access to an inland waterway, etc.
- ❖ easy access to the marina at night and under fog and storm conditions
- ❖ minimum access channel of 7 feet

Small Sailboats
- ❖ access channel very short or wide enough to permit easy tacking
- ❖ access channel oriented essentially at right angles to prevailing winds
- ❖ minimum channel depths of 5 feet
- ❖ relatively protected waters within 1 mile of the marina
- ❖ open waters of at least 1 mile in diameter within 1 mile of the marina, with few shoreside obstructions that would cause variations in wind velocity and direction. (This requirement is for sailboat racing activity.)

❖ FIGURE 6.3 Water access requirements for typical boat uses. [Source: Clinton J. Chamberlain, *Marinas: Recommendations for Design, Construction, and Management* (Chicago: National Marine Manufacturers Association, 1983), 3.]

land uses—hotel, golf course, residential units—exert strong influences on whether or not the development is viable.

GENERAL DESIGN PRINCIPLES

1882: Indeed, if there were some places to eat and shop, working around these docks and warehouses wouldn't be half bad.
1992: Imagine . . . take away all the food and shops, and this marketplace pavilion easily could be a 19th-century waterfront warehouse.
—Cartoons by Roger K. Lewis satirizing Baltimore's Inner Harbor

Four principles guide the design of marinas:

1. The geography determines the engineering.
2. The engineering determines the profile.
3. The profile determines the layout.
4. The layout determines the architecture.[20]

❖ Boats in Brazil. [Source: Design Workshop, Inc.]

GEOGRAPHY— The major cost in building a marina comes from dredging, locks, bulk-
ENGINEERING heads, breakwaters, and piles.[21]

Dredging   Dredging changes the bottom profile of the basin to allow deeper-draft boats to dock in the marina. Most pleasure boats need 2 feet of clearance below the propeller at low tide. Most boats can be accommodated with a depth of 7 feet at mean low water.

Dredging can cause siltation problems if not done properly. The basin bottom should slope slightly toward the entrance to encourage a natural flushing action. Deep-water marinas, especially those that are enclosed, can have severe water quality problems because of the lack of natural flow. Installation of aeration systems may be necessary.

If the material being dredged has a high clay or organic silt content, it will tend to trap chemical contaminates, such as hydrocarbons and heavy metals. Bottom testing is necessary to confirm their presence. Permit granting is easier for on-site rather than off-site disposal, which must be done where the material being dredged cannot erode away or leach out.[22] Material dredged from the bottom can be used as fill in the area next to the basin. Savings can accrue when only part of the marina basin is dredged. This means that larger boats are limited to the dredged parts of the marina, while the smaller-keeled boats are berthed in the undredged spots. Because of the high cost of disposal of fill material, the ideal relationship occurs when the amount of dredged material equals the amount of fill needed.

In general, the degree of difficulty in getting a dredging permit increases proportionately with the amount of dredging to take place.

Locks   Locks may be the answer where a site is otherwise inaccessible. They are necessary where the tidal range is greater than 12 feet or where there is a major change in elevation between the basin and open water. Because of the expense, locks are rarely economical in marinas of fewer than 500 boats. Locks can cause problems due to excessive waits to get in or out of the marina.

Bulkheads   A bulkhead is "a retaining wall that is backed with solid fill and erected along the water to extend the upland out to the bulkhead line; serves as protection against tidal or watercourse erection of land."[23] Bulkheads prevent erosion of the shoreline as well as provide safe, convenient access to the water part of the marina. A less expensive alternative is revetments, made of concrete and laid at the shoreline's natural angle of repose. Revetments provide better wave action and are more environmentally friendly to fish. In some cases, vegetation can be used as an inexpensive and attractive alternative. Bulkheading precludes development of the beach area, a potentially popular amenity, and should not be done unless absolutely necessary.

Bulkheads are of either sheet or gravity types. The former uses sheeting made of steel, concrete, or wood that is anchored by piles. The latter is made of precast concrete and retains the shoreline by means of weight and shape. Gravity bulkheads allow easy access to boats but, in reflecting the waves, cause greater wave turbulence at the shoreline.

Breakwaters Breakwaters are used to shield the marina from wave action. Potential wave action is simulated by engineers to determine the extent of breakwaters needed. Improper location of breakwaters can reduce natural flushing, exacerbate erosion problems, and encourage dangerous currents. Breakwaters are commonly constructed of a long, narrow strip of rubble. Floating breakwaters are less expensive to construct, though more expensive to maintain, and do not impede water flow. They are not suitable for areas that suffer from severe weather conditions.

Piles Piles are used to support fixed piers and bulkheads and to anchor floating piers. They need to be durable, strong, and straight , and tend to be made of timber, concrete, steel, or a combination thereof, such as PVC-jacketed concrete.[24]

ENGINEERING— PROFILE The four basic marina types are offshore, recessed, built-in, and land-locked.[25] They can be seen in Figure 6.4.

Offshore Marina Because the offshore marina requires minimum bulkhead wall, land take, and dredging, it can be the least expensive type to build. Many, however, require expensive breakwaters, the cost of which, in deep water, can negate cost savings in other areas. It is vulnerable to weather, currents and, on rivers and estuaries, is a navigation hazard. It is also subject to silting by littoral drift—the movement of sand by wave action. It offers minimum enclosure and has the least impact on the environment. The offshore marina, however, presents few opportunities to place land uses directly by the boats.

Recessed Marina When conditions on the sea bottom do not allow for an offshore layout, a recessed marina may be the economical option. Dredging takes earth from

❖ FIGURE 6.4
Basic marina
types. [Source:
Donald W. Adie,
*Marinas: A
Working Guide to
Their Development*,
3rd ed. (New York:
Nichols, 1984),
95.] Reprinted by
permission of
Butterworth-
Heinemann
Publishers, a
division of Reed
Educational &
Professional
Publishing, Ltd.]

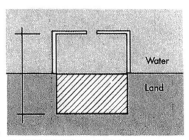

OFFSHORE MARINA

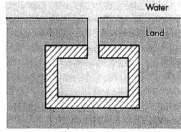

LAND-LOCKED MARINA

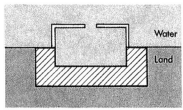

RECESSED MARINA

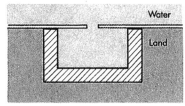

BUILT-IN MARINA

the original shoreline and deposits it offshore to raise the bottom to an appropriate level. Recessed marinas constitute a navigation hazard for passing craft.

Built-In Marina   The built-in marina offers the advantages of an uninterrupted shoreline, a large land-water interface, and considerable enclosure. Hence, it offers excellent safety and affords opportunities for many slips. However, it requires a large amount of land, a long bulkhead wall, and significant dredging. This makes it more expensive than the categories noted above. Views to the open water are maintained, as are opportunities for development located close to the boats. Water stagnation is a potential problem because of poor water flow.

Landlocked   The landlocked marina is both the costliest and the safest type of marina.
Marina   It offers maximum enclosure and minimum interruption of shoreline (hence the safety factor), yet requires maximum bulkhead wall and dredging (hence the cost). The distance from open water can be inconvenient. Some means of circulating the water is necessary to prevent stagnation. From a revenue-generating perspective, this layout offers maximum frontage for boat slips.

No matter the type, the amount of land area required should be equal to the water area. In the water, 77 percent of the area can be used for mooring, while the remaining 23 percent is needed for clearances. Parking can take anywhere from 22 percent[26] to 40 percent[27] of the land area. The remaining land can be used for other purposes. The ratios of boats to cars and people to cars are highly characteristic of individual marinas and must be determined case by case to estimate the numbers of boats, cars, and people to be accommodated. As a rule of thumb, marinas plan on between one-half to two parking spaces per boat slip, with a parking density of 90 cars per acre.[28]

Entrances to marinas should be built taking local wave conditions into account. The entrance should be turned away from the prevailing wave direction, at least 4 times the width of the largest berthed boat, and perpendicular to prevailing winds if sailboats are stored in the marina. Care must be taken to minimize littoral drift at the entrance, which can impede access and require expensive dredging.

Turning areas are needed when facilities such as fueling docks are part of the marina. The amount of space required will depend on the type of boat and the skill of the sailor. For example, if the marina caters to sailboats and prevailing winds are strong, the turning area should be larger than average. Generally speaking, the narrowest dimension of a turning basin should be 2¼ times the length of the marina's longest boat.

PROFILE— LAYOUT It is, unfortunately, common for mooring circulation and layout decisions to be made after the shape of the basin is determined. The best basin shape is rectangular, which allows for the greatest density of boats with the easiest maneuvering. More effective and efficient designs occur when mooring decisions are made early in the process as part of the overall development and design strategy.

The basic choice in mooring layout is whether to have fixed or floating piers.[29] Which type to select depends on the degree of water level fluctuation, the amount of money available, and how important safety is to the users. Fixed piers are stronger, more stable, and easier and cheaper to maintain. Floating piers are safer where there are major water level fluctuations. They also permit relatively easy expansion and modification. Floating docks have frames made of wood, concrete, or metal.[30]

The layout is determined by the site constraints as well as the demands of the expected market. The slip or berth—the water space between two piers—is the safest way to store boats. Slips are usually reached by piers or walkways that extend from the shore or bulkhead line. The piers can be fixed or float over the water (Figure 6.5). The latter tend to be attached to piles such that they rise and fall with the water level.

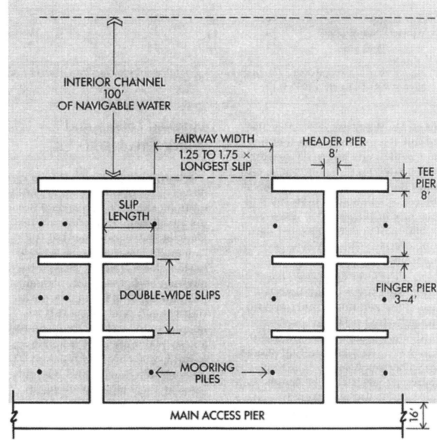

❖ FIGURE 6.5 Slip layout. [Source: Patrick L. Phillips, *Developing with Recreational Amenities: Golf, Tennis, Skiing, Marinas* (Washington, D.C.: Urban Land Institute, 1986), 160. Reproduced with permission of the Urban Land Institute.]

Smaller finger piers allow access to the boats, which are stored perpendicular to the main or header piers. Tee piers help protect boats from wave action.

Slips are either single- or double-wide (for storage of two boats). Piles can be used instead of finger piers as an alternate method of storage (see Figure 6.6). Storing the boats with the stern to the quay, jetty, or pontoon with the bow tied to piles is inexpensive, though not as convenient for embarking as alongside jetties or pontoons. Alternatively, the bows can be moored to anchors or buoys. This is also economical and is particularly suitable for large yachts, where the gangway is attached to the stern. A potential problem involves propellers becoming entangled.

Storing boats alongside finger piers or catwalks is convenient for embarking and disembarking. Where more than one yacht is moored per

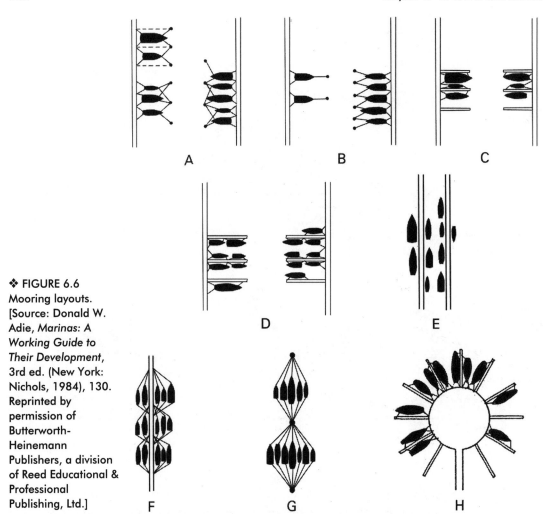

❖ FIGURE 6.6
Mooring layouts.
[Source: Donald W.
Adie, *Marinas: A
Working Guide to
Their Development*,
3rd ed. (New York:
Nichols, 1984), 130.
Reprinted by
permission of
Butterworth-
Heinemann
Publishers, a division
of Reed Educational &
Professional
Publishing, Ltd.]

finger, flexibility in accommodating different lengths of boat is greater;
however, the finger piers must be wider. When boats are placed in a single
bank alongside the quay, they are similarly convenient for embarking and
disembarking. Flexibility is offered for accommodating different lengths
of boat. Boats can also be placed alongside the quay, three or four abreast.
The economies of this setup are balanced by the necessity for crews from
the outer yachts to climb over the inner boats.

Mooring between piles is the cheapest system because of the high density involved. However, there is no access to dry land and leaving the
mooring is difficult.

The safest arrangement is when the long axis of the boat is parallel to the prevailing winds and when boats are secured on all four corners. Finger piers on both sides of the boat are the most convenient layout for owners. The double-wide slip arrangement saves the marina manager money and space and offers the greatest flexibility. However, because the boats are not separated by piles or piers, they are subject to damage from both wave action and other boats. Finally, star finger berths offer an interesting alternative.

LAYOUT— ARCHITECTURE Architects must take into account the circulation pattern, the social interests of the boaters and the need for support facilities. The variety of potential services and facilities that can be part of a marina development are noted in Table 6.2. The International Marina Institute publishes annual data on marinas, including destination marinas. Their 1998 report includes data from 20 destination resorts. Some 83 percent of destination marina resorts have restaurants, three-quarters offer dry rack storage, and almost four out of ten have haul-out and repair services. In addition, a third have free public boat launch facilities.

❖ Marina layout.

❖ TABLE 6.2 Marina Services and Facilities

Water Related	Land Related
MARINA SERVICES	
Boat launching	Boat sales
Mooring service	Boat repairs
Water taxi service	Marina supply sales
Transient boat service	General supply sales
Waste collection	Trailer storage
Fueling	Parking
Boat towing	Overnight accommodation
Fire and rescue services	Food service
Navigation and weather information	Concessions
Recreational services	Utility services
MARINA FACILITIES	
Open and covered mooring	Boat building and repair
Boat launch ramp	Boat dry storage
Marine railway	Trailer storage
Crane lift	Restaurant
Dry dock	Hotel
Fueling pier	Picnic areas
Anchorage services	Convenience store
Marine service station	Boat washing
Entrance and exit channels	Parking
Swimming area	Swimming pool
Water skiing course	Camping
Basin flushing system	Beach area
Storm and wave protection	Club room
	Marine supply sales
	Public toilets and showers
	Recreational facilities
	Bait shop
	Seafood sales

Source: U.S. Environmental Protection Agency Coastal Marinas Assessment Handbook (Atlanta: U.S. Environmental Protection Agency, 1985), 3–14.

Circulation   Consideration must be given to the separation of various marina user
Pattern   groups. Users can be divided into social and service traffic and by destination.[31] Cars with boats need to be directed to a launch area, while visitors
and owners not towing boats are diverted to the clubhouse and parking.
While parking should be reasonably close to the slips, many operators
question the wisdom of using valuable waterfront land for parking.

Social Interests   It is often said that boaters, like tennis players, place few demands on
facilities. Because of their love for the activity, they are willing to put up
with and may, in fact, enjoy being around the maintenance side of marinas. However, marinas may also seek to attract nonboaters to retail out-
lets, hotels, and restaurants. In this case, care must be taken to separate
the attractive elements of boating and the necessary but less attractive
service elements. Facilities might include restaurant and store operations,
hotels, clubhouse, picnicking, and camping. In resorts, marinas must be
developed to serve more than the needs of boaters. Adding facilities to
make the marina look more like a fishing village and less like a boatyard
increases its attractiveness and provides more income opportunities. Care
must be taken to avoid conflicts between the recreational uses of the facility and the more industrial aspects of boat maintenance.

Adie suggests that three questions be asked to determine what facilities can and should be offered:

1. What is possible, given the physical characteristics and environmental limitations of the site?
2. What is popular in terms of market demand?
3. What is profitable for the operator?[32]

Support Facilities   A variety of support facilities will be needed, depending on the type of
marina development, including toilet/showers, boat service center, boat
launching equipment, boat sewage disposal and water take-on, firefight-
ing equipment, and boat storage facilities. Instead of using valuable waterfront land for winter storage, perhaps parking lots can serve. An increasingly popular method of storing boats is dry stack storage, wherein boats
are warehoused in stacks of up to three boats and raised and lowered by
forklifts. In a well-managed system of stack storage, 25 boats can be
launched in an hour. This system offers advantages to both marina operator and boat owner.[33] For the operator, dry stack boat storage:

❖ Maximizes storage density.
❖ Improves security by allowing employee-only access to the rack
   storage area.

quick getaways 6.5

Dry Stack Storage

The scarcity of marina land and the greatly increased legal and environmental requirements of marina development keep many marina owners from expanding their holdings. An alternative is on-site dry stack storage.

The multistory storage of boats on a site can provide additional revenue to a marina if land is scarce and further expansion is impossible. Dry stacks of boats can be built up to five levels. Boats are stored on shelves, making the structure look like a group of small storage organizers in a workshop. A powerful forklift machine picks up boats one by one from the loading area and places each into a rack.

Many factors affect the cost of a proposed dry stack storage facility. The five most important factors are:

1. *Regulations from local and state building departments*—These agencies determine the height requirements, road and wind loads, landscaping layouts, onsite parking regulations, and other requirements that directly affect the degree of development allowed.
2. *Soil conditions*—Areas with more porous soils usually mean that piles must be driven into the ground and that special spread-concrete footings and beams provide the necessary foundation.
3. *Location*—The site affects the amount of ingress and egress, costs of construction materials, and local labor rates.
4. *Fire safety regulations*—It may be necessary to provide a wet sprinkler system for each level of the rack, depending on municipal and state requirements.
5. *Storage requirements of the owner*—The particular plan of the owner directly affects the project. Such factors as how many levels the facility will contain, the size of the boats to be stored, what type of system will be installed, and, especially, whether the facility will be fully enclosed, partially open, or completely open are key factors affecting the layout.

Source: John Simpson, "Appraising Proposed Marina Dry Stack Storage," *Appraisal Journal* 66, no. 3 (July 1998): 269–273.

Question: In what types of marinas is dry stack storage appropriate?

❖ Improves profitability when water space is limited by removing from the water boats under 30 feet for dry storage, thereby catering to the larger, higher-profit-generating boats.

❖ Can mean easier permits than wet storage.

❖ Gives a faster return on investment than does dock storage.

The boat owner, in turn, gets more protection and lower rental than in wet slips. In one study, the price elasticity of demand for wet slip storage was calculated at −0.23—that is, a 10 percent increase in the price of wet slips results in a 2.3 percent reduction in demand for wet slips. The demand for wet slips compared to dry slips increases as boat size and boater income increases.[34]

Guidelines for pump-out stations vary from 1 per 100 (industry consultants) to 1 per 400 (U.S. government) boats. The tendency is to provide a solitary, stationary sewage pump-out station. However, pump-out capability can be provided at each slip at the relatively low cost of $250 per slip (1995 figures) during new construction.[35]

Handicap Access

Marina operators have slowly become more conscious of the need to make their facilities accessible to people with physical disabilities. This means developing a route that offers a safe and unobstructed path to all elements of the facility.[36] Of primary concern to marinas are toilet facilities, parking areas, and gangway or ramp access to dock systems.

Toilet facilities must allow for the maneuvering of a wheelchair and the presence of other people in the stall at the same time. An approach 4 feet wide and a door at least 3 feet wide are required. A 5-foot diameter of clear space within each stall is needed for turning purposes. Door locks, toilet fixtures, grab bars, and cost hooks must be within easy reach.[37]

Parking spaces must be designated for use by people with physical disabilities when 15 or more parking spaces are developed. Here are general guidelines:

No. of Parking Spaces	Spaces Required for Handicapped
15–25	1 space
26–40	5% but not fewer than 2 spaces
41–100	4% but not fewer than 3 spaces
101–200	3% but not fewer than 4 spaces
210–500	2% but not fewer than 6 spaces[38]

The designated spaces should be those closest to the activity. If the parking spots cannot be located less than 200 feet from the activity, a drop-off area needs to be created within 100 feet of the activity. Parking spaces can be 12 feet wide for perpendicular or diagonal parking layouts or consist of 8-foot-wide spaces separated by a 5-foot-wide aisle to serve two vehicles.

A curb cut at each space allows people to access the sidewalk without having to enter the vehicular traffic flow.

Gangway access should be as short and direct as possible. Walkways must be a minimum of 3 feet wide—6 feet is preferred—with a slope not to exceed 1:20. Handrails on both sides of a ramp or stair assist people who favor one side of the body. A ramp is defined as a "pathway with a slope of greater than 1:20."[39] Due to large tidal changes, the primary access to marinas is often a relatively steep slope. This presents the major difficulty for marinas attempting to make their facilities accessible. Commonly, regulations indicate that ramps should not be greater than 1:12. This, however, may be too steep for people in wheelchairs. A ramp 4 feet wide with rails on both sides and a landing for resting every 32 feet allows people in wheelchairs to negotiate the slope while gripping both rails to ease the way up or slow the descent.

SUMMARY

The importance of water as the basis for a number of recreational developments was noted. This chapter focused on beach resorts and marinas. The development process for a beach resort needs to consider six elements: sea, seashore, beach, back beach, coastal stretch, and the surrounding country. For a marina, the market must be analyzed, a market strategy and marina concept developed, and an initial site identified. Feasibility analyses are conducted and a preliminary design sketched out. Finally, the marina is developed according to certain design principles— the geography determines the engineering, which, in turn, determines the profile, which determines the layout, which determines the architecture.

ENDNOTES

1. Dean Schwanke et al., *Resort Development Handbook* (Washington, D.C.: Urban Land Institute, 1997), 143.
2. Lynn C. Harrison and Winston Husbands (eds.), *Practicing Responsible Tourism: International Case Studies in Tourism Planning, Policy, and Development* (New York: John Wiley & Sons, 1996), 74.

3. A. H. Paul, "Weather and the Daily Use of Outdoor Recreational Areas in Canada," in J. A. Taylor (ed.), *Weather Forecasting for Agriculture and Industry* (Newton Abbot, England: David and Charles, 1972), 132–146.

4. Amanda Brown, "Too Many Coastal Waters Fail Germ Test, Says Minister," *PA News*, 19 November 1998.

5. Henry Lee Morgenstern, "Clouds over the Coral," *Earth Action Network* (March 1999): 36–43.

6. Patrick L. Phillips, *Developing with Recreational Amenities: Golf, Tennis, Skiing, Marinas* (Washington, D.C.: Urban Land Institute, 1986), 235.

7. Ibid.

8. Ibid.

9. Ibid., 234–237.

10. Valene L. Smith and William R. Eadington, *Tourism Alternatives: Potentials and Problems in the Development of Tourism* (Philadelphia: University of Pennsylvania Press, 1992).

11. Phillips, *Developing with Recreational Amenities*, 141.

12. U.S. Environmental Protection Agency Coastal Marinas Assessment Handbook (Atlanta: United States Environmental Protection Agency, 1985), 3.5.

13. Schwanke et al., *Resort Development Handbook*, 145.

14. Phillips, *Developing with Recreational Amenities*, 149.

15. U.S. Environmental Protection Agency Coastal Marinas Assessment Handbook, 3.2.

16. Ibid., 3.8–3.9.

17. Doug Henschen and Peter Shroeder, "Marinas Good Guys: Finalists for the 1994 National Marine Manufacturers Association's Environmental Responsibility Awards," *Lexis-Nexus Academic Universe* 57, no. 11: 25.

18. J. C. Swanson and M. L. Spaulding, "Marina Boat Carrying Capacity: An Assessment and Comparison of Methodologies," paper presented at the 1990 National Marina Research Conference, International Marina Institute, Chicago, 1990.

19. Phillips, *Developing with Recreational Amenities*, 144.

20. Phillips, "Water-Based Recreation Site Complexes," *Developing with Recreational Amenities*, 227.

21. Donald W. Adie, *Marinas: A Working Guide to Their Development*, 3rd ed. (New York: Nichols, 1984), 95.

22. Schwanke et al., *Resort Development Handbook*, 146.

23. Neil W. Ross, "Dredging Successfully," *Boating Industry Magazine* (March 1988), 18.

24. Appraisal Institute, *The Dictionary of Real Estate Appraisal*, 3rd ed. (Chicago: Appraisal Institute, 1993), 312.

25. Phillips, *Developing with Recreational Amenities*, 167.

26. Ibid., 150.

27. Adie, *Marinas*, 111.

28. Phillips, *Developing with Recreational Amenities*, 158.

29. Ibid.

30. Schwanke et al., *Resort Development Handbook*, 146.

31. Appraisal Institute, *Dictionary of Real Estate Appraisal*, 16.

32. Adie, *Marinas*, 69.

33. Paul E. Dodson, "Introduction to Dry Stack Boat Storage," in *Marina Investment and Appraisal Course* (Wickford, R.I.: International Marina Institute, 1990), 1–3.

34. Fred Bell, "Demand and Marketing, Part A: Comparison of Dry Stack and Wet Slip Demand," in *Dry Stack Marina Handbook*, 2nd ed. (Wickford, R.I.: International Marina Institute, 1992), section 6, 4.

35. Bruce O. Tobiasson, "Marina Design and Development with an Environmental Conscience," handout at International Marina Institute FMM School, 1995, 16.

36. Bruce O. Tobiasson, "Handicapped Access in Marina Design," paper presented at the 1989 National Marina Research Conference, International Marina Institute, 1989, 107–108.

37. Ibid., 113.

38. Ibid., 108.

39. Ibid., 111.

Chapter 7
GOLF- AND TENNIS-BASED RESORTS

INTRODUCTION

*It looks like an excellent exercise. But what's the little white
ball for?*
—ULYSSES S. GRANT

Golf course design is examined in relation to the reason for developing the
course. Important practices for each stage of the development are noted,
as are the characteristics of the various types of golf courses. Design principles are outlined that combine concern for the environment with attractiveness to the market. Similar consideration is given to tennis.

Golf is a universal pastime. It is estimated that 15 million golfers are
vying for position on 3500 golf courses in Asia. Of the 16,000-plus golf
courses in the United States, over 1300 are resort or real estate/resort
courses.[1] The popularity of golf has increased tremendously over the past
50 years—from 3.5 million U.S. golfers in 1950 to 26.4 million in 1998.
This has resulted in its being enjoyed by an increasingly broad section of
society. However, although the industry gains 1.5 to 3 million new golfers
per year, it also loses nearly an equal number because the game fails to
convert those with an interest into committed golfers. The industry has
been unable to sell golf as an experience. The number of golfers and
rounds played is expected to increase at a rate of 1 to 2 percent a year over
the next decade.[2]

Golf courses can serve many purposes. Because of their attractiveness
to growing numbers of people, they may help the marketing effort in selling a resort or residential community. The design of the golf course is
dependent on the strategic role it is meant to play within the resort. If the
primary purpose of the course is to sell real estate, buildings should be
designed to take advantage of views. There should be maximum real
estate frontage on the fairways, as these sites command premium prices.
By some estimates, golf course frontage can result in an 8 percent premium in the price for a home. In contrast, in one study, a home one-tenth
of a mile from the golf course gate had a 3.7 percent reduction in its value
compared to golf course frontage.[3]

Water elements should be planned as both scenic amenities and as golf
hazards, and the most valuable land should be kept for uses other than golf.

Courses can also be used in the marketing effort to sell homes or condominiums. An estimated 80 percent of all new and planned golf courses
are associated with residential developments.[4] In these kinds of cases, the
course should be developed early in the development process, designed to

support tournament play, and planned for photogenic and outstanding holes that take advantage of site characteristics. This, obviously, costs more to build than the typical golf course.

Where the objective is to provide a high-quality amenity to the real estate target market, the course must be developed with the average golfer in mind. The integrity and playability of the course become the major design consideration. The integrity of the golf course is "the degree to which golfers perceive that surrounding land uses visually or physically impinge on their game."[5] The course might be built in stages as real estate expands. Golf courses undoubtedly raise land values and can evolve into profit centers themselves.

Concerns over the negative environmental impact of golf courses are increasing. The issues revolve around three concerns: land use changes and soil erosion, the use of chemical fertilizers (controlling pests requires upwards of 9 pounds of pesticides per acre), and the extensive use of water. The positive environmental aspects of golf courses, on the other hand, include:

- ❖ *Reduced runoff*—Turf on golf courses helps reduce water runoff, erosion, and flooding.
- ❖ *Groundwater recharge*—A 150-acre course can recharge the water table with a net 90 million gallons of rainwater each year.
- ❖ *Water filtration system*—Water that has moved through a golf course is purer than it was before it reached the course.
- ❖ *Effluent water*—Golf courses can be irrigated with effluent water that is filtered by the soil and vegetation before returning to the aquifer.
- ❖ *Oxygen production*—A 150-acre golf course produces enough oxygen for 118,000 people per day.
- ❖ *Temperature*—The cooling effect of a course is equivalent to several hundred tons of air conditioning.
- ❖ *Noise abatement*—Turf absorbs and deflects sound.
- ❖ *Wildlife*—Courses maintain natural habitats for wildlife.
- ❖ *Allergy control*—Turf helps trap dust and reduces pollen levels.
- ❖ *Fire breaks*—Turfgrass offers a buffer zone to help prevent the spread of wildfire.
- ❖ *Open space*—Many developments require a certain amount of open space. In some cases, golf courses can qualify as open space to help meet this requirement.[6]

The high cost of construction and maintenance means that development must be approached carefully.

quick getaways 7.1

Golf Courses: Living Laboratories

Golf courses are becoming living laboratories for understanding how to develop land in an environmentally friendly way. At Purdue University's Kampen Golf Course, research projects are underway that show how to reduce the negative effects of residential and commercial development. Other projects are exploring:

- the natural ability of microbes in golf course turf to digest polluting chemicals in water runoff, turning them into harmless substances
- the best way to plant trees in areas where construction has removed them
- how to better maintain wildlife in the out-of-play areas of golf courses

These experiments will help reduce the objections of many environmentalists to golf courses.

Golf courses are turning out to be a way to clean the highly polluted water that comes from automobiles. They are also becoming a way that humans and wildlife can coexist without harming the animals' environment.

Source: "Golf Courses Become Living Laboratories," Futurist 33, no. 3 (March 1999), 7.

Question: Are golf courses good or bad for the environment? Explain.

GENERAL GUIDELINES

Golf is the engine that drives most resort destinations.
—DOUGLAS GEOGA
President of Hyatt Hotels Corp.

In the 1960s, the cost of developing a golf course was easily recouped through the premium prices charged for fairway frontage and the general marketing appeal of the amenity. Rising interest rates and inflation in the 1970s changed that picture. The increasingly high development costs led developers to reduce construction and maintenance costs and look for sources of additional revenue. For example, more courses are being designed with water conservation in mind, reusing wastewater for irrigation. Courses are also being designed to speed play, thereby increasing course capacity, daily rounds, and revenue.

OWNERSHIP Golf courses can be privately or municipally owned. Private clubs are open to members only or to the public on a daily fee basis. Today, it is common for a golf course to be part of a development mix that includes various housing products: primary homes, vacation residences, a resort hotel, and condominiums. This means that the old development model is no longer appropriate. Traditionally, the course was built early in the development of the project, the cost was covered through sales of frontage home sites, and the developer operated the course for a few years before turning management and maintenance over to the residents of the project. The new model involves limiting the up-front development costs, maximizing cash flow and the marketing impact of the amenity, and transferring ownership in a planned and orderly manner.[7]

In Japan, where land is at a premium, most of the courses are mountainous.[8] Flat land is used for growing crops, and the towns and cities are constructed on flat land because most of the people, because of spirits, do not like to live in houses in the mountains or even in the foothills. As a result, golf courses do not have house lots around them, as is common in North America.

At a self-contained resort, the golf course must be more of a stand-alone attraction than when it is part of a larger community of various housing products. Frontage development becomes less important and might even be discouraged. Oceanfront holes, uneconomic in most development projects, might be constructed for a memorable guest experience.

Courses can be operated in one of three ways: daily fee, nonequity private club, and membership-owned equity club.[9]

Even within a real estate development, developers may open the course to the general public on a daily fee basis during the early years of the project life. Cash flow helps sustain the development while helping stimulate interest in the development. An upscale daily fee facility can become a permanent part of the overall concept.

In a nonequity private club, members pay an initiation fee and annual dues. The club may be open to nonmembers at a higher fee. The developer keeps control of the course and hopes to operate it at a profit.

quick getaways 7.2

Golf Communities

A golf course in a residential community may not only be an amenity for the residents but rewarding to the golf community developer. The rate of new golf course construction has increased significantly in the 1990s, from an average of about 150 a year to more than 400 a year.

Of the golf course development projects completed in 1998, about 40 percent were part of housing developments. Golf courses help residential builders sell homes to all types of buyers, not just people who play golf. With regard to the number of golfers who actually live on a golf course, the National Golf Foundation reports that approximately 3.7 million, or 15 percent of all golfers, are permanent residents of a golf course community. Eight out of ten of the 15 percent who live in a golf course community own their own residences, and another 3 percent of golfers own a residence on a golf course that they use as a vacation home or rent out as investment property.

Much of the growth in construction of golf course housing communities has been in Frost Belt states such as Michigan, Ohio, Indiana, Wisconsin, and Illinois. These areas have a good supply of land that is relatively inexpensive and suitable for golf course development.

Source: Ashok Chaluvadi, "Golf Communities," *Housing Economics* 47, no. 7 (July 1999): 6–7.

Question: **What are the possible roles of a golf course as part of a resort development?**

In the equity arrangement, members buy an equal share in the ownership of the club, the pricing being tied to the cost of the land and the improvements. As noted in Chapter 3, recreational amenities can be operated in all three ways, depending on if and when the developer transfers control to the residents of the development.

PLANNING AND DEVELOPMENT

*The ideal site is in a valley where the land rolls every 200 to
250 yards with grades of less than 10 percent, good sites for
greens, a change in elevation of about 50 to 100 feet, well-
drained sandy soil that dries quickly after rain, tall existing
trees of a species suitable for golf and lakes already there.*
— DESMOND MUIRHEAD
Article in *Urban Land,* January 1994

LANDSCAPE ARCHITECT A landscape architect is "one whose profession is to plan the decorative arrangement of outdoor features."[10] In the development of a golf course, their responsibilities are threefold:

1. to assist the developer/client to attract visitors through design
2. to provide the visitors/users with a rich and memorable experience
3. to protect the natural resources

SIZE OF PROPERTY Many developers underestimate the amount of land needed for a golf course.[11] While 120 to 130 acres might suffice for a regulation 18-hole course on a flat site with few facilities, the same course on more difficult terrain might need upwards of 150 acres. It goes without saying that the latter alternative is more visually pleasing and recreationally challenging to the golfer.

❖ New mountain golf courses, Maroon Creek, Aspen, Colorado. [Source: Design Workshop, Inc.]

SHAPE OF PROPERTY Irregularly shaped pieces of land make for potentially more interesting and safer golf courses compared to square or rectangular sites. Regular developments are more likely to have a number of parallel holes. Long, narrow sites restrict the options of the developer. Road crossings also reduce the attractiveness of a site. The orientation of the course is another item to consider. A long, narrow course oriented northwest-southeast means that the holes face the morning or afternoon sun, making play more difficult. A north–south orientation is preferred.

TOPOGRAPHY The topography of the site has the greatest impact on the quality of the finished golf experience. Gently rolling land is preferred, as flat land is boring and hilly land is tiring on players, slows play, requires numerous blind shots, and is expensive to maintain. The ideal site should have both sloping and flat areas, with tees, greens, and fairways adapted to the contours of the land. Steep slopes reduce the viability of the site. They can be graded, of course, but at significant cost. Many courses offer excavated lakes and ponds, the extracted fill being used to provide little hills. A varied topography offers large views that increase the selling price of real estate lots.

Designers begin by looking at the existing contours of the land to identify suitable areas for tees, greens, and fairway landing areas where well-hit balls can come to rest without rolling out of bounds. According to the Urban Land Institute, "The best holes will drop in elevation from tee to landing area and landing area to green."[12] Because the golfer can easily see the hole, play is faster and more enjoyable.

NATURAL HAZARDS Hazards such as streams, ravines, ponds, and rolling terrain make the course more interesting aesthetically and more challenging, from a golfing perspective, and reduce construction costs, as fewer artificial hazards must be constructed.

SOIL CHARACTERISTICS Soil fertility depends, to a large extent, on the previous use of the land. For example, a course built on a run-down farm that was intensively cultivated and poorly fed will need more frequent fertilization to bring it up to the level required for a golf course.

Several types of land that cannot be used for other development can make excellent golf courses. Examples include wetlands, floodplains, drainage channels, and dry streambeds.[13] The drawback is that construction costs in sites with a high drainage table are considerably higher.

Insufficient attention to drainage problems can be costly. A widely quoted story in golf circles is about the superintendent who was asked what it takes to keep a golf course looking good. The reply was, "About 5 percent common sense and 95 percent drainage, and if you don't have much common sense, then put in more drainage."[14] Wet conditions on a site with inadequate drainage can reduce the number of rounds that can be played during the season. Revenues are reduced, the round of golf is less attractive to the players, and the course is more expensive to maintain. The drainage systems needs to take into account runoff from real estate development around the course. On the other hand, golf course water features offer biological filtering as part of a comprehensive stormwater management program.

It is said that a site can never have too much topsoil. Topsoil is crucial to the healthy growth of turfgrass. The best type is well-drained, sandy loam. If major grading has to take place, the topsoil should be removed first, stored nearby, then spread over the graded areas. In coastal areas, alluvial soil allows for low-cost development. Peat and many soils, on the other hand, are unstable and high in organic compounds. Clay soil reduces the cost of constructing ponds but causes problems if the rate of percolation is insufficient for proper drainage. On the other hand, high percolation rates increase the need for water and fertilizer. Rock outcroppings add visual appeal to a course, but rocky soil increases development costs.

VEGETATION Next to slope, vegetation is the most important influence on the overall character of a course. Wooded areas, for example, enhance the visual and ecological appeal of a course by separating fairways. At the same time, they provide opportunities for compatible recreational uses such as walking, cross-country skiing, and bicycling. On heavily wooded sites, a new course looks more mature than it is. If the area is too heavily wooded, however, the cost of clearing it will be high.

CLEARING REQUIRED Clear sites offer the advantage of lower site preparation costs and fewer environmental challenges. However, landscaping costs are higher and the site will look unfinished for several years. The cost of clearing a site is heavily dependent on the type of vegetation to be cleared and how easily it can be disposed of. Large, mature trees are expensive to clear. It may be possible to sell marketable trees to loggers. The remaining smaller trees and other vegetation must then be cleared. If burning is not allowed, the disposal cost can be high, as the material must be chipped and removed from the site.

MARKET Four important market-related items must be considered in designing a course:

❖ relationship within the project between golf and real estate
❖ ability levels and diversity of players
❖ overall level of demand for the course
❖ frequency of play by the same group of users[15]

For example, courses in second-home communities are typically designed with single fairways to provide maximum fairway frontage for premium lot prices. Resort hotel courses are designed to attract serious golfers. The core or parallel fairways layout helps protect the integrity of the course for these people. At resorts that do not have many repeat guests, the visibility of the green and all major hazards from the tee is important. While golfers who play the course often become aware of greens and hazards placement, the one-time-only golfer is not and needs assistance to prevent the experience from becoming too frustrating. To improve visibility, holes should drop in elevation from tee to landing area and from landing area to green. Where the resort features golf, a number of signature holes should be built to produce a memorable experience for the golfer. Where time is an issue, variety, multiple tees, and large greens take on greater importance.

LAND COST The cost of building a top-rated golf course runs between $200,000 and $400,000 a hole. This translates into $3.6 million and $7.2 million—perhaps as much as 10 to 12 percent of the total cost of building the resort.[16] These figures include clearing, grading, drainage, construction of tees, fairways, greens, sand bunkers, irrigation system, and cart paths, seeding, and grassing.

WATER SUPPLY A regulation 18-hole golf course needs between 1.5 and 3.5 million gallons of water per week.[17] The amount depends on the type of turf, the irrigation system, and the climate. Water quality is another concern. The concentration of soluble salts should be less than 2000 parts per million for grass to grow well. More and more courses are using treated wastewater for irrigation purposes. In addition, research at places like the turf management department at Colorado State University is focusing on native grass species, such as wheatgrass and blue grama, that can keep their drought-resistant characteristics on golf courses.

Well water can be routed into reservoirs that are utilized as water hazards on the course. In a similar vein, streams and rivers can be tapped as a source of irrigation water. "The limiting factor in this type of arrangement is the period of lowest flows in the stream's watershed."[18] In dry periods, stream sources can be supplemented by well water. The vertical difference between the average elevation of the lake and the highest point on the course determines the extent to which costly pumping is required.

Irrigation System   Irrigation systems for golf courses were introduced in the late 1800s. Since then, they have become increasingly complex. The amount of coverage has to balance the need for irrigation and the cost of the system. In desert areas, the system has to cover the entire course, from fairways to greens and tees. In other places, either a single-row or double-row fairway system is sufficient.[19] A single-row system places sprinkler heads down the middle of the fairway. Less piping and fewer heads are needed, making this a less expensive option than a double-row system. The decision of whether to install a single- or a double-row system depends on the width of the fairways. The amount of water used can vary from 800 gallons per minute (gpm) for a single-row system to 1600 gpm for complete coverage of all elements of the course.

Systems can be either automatic or manual. The former is more expensive to install but less costly to operate than the latter. The irrigation system for Terravita in Scottsdale, Arizona, uses an on-site weather station to measure daily evaporation and adjusts each sprinkler's run time to replace only the amount of water that is needed.

CLIMATE   Climate affects the length of the season and the costs of maintenance. Courses in moderate climates accommodate more rounds of golf per year while incurring relatively high maintenance costs year-round. In the Palm Springs area, for example, the highest irrigation costs occur during the off-season. Northern courses have lower maintenance costs compared to those in other geographic regions during the cold season.

Arid   While many critics claim that it is irresponsible to build golf courses in arid parts of the world, others argue that in places like the southwestern United States, golf courses serve two major roles: flood control and groundwater recharge.[20] In Scottsdale, natural washes, called arroyos, are fairly common. While arroyos are usually dry, during summer and winter rains they can turn into raging torrents in minutes. Because any kind of development increases runoff, care has to be taken to ensure that the increased water flow does not adversely affect developments and habitats downstream. The solution is to use a golf course as a means of drainage by directing drainage channels onto the course itself and building them into its features. Because the soil in the area readily absorbs water, a number of waste bunkers are strategically built around the course. Most of the year, they act as regular hazards. However, when the rains come, they fill with runoff, which then percolates back into the groundwater or is released slowly into the arroyos.

In Sun City, Arizona, the problem was that the soil was so tightly packed that runoff would take too long to be absorbed. Designers created 17 lakes on the Sun City Grand course for runoff deposit, where the water is used for groundwater recharging. In total, the lakes allow up to 4000 acre-feet of water annually to reach the groundwater table below.

MAINTENANCE   Maintenance is the largest single cost item for a course. "Maintenance costs will depend on a wide variety of factors, including the course's location, length of season, type, market size, and purpose."[21] According to the American Society of Golf Course Architects, maintenance costs can run anywhere from $250,000 to $650,000 a year. This does not include operation of the clubhouse and the fleet of golf carts. The task is to balance the higher quality of the course with the increased maintenance costs required to produce that quality. At some point, spending more money on maintenance does not produce a corresponding increase in course quality.

A major factor in maintenance costs is the type of grass selected. In northern latitudes, it is generally accepted that bentgrass provides the best playing surface. This type is less practical in the South because of summer heat stress. Bluegrass is criticized for not having the color contrast or playing conditions of bentgrass but it tolerates heat better and requires less pesticides, fertilizer, and water. Maintenance savings can be $80,000 a year.[22] The point is that maintenance costs should be considered when designing a course.

The way a course is maintained also has an impact on operations. "When greens are kept fast, fairways lush and narrow, roughs long and sand bunkers soft . . . play will be difficult and slow."[23] The visual effect of the course also has a major impact on how enjoyable the experience is.

quick getaways 7.3

Designing Greener Golf Courses

In 1996, *Environment Principles for Golf Courses* was published by the American Society of Golf Course Architects for all golf courses in the United States. The principles were developed by a committee of 25 people from 16 groups, including the U.S. Environmental Protection Agency, the American Society of Golf Course Architects, the United States Golf Association, Audubon International, and the National Wildlife Federation. The representatives' goal was to identify general environmental measures, beyond those required by law, that are applicable nationwide.

The principles are centered around factors to take into consideration when planning, designing, and constructing new golf courses. In the design stage, for example, installation of irrigation systems that reuse wastewater may be an option, depending on factors such as soil, climate, and groundwater. Overall, the design should stress the importance of the efficient use of water and the ability to reuse it if necessary. The preservation of wildlife habitats and aquatic animals should also be incorporated in the design and planning processes of new golf courses.

These are just a few of the measures that can make municipal golf courses more environmentally friendly. The payoff can be an improved facility for the benefit of the golfers, the local government, and the community in general.

Source: Bob Shapard, "Environment at the Forefront: Keys for Greener Municipal Golf Courses," *American City and County* 112, no. 4 (April 1997): 52–59.

Question: How can a golf course be environmentally friendly?

GOLF COURSE TYPES

> *God created golf holes. It is up to the architect to discover them.*
> —DONALD ROSS
> *Golf Course Design*

Five basic golf course types serve as the models for constructing a course.[24] They are illustrated in Figure 7.1. Which one is used depends on the objectives of the project and the characteristics of the land available.

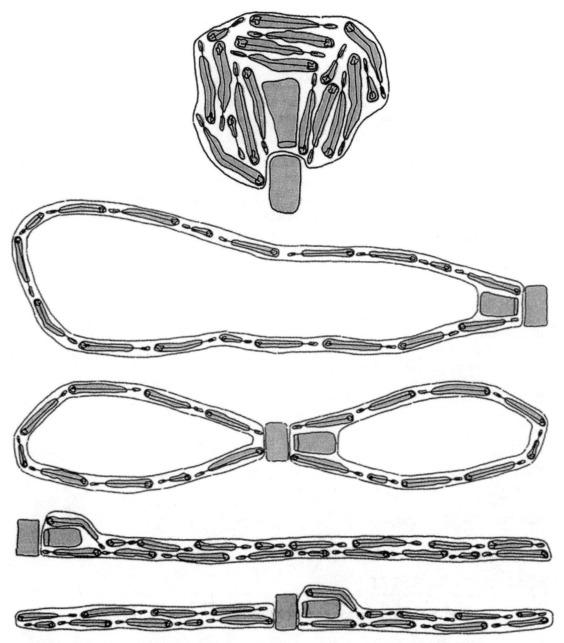

❖ FIGURE 7.1 The five basic types of golf course. [Source: Patrick L. Phillips, *Developing with Recreational Amenities: Golf, Tennis, Skiing, Marinas* (Washington, D.C.: Urban Land Institute, 1986), 35–36. Reproduced with permission of the Urban Land Institute.]

Each model is based on the idea of the regulation course which, in turn, is based on the concept of par. Par is "the score for a given hole produced by error-free golf, or the score an expert golfer would be expected to make."[25] Ordinary playing conditions are assumed and two putting strokes are allowed. On a par 4 hole, for example, the golfer would reach the green in two strokes. The United States Golf Association has established the following distance standards for par:

Par	Men	Women
3	up to 250 yards	up to 210 yards
4	251–470 yards	211–400 yards
5	471 yards +	401 yards +

THE REGULATION GOLF COURSE

The regulation golf course has a par between 69 and 73, with 72 considered ideal. The course probably has three sets of tees ranging from 5200 to 7200 yards in length for golfers of varying ability. The holes making up the course are a combination of par 3s, 4s, and 5s, and generally consist of four par 3s, ten par 4s, and three par 5s. In keeping with the objective of making the course fair and enjoyable to play, the holes should be evenly spread along two circuits of nine holes each.[26]

CORE GOLF COURSES

In a core golf course—the oldest and most basic design—the holes are designed together and either in a continuous sequence with starting and finishing holes at the clubhouse or in returning nines with two starting and finishing holes at the clubhouse. It requires about 140 acres and gives 10,000 feet of lot frontage. It consumes the least amount of land and offers the least course frontage. The core course can offer the greatest integrity or golf experience because the emphasis is on golf rather than real estate development. This is the case because the only real estate potential is around the periphery of the course. The core course is also the most efficient layout, as play is quick and the course comparatively inexpensive to maintain.

SINGLE FAIRWAY CONTINUOUS

The single fairway continuous 18-hole course comprises holes strung together in a long loop. It takes about 175 acres, offers 46,800 feet of lot frontage, and requires a minimum width between developed areas of 300 feet.

The course takes the maximum land area, offers maximum fairway frontage, and has the least operational flexibility. Because there is only one starting point, only one foursome at a time can start the course. This means that it can take up to four hours to fill the course completely. A shorter round of nine holes is difficult or impossible to play. In addition, play is slower because golfers must avoid out-of-bounds situations on both sides of the fairway. (The penalty for hitting a ball out of bounds is two strokes.) The layout does, however, allow maximum flexibility of layout because of its few fixed elements; only the clubhouse and the starting and closing holes have fixed positions. The course can, thus, be designed around difficult terrain.

SINGLE FAIRWAY WITH RETURNING NINES The single fairway 18-hole course with returning nines uses about 175 acres and offers 44,400 feet of lot frontage with a minimum width of 300 feet between developed areas. It is second in fairway frontage and a close second in use of land. Some savings can be gained on land use because of the concentration of holes and tees at the first, ninth, tenth, and eighteenth holes. Playing flexibility and the number of rounds that can be played each day are maximized because of the returning nines. Two parties of four can start at the same time, one group on the first hole and one on the tenth, and cross over after playing nine holes. Because of this, the entire course can be filled, with a foursome on each hole, in about two and one-half hours. Maintenance costs are moderately higher than are double fairways and core courses because tees and greens cover a larger area.

DOUBLE FAIRWAY CONTINUOUS The double fairway continuous 18-hole course uses approximately 150 acres, offers 25,000 feet of lot frontage, and requires a minimum width of 500 between developed areas. It uses one-sixth less land than a single fairway course. The double fairways mean the layout is less flexible. In particular, it is more difficult to work around existing vegetation. The course is, however, well suited for long, narrow sites.

Maintenance costs and time are reduced because of the double fairways. The course's parallel nature can make it boring, so special care must be taken to design interesting holes.

DOUBLE FAIRWAY WITH RETURNING NINES The double fairway 18-hole course with returning nines uses about 150 acres of land, with 500 feet being the minimum width between developed areas. It offers 24,200 feet of lot frontage. It uses one-sixth less land than a single fairway course and offers more integrity than a single fairway course lined with housing development. The returning nines, as before, offer the flexibility of two foursomes starting at the same time. Maintenance costs are less than for a single fairway and supervision is easier.

In summary, continuous layouts increase frontage but decrease operational flexibility. Returning nines offer much greater flexibility at the cost of some frontage. Single fairways give the designer maximum flexibility, as far as the layout is concerned, while delivering maximum frontage. The downside is that maintenance costs are higher and the quality of play for the golfer may be lessened. Double fairways save on maintenance costs while providing golfers with a better golf experience—at the cost of frontage development.[27] These comparisons are summarized in Table 7.1.

Good design can make the experience better for both homeowner and golfer. When trees are placed between lots set at an angle to the fairway, both groups benefit. Golfers tend to see trees rather than houses, while homeowners, because the angle screens views of homes on the other side of the fairway, also see more vegetation. This concept is illustrated in Figure 7.2.

❖ TABLE 7.1 Comparison of Golf Course Types

Type of Course	Land Consumption	Frontage	Flexibility/ Capacity	Maintenance Cost	Integrity
Core	low	low	low*	low	high
Single fairway continuous	high	high	low	high	low
Single fairway with returning nines	high	high	high	high	low
Double fairway continuous	medium	medium	low	medium	medium
Double fairway with returning nines	medium	medium	high	medium	medium

*Low if continuous, high if returning nines.

Source: Patrick L. Phillips, *Developing with Recreational Amenities: Golf, Tennis, Skiing, Marinas* (Washington, D.C.: Urban Land Institute, 1986), 37. Reproduced with permission of the Urban Land Institute.

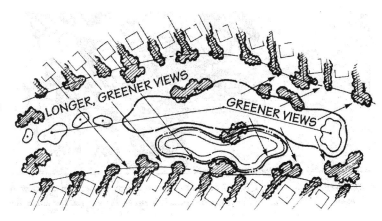

❖ FIGURE 7.2 Placement of trees on angled lots. [Source: Robert Muir Graves and Geoffrey S. Cornish, *Golf Course Design* (New York: John Wiley & Sons, Inc., 1998), 147. Reprinted by permission of John Wiley & Sons, Inc.]

quick getaways 7.4

Teeing Off into the Future

The use of computers has changed the way golf courses are designed. In the future, technologies such as geographic information systems and virtual reality will allow an architect to design, build, and even play a golf course without moving a single ounce of earth or leaving the office. Golf simulation games are available for home video and reflect how the game might be played in the future.

Advancing technology will also increase the ability of many golfers. Technology is available that incorporates extensive biomedical research to help individuals develop the optimal golf swing. New technology will also improve the equipment that golfers use.

It is safe to say that with the advances in technology of the past 20 or 30 years, the game of golf is not safe from change. There will always be a better way to design a course or make the course more user friendly.

Source: Anthony S. Akins, "Golfers Tee Off into the Future," *Futurist* 28, no. 2 (March/April 1994): 39–42.

Question: How will technology change the way golf courses are developed?

While courses tend to follow one of the above models for most holes, they tend to incorporate elements of other designs for several of the holes to accommodate specific elements of the site.

OTHER Various other types of course have been developed to accommodate smaller pieces of land or to allow for completion of a round of golf in a relatively short period of time. Some of these options are nine-hole regulation (including multiple tees, which allow the hole to be played in different ways); 18-hole executive, which allows completion of a round in about half the usual time; the par 3, consisting entirely of par-3 holes; the 27-hole regulation laid out in three returning nines, popular in resorts where there is concentrated demand for play in the morning hours; and the 36-hole regulation, which can be an 18-hole continuous and two returning nines.

These last two options require greater capital investment but offer much more course capacity for the money invested.

Typically, a resort will need a challenging regulation 18- or 36-hole course with an executive or par 3 course as a supplement.

GOLF HOLE STYLES Golf holes are the essence of a course. The style of holes can be defined as penal, strategic, or heroic on the basis of type, placement, and number of hazards. These styles are illustrated in Figure 7.3.

Penal The majority of holes built early in the twentieth century were in the penal style and patterned after British courses. Hazards are scattered at random around these holes in a manner that is unfair, given the inconsistent play of the average golfer. This makes the hole relatively easy for the better golfer and difficult for beginner or older players. Long, accurate tee shots are required over hazards to land in a relatively small landing area. In short, every poorly played shot is severely penalized. As a result, play tends to be slow.

Strategic Most holes today are designed as strategic—that is, the green may be approached in several ways, each with a different degree of risk and

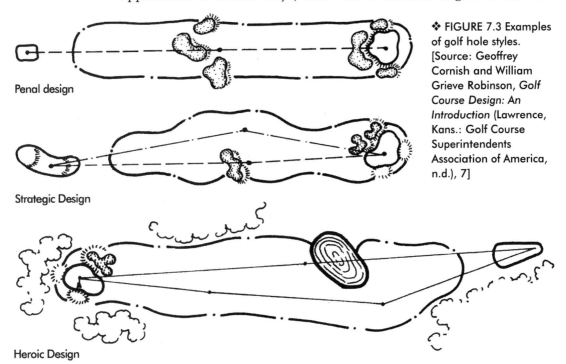

Penal design

Strategic Design

Heroic Design

❖ FIGURE 7.3 Examples of golf hole styles. [Source: Geoffrey Cornish and William Grieve Robinson, *Golf Course Design: An Introduction* (Lawrence, Kans.: Golf Course Superintendents Association of America, n.d.), 7]

reward. Safer shots will cost a stroke or two, but errors are not as severely punished as in the penal style. Golfers must play position to score well. The result is a thinking-person's course that plays faster than a penal design. The bite-off hole (Figure 7.4) is an excellent example of strategic design.

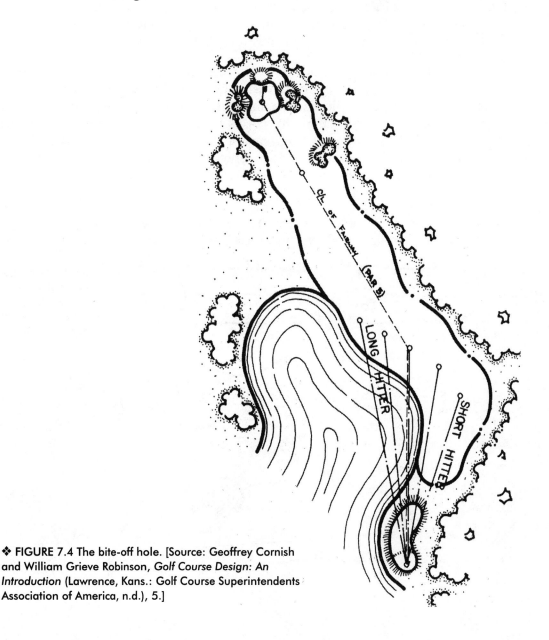

❖ FIGURE 7.4 The bite-off hole. [Source: Geoffrey Cornish and William Grieve Robinson, *Golf Course Design: An Introduction* (Lawrence, Kans.: Golf Course Superintendents Association of America, n.d.), 5.]

❖ Regulation golf course. [Source: Design Workshop, Inc.]

Heroic The heroic style is a combination of the other two. Golfers must choose between alternate routes to the pin, with one much more difficult than the other. Failure is punished more severely than under the strategic model. The reward for taking the more difficult route is typically a birdie (one below par) or an eagle (two below par).

The typical course today consists mainly of strategic holes with a sprinkling of heroic holes, usually around water hazards.

DESIGN PRINCIPLES

All artificial features should have so natural an appearance that a stranger is unable to distinguish them from nature itself.

—DR. ALASTAIR MCKENZIE
Designer, Augusta National

In order of importance, the factors to consider when designing a golf course are:

1. *safety*—to golfers and passersby
2. *flexibility*—different lengths of tees to handle golfers of varying abilities
3. *shot value*—variety of shots, lengths, and targets

4. *fairness*—placement and severity of hazards
5. *progression*—sequence of holes
6. *flow*—movement of golfers around the course
7. *balance*—distribution of par
8. *maintenance costs*
9. *construction planning*
10. *aesthetics*
11. *tournament qualities*[28]

An item higher on the list takes precedence over one below it. For example, the primary issue is safety. The next six items, flexibility through balance, deal with designing the course for play and making the experience as pleasant as possible. Maintenance costs, because they are ongoing, are more important than the one-time cost of construction. Aesthetics, while important, is of less concern than the factors preceding it on the list. Finally, the one to two weeks of tournament play annually is of less concern than the other factors noted above.

SAFETY Courses should be designed with golfer (and passerby) safety in mind. Many golfers tend to slice the ball, playing it to the right of where they meant it to go. For this reason, out-of-bounds on the right can be dangerous to people and homes (Figure 7.5). Several measures, as indicated in Figure 7.6, can be taken to increase the safety of the experience:

❖ Tees can be staggered so that players on adjoining holes do not slice into the same area.

❖ Safety buffers, such as bunkers, rough, trees, and other vegetation, can be installed. A rule of thumb is that over 90 percent of all shots fall within 15 degrees of the line of the desired shot. This can be used as a guideline for the placement of double-fairway holes.

❖ The risk associated with blind shots—which occur when the golfer is unable to see the likely path of the shot—can be decreased by cutting down the obstruction, raising the tee to allow the golfer sight access to the route of the shot, or installing a periscope on a pole so the player can check for people in the path of the shot.

❖ Keeping out-of-bounds areas on the hook or left side of the shot means that courses play clockwise.

❖ Having the right side of the impact area higher than the left means that sliced balls are caught by a mound and kept in play.[29]

❖ FIGURE 7.5 Many golfers have a tendency to slice.
[Source: Geoffrey Cornish and William Grieve Robinson,
Golf Course Design: An Introduction (Lawrence, Kans.:
Golf Course Superintendents Association of America,
n.d.), 8.]

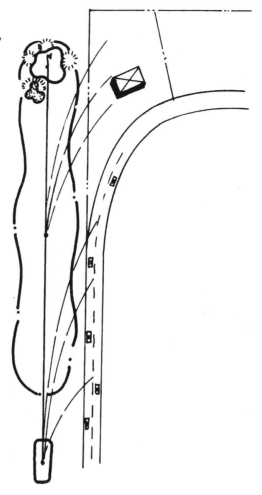

DESIGN FOR PLAY

Flexibility

The course should be built for all golfers. Variations in handicap can be accommodated by placing multiple tees at different distances from the hole. Tees serve as the control points for each hole. They are often as large as greens, with several starting points to handle golfers of varying strength and ability.

Five sets of tees are common—the forward tee of 140 yards for novices; the intermediate tee at 175 yards for advanced female, junior, and senior players; the main tee of 210 yards for average males and advanced seniors; the back tee of 240 yards for advanced golfers and female professionals; and the pro tee of 270 yards for tour golf pros. On courses 5000 feet above sea level, the ball will carry 10 percent farther.[30]

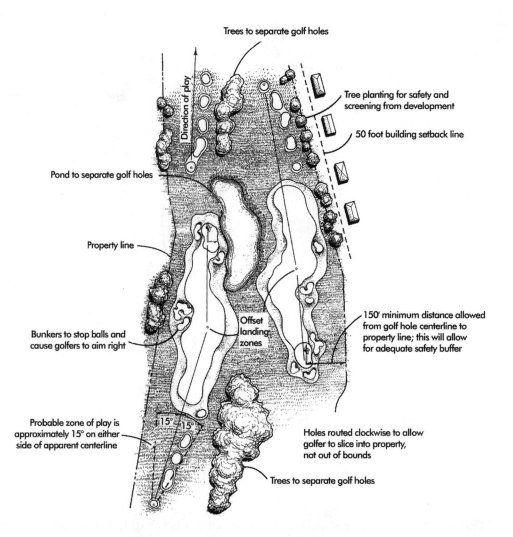

Trees to separate golf holes

Tree planting for safety and screening from development

50 foot building setback line

Direction of play

Pond to separate golf holes

Property line

Bunkers to stop balls and cause golfers to aim right

Offset landing zones

150' minimum distance allowed from golf hole centerline to property line; this will allow for adequate safety buffer

Probable zone of play is approximately 15° on either side of apparent centerline

15°   15°

Holes routed clockwise to allow golfer to slice into property, not out of bounds

Trees to separate golf holes

❖ FIGURE 7.6 Design safety elements. [Source: Michael J. Hurdzan, *Golf Course Architecture: Design, Construction, Restoration* (Chelsea, Mich.: Sleeping Bear Press, 1996), 25.]

Tee placement also depends on the amount of play. The more the course is played, the larger the tees. A common rule of thumb is to build a tee area of 100 to 200 square feet per 1000 rounds of golf per year.[31] Because of practice swings on both the first and the tenth holes, these tee areas need to be larger. Similarly, on a par 3 where the tee shot is played with an iron, the playing surface is subject to more wear and tear and a larger tee area is needed.

❖ Golf instruction, Aspen, Colorado. [Source: Design Workshop, Inc.]

Shot Value   The value of a shot to the golfer depends on its length, the target size, the difficulty of the hazards, and the position from which the shot is played. Difficult hazards on a short hole can counterbalance easier hazards on a longer hole. Designers can mix and match these criteria to create shots that most golfers can successfully make. Collectively, the shots taken make up the round of golf. A good layout means that every club in the bag should be used. Theoretically, the best round is played by the best all-around player rather than by the best putter or driver.

Fairness   A golf hole is said to be unfair "if there is but one route to the hole, which must carry a severe hazard, and the required shot is beyond the ability of most golfers."[32] Various features are situated around the course to add to the strategy of play. Sand, water, trees, and rough are all used for this purpose. "The basic principle of hazards is to allow the golfer a reasonable chance of recovery."[33] The use of sand in bunkers is a link to the past practice of locating courses on seaside links—where, it is said, livestock crouching against the dunes for shelter formed bunkers. Today, the bunkers provide a visual contrast to the predominance of green while being useful for stopping errant shots. The most aesthetically pleasing bunkers feature sand surfaces that slope upward and turf hanging over the edges. Bunkers of this sort, however, require mowing by hand. Softer slopes and curves provide good-looking bunkers that can be maintained by riding mower. Bunkers range from 1000 to 3000 square feet when close to the green and up to 4000 square feet on a fairway.

Water is a more punishing hazard than sand, as a shot into the water means a penalty stroke rather than "just" a difficult shot out of the bunker. However, apart from its aesthetics, water can speed play, as the golfer takes another shot instead of a well-thought-out difficult stroke.

Trees enclose the course in addition to functioning as a safety factor by providing a vertical target for errant balls. Placed behind a green, they aid depth perception. They can also provide shade, act as a windbreak, and add to the visual appeal of a course.

The rough areas on either side of the fairway are also hazards. The rough tends to get deeper the farther one moves from the fairway. This penalizes the poor shot well off the fairway. In some situations, wind can be a hazard and must be taken into account. To be fair to the golfer, designers avoid building consecutive holes into the prevailing wind.

While hazards can add to the interest of play, their number and placement also affect the speed at which rounds can be played. Most hazards, landing areas, and putting surfaces should be visible from the tee. Seeing the layout of the hole invites the golfer to think, thereby emphasizing the strategic nature of the game. Additionally, the enjoyment of a good shot is enhanced if the golfer can see the ball land.

Progression   Progression refers to the way the holes are sequenced around the course. A satisfying golf experience means the golfer experiences as wide a number of shots and holes as possible.

Holes should be located in relation to natural features. Tee areas require flat land; greens can be located at the base of slopes that provide aesthetic backdrops. Avoiding consecutive holes of the same par is preferred for the sake of variety. However, this guideline may need to be adjusted to the natural features of the course. Designers prefer not ending a round with consecutive par 3s or par 5s.

Because of the fatigue factor, most golfers prefer a course that slopes downhill on the final holes. A water hazard around the clubhouse makes for a dramatic setting to end the round.

The difficulty of the holes should increase slowly to culminate in challenge at holes 7, 8, and 9. Difficulty should then drop, then slowly rise again before topping out at holes 16, 17, and 18 with a par 3, 4, and 5.[34] Excitement is added if players have a chance to catch up on the final few holes by taking additional chances—taking more difficult routes to the pin to cut strokes off the score.

Flow   Flow refers to the movement of golfers around the course. Speed of play is largely a function of the quality of course maintenance. However, speed can be increased by reducing the number of hazards and shortening the hole relative to par. The first holes to be designed are those around the clubhouse—holes 1, 10, and 18. To avoid slow play off the opening holes, the first and tenth holes should be of medium difficulty and maximum visibility. A par 4 or par 5 that avoids narrow fairways, water, and other traps near the green is ideal. Starting a round with a medium-length par 5 and leaving long par 3s to the middle of a round helps flow. Widening the fairway minimizes the rough, which, being more difficult to play from, slows play.

Balance   Balance refers to the "equality or distribution of par, shot value, and golf course length."[35] Courses are generally balanced such that the first set of nine holes is equivalent to the second nine. In courses with returning nines, golfers may start on the first or the tenth hole. Even on an 18-hole course, many golfers play only the first nine. Designers therefore like to ensure that both nine-hole experiences are balanced with respect to difficulty and style.

COSTS
Maintenance   Long-term maintenance is a balance between cost and quality—how much quality golfers are willing and able to pay for. Decisions made during design and construction of the course affect later maintenance costs. Consider, for example, the green. The modern green is raised above the level of the fairway. This allows air to circulate across the turf, thus helping ice melt in the spring and the green to drain faster after rain. Prior to World War II, greens averaged 5000 square feet. Larger greens became popular, growing to 12,000 square feet.[36] As a result, maintenance costs escalated while play slowed because of the increased attention paid to putting. Today's greens are somewhere between these two extremes and allow for several pole positions to even wear and tear while reducing maintenance costs.

A green serves several purposes. It acts as a target area for incoming balls on their way to the hole. It should not only receive but also hold a well-struck shot. It provides a consistent putting surface to test the putting skills of the player. It must be designed with maintenance costs in mind while being playable as many days of the year as possible.[37]

Greens should be located downhill from the tee although, as noted above, the green itself is deliberately elevated 1 to 3 feet from its immediate surroundings. A natural backdrop—trees or a creek—provides an excellent setting. Greens typically vary from 5000 to 8000 square feet, large enough for 14 hole locations. Changing the position of the pole helps ensure even wear on the green. The size of the green should also reflect the difficulty of the hole; the more difficult holes require larger greens. Likewise, the longer the approach shot called for, the larger the green.

Greens tend to slope from back to front at a gradient at least 2 percent.[38] This increases visibility from the tee while helping hold the approach shot to the green. Difficult greens slow play even more, given that putting is the slowest part of the game. Overly large greens slow play in that they call for very long putts.

The amount of fairway—the playable area from the tee to the green—also influences maintenance costs. The landing area on the fairway should be wide and flat enough to ensure a predictable finish to the shot. Typically, this means an area between 120 and 150 feet wide. Shorter holes have a narrower fairway. If the fairway is too narrow, balls can land in the rough and play is slowed. The lower cost of maintaining the rough has to be balanced against the higher cost of fairway maintenance and golfer frustration with slow play.

Mounds are another example. Gentle mounds reflect the Scottish roots of the sport. For the golfer, mounds assist in depth perception. Steep mounds require hand mowing and result in higher maintenance costs (Figure 7.7).

Construction Planning When the course is being planned, it is up to the designer to present cost-benefit analyses of major design features so that owners can weigh the cost of the feature (and its longer-term maintenance cost) against benefits to the players.

AESTHETICS Designers are expected to use principles of art—harmony, proportion, balance, rhythm, and emphasis—in making their courses enjoyable to play.[39] Figure 7.8 illustrates the application of these principles.

❖ FIGURE 7.7 Gentle mounds permit machine mowing. [Source: Geoffrey Cornish and William Grieve Robinson, *Golf Course Design: An Introduction* (Lawrence, Kans.: Golf Course Superintendents Association of America, n.d.), 13.]

TOURNAMENT QUALITIES
For a successful tournament, a course needs "at least 6800 yards for a men's tournament and 6000 yards for a ladies' event, [to] have relatively small but good landing areas, [to] provide at least four competitive pin positions on each green, and [to] have a large practice area."[40]

The needs of the spectators, or gallery, also must be anticipated with respect to parking, movement, seating, restrooms, first aid stations, and television camera locations.

ACCESSIBILITY
Since the 1990 Americans with Disabilities Act (ADA) was passed, golf course managers are feeling increased pressure to make their courses accessible to people with physical disabilities. While federal guidelines exempt private courses, the definition of *private* is limited. If a course ever opens its grounds to the public—for a tournament, for example—it may be regarded as coming under federal guidelines. Because golfers with physical disabilities are estimated to comprise 12 percent of the golfing population, or 10 to 15 million people, it makes economic as well as altruistic sense to open courses to this segment of the market.[41]

Course superintendents have two primary concerns. They fear that wheelchairs and other vehicles will damage fragile greens. They are also worried about slow play.

❖ FIGURE 7.8 Integrating art principles with golf course design. [Source: Geoffrey Cornish and William Grieve Robinson, *Golf Course Design: An Introduction* (Lawrence, Kans.: Golf Course Superintendents Association of America, n.d.), 17–19.]

The basic approach is to ensure that at least one tee and one route to the green on each hole be accessible to golfers with physical disabilities.

CLUBHOUSES Many golf courses suffer because the clubhouse is too large for the membership base and so is too expensive to operate for the income generated. A resort setting may need a relatively small clubhouse of 4000 square feet that emphasizes the pro shop and lockers. Clubhouses tend to be built on visible, centrally located sites. They should be near the first and tenth tees (the ninth and eighteenth greens), with a practice green and driving range nearby. On a hilly site, it is best to locate the clubhouse between the highest and lowest points so golfers can avoid long climbs on continuous courses on the back nine. The separation of vehicles and pedestrians, the location of maintenance facilities and storage areas, and the relationship between the course and real estate units must also be considered.[42]

A major concern occurs when the clubhouse is used by resort guests, homeowners, and nonresidents. Market segments can be separated spatially by assignment. Additionally, access can be managed by the user group through, for example, giving residents preference for golf starting times.

One useful approach is to design the clubhouse facilities to grow as demand grows. Using a modular approach, facilities can be small at first and expand as the project matures. This conveys the impression of an active clubhouse while allowing for the phasing-in of capital expenditures at a pace consistent with revenue generation.

Practice facilities can take from four to six acres. This is twice the size of an average hole. Typically, they include a driving range, putting greens, target greens for practicing approaches to the green, and practice bunkers. The driving range should not be oriented directly east–west, as the sun will get in the eyes of golfers.

Several principles guide clubhouse design:

❖ To ensure that the floor plan and building functions act in concert, the clubhouse operator should be part of the design process.
❖ The clubhouse should be integrated with and complement its setting.
❖ The design should incorporate elements of the immediate surroundings, local traditions, and materials to make it unique to the area.
❖ The clubhouse should have a personality and character that gives it a sense of place and tradition that is comfortable and inviting to the members.
❖ Traditional architecture helps the clubhouse age gracefully without seeming out of touch with fads.[43]

A Checklist for Development

The design, construction, and maintenance of a simple golf course have evolved into a complex process. Today's environmental issues, economic issues, and the demands established by the objectives of the project all require careful consideration.

Each golf course is unique with respect to construction and maintenance. However, certain major steps are common in the development of almost every course:

1. Conduct a feasibility study to verify the need for a golf course.
2. Assemble a team of qualified professionals led by a golf course architect to address the complex issues involved in planning, design, and construction.
3. Determine the environmental issues that may be involved.
4. Confirm site suitability and goals for the project with the client.
5. Develop a conceptual plan that addresses all environmental issues and design criteria.

Pro Shop   The pro shop—the area where golf clubs and bags, clothing, balls, and other accessories are sold—is a large part of the clubhouse in a resort, though likely to be smaller than in a primary-home community. In the latter case, clubs and bags, which require considerable display space, are more likely to be sold than in a resort setting. While pro shops in resorts have higher sales-per-round-played figures than those in primary-housing communities, the sales are more likely to be balls and smaller accessories.

Golf Carts   Despite the cries of protest from purists, most courses allow, and even promote, the use of golf carts, which can provide significant revenue while making the game more accessible to more people. Carts can be powered by electricity or gasoline. In addition to a secure storage area, provision has to be made for recharging or fueling the carts. Earlier courses allowed

6. Arrange a presubmission meeting with the regulatory agencies and interested local citizen and environmental groups to review and receive input on the conceptual plan.
7. Refine the concept based on the input received and develop a final master plan.
8. Submit the master plan for required approvals.
9. Stake out the golf course.
10. Develop a thorough set of construction plans and specifications for the golf course.
11. Submit construction documents for regulatory review and permitting.
12. Hire a qualified golf course superintendent prior to the commencement of construction to provide management and administration for the project.
13. Undergo a bidding or negotiation process for the construction of the golf course.
14. Start construction.
15. Perform site inspection visits to ensure that the course is being constructed in accordance with the plans and intent of design.
16. Implement responsible management practices for maintenance prior to the completion of construction.
17. Complete construction of the golf course.
18. Prepare the golf course for opening.
19. Open for play.

Source: Bill Love, *An Environmental Approach to Golf Course Development* (Chicago: American Society of Golf Course Architects, 1999), 41.

Question: How does this checklist compare with procedures identified in the text?

carts on the fairways and had paths only around high-traffic areas like tees and greens. Recent trends have extended the paths the entire length of the course. This helps avoid wear and tear and controls traffic on the course. Fairway damage is also reduced, and golfers can return to the course sooner after heavy rain.[44]

It is important that the way the course will be played should be taken into account when laying out the golf cart path. For example:

❖ As many golfers tend to slice the ball, cart paths should be on the right side of the fairway. An exception is a dogleg that plays right to left. On such a hole, the shortest distance to the hole is along the left side, and most players will shoot in that direction. If the cart path is on the longer, right-hand side of the fairway, golfers may find it so far away from their ball that they ignore the path and drive across the course.

❖ As a rule of thumb, the distance from the center of the path to the center of the fairway should be 90 feet, although this is shorter at tees and greens.
❖ A wavy path is more aesthetically pleasing than a straight line although, if the line is too wavy, drivers cut corners.
❖ Paths should cross the hole as little as possible.
❖ Parking areas are needed at tees, greens, and practice areas.
❖ While it is tempting to utilize two-directional paths down the middle of a double fairway as a way of cutting costs, holes that are too close together can act as a hazard for golfers playing out from the clubhouse; they will be forced to face balls hit by golfers playing back to the clubhouse.
❖ Low mounds can be used to camouflage paths.
❖ To comply with the ADA, paths must allow for exits every 75 yards.[45]

REMODELING Changes in equipment have resulted in players being able to hit balls farther and more accurately; courses that once were challenging can lose much of their original luster. Attempts to redesign the course, or parts of the course, should be made in the context of a master plan. To keep the course in continuous play, most plans spread the work over two to four years. Here is a typical schedule:

❖ *First year*—Prepare master plan.
❖ *Second year*—Remodel first nine holes and automate irrigation system. Clear area for new practice range and maintenance area.
❖ *Third year*—Open remodeled nine holes. Remodel second nine holes and automate irrigation system.
❖ *Fourth year*—Open second remodeled nine. Construct new maintenance building, entrance road, and parking lot.[46]

The remodeling should be done at a time of the year when the number of players is reduced—fall in the north and summer in the south.

Specific elements might include the establishment of multiple tees, eliminating blind shots on fairways, developing gentler contours on bunkers to reduce hand mowing, installing completely automated irrigation systems, offering more variety in the greens with more pin placements and gentle undulations to make mowing less likely to scalp the grass, a long-term tree planting program, and the incorporation of cart paths.

TENNIS

Good shot, bad luck and hell are the five basic words to be used in a game of tennis, though these, of course, can be slightly amplified.

—VIRGINIA GRAHAM

INTRODUCTION Tennis facilities are a favorite amenity choice for a resort. From the developer's perspective, the requirements for land and the costs of development and maintenance are relatively small, regulatory and permit issues are few or nonexistent, and tennis and golf share a complementary market.

In real estate settings, tennis courts can speed sales because so many people enjoy playing the game.

SITE SELECTION While tennis courts can be located more flexibly than other amenities, they tend to be conceived as part of the centralized core of facilities serving a large real estate project. Resident access is thus protected, while parking and clubhouse facilities can be shared with other amenities.

Climate has a dramatic effect on usage. In desert climates, it makes sense to install lights so guests can play in the cooler evenings. Indoor facilities may be appropriate in wet or cold climates. Climate can also affect the type of court surface to be used.

An acre of land can, theoretically, accommodate six single courts, each 60 by 120 feet. In reality, this crowded configuration would make for a very unpleasant experience. Three courts can be comfortably placed on an acre of land, with enough space left over for parking, seating, and landscaping. The best sites are flat, rectangular, and built to avoid direct sun in the players' eyes. A dark background behind the players helps them see the ball.

A private outdoor tennis club can handle between 30 and 60 players per court. This is a useful ratio for determining the number of courts to build in a resort setting. Capacity can be increased by one-third by adding lights. A reservation system helps push capacity closer to the upper figure of 60 players per court.[47]

PLANNING AND DESIGN Tennis courts tend to be developed in clusters. A variety of cluster options is available (Figure 7.9). Maximum efficiency in space and building costs comes when courts are developed in clusters of eight or ten. Built side by side, courts should be 12 feet apart. Each additional court adds 48 feet of width to the battery of units—36 feet for the width of a doubles court plus

LAYOUT DESCRIPTION	IN-BOUNDS (Sq. Ft.)	OUT-BOUNDS (Sq. Ft.)	TOTAL (Sq. Ft.)	
STANDARD SINGLE UNIT	2808	4392	7200	
2 Courts End-to-End	5616	8784	14,400	
2 Courts In Battery	5616	7344	12,960	
3 Courts In Battery	8424	10,296	18,720	
4 Courts In Battery	11,232	13,248	24,480	
2 Batteries of 2— End-to-End	11,232	14,688	25,920	
2 Batteries of 3— End-to-End	16,848	20,592	37,440	
6 Courts In Battery	16,848	19,152	36,000	

❖ FIGURE 7.9 Tennis court configuration options. [Source: Patrick L. Phillips, *Developing with Recreational Amenities: Golf, Tennis, Skiing, Marinas* (Washington, D.C.: Urban Land Institute, 1986), 92. Reproduced with permission of the Urban Land Institute.]

the 12 feet of separation. Adding courts means that the average space needed per court is reduced. Placing courts end to end is not recommended unless they are separated by screens or fences.

The objective in orienting the course is to avoid players having the sun in their eyes. In northern resorts, play is concentrated in the nine nonwinter months. The sun tends to ride high in the sky and play is equally divided between morning and afternoon. The court should be oriented with the long axis aligned north and south. In southern areas, play occurs year-round. In the winter months, the late-afternoon sun can hang low in the sky. The best approach, therefore, may be to orient the court northwest–southeast at a 15- to 20-degree angle to true north to prevent players on the north side of the court from looking directly into the sun.

Orientation is less of a factor in other elevations and climates. In a Rocky Mountain resort setting, for example, play tends to occur in the midmorning to midafternoon of the summer, when the sun is high in the sky and less likely to bother players. It is more of a factor when the court is to be used for a major annual event. In this case, the court should be oriented relative to the position of the sun during the one- or two-week period of the tournament.[48]

Surface   The original court surface in England was grass. Today, 14 types of surface are divided into two major categories: porous and nonporous. Nonporous surfaces can be cushioned or noncushioned, and can be compared on the basis of cost and play factors. The initial cost, the cost of repairs and maintenance, and time before resurfacing vary greatly. Fast-drying porous surfaces are relatively expensive, require daily and yearly care, and need to be resurfaced annually. Clay, on the other hand, is much less expensive and needs resurfacing only every five years. However, it takes longer to dry after rain and, therefore, limits play where a great deal of rain falls.

Porous courts can be fast drying, clay, or grass. They all allow moisture to drain through their surfaces, and their softness makes them easy on players' legs. Grass courts look wonderful but cost a lot to build and maintain; they need daily maintenance (watering and rolling) and are susceptible to damage. In contrast, clay courts are less expensive to build and last a long time, but they play slower than grass and have rather high maintenance requirements.

Nonporous courts last a long time, are easy to maintain, and dry quickly. Noncushioned courts play fast and are hard on players' feet, legs, and backs. Unlike on porous courts, however, players do not slide.

Nonporous cushioned courts offer the maintenance advantages of nonporous surfaces and the player comfort benefits of porous courts. Synthetic turf surfaces require more maintenance than other nonporous courts but less than porous surfaces; they also offer a long-lasting finish.

Player preference should be a major factor in selecting the court surface. Easterners tend to prefer clay courts, while westerners lean toward hard courts. Older players probably prefer softer surfaces to hard. Climate also plays a part. In hot areas, it is wise to select a surface that stays relatively cool, does not glare excessively, and does not crack or soften in the heat. In northern areas, the effect of frost can be a concern.

Fast-drying indoor courts require watering daily, perhaps requiring the installation of extra ventilation to avoid condensation.

Lights As noted earlier, lighting can increase the capacity of a court by a third and is especially important in hot climates, where play may be unbearable during the day. The quality rather than the quantity of lighting is important. Lights should be placed along the length of the court and mounted between 15 and 35 feet above the surface. Lights can be either incandescent, fluorescent, or high-density discharge (HID). Incandescents are relatively inexpensive to install but expensive to maintain. The lamps have a short life and are inefficient when in use. However, they give good color and need no warm up. Fluorescent lights are efficient, last a long time, and give good color. HID lights are also efficient and last a long time, but they take several minutes to warm up to maximum brightness.

Indoor Structures Indoor facilities today commonly offer racquetball and squash courts together with exercise and fitness areas. An indoor tennis court might complement such a facility. While most structures are made of prefabricated steel, air-supported fabric bubbles are half the cost to build—but they have shorter lives. Tension-supported fabric structures with open or closed sides are also used to cover courts.

Support Facilities Support facilities are necessary (and profitable) as a complement to tennis courts. Areas for clinics and instructional programs in addition to practice sessions offer a full-service program to the guest. At some resorts, circular facilities have ball-spraying machines serving balls to players in pie-shaped alleys. Videos can be taken of the players to help them improve their stroke.

One tennis court is much like another. Differences are more likely found in the quality of the support facilities. Shading, viewing areas, landscaping, drinking fountains, and other amenities can help a resort stand out from the rest.

A clubhouse overlooking the courts can be an attractive place for players to relax over a drink or meal and to watch others in action. Locker rooms should have one shower for every one and one-half to two courts and be equipped with five to seven lockers per court.[49]

MANAGEMENT In resort settings, the developer either retains ownership of tennis facilities after the project is built or sells or leases them to the operator of the resort. As with golf courses and marinas, the trend is toward contracting with management companies that specialize in the recreational activity. A tennis pro is similar to the golf pro and takes responsibility for all aspects of the operation, including maintenance, the pro shop, and instruction. Many argue that the pro is inexperienced in retailing and should be restricted to instruction. At larger resorts, the shop is usually run by experienced retailers because of the potential profits from lines of clothing.

At a resort that includes residential units, dealing with two market segments—residents and resort guests—can be problematic. This situation can be handled as it is with golf—by giving residents priority scheduling and setting different fee structures for each.

SUMMARY

The design and layout of a golf course depends on the reason for developing the course. All courses, however, should express certain design principles so as to be environmentally sensitive while allowing the operator to make a profit. The same is true for tennis courts at a resort.

ENDNOTES

1. Jeff Highley, "Tee Time: As an Amenity or Profit Center, Golf Boosts Bottom Line," *Hotel and Motel Management*, 7 September 1998, 34–37.
2. National Golf Foundation, *A Strategic Perspective on the Future of Golf* (Jupiter, Fla.: National Golf Foundation, 1999).
3. Paul K. Asabere and Forrest E. Huffman, "Negative and Positive Impacts of Golf Course Proximity on Home Prices," *Appraisal Journal* (October 1999) vol. 6414: 351–355.
4. Dean H. Burgess, "Lending to Golf Course Communities," *Journal of Commercial Bank Lending* (March 1991) vol. 74: 19–30.
5. Dean Schwanke et al., *Resort Development Handbook* (Washington, D.C.: Urban Land Institute, 1977), 156.

6. Mark Hazard Osmun, "Spanish Bay: Golf Course Developers as Environmental Heroes," *Urban Land* (July 1997) vol. 56: 40.

7. Patrick L. Phillips, *Developing with Recreational Amenities: Golf, Tennis, Skiing, Marinas* (Washington, D.C.: Urban Land Institute, 1986), 33.

8. Desmond Muirhead, "Changing Times: Building Golf Courses in the 90s in Japan Is a Different Story: The Focus Is on the Bottom Line," *Executive Golfer* (June 1997): 46–50.

9. American Society of Golf Course Architects, *Handbook: Tips for Real Estate Development* (Chicago: American Society of Golf Course Architects, n.d.).

10. *Funk and Wagnalls Standard Encyclopedic Dictionary* (Chicago: J.G. Ferguson Publishing Company, 1965).

11. Schwanke et al., *Resort Development Handbook*, 153.

12. Phillips, *Developing with Recreational Amenities*, 41.

13. Schwanke et al., *Resort Development Handbook*, 153.

14. Michael J. Hurdzan, "Design and Maintenance: A Crucial Marriage: Part 1 of 2," *Golf Course News* (September 1997): 24–25.

15. Schwanke et al., *Resort Development Handbook*, 157.

16. Highley, "Tee Time," 37.

17. Schwanke et al., *Resort Development Handbook*, 155.

18. Phillips, *Developing with Recreational Amenities*, 44.

19. Ibid., 71.

20. Greg H. Nash, "Beautiful, Fun, and Functional: Desert Golf Courses Solve Flood-Control Problems in the Southwest," *Golf Course Management* (February 1996) vol. 56: 122–124.

21. Phillips, *Developing with Recreational Amenities*, 79.

22. Michael Hurdzan, "Design and Maintenance: A Crucial Marriage: Part 2 of 2," *Golf Course News* (October 1997) vol. 73: 13–14.

23. Hurdzan, "Design and Maintenance: Part 1," 24–25.

24. Phillips, *Developing with Recreational Amenities*, 79.

25. Ibid.

26. Schwanke et al., *Resort Development Handbook*, 155.

27. Phillips, *Developing with Recreational Amenities*, 37.

28. Michael J. Hurdzan, *Golf Course Architecture: Design, Construction, Restoration* (Chelsea, Mich.: Sleeping Bear Press, 1996), 23–43.

29. Ibid., 25.

30. Ibid., 31.

31. Phillips, *Developing with Recreational Amenities*, 57.

32. Ibid., 32.

33. Ibid., 58.

34. Hurdzan, *Golf Course Architecture*, 33.

35. Ibid., 35.

36. Geoffrey S. Cornish and William Grieve Robinson, *Golf Course Design: An Introduction* (Lawrence, Kans.: Golf Course Superintendents Association of America, n.d.), 11.

37. Hurdzan, *Golf Course Architecture*, 15.
38. Phillips, *Developing with Recreational Amenities*, 58.
39. Cornish and Robinson, *Golf Course Design*, 17.
40. Hurdzan, *Golf Course Architecture*, 41.
41. John Torsiello, "Access Guidelines to Ensure All Courses Are Up to Par," *Golfweek* (June 1996) vol. 28: 21, 29.
42. Schwanke et al., *Resort Development Handbook*, 161.
43. Mark deReus, "Golf Clubhouse Design," *Developments* (June 1993): 16-19.
44. Phillips, *Developing with Recreational Amenities*, 74.
45. Robert Muir Graves and Geoffrey S. Cornish, *Golf Course Design* (New York: John Wiley & Sons, 1998), 147.
46. American Society of Golf Course Architects, *Handbook*.
47. Phillips, *Developing with Recreational Amenities*, 91.
48. Ibid., 92.
49. Ibid., 104.

Section 2
OPERATIONS AND MANAGEMENT

Chapter 8
MARKETING THE RESORT EXPERIENCE

MARKETING DEFINED

Marketing . . . is the whole business seen from the point of view of its final result, that is, from the customer's point of view. Concern and responsibility for marketing must, therefore, permeate all areas of the enterprise.

—PETER DRUCKER
People and Performance

The American Marketing Association defines marketing as the "process of planning and executing the conception, pricing, promotion, and distribution of ideas, goods, and services to create exchanges that satisfy individual and organizational objectives."[1] This indicates that marketing is much more than advertising, much more than sales promotion. Marketing encompasses the development of the concept, product, or service through how it should be priced, promoted, and made available to people. It works only if an exchange is made between buyer (the individual) and seller (the organization) that benefits both. The buyer receives something of value and the organization receives revenue.

One definition brings together the financial concerns of management and the need to satisfy consumer needs. It encompasses three items:

1. determining the needs and wants of consumers
2. creating the mix of products and services that will satisfy these needs and wants
3. promoting and selling the product–service mix to generate a level of income satisfactory to the management and stockholders of the organization[2]

Inherent in these definitions are several ideas. First is the focus on the guest. Marketing is a way of thinking about the business that makes the satisfaction of guest needs paramount. Second is the practical implication that businesses cannot be all things to all people; it cannot satisfy all the needs and wants of all the people. Some choice must be made as to which segments of the market are to be targeted. Third is an appreciation of research to determine guest needs and wants. The idea of sequential steps—that products and services are developed only after guest needs and wants have been identified—is a fourth idea. Guest satisfaction is the fifth idea. It is not enough to promote and sell the service. The resort must not only bring guests in, it must bring them back. Finally, the idea of exchange means that the satisfaction of guests' needs must bring economic benefit to the resort.

In this chapter, the steps involved in laying out a marketing plan are noted. Sufficient detail is given to allow the reader to put such a plan together.

DEVELOPING A MARKETING PLAN

No great marketing decisions have ever been made on quantitative data.

—JOHN SCULLEY
CEO, Apple Computer, *The Intuitive Manager*

Six steps are involved in the development of a marketing plan:

1. Conduct a marketing audit.
2. Select target markets.
3. Position the property.
4. Determine marketing objectives.
5. Develop and implement action plans.
6. Monitor and evaluate the marketing plan.[3]

CONDUCT A MARKETING AUDIT The marketing audit comprises analyses of the guests, the property, and the competition. Given the foregoing definitions of marketing, it is appropriate to look first at guests.

Guests The purpose of analyzing guests, property, and the competition is to develop a profile of the customers and to evaluate, in an unbiased way, how the operation stacks up relative to the competition in providing what they want.

Information about the guests breaks down as follows:

❖ Who are they?
❖ Where do they come from?
❖ When do they visit, and when is the decision to visit made?
❖ How do they reach us?
❖ Why do they come, and how satisfied are they when they leave?[4]

This information can come from sales histories, employees and management staff, the guests themselves, and outside research sources.

The information collected breaks down into how many people stay at the resort, how much they spend, what they spend it on, and how business is spread throughout the year. From this analysis, one can see when business is strong and, more important, when it is weak. In addition, specific objectives can be set to improve sales of specific items or numbers of guests.

Management and staff can provide information about the guests because they are constantly in contact with them. While such data are not scientific, they can give a picture of what is selling and why, what guests like and do not like, and what types of people visit at different times during the season. In addition to providing useful information, asking the opinion of employees makes them feel important and can serve as a motivational tool.

More formal questionnaires can be used to collect information on the guest base. The key in developing a questionnaire is to develop the research objectives first, decide on the questions that will yield the desired information, select an appropriate research methodology, and conduct the research. A simple category of data that is easily collected and very useful is guest zip codes. The key to increasing sales and guest count is to identify the characteristics of current guests and to use that profile as a basis for attracting more people.

One way to get this information is from a focus group.[5] A focus group consists of six to ten former or current guests, supervised by a discussion leader, who express their feelings about aspects of the operation. Questions range from the general to the specific and concentrate on motivations, feelings, and gut-level issues. Although not statistically reliable, such sessions can indicate a great deal about what motivates customers.

Customer comment cards are a favorite way of collecting information. A positive bias is probably built into any research conducted in the resort. Most guests will not complain while on the property unless something is really wrong. An average or mildly unpleasant experience may not result in negative comments until the guests leave the resort.

Property The property analysis is an unbiased evaluation of the strengths and weaknesses of the operation. A typical checklist evaluates the property and the competition with respect to the following factors:

- ❖ variety of services
- ❖ appeal of services
- ❖ quality
- ❖ consistency
- ❖ pricing
- ❖ service speed
- ❖ service quality

❖ service friendliness
❖ cleanliness
❖ promotional activity
❖ visibility
❖ image
❖ atmosphere
❖ facility[6]

The problem is that such a list does not indicate how important these things are to guests. A better starting point is to look at the resort from the guest viewpoint. By identifying the factors important to guests and using them as a checklist to evaluate both the operation and the competition, a focus on the guest is assured. For example, if a resort features an excellent spa but that factor is unimportant to the guests, is the spa a strength, a weakness, or a neutral factor?

Some resorts use mystery shoppers to evaluate the operation. These people should always remain anonymous and conduct random evaluations. Management receives a report on the exterior, interior, and signage of the facility in addition to comments on the appearance, performance, and service provided by the employees.

Competition A competing facility is any operation that seeks to attract the business being sought by the resort under consideration. A competitive analysis compares such facilities with the operation under study. The purpose of the analysis is to discover:

❖ profitable market segments being served by competitors that are not being served at the operation under study
❖ some competitive benefit or advantage the property has that cannot be matched by the competition
❖ weaknesses in the marketing strategy of the competition that can be capitalized on[7]

A competitive analysis involves getting as much relevant information as possible and includes staying at competing facilities and evaluating their advertising.

SELECT TARGET MARKETS The idea behind the selection of market segments is that people differ in what they want from a resort experience and that it is not possible to be all things to all people. Market segmentation involves dividing a heterogeneous market into smaller homogeneous segments. While the members of

❖ Segmenting the market. [Source: Design Workshop, Inc.]

a segment share characteristics, they differ from people in another market segment. Operators can more effectively target marketing efforts to people who are most likely to patronize the resort.

Segmentation Variables

Marketers segment the market on the basis of one or more variables. The major variables used are geographic, demographic, psychographic, usage or behavioral, and benefits sought.

❖ *Geographic segmentation* involves identifying the geographic limits of the trading area and appealing to people within those boundaries.

❖ *Demographic segmentation* involves dividing the market on the basis of age, income, gender, annual income, family size, stage in the family life cycle, educational level, occupation, ethnicity, religion, nationality, and social class.

❖ *Psychographic segmentation* divides people based on their attitudes, interests, and opinions.

❖ *Usage or behavioral segmentation* divides people based on how much they use the product or service. A typical division is into light, medium, and heavy users.

❖ *Benefit segmentation* separates people on the basis of the benefits they seek from the resort experience.

Market segments should be selected on the basis of size, likelihood of growth, competitive position, the cost of reaching the segment, and how compatible the segment is with the company's objectives and resources.

Revenue Grid For an existing business, a revenue grid and an analysis of activity can be helpful in selecting workable market segments. A revenue grid identifies how much revenue is brought in from the various segments of the market presently being served. A useful rule of thumb in marketing is to attract guests similar to those already being attracted. For some reason, the resort attracts a certain kind of clientele. An examination of the existing guest base broken down by the sales each segment brings in is an excellent start to identifying future potential. In other words, find out who the guests are and seek more people with similar characteristics.

As noted above, an analysis of business activity tells when business is good and, more important, when it is bad. This can suggest areas of importance for increasing sales. The marketplace can then be searched for prospective market segments consisting of people who go on vacations when the operation needs the business. The segments are then evaluated relative to the criteria noted above to determine their suitability.

POSITION THE PROPERTY

Positioning Statement

The image that customers have of an operation is its position in the marketplace. A positioning statement is the company's attempt at developing the desired image. A good statement accomplishes several things. First, it creates an image in the minds of the customers as to what the resort stands for. In the resort business, as in any other, people make decisions based on their perceptions rather than on the reality of the situation. If the image is positive—that the resort offers good value—they may decide to stay there. However, image alone will not induce the guest to buy. A variety of promotional means are used to convey an image to the guest.

The actual resort experience offers a reality check to the guest. It may be less gratifying than expected. The result is a disappointed customer. The image portrayed by the resort must be positive enough to encourage people to visit the operation. The actual resort experience must be equal to or greater than the image for the guest to leave satisfied.

Segmentation in the Timeshare Market

Timeshare resorts vary from region to region due to seasonality, resort type, and location characteristics. The Florida market is the most significant and highly developed U.S. market. The attractiveness of the destination is a result of its warm climate and easy accessibility from central and eastern states. Because Orlando and central Florida cater to a family market, most units have two or three bedroom. The highly competitive nature of the industry in this region means that new companies seeking to enter the market encounter significant barriers. On the southeast coast of Florida, most timeshares are hotel conversions and are sold as studio units. Visitors come from Latin America, Europe, Canada, and the eastern United States. This market mix dictates the need for a flexible marketing strategy that utilizes minivacations as the major method of generating leads. There appears to be development opportunity in two areas: beachfront properties and association with major branded hotel companies.

Timeshare resorts in the Northeast and Southeast are found in both mountain and beach areas. Many owners live in the region and value its diversity. In the North, demand is high for exchanges between New England ski resorts and Cape Cod beach resorts. Because of short driving distances and the variety of outdoor recreational opportunities, vacation owners in the mid-Atlantic states tend to return to the region rather than exchange elsewhere.

The central region of the country is the smallest in terms of both number of resorts and sales volume. Lakefront and ski areas are the favored locations. Owners tend

Second, the positioning statement describes the benefits the resort offers to the guests. Resorts offer features, but people buy benefits. Guests, in fact, "buy" a bundle of benefits. When staying at a resort, individuals look to different aspects of the experience for satisfaction. For some, a large variety of recreational choices is important. For others, price

to return to their home resort or exchange within the region for reasons similar to those noted for mid-Atlantic owners.

In the Mountain region, timeshares are concentrated in the ski areas of Colorado and Utah and the desert regions of Arizona and Las Vegas. The Rocky Mountain region targets skiers in the winter and families in the summer. Expansion is limited by the relatively remote locations, seasonality, and, in the mountain areas, limited building sites. The Las Vegas market comprises mainly one-bedroom and studio units. As the town continues to seek a reputation as a family destination, the market for two- and three-bedroom units is growing.

The Pacific region is the fastest-growing in the United States. Hawaiian resorts draw primarily from California and Japan. Hawaii has the advantages of an upscale reputation, year-round demand, and a high level of repeat visitors staying a relatively long time. These factors eliminate the need for seasonal pricing. Because of the high cost of ownership and travel to the islands, a large percentage of sales are biennials.

The three major timeshare areas in California are Lake Tahoe, the southern coastal area, and the Palm Springs area. The first is a year-round destination that markets primarily to residents of northern California. The limited population base and high repeat visitation means that many visitors have already been approached regarding vacation ownership. Resorts have been hamstrung in their ability to market to families because of environmental restrictions on units with full kitchen facilities. This has also limited exchange opportunities.

The southern coastal area has a large population base. However, land is limited and development costs are high. Growth opportunity will probably come from branded vacation ownership projects that can use their competitive advantage in the marketplace. Palm Springs uses its proximity to the large population base in southern California, its reputation as a resort destination, the warm weather, and the profusion of golf facilities as major selling points. The desert location means that there is a strong seasonal demand, peaking in the winter months. Day trips and minivacations marketed to people in southern California are favored methods of encouraging sales.

Source: The United States Timeshare Industry: Overview and Economic Impact Analysis (Washington, D.C.: American Resort Development Association, 1997).

Question: In what ways must the marketing of timeshares vary in different parts of the country?

is a major concern. Still others emphasize privacy. Because people buy benefits, the operation must communicate the benefits it offers to its potential customers.

Third, the positioning statement differentiates the property from the competition. Everyone offers "atmosphere" and "value." But just what is it

❖ The importance of image, Torre del Remei, Bolvir, Spain. [Source: Design Workshop, Inc.]

that makes one resort different from another? Why should I come to your place rather than the resort across the state?

The key is to find a difference, an advantage, that is difficult for the competition to replicate. Every business seeks a unique selling point or a competitive differential advantage, something that makes it different from the competition and can be used to advantage. The nature of business means that unique selling points are subject to the principle of perishable distinctiveness. If one resort develops an advantage that makes it especially attractive to customers, the competition becomes aware of that advantage and seeks to copy it, thus neutralizing the previously unique selling point. That which made the resort distinctive is gone; it was perishable. "What can separate me from my competition that is difficult, if not impossible, to copy?" This is the third element that must be addressed by a positioning statement.

It should readily be seen that a positioning statement can come only after an analysis has been made of the market, the property, and the competition. The key is to identify what the target market wants from a resort experience (the benefits) and how the operation is perceived as providing these benefits compared to the competition.

Perceptual Maps Perceptual maps can be useful tools for developing a positioning statement. A perceptual map is a visual representation of two elements: the relative importance of benefits to guests and their perception of how well a facility provides these benefits. In essence, customers from the market segment being sought are asked two questions: "What things are important to you when vacationing?" and "How well do you think resort X does in providing these benefits?" The benefits guests consider important can be identified via informal discussions or a focus group session. The focus group can identify what the members like and dislike about the resort and the competition. The results are qualitative rather than quantitative. They do not disclose percentages, but they do indicate gut issues. A list of benefits sought when planning a vacation can be obtained from focus groups.

This list can then be used to construct a questionnaire to be presented to a sample of present and prospective guests, who are asked to rate the importance of these items to them on a scale of 1 (very important) to 5 (not important). The guests are then asked if the resort provides these things, again on a scale of 1 (totally) to 5 (not at all). The resulting scores can be placed on a matrix, as in Figure 8.1.

Crosshairs are drawn on the graph such that half of the items are above the horizontal line and half below, and half of the items are to the left of the vertical line and half to the right. The result is four quadrants. In the upper right section, quadrant 1, are items that are not important to the guest and that they think the resort does not satisfy.

In quadrant 2 are factors that, again, are not important to the guests. However, they think the resort provides these. Quadrants 3 and 4 are made up of factors that guests consider important. In quadrant 3 are factors they perceive the resort does not do a good job of providing. In quadrant 4 are factors the guests think the operation does do well on.

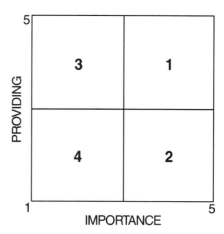

❖ FIGURE 8.1 Perceptual map.

From these findings, the resort can identify where it stands in the minds of its customers and determine appropriate actions. The factors in quadrants 1 and 2 should be ignored. Guests say these items are not important to them. If they are not important to customers, they are not important to the resort operation. Resorts tend to want to play to their strengths.

The facility that markets to guests on factors not important to them will not attract those people. The important items are in quadrants 3 and 4. These factors are important to guests.

At this point, a reality check is necessary. How accurate are the guests' perceptions? The answer determines the appropriate action. Where the image is negative but the actual situation is positive, the resort needs to improve the image. For example, it may be that special deals are offered but customers are unaware of them. Where the image is negative and the actual situation is negative, or when the image is positive but the actual situation is negative, the product or service must be changed. For example, if people believe that consistency of service is a problem and it really is a problem, service must be improved so that it is consistent. Similarly, if the perception is that many recreational opportunities are available but, in reality, they are not, that also must be changed. If customers are drawn to a resort expecting a variety of recreational opportunities, the visit will show that they are lacking and the guests will be dissatisfied. Finally, where the image is positive and the actual situation is positive, the resort has the basis for a positioning statement.

Similar perceptual maps can be drawn for the competition to determine just where, in the minds of the guest, the resort is perceived as doing a better job of providing benefits important to them. The resulting positioning statement will be based on research that has identified the benefits guests look for, what is provided to satisfy these desired benefits, and how the resort differs from the competition in providing these desired benefits.

In essence, the positioning statement says: "For _____ seeking _____, we provide _____." The first blank should be filled with the segment of the market being considered, the second blank with the benefits being sought, and the third space with what the resort will provide to satisfy guests.

DETERMINE MARKETING OBJECTIVES

Criteria

The act of setting objectives increases the likelihood of their achievement. The reason is that management now has something to work toward. Developing objectives gives managers a way to determine the extent to which they are moving forward and to change strategies if positive movement is not being made. It allows for a way of keeping score. This in itself

The Teen Market

Research by Hyatt Hotels shows that teenagers like to go on vacation with their families but, when at the destination, want to get away from their parents and be with other teens. Seventy-nine percent of 500 teenagers surveyed said they wanted to meet and spend time with other teens while on vacation. Romance is important, with 77 percent of the boys and 57 percent of the girls hoping to find it on vacation. Nearly half say their parents drive them crazy.

Twelve percent of the teens had their own hotel room on their last vacation; 47 percent shared a room with parents, and 27 percent shared a room with a sibling. In order of importance, teens are interested in shopping, sightseeing, sports, group barbecues, and beach parties.

Based on their research, Hyatt identified five segments of the teen market:

- *All-Americans*—This group makes up 27 percent of the market. They are conservative, wholesome, and family oriented. They obey their parents and have a say in planning the family vacation. Likely to be girls, they enjoy nature walks, seminars, sightseeing, and cultural activities.

- *Lone rangers*—Mostly boys and representing 12 percent of the market, teens in this segment are smart, solitary, and come from small, high-income families. They have their own room when on vacation. They like to bike, hike, play video games, and work on a personal computer in their room.

- *Moody blues*—These teens, 28 percent of the sample, are miserable. They get bored and depressed when on vacation, avoid organized activities, and are uninterested in meeting other teens.

- *Young and restless*—This 20 percent of the group are headstrong, lively, and impulsive. They like romance, organized activities, sports, and sneaking around. They are likely to be boys.

- *Hot shots*—This 12 percent of the group tend to be older teenage boys who prefer beach and ski vacations and are athletic, adventurous, and independent. They often take a friend on vacation, sharing a room with that person.

Source: "Hotel Chain's Teen Survey: The Good, the Bad, and the Miserable," *Travel Weekly*, 1 June 1992, p. 15.

Question: Can you design a resort program aimed at teenagers? Also design a brochure to attract them to the resort and its teen program.

is a motivational tool as well as a method of assigning responsibility and rewarding the achievement of results.

To be useful, objectives should be set for each segment of the market to which the resort is appealing. Each market segment is different in terms of activity and spending patterns and the extent to which the operation is presently successful in its marketing effort. Second, objectives should be results oriented. This usually means specifying an improvement in volume, revenues, or market share. Only by identifying the desired results can management set targets and, later, measure to see whether the effort has been successful.

Objectives should be set in quantitative rather than qualitative terms. The problem with qualitative objectives (for example, "improve service") is that their measurement is open to subjective judgment.

Each objective should contain a time element. It is not enough to say that the spa operation wants to increase its customer count by 100 guests per week. A time limit must be set as to when this objective should be achieved.

Life-Cycle Curve   Objectives have to be set consistent with where the operation is in the product life-cycle curve. The concept of a product life cycle is that a business goes through stages during its lifetime. A business is introduced into the marketplace and will grow, mature, and decline. Different marketing objectives are appropriate at different stages of the life cycle. In the introductory stage, the key is to create awareness and trial on the part of guests; in the growth stage, sales are rising at an increasing rate and market share should be maximized; in the maturity stage, sales are increasing but at a decreasing rate and profits should be maximized while market share is defended. Finally, in the declining stage of the life cycle, sales are decreasing, expenditures are reduced, and as much is extracted from the business as possible.

Buying Process   It is important to set objectives that are consistent with where guests are in their buying process. The concept of a buying process is that potential guests go through a series of stages before making a purchase. They must first be made aware of the existence of the resort. Then they need to have information outlining the property's benefits to them. At this point, if the advertising campaign is successful, guests form a positive attitude about the resort, develop a preference for it, are convinced they should go there, actually visit the place, and, if satisfied, return. The objectives set vary depending on where the market is in the buying process.

At the awareness stage, the objective is to expose people to the operation. Success can be measured by identifying the number of people exposed to the message—number of readers, viewers, and so on. At the knowledge or comprehension stage, when guests are trying to identify what the resort can offer them, the objective is to transmit information. How well this has been accomplished can be determined by measuring the percentage of readers or viewers who remember essential parts of the message.

The objective in the attitude stage is to change people's attitudes about the operation. The success of a program can be determined by measuring consumer attitudes before and after the campaign to determine whether or not a change has occurred. Similarly, during the preference stage—where the objective is to create a preference in the mind of the customer—preference surveys before and after the campaign can be done. It may be, for example, that prior to the campaign, one resort places sixth out of ten on a list of preferred operations. If the resort places third after the program, the campaign can be called a success.

The conviction stage seeks to have guests do something. The number of actions taken—phone reservations made, for example—can be measured. Purchase is measured by the number of people who actually stay at the resort or buy a specific service. Finally, adoption—where the objective is repeat purchase—can be measured by the percentage of customers who are repeats.

DEVELOP AND IMPLEMENT ACTION PLANS

The implementation of an action plan involves the development and execution of a specific marketing mix for each segment of the target market. It involves developing the means to carry out the job, developing a budget to accomplish the plan, and assigning responsibility for the plan.

The marketing mix has been variously defined by several authors. Originally comprising product planning, pricing, distribution, promotion, servicing, and market research, it has been standardized into the "four Ps" of product, price, promotion, and place. Other elements have been suggested to modify the four Ps specifically for the hospitality industry. It is suggested that the marketing mix for resort operations consists of four elements: product-service mix, price, promotion-communication mix, and place-distribution mix.[8] The selected mix varies depending on the industry, the position of the operation in the marketplace, and how it fares presently relative to the competition.

Product–Service Mix

The product-service mix consists of the products and services offered by the operation in an attempt to satisfy guest needs. It covers recreational options, quality, reputation, image, furnishings and decor, exterior structure and interior layout, and service features of the operation. It includes elements that the guest pays for either directly or indirectly. In the restaurant, for example, the price charged for the steak on the plate covers not only the meat itself but also the plate it is served on, the napkins used, background entertainment, and even the view from the table—the price of which is reflected in the cost of buying the facility. Even the status of visiting a particular restaurant is something that is paid for in increased prices.

The following factors are associated with successful new products and services:

❖ the ability to identify customer needs
❖ use of existing company know-how and resources
❖ developing new products in the company's core markets
❖ measurement of performance during the development stage; screening and testing ideas before spending money on development
❖ coordination between research and development and marketing
❖ an organizational environment that encourages entrepreneurship and risk taking
❖ linking new product development to corporate goals[9]

Price   Several points regarding price bear mentioning. First, the importance of price comes from its role as half of the price–value relationship that customers seek. If, in the minds of the guest, the value received is less than the price paid, the experience is viewed negatively. Second, in the resort business, much of the pricing process is product driven—that is, resorts have a particular facility that has fixed and variable costs, and management has to meet these costs by finding a segment of the market willing to pay the price for the product or service being offered. However, it should always be remembered that the customer is the final arbiter of whether the price charged is acceptable. The latter concept, consumer-driven pricing, is often ignored in the resort industry.[10] The point is that the customer, not the product cost, determines whether an item will sell.

Promotion–
Communication
Mix   The promotion-communication mix consists of all the communications between the company and the customer and comprises media advertising, word of mouth, merchandising, promotion, public relations, publicity, and personal selling.

In the communications process, a target market is identified, objectives set, the theme of the message established, the promotional mix

❖ Promoting the facility, River Run Village, Colorado. [Source: Design Workshop, Inc.]

determined, appropriate media selected, and a budget established. It is important to set controls at each step of the way to determine whether or not the campaign is on track.

To determine whether or not the correct target market has been chosen, the operator must answer the following questions:

❖ Do I know what my guests want?
❖ Do I know what the marketplace wants?
❖ Do I know the characteristics of the target market I want to attract?

For control purposes objectives should be SMART—that is, they should be *s*pecific, *m*easurable, *a*chievable, *r*ealistic, and *t*ime-bound. To make the objective specific, it is necessary to quantify it. It is not enough to "increase awareness"; it is necessary to "reach 1000 prospects." The sheer fact that a specific target has been set increases the chances of reaching it.

Similarly, objectives must be measurable. An objective of "increasing awareness" cannot be measured; it is too vague. It is possible, however, to determine whether or not 1000 people have been exposed to a promotional message. Newspapers count circulation, radio stations count listeners, and direct mailings can be tabulated.

If objectives are not achievable, setting them is a meaningless exercise. They must also be realistic in the eyes of the people whose job it is to meet them. If objectives are set at an unrealistically high level, the people charged with the task meeting them will not even try, realizing that it is impossible. Finally, objectives must be time-bound—that is, a time frame within which the objective is to be achieved must be specified. If it is not, no one can determine whether or not the objective has been reached.

A variety of themes can be developed as part of a promotional campaign. The proper message is one that is desirable, believable, exclusive, and action oriented. It must make the customer want what is being offered, it has to be believed, it should belong to one operation and no other, and it should induce action on the part of the customer.

The major elements of the promotional mix are:

❖ *advertising*—any paid form of nonpersonal presentation and promotion of ideas, goods, or services by an identified sponsor
❖ *personal selling*—oral conversations, either by telephone or face to face, between salespersons and prospective customers
❖ *sales promotion*—short-term incentives to encourage purchase or sales of a product or service
❖ *merchandising*—materials used in-house to stimulate sales, including brochures on display, signs, posters, tent cards, and other point-of-purchase promotional items
❖ *public relations and publicity*—the nonpaid communication activities involved in maintaining or improving relationships with other organizations and individuals[11]

Various elements of the promotional mix involve the use of paid or unpaid media. The key control question is this: "Is my message in a place where it will be seen, read, or heard by my customers?"

The place of budgeting in the promotional process depends on the approach to promotion taken by the operation. In a bottom-up approach, objectives are set, the methods of reaching the objectives determined, and a budget agreed on. All too often, however, a top-down approach is used whereby the budget is determined first and objectives set relative to the amount of money available. Budgets can be set according to industry standards, to what the competition is spending, to the amount of money available, or to meet the agreed-on objectives. The best and most difficult method of establishing a budget is to identify the objectives and set a budget sufficient to meet them—and that the business can afford. Promotion is more art than science. There is no scientific way to determine how many advertisements it will take to produce x number of customers. For this reason alone, the tendency is common to view budgeting as a top-down effort.

If promotion is communication, it does not work unless communication occurs, unless the object of the communication receives it and responds. If each step of the process has been controlled, the chance is greater that the campaign will be a success and that customers will respond to an advertisement, sign up for an activity suggested by a resort employee, or take a lesson based on a tent card in the room.

This final part of the control process is vital. Did the promotion do what it was intended to do? Can the impact on sales be traced to a particular effort? Only through such tracking can a cost–benefit analysis be done in an effort to measure the effectiveness of the various parts of the promotional effort.

Advertising. When planning newspaper or magazine advertisement copy, layout and photographs and sketches must be considered. The copy consists of the headline and body text. The headline of the ad must catch the reader's attention, while the body includes the details. A good advertisement starts with a headline that is enticing, provocative, and attention grabbing. A clever punch headline with few words is preferable to one that attempts to tell the entire story.

Choosing an unusual size and shape is one way to make an ad stand out. If most other ads are quarter-page vertical, a quarter-page horizontal space may attract more attention.

Suppress the urge to crowd as much information as possible into an ad. The most successful ads tell a simple story in clear, concise language. Ads jammed with too many facts and figures are unlikely to be read.

All ads create impressions. A simple test can determine what stands out most in an ad. The ad is turned upside down to see what is most noticeable. People are used to reading left to right, top to bottom. Once a page is turned upside down, the mind's eye becomes disoriented, and the viewer cannot read according to learned methods. At first, the ad may look like a big blur, but later the viewer will be able to detect the most outstanding element in the ad, the one that will have the most impact on readers. If that element is not the one intended, the ad needs to be redesigned. If the big blur remains and the viewer finds it difficult to determine any outstanding element, the ad needs to be redesigned. A catchy headline, a strong graphic, a bold price, or any other single element should be prominent.

Radio is an immediate medium for quick news and information. Advertising time can readily be bought and commercials produced quickly for relatively low cost. Radio uses words and sounds to describe products and services and special occasions. Radio plays on the imagination of the listeners because it cannot show or demonstrate products or services. The advertising message usually must remind people of things they know. New, unique, or complicated ideas may be difficult to express. Radio is a transient medium. Messages cannot be kept for later reference. Listeners, for example, must remember addresses and telephone numbers. Coupon offers are out.

Unquestionably, television is the powerhouse medium. It combines the advantages of sight, sound, immediacy, dramatization, and emotional involvement of the viewers in a way that no other medium can match. It is also expensive. Television can make customers aware of what is offered at a price that requires considerable planning and budgeting. A resort may play commercials over its own closed-circuit system.

Signs and billboards can be found on location, on highways, and on buildings. The message should be brief yet eye-catching. Gigantic signs are now being constructed that swing and shimmer at the slightest touch of wind. Changeable copy panels make it possible to advertise daily program updates.

Direct mail offers a number of advantages to the guest activity programmer. This form of advertising has a high degree of control, as the manager decides to whom the message is sent. The number of pieces mailed can be tailored to the available budget. Direct mail is highly audience selective in that the mailing lists are developed from in-house customer rosters or from names obtained from mailing-list houses, which can break enormous lists down into narrow segments. Direct mail is increasing in popularity because it permits high target market selectivity.

The message can be personalized to different market segments. There is some question as to whether or not direct mail is cluttered. Certainly, people are unlikely to be doing anything else when they read their mail. On the other hand, so much mail is now regarded as junk that any and all nonpersonal mail stands a good chance of being thrown out unopened unless the piece is carefully designed. The ability to assess responses from a mailing by enclosing a coupon or a phone number allows easy measurement of the results of a campaign.

Direct mailings, on the other hand, tend to have a high discard rate, high total cost, and long lead time. A rule of thumb is that a direct mailing gets a 1 to 3 percent response rate. This means that for every 100 letters

quick getaways 8.3

Eco-Advertising

Here are some advertising support strategies based on positive environmental themes:

- Reinforce performance benefits with environmental benefits.
- Portray environmentally responsible behavior as cost conscious—saving money and more.
- Emphasize quality, durability, and longevity.
- Help customers minimize waste.
- Provide customers with a way in which to repair and upgrade products.
- Develop reusable products.

Source: Robert Rebak, Greener Marketing and Advertising: Charting a Responsible Course (Emmaus, Penna.: Rodale Press, 1993).

sent out, the operator will receive an average of only two responses. To get 100 customers with this response rate would require a mailing of 5000 pieces. The response rate can be improved by raising the quality of the list and by carefully targeting the needs of the recipients.

Personal Selling. Resorts attempt to sell timeshares in many ways: directly to owners or from owner referrals, rental and exchange guests, walk-ins, guests on minivacations, and from contacts made off-premises.[12]

Over one-third of on-site sales are generated from off-premise contacts. This is a fairly expensive way of generating sales, the marketing costs being 16 percent of net sales. Less than 20 percent of net on-site sales are generated from people taking minivacations, which have a marketing cost of 14 percent of net sales. Sales to existing owners, owner referrals, and rental guests each represent approximately 10 percent of all sales. The marketing cost as a percentage of net sales for each is about 7 percent. The importance of the sales generation method has to be measured against its cost. The marketing costs for off-premises contacts and minivacations are much greater than for the other methods noted above.

The average rate of rescissions—where sales are not consummated—is about 18 percent.[13] Obviously, the greater this rate, the more gross sales are required to make a given volume of net sales and the greater the marketing effort needed.

Promotions. Sales promotion consists of short-term incentives to encourage the purchase of a product or service. Consumer promotions may include coupons, premiums, patronage rewards, contests, sweepstakes, and games. Promotions may be open or contingent. Open offers do not require the guest to do anything other than buy the product. Special activities and discounts are examples of open offers. The advantage to the resort is that open promotions have broad customer appeal, as no effort—to redeem a coupon, for example—is required. On the other hand, the manager has no idea how many people will take advantage of the promotion. More people may show up than anticipated, creating bad will if the item being promoted is not available or high costs if it is.

A contingent offer requires the customer to do something—clip a coupon or make a specific purchase. The redemption rate is more easily controlled, although fewer customers will be attracted. This method is preferred for cost-control reasons. Because of their short-term nature—good promotions have an expiration date—they can stimulate sales during the period of the promotion. Promotions cannot be used as the sole or even the most important part of the marketing effort. If the business depends too heavily on promotions, customers may wait for the next promotion before they buy.

Coupons are certificates that give the customer a savings when they purchase a product, as in a two-for-one lesson purchase. Coupons offering free products are used to generate customer trial. The measure of success is whether or not the customer count increases. A successful trial promotion gets customers to buy something they would not ordinarily order.

In setting up a promotion, the objective needs to be determined, the target market selected, a strategy for implementing the promotion outlined, ways to promote the promotion identified, and evaluation methods set. The purpose or objective of the promotion needs to be determined up front. The objective can be thought of as the problem to be solved. Typically, promotions are used to attract new customers, keep existing customers happy, accelerate slow periods, or spotlight specials. The implementation of the promotion differs with the objective.

Merchandising. Merchandising consists of materials used in-house to stimulate sales. The difference between merchandising and promotions is that promotions are used to get customers in the door, whereas merchandising occurs once the customer is inside the resort. Merchandising includes brochures on display, signs, posters, tent cards, and point-of-purchase promotional items. The purpose of merchandising is twofold: to retain a resort's loyal customer base and to increase the percentage of total business generated by these loyal customers.

Public Relations and Publicity. Public relations includes everything that a resort does to maintain or improve its relationship with other organizations. Publicity is the use of nonpaid communications, such as press releases and press conferences. Businesses have a number of publics—individuals and organizations with whom and with which they interact. These range from employees and their families, unions, and owners to customers, competitors, government, hospitality schools, and the media. The job of public relations is to represent the operation favorably to these publics.

A good press release answers the questions *who, what, when, where, why,* and *how.* Ideally, this information is summarized in the opening paragraph. In addition to being newsworthy, the press release should be dated, list a contact person and phone number, indicate when the information can be released (usually, it is "for immediate release"), be typed double-spaced, have an eye-catching headline, be printed on letterhead, be no more than two pages in length, and be factual.

The value of public relations is that although the organization gives up total control of the message, the resulting message is persuasive because it is perceived as more objective than a commercial advertisement. Word-of-mouth publicity is by far the most desirable form of advertising. It means that someone was sufficiently impressed with the resort to discuss it with others. An endorsement by a friend is usually enough to cause a person to try a place.

Potential customers are bombarded with every sort of advertising every day. Understandably, people tend to be skeptical and often discount an advertiser's claims. In short, there is a gap between what advertisers say and what customers believe. There is, however, little or no gap when a friend recommends an activity to another friend. The friend has no motive for profit or gain; therefore, the suggestion is appreciated and believed. While its power has been demonstrated time after time, positive word of mouth takes too long to translate into sufficient numbers of guests to

ensure the financial success of the establishment. It has been argued that
the role of advertising is primarily to expose people to the facility's existence and that only word of mouth can induce actual patronage.

**Place–
Distribution Mix** The channels that connect the company and its various customers are
referred to as the distribution mix. Channels can either be direct or indirect. A direct channel of distribution means that the resort communicates directly with its guests. In indirect distribution, one or more inter-
mediaries moves messages between the resort and its customers. For
example, a property may decide to be part of a tour package being promoted by a tour operator. The decision to accept credit cards also
brings an intermediary—the credit card company—between the resort
and the customer.

Several factors must be considered before deciding on the form of distribution. If a distribution network already exists or is proposed, it may be
in the interests of the operator to use it. If a tour operator aggressively
advertises the resort as part of a package, the resort may be able to utilize
scarce advertising dollars elsewhere.

People in the indirect channel of distribution between the resort and
the guest make money by helping generate sales. They do not get paid
unless a sale is made; thus, the selling cost for the resort is variable. This
compares to the selling cost for direct distribution, which is fixed. The
promotion is directed by the operator directly at the customer and must
be paid for in full whether it attracts one customer or 1000. On the other
hand, it must be remembered that everyone between the resort and the
guest must get a cut of the selling price charged by the operation. If a
room sells for $160 and the resort sells it directly to the guest, the resort
receives $160. However, if a credit card is used, a percentage of the sale is
paid to the credit card company and the bank handling the collection. The
bus operator willing to bring in two busloads of tourists three times a
week during the season will pay less than $160 per room because it is
buying in bulk and expects to pay less by buying wholesale. Every resort
manager would prefer to sell every room for the retail price. At times
during the week or the year, however, the business is not there to pay the
full asking price. This is when, and only when, discounts paid to interme-
diaries can be justified.

The key for the operation is to know when it wants the business and to
understand the cost structure sufficiently well to realize how low it can
price the product and still make money. As a minimum, it is important to
know what the break-even point is. The break-even point for a resort facil-

ity is the point at which no profit is made and no loss is incurred. At the break-even point, total revenues exactly equal total costs. The important distinction here is that after the break-even point, the only costs incurred by the operation are variable costs. If break-even can thus be assured, the product can be priced to cover variable costs. Anything over the variable cost is profit.

A third factor to consider is the image of the intermediary. The image of the people or organizations distributing the product represent, for the customer, the image of the resort being sold. Operators should ensure that this image is consistent with the one they want to portray.

Direct sales are made through employees of the resort. These people, by virtue of their employment by the operation, should be more motivated to ensure the success of the resort than others in the channel who are not employees. Operators must determine the needs and wants of those in the channel to ensure a match between what the guest wants and what the resort has to offer.

A final factor to consider is who has the power in the channel. To the extent that a resort relies on a tour operator to bring in a significant amount of business, that operator has increased power to demand better prices and services at the risk of taking the business to another resort.

Budget A crucial part of the action plan is the budget developed to carry it out. Various means are used to develop a budget. A common approach is to base the budget on a percentage of sales. This option can work with businesses with a high percentage of repeat business. However, if sales go down in a particular year, the following year's marketing budget will be cut when it should probably be increased.

Another option is to spend in line with what the competition is spending. This effectively puts the resort's fate in the hands of the competition, which may not know what it is doing. A third option is to spend what the business can afford. This approach is a reactive way of deciding action plans.

The fourth approach is the best but also the most difficult. Action plans are developed and an amount budgeted to ensure their completion. The desired budget may have to be modified in light of the amount of money available. However, the point is to first determine how much money is needed to do the job and then determine if the business can afford it, rather than vice versa.

For example, timeshare developers spend a great deal on sales and marketing—about 45 percent of net sales. Total costs are broken down into three areas:

❖ marketing costs—24 percent of net sales
❖ sales commissions—17 percent of net sales
❖ other sales costs—4 percent of net sales[14]

MONITOR AND EVALUATE THE MARKETING PLAN

It is easy to see when a marketing plan is successful—more guests come in more often and pay higher prices. Equally, it is easy to determine when a plan has not worked—fewer guests come in less often and spend less. What is difficult, however, is to determine why the plan succeeded or failed. The exciting part of putting a marketing plan in place is the operation of the plan, but the most important and most overlooked part is determining whether or not it was successful and how and where it succeeded or went wrong. Even when the plan is evaluated, this is often done after the event as a kind of postmortem. This may be useful in helping ensure the success of the next marketing effort. It does nothing for the existing campaign.

The marketing plan must be monitored at each step to ensure that it is on track, and corrective action must be taken at each step if it is off track.

SUMMARY

Marketing is the process of planning and executing the conception, pricing, promotion, and distribution of ideas, goods, and services to create exchanges that satisfy individual and organizational objectives. The marketing plan can be developed according to the following steps: conduct a marketing audit, select target markets, position the property, determine marketing objectives, develop action plans, and monitor and evaluate the plan.

ENDNOTES

1. "AMA Board Approves New Marketing Definition," *Marketing News*, 1 March 1985, p. 1.
2. Robert D. Reid, *Hospitality Marketing Management*, 2nd ed. (New York: Van Nostrand Reinhold, 1989), 8.
3. James R. Abbey, *Hospitality Sales and Advertising* (East Lansing, Mich.: Educational Institute of the American Hotel and Motel Association, 1989), 34.
4. Tom Feltenstein, *Foodservice Marketing for the '90s* (New York: John Wiley & Sons, 1992), 51-54.
5. Ibid., 29.
6. Ibid., 23.
7. Abbey, *Hospitality Sales and Advertising*, 37.

8. Abbey, *Hospitality Sales and Advertising*, 20.

9. Robert C. Lewis and Richard E. Chambers, *Marketing Leadership in Hospitality: Foundations and Practices* (New York: Van Nostrand Reinhold, 1989), 327.

10. Ibid., 354.

11. T. F. Chiffriller, *Successful Restaurant Operation* (Boston: CBI Publishing, 1982), 278.

12. *Financial Performance 1999: A Survey of Timeshare and Vacation Ownership Resort Developers* (Washington, D.C.: American Resort Development Association, 1999), 59-61.

13. Ibid., 66.

14. Ibid., 21.

Chapter 9
RESORT OPERATIONS

Introduction

Design

Operations

Retail

Ecolodges

Summary

Endnotes

INTRODUCTION

*So many women ran the hotels in the Catskills, strong women
like Jennie Grossinger, Lillian Brown. It came out of that old-
country tradition where the women ran the business and took
care of all the practical matters so the man could study.*
—MYRNA KATZ FROMMER AND HARVEY FROMMER
It Happened in the Catskills

The operation of a resort differs in many significant ways from that of a
traditional hotel. This chapter assumes the reader is familiar with basic
hotel operations. It concentrates on what makes condominiums, vacation
ownership, and timeshare properties different from traditional hotels.

DESIGN

*A movement is underway in resort design. Its emergence
demands that developers, planners, and architects focus on
regional specificity. . . . This movement studies a resort in
terms of its site-specific and regionally unique qualities; its
history, culture, climate. . . . The inherent site qualities form
the basis of a design philosophy.*
—JOHN COTTLE
Cottle Greybeal Architects

Vacation ownership resorts began in the 1970s with motel conversions
and timeshare interests in existing but unsold condominium apartments.
Today, these resorts are purpose-built, and their layout and design are
comparable to any luxury resort.

Most vacation ownership units have two bedrooms and two full baths
and can sleep up to six people. One-bedroom units typically sleep up to
four people, while studio units sleep no more than two.[1]

Recent designs include the lockout unit, consisting of two bedrooms
and two bathrooms or three bedrooms and three bathrooms, which is
designed such that the owner can occupy the living room and one or two
bedrooms while renting out the remaining space. Features such as ter-
races, balconies, wood-burning fireplaces, hot tubs, and whirlpool baths
are becoming increasingly common.

Public spaces in a vacation ownership resort can include hospitality
areas consisting of a check-in desk, concierge desk, and cashier, game
rooms, restaurants, and stores.[2] In fee-simple resorts organized as condominiums (where owners actually own the weeks they buy forever), the
public spaces are common areas owned jointly by all unit owners. It is not

quick getaways 9.1

Converting Hotels into Timeshares

It is challenging to convert a hotel into a timeshare because the two products are very different. Developers use the hotel's basic structure and redo the interior. One such operation was the Kauai BeachBoy Hotel in Kauai, Hawaii, which was converted into 108 Hawaiian-style units. The bedrooms were made larger and more spacious. In the center bay, the bedroom was torn out and a kitchen put in and made a central part of the living room. Designers had to take into account the Resort Condominiums International and Interval International requirement that, for two-bedroom units, one bedroom must be accessible from the living room and not through a bedroom.

At Bluebeard's Castle in St. Thomas, U.S. Virgin Islands, the target market of couples meant that units were required to sleep two rather than six or eight. To give an illusion of greater space and the perceived value of two rooms, a partition wall was designed to divide bedroom and living room. Available plumbing was utilized to transform a large entry closet into a kitchenette.

On Clearwater Beach in Florida, an older beach motel was converted to a Ramada Vacation Suites. Three hotel rooms were converted into one-bedroom units with an attachable studio, and two-bedroom units. A major problem in most conversions is space maximization. Solutions include recessed televisions and fireplaces, added shelves, and desk space that doubles as a makeup table.

A different challenge was an urban timeshare project in New York City: the conversion of the Park Central Hotel to The Manhattan Club. The developers cut the property in half horizontally. The timeshare portion is the top half of the building. People entering the timeshare elevator do not even know they are in a hotel because the elevator passes those floors. Units consist of one-bedroom apartments with two hotel windows.

Source: M.A. Baumann, "Transforming Hotels into Timeshares Can Be a Tricky Task," *Hotel and Motel Management*, 1 November 1999, pp. 74, 82.

Question: **Why is it difficult to convert a traditional hotel into a timeshare project?**

uncommon for developers to retain ownership of some or all of the profit centers in the resort.

The lobby must be able to accommodate large numbers of people and luggage during weekly arrival and departure times. Some provision must be made to store the luggage of guests who arrive prior to official check-in times.

The outdoor landscape is important to creating an ambience that enhances the overall experience of the guest. Extensive use of exotic plants has given way to the use of native flora. This movement reflects an increased concern for the environment.

OPERATIONS

RESERVATIONS AND THE FRONT DESK

Front office procedures at whole and interval ownership resorts have much in common with those at traditional resorts. Front office personnel take reservations over the telephone; they accept transient guests; they deal with such things as computer systems, key control, and keeping accurate guest records. In other ways, the tasks are very different.

Reservations

While reservations at a traditional resort might come in via a toll-free number or direct calls from prospective guests, at interval ownership resorts they can, in addition, come from an exchange company or a vacation club. In a traditional resort, the number of rooms available for rent is determined by management. In a vacation ownership resort, the number of units available is determined by the number of owners who want to rent or exchange their units.

The person reserving the unit may own a specific unit, own the right to stay in an unspecified unit, be the guest of an owner, or "just" be a regular tourist looking to stay at a resort. In each case, the person brings a different level of knowledge and expectation to the telephone encounter. Staff need to be able to handle this variety of guest types. Typically, one-third of all incoming calls are reservations, while the remainder involve questions, confirmations, and owner-related questions and problems.

Three types of people place reservations at whole or interval ownership resorts: owners, guests of owners, and renters. Owners may or may not have placed their units in a rental program. The former may be required to reserve their own units anywhere from 30 days to one year in advance. Advance notice allows management to determine availability on a seasonal basis. Owners who have not placed their units in the rental pool may also be required to call ahead to reserve the unit. Because they have maintenance agreements with the resort, calling ahead allows them to confirm that the unit has not been scheduled for deep cleaning and is in shape for them to take occupancy.

The second type of people who place reservations are guests who have been given permission by the owner to occupy the unit. It is important that the resort accept bookings from one and only one owner contact person in order to avoid double bookings. Third, are renters—transient guests who have booked a resort stay. Rentals may come in through the resort's reservations office or from an outside real estate agency. Few reservations come from retail travel agents (unlike traditional resorts) because few central reservation systems can link individual agents to resorts. If few units are available for rent, it may be unprofitable for the resort to operate a rental program.

Many owners put their units into a rental pool in an attempt to recoup their investment. Most states prohibit developers from guaranteeing rental income. Nevertheless, when owners are in a rental pool, they may put pressure on management to keep the unit occupied and bringing in revenue all the time.

Reservationists Employees who take reservations at vacation ownership resorts have a much more complicated task than do their counterparts at traditional resorts, which feature few room types. The task is to simply match the needs of the guest to a relatively small list of variables. Vacation ownership units vary greatly in terms of size, view, appliances, and decor. Matching individual guests to all of the units available is more complex and requires greater product knowledge on the part of the employees. Repeat renters tend to book a specific unit rather than wait to be assigned a unit at check-in, which is typical at a traditional resort.

A number of computerized reservation systems specific to vacation ownership resorts have been developed by software companies. Such programs help track guest deposits, manage correspondence, and pay revenue to owners. Additional modules link reservations to the Internet and encourage revenue equalization by having units with less revenue or room nights booked to appear first on a list of available units.

Check-In Some resorts have separate check-in facilities for owners. Owners do not expect to be treated like guests—they want to be treated like owners! This places additional pressure on employees to give exceptionally high standards of service.

Work patterns at interval ownership resorts differ from those at both whole ownership or traditional resorts. At the former, guests check in and out on turnover days. Typically, check-out occurs on Saturday or Sunday. Some resorts stagger these days over Friday, Saturday, and Sunday to balance employee workload. On turnover day, all units have to be cleaned in a matter of hours. Timeshares hire temporary or contract employees to handle the specific work patterns of timeshare units. This makes for a difficult management situation due to the constantly changing staff. The balance between nightly rentals and interval owners is an issue traditional resorts do not have to deal with.

Billing Other differences relate to overbooking and payment of the bill. Interval and whole ownership resorts rarely overbook. There is an expectation that guests show up. To encourage this, advance deposits and full payment on arrival are common at whole ownership resorts.

Key control can be a problem at interval resorts. It is expected that guests turn in keys at departure. Owners may feel that it is legitimate for them not only to hang on to their keys but also to make copies of them to hand out to friends. Electronic locks, which can be programmed after each guest leaves, alleviate this problem.

Owner Relations Large whole ownership resorts have a separate department dedicated to owner relations. Interval ownership resorts have difficulty giving such personal attention because of the large volume of owners. This latter group of owners does not typically have the same level of feeling toward the unit as do whole owners. Service expectations, however, remain high. Exchange guests rank each property they stay at. These ratings affect the resort's ranking by the exchange organization, which, in turn, influences the trade value of the resort to others. Thus, guest satisfaction has a direct impact on the attractiveness of the property to others.[3]

HOUSEKEEPING There are major differences in the way traditional resorts and ownership properties operate relative to housekeeping. The principal differences are in:

- ❖ size and location of units
- ❖ guest arrival and departure patterns
- ❖ staffing patterns
- ❖ owner relations

Size and Location of Units While the standard hotel room measures 400 square feet and includes a sleeping area and a bathroom, the typical condominium unit has over 1000 square feet and includes three bedrooms, two bathrooms, a kitchen, and a living/dining area. Many also include fireplaces and balconies. Thus, while a standard room can be cleaned in 30 minutes, it may take up to 90

❖ Comfortable lodging,
Aspen, Colorado. [Source:
Design Workshop, Inc.]

minutes to clean a condominium unit. The daily standard for a hotel housekeeper may be 15 to 20 rooms per day; for a resort condominium housekeeper, the number may be closer to 5 units per day.

The problem is not just the size but also the complexity of the cleaning task. Units may include tubs with glass enclosures rather than shower curtains, Jacuzzis enclosed with glass or mirrors, fireplaces and grills, ovens, dishwashers, and refrigerators.

While hotel rooms are located in an enclosed building, condominium units in a resort may be spread over several acres. Problems of transporting materials and supplies over distances in all types of weather are intensified.

Guest Arrival and Departure Patterns
In a traditional hotel, guests come and go during the week. In a vacation ownership resort, most guests arrive and depart on the same day. This exchange day or turnover day creates unique problems for housekeeping.

All units in the property have to be cleaned in a matter of hours. It is important to have a system that choreographs activities to ensure a smooth turnover. This might mean, for example, that supplies are made up into goodie bags for easy distribution to individual condominiums. There has to be a plan for dealing with early arrivals. This might include giving tours of the property, having a welcome party, or giving beepers to guests to let them know when units are available for occupancy.

Staffing Patterns The pattern described above means that many housekeepers are needed—but for only one day a week. Even when some units are rented on a daily basis, the number of housekeepers needed is much lower than the number required on exchange day. This situation can be addressed through staggered cleaning schedules, utilization of part-time employees, or using outside contractors.

Depending on the minimum stay requirement, some guests may stay for a week while others leave after three or four days. Staggering departures in this way can spread out the work for the housekeeping staff. Some resorts offer a midweek cleaning on the third or fourth day of a weeklong stay in conjunction with a "daily refresh," which can include emptying the trash, straightening the bed, and delivering towels. Additional services are made available for a fee.

Part-time employees can be used to supplement a small full-time staff. Using part-timers offers flexibility of schedule and lower costs through not providing benefits. Special efforts are necessary to make part-time workers feel part of the team. Their use also necessitates constant training to bring new employees up to speed on the standards of the resort.

Mastercorp is an example of an outside contractor that provides housekeeping service to resorts. The company recruits and hires for and manages all housekeeping and laundry services. The resort has limited control over Mastercorp employees. This is not a problem if standards are met. Problems, however, may take longer to resolve to the satisfaction of guest and resort management because of the presence of the outside contractor. The guest, on seeing a housekeeping employee, believes that person to be an employee of the resort. The employee has to answer to the guest, resort management, and the contractor. Communication is more complex and problems more difficult to resolve.

Owner Relations Some owners develop strong feelings toward the person taking care of their unit and want assurance that that individual will always handle their unit. The advantage of this arrangement is that a specific person becomes familiar with the layout and requirements of particular units and can be expected to do a better job than someone who rotates into the unit every other day. Difficulties arise when owners treat the housekeeper as a personal maid or give them cleaning instructions at odds with policies of the resort.[4]

MAINTENANCE AND ENGINEERING

Role of Owners

Because of the interest and involvement of owners, there is more pressure on the maintenance department of a vacation ownership resort compared to a traditional property. While hotel guests pay for the expense of repairs indirectly through their room rate, whole ownership resort owners pay directly for all maintenance and repairs on their unit and share in the expenses of the common units. The maintenance responsibilities of the owners are usually spelled out in the owner's agreement. This might detail the standards that owners must maintain for repairs, interior decorating, and furnishing. If the standards are not met, the unit may be taken out of the rental program. As a rule of thumb, the more permanent residents there are, the less maintenance is required.

Because units are not standardized, it is difficult to specify the same bedding, seating arrangements, and decor for each. However, it is possible to enforce quality standards on all items within the units.

Owners either rent out their unit through resort management, do not rent out the unit because it is used as a second home, or rent out the unit themselves or through a third party. The first group tends to contract repair and maintenance services to the management company of the resort. This certainly makes sense for owners in terms of convenience and cost. The management company can respond faster with a staff familiar with the units. At the same time, they can likely offer services at a cost that is lower than that of outside contractors. The second group typically do their own work, while the latter group usually have work done by the same agency that rents the unit. Interval ownership resorts usually hold back two weeks during the year when the unit is not rented. Major repairs and heavy maintenance are done at this time.

Maintenance is usually regarded as a support center that is an expensive necessity. In ownership condominiums, the maintenance function is often run as a break-even proposition. It does, however, have the potential to be a profit center. Operational costs are passed on to owners, while the department collects revenue for services rendered to owners. Management may charge an annual fee to do the following:

❖ Recycle ice maker.
❖ Adjust refrigerator settings.
❖ Reset breakers.
❖ Unstop garbage disposal.
❖ Plunge toilet.
❖ Adjust sink and tub stoppers.
❖ Replace faucet knobs.
❖ Desuds the dishwasher.
❖ Tighten door hinges.
❖ Inspect the heating and air conditioning system.
❖ Replace air conditioning filters.
❖ Replace light bulbs.

Common Areas   As noted earlier, owners pay for work done on their individual units, while expenses for common areas are shared. Common areas include:

❖ land, grounds, private roads, parking areas
❖ foundations, main walls, roofs, lobbies, building entrances and exits
❖ central services such as power, light, gas, water
❖ elevators
❖ laundry and storage rooms
❖ recreational amenities

❖ Guest Services, Little Nell, Aspen, Colorado. [Source: Design Workshop, Inc.]

Common areas may be general (such as those noted above) or limited. Limited common elements are those to which only a single owner has access. Examples include a balcony and a lock on a door. While the owner has exclusive use of each, the former can be seen by others, while the latter is included because the association may need to access the room in the event of an emergency.

Major Repairs Repairs can be expensive. The resort needs to specify priorities for determining the order in which repairs must be completed. The order of general priorities should be:

1. systems critical to life, health, and the property (asbestos removal)
2. systems critical to the property's daily operation (furnace, air conditioning)
3. systems that would cause damage to other systems if they failed (drains, leaks, broken windows)
4. systems that would cause major inconvenience to owners (electrical system)
5. systems that would cause minor inconvenience to owners (minor furniture scratches)
6. systems requiring replacement for cosmetic reasons (out-of-style wallpaper)

Monthly Assessments Monthly assessment fees are negotiated with the board and charged to individual owners. They are intended to support ongoing upkeep so as to increase the attractiveness of the resort and maintain the value of the property.

A system has to be set up to ensure that all work is properly billed. When a repair request is received, a work order is generated that is used to schedule labor and create an invoice, which is sent to the owner as part of her statement. Many companies have a policy of calling the owner if expenses exceed an agreed-on limit.

Renovations Resorts usually undertake renovations for one or more of the following reasons:

❖ higher service expectations on the part of owners
❖ increasing levels of technological comfort
❖ keeping up with competition
❖ greater environmental awareness

quick getaways 9.2

Revenue-Generating Programs for Resorts

Timeshare resorts are increasingly looking at new ways to generate revenue. Here are four options:

➤ *Resort activity programs*—Activity programs help create a friendly atmosphere and bring owners back for more. Owners are kept entertained and are given the opportunity to meet vacationers with similar interests. However, they do not generate large amounts of revenue and are time-consuming to organize. Popular programs offer an authentic or educational experience unique to the region. Sandstone Creek Club resort in Vail, Colorado, offers microbrew parties ($3250 annual profit), ice cream parties ($3750 annual profit), and wine-tasting events ($2500 annual profit). Stoneridge Recreational Club Condominiums operates an 18-hole mini-golf course that makes a $6000 annual profit.

➤ *Small-scale rental programs*—Rental programs are easy to start up and operate. They offer a larger profit potential, dollar for dollar, than activities. Owners get the advantage of on-site convenience while resorts make maximum use of their facility. Replacing equipment can be costly and some rentals involve a degree of liability. Safety and security have to be the primary concern. Rental agreements need to be drawn up in such a way that they protect the resort. To avoid these issues, it is wise to work with an outside rental company.

Prior to the actual renovation, the scope of the project must be determined. Long-term objectives must be identified, a projects list generated, costs and benefits numerated, and projects chosen. An outside expert may be brought in to prepare the design, act as an inspection agent, or act as an independent arbitrator in the event of a dispute. A decision must be made on how the project will be funded—from existing funds or via a special assessment. Reserves are funded through annual fees or as part of the regular monthly assessments. Some states mandate the collection of reserves. Permission from the owners is usually required before reserves

Nob Hill Inn, in the middle of San Francisco, has no room for parking. The resort made a deal with the parking garage next door; the resort would charge guests $3.00 more than the cost of renting parking spaces and take in $3000 in annual revenue. The Vacation Owners Association at Olympia in Wisconsin contracts with a movie rental outlet to supply the resort with videos, which are rented from the front desk. Stonebridge Resort in Idaho rents its recreational center for parties during its off-hours and clears $2000 profit per year.

- *External concierge services*—Resorts make a commission from local tour companies when owners sign up for a sightseeing tour. While owners receive discounts, the cost burden falls on the outside company. However, resort management has to spend time up front in developing relationships with local businesses. Showing sightseeing companies the potential buying power of the owners at the resort helps build partnerships. It is important to check that the certificate of liability insurance held by the outside vendor covers the resort owners. Nob Hill earns annual commissions of $6000 selling sightseeing tickets to its owners.

- *Vendor rebates*—Partnering with preferred suppliers generates discounts for resort owners and offers potential revenue streams through tours, tickets, and logo items. The profit margin can be greater than that obtained through rental programs. Owners receive discounts while an outside party pays the cost. However, start-up costs can be high, and resorts may need to develop a special accounting program to handle the finances. The Arroyo Roble Resort in Sedona, Arizona, signed up with RCI's Preferred Alliance program (a major timeshare exchange company) to have AT&T as the long-distance provider at the resort. They generate $1000 in annual profits based on a commission of 50 cents for every operator-assisted call and a loyalty bonus of $5.00 per unit. In other programs, resorts receive a 75-cent commission for every Pizza Hut order delivered to the resort and $2.00 for every disposable Kodak camera sold on site.

Source: "Little Things Mean a Lot," *RCI Premier* (November/December 1999): 32–35.

Question: What are some additional revenue-generating options for timeshare projects?

can be spent. When a special assessment is needed to complete the work, the cost of the project is divided among and charged to the owners. Finally, a contractor is selected.

During the planning phase, it is critical that a communications program be targeted toward owners to explain the costs and benefits of the project. Communication is key to getting the support of the owners, who will be more interested in what is being proposed than are guests.

Employees may need to be retrained in new procedures after the renovation. If, for example, a pool has been resurfaced, maintenance proce-

❖ The importance of retail, Muju, South Korea. [Source: Design Workshop, Inc.]

dures may be different. Owners will also expect higher standards of quality to go along with the new facilities. A festive reopening will help generate positive feelings from owners.[5]

RETAIL

A good store is by definition one that exposes the greatest portion of its goods to the greatest number of its shoppers for the longest period of time.

—PACO UNDERHILL
Why We Buy

Retail sales are a significant part of most resort operations. Merchandise sales account for about 13 percent of total revenue for resort golf facilities in the United States,[6] while ski clothing and equipment sales make up 6 percent of total sales at North American ski areas. Rentals account for an additional 4 percent of revenue.[7]

Retail stores have three distinct aspects:

❖ design (the premises)
❖ merchandising (what is put on the premises)
❖ operations (what employees do)[8]

These three items are interdependent. Decisions regarding one affect the other two. Strengthening one area takes some pressure off the others. If one is weakened, it shifts more burden onto the remaining two. Consider, for example, a store selling bottles of sunscreen. It is time-consuming for employees to stock all those bottles in perfectly straight rows. If the store were to replace the shelves with bins, a clerk could just roll a trolley of merchandise to the aisle, open the bin, and dump in the goods. This strategy would have to be considered in light of the overall impression the store wishes to give. Management would have to ensure that customers did not perceive the bins as indicative of lower quality.

LAYOUT AND DESIGN

Time

The most important factor in determining how much people will buy is the amount of time they spend in the store (assuming they are buying and not waiting in line). Another crucial element is the interception rate—the percentage of customers who have some contact with an employee. The more shopper–employee contacts that take place, the greater the average sale.

On the other hand, the most important factor in determining customer satisfaction is waiting time. The longer shoppers wait in line, the lower their impression of overall service.

Layout

Retail space should take the physical characteristics of customers into account when designing the physical layout of the store. Consider the following:

❖ Most people have two hands that, at rest, are approximately 3 feet off the floor.
❖ People focus on what is directly in front of them. This means that displays should be offset to one side so that they can be more easily seen from an angle. *Endcap* refers to the display of merchandise on the end of store aisles. To fully appreciate the displays, customers need to walk sideways! Placing shelves or racks at an angle—chevroning—positions the shelves at a 45-degree angle rather than a 90-degree angle to the aisle. The problem is that chevroning shelves takes up about one-fifth more floor space than the usual configuration. As a result, a store can show only 80 percent as much merchandise.

Peripheral vision is determined, in part, by environmental factors. Sight lines should be taken into consideration; merchandise should not be placed so it cuts them off. The *capture rate* refers to how much of what is on display is seen by shoppers. The reliable zone, that placement area in which shoppers will probably see the merchandise, extends from slightly above eye level down to about the knee level.

Large items are the only merchandise that should be displayed above or below the reliable zone. Tipping the bottom shelf up slightly helps visibility.

- ❖ People would rather look at people than objects. The number-one thing people look at is other people. The most effective signs in fast-food restaurants are those that sit on top of the cash registers—more or less at the level of the cashier's face.
- ❖ People go in predictable paths, speed up, slow down, and stop in response to their surroundings. People in North America tend to walk to the right immediately on entering a store, so this is an area of prominence in which to place products. This right-moving tendency is linked to the side of the road on which people drive. In Great Britain and Australia, on the other hand, people tend to walk to the left.

Transition Zone   When people cross the threshold of a store, they do not come to an immediate stop. Their momentum carries them into the store through a transition zone. Getting them to pay attention to displays at the entrance requires some thought on the part of the retailer. A slightly creaky door, a squeaky hinge, or special lighting on the doorway can clearly mark the division between the store and its outside environment. Merchandisers are advised to avoid trying to accomplish anything important there and to take steps to keep the transition zone as small as possible.

Several opportunities are presented in the transition zone. An employee can greet customers and acknowledge their presence. Shoplifting can be discouraged. The easiest way to do this is to make sure employees acknowledge the presence of every shopper with a simple hello.

Basket Placement   Baskets are usually placed immediately inside the store entrance. In many cases, customers rush through the transition zone, bypassing the baskets. At one store, employees were trained to offer baskets to any customer holding three or more items. Most gratefully accepted this gesture and took the basket. As more people used baskets, the average sale increased. Baskets, in fact, should be scattered throughout the store where they are most needed by customers. The stack should be at least 5 feet high to ensure visibility and prevent shoppers from having to bend to get one. Shoppers hate to bend, especially when their hands are full.[9]

MERCHANDISING

Retail Competition   Resort retailers have to compete with major retail stores and chains for their guests' business. Golf pro shops, for example, rank first in only one consumer category—gloves—where they are the outlet of choice of 21 percent of all golfers. When it comes to other purchase categories (balls, clubs, bags, apparel, and shoes), their market share slips to between 9 and 14 percent.[10] Resort retailers have to compete with department stores, which are devoting more and more space to golf-specific clothing. As retail companies come out with casual lines, they intensify the struggle to find shelf space in the pro shop and resort retail store. Liz Claiborne has already taken the lead from Ralph Lauren—whose Polo line went from department store to pro shop favorite—by placing its LizSport line at private clubs and resorts around the country.

Department stores are looking to delve further into weekend casual sportswear. Callaway is one of only a handful of companies, including Brooks Brothers, creating golf lines exclusively for department stores. Years ago, golf discount stores took a chunk out of the pro's hard goods business but did not compete in the apparel area. Now, the department stores and specialty stores are threatening to cut into that business as well. Many pro shop owners and buyers feel betrayed by the defection of golf apparel companies and are sometimes less apt to do business with them. Department stores get greater variety than do resorts because of the volume they deal with.

Resort shops do have one major edge: cresting. Logoed apparel comprises 90 percent of menswear. On the other hand, there is not much logoing in womenswear. As a result, this is where the competition is. The resort retailer must compete on the basis of service, attention, and experience while emphasizing their potential to provide consumers with immediate gratification in their stores.

Vendors   Carrying all the major lines is impossible, so resort retailers have to be selective in their choice of vendors and items they carry. The average number of lines carried in golf resort stores ranges from two (gloves and rainwear) to seven (men's shirts). Most carry three to four brand names in clubs.[11] In choosing vendors, resorts should consider the following:

* *Marketing and pull-through*—Has a line been nationally advertised? Does it have adequate consumer awareness? Is the name recognizable?
* *Pricing policy*—How willing is the company to work with the resort store on pricing, closeouts, dating, and terms?
* *Execution*—How easy is it to do business with the company? Does the paperwork match what's in the box? Does the company ship completely and on time?
* *Customer service*—Are the customer service people talented, aware, and able to answer questions? Customer service can make or break a company.

❖ *Sales staff*—How talented is the sales staff in advising the buyer how to invest? Does the representative have an awareness and understanding of the resort retail business?

❖ *Logos*—Does the company logo in-house or out? This may seem a minor point, but when a good portion of your business depends on selling your name, excellent logo service is critical.

❖ *Commitment*—What is the company's commitment to the industry? Does it understand the needs and problems of the resort retailer? Is it willing to work with you? Vendors have to understand the personal nature of the resort business, where smaller orders and more exact deliveries are the norm.[12]

TRENDS IN THE GOLF STORE

Apparel accounts for almost 40 percent of total dollar sales at golf resorts. Approximately half of all apparel revenue comes from men's shirts. Women's shirts account for about 6 percent of total sales and 15 percent of all apparel sales. A major reason for this discrepancy is the inattention retailers (especially in golf resorts) have paid to the female customer. This subject is addressed in greater detail later in this chapter.

Clubs account for just over 20 percent of all sales in golf resorts, the same proportion as balls and headwear together. Shoes and gloves combine for about 10 percent of sales, while bags account for 3 percent.[13]

Apparel

Consumers are looking to department stores for more of their leisure fashion needs. This has always been true for men's slacks and shorts and for women's apparel in general. Perhaps, as a result, retailers have become more selective in the manufacturers they carry. Ashworth, Izod Club, Gear for Sports, and Polo Ralph Lauren are the top manufacturers in brand penetration.[14]

Clubs

Clubs are becoming lighter and longer. The increased popularity of titanium woods resulted in a corresponding decrease in sales of standard-sized metal woods.

Balls

The golf ball market is dominated by four major brands: Titleist, Spalding, Wilson, and Maxfli. Distance (95 percent) and durability (72 percent) topped the list of golf ball characteristics retailers believe are the most important to their customers.[15] Recent years have seen the increased popularity of corporate logo ball sales.

quick getaways 9.3

Golf Shop Merchandising

Here are ten strategies for golf shop merchandising success:

1. Make sure every golfer has to walk through the shop.
2. Welcome everyone into the shop.
3. Find the personality of the shop and make the most of it.
4. Know the audience.
5. Ask open-ended questions of customers and listen to them.
6. Use product knowledge to increase sales.
7. Create displays that show the customer how to use or wear the products.
8. Offer special services to cater to customers.
9. Thank customers for their business.
10. Communicate with the staff.

Source: Lisa Michaels, "Making the Difference: Tips on How Golf Shops Can Compete with Department Stores," *Golf Product News,* May/June 1995, 32–33.

Question: What other merchandising strategies can be added to this list?

Footwear   The average golf resort store carries two lines of footwear, and Foot-Joy is one of them. Foot-Joy and Etonic are the major brand penetration leaders. Recent innovations include waterproof leathers and new colors. This latter development has encouraged more players to buy an extra pair of golf shoes to match a particular wardrobe. Men are asking for shoes with waterproof guarantees (two-year guarantees are popular), while women are demanding more color varieties to accessorize outfits.

Gloves   Foot-Joy has 40 percent of the market and is carried by 83 percent of all golf shops. Etonic is second, with 46 percent penetration.

Bags   The market for bags is not dominated by a brand name as it is with clubs and shoes. The key for consumers is innovation. The trend is toward light-weight, high-tech bags. Embroidered bags are a relatively untapped source of potential business.

GETTING YOUR MESSAGE NOTICED The key to getting your message across is, first, to attract the attention of the audience. Once that is accomplished, the message has to be presented in a way that is clear and logical; it must have a beginning, a middle, and an ending.[16] People absorb information a little at a time. If they are told too much too fast, the result is information overload. If customers are confused, they will miss the message altogether.

By walking through the store as a customer, retailers can see what shoppers will do and what they will look at in different places in the store. Where people are walking fast, the message has to be short and have immediate impact. Where people are browsing, on the other hand, more detail can be given. At the cash register, where they stand still, there is an opportunity for a longer message.

For example, the shoe department offers an opportunity to promote other products. When the clerk goes off to find a particular shoe, the customer is left (usually shoeless) with nothing to do. The customer could be given promotional reading materials. Research has shown that 25 percent of the diners in fast-food restaurants read table tents, compared to only 2 percent of diners in family restaurants.[17] The reason is that, in family restaurants, most parties are groups of two, three, or four. They are too busy talking to read. Many fast-food customers, on the other hand, are on their own and looking for a distraction.

Signs should interrupt the existing natural sight lines in any given area. Retailers should put themselves in the shoes of the customer and identify where they are looking—that is the perfect spot for a sign. The principles of good design are as follows:

❖ no extra words
❖ the right sign at the right place
❖ enough signs that customers don't feel ignored or underinformed
❖ not so many signs that there's clutter or confusion[18]

Merchandise Placement Because North American shoppers search right and most are right-handed, merchandise should be displayed just slightly to the right of where customers stand. The most popular brand should go dead center, the brand the store is trying to build just to the right of it.[19]

Positioning the most popular items halfway down the aisle encourages shoppers to pass other items on the way to their purchase. Similarly, a large graphic or hanging on a rear wall seems to pull shoppers toward it.[20]

According to Underhill, "almost all unplanned buying is a result of touching, hearing, smelling, or tasting."[21] Let people know that it is all right for them to touch. Many people, for example, are reluctant to mess up a neat display of sweaters. When sweaters are displayed in several shades, it is wise to place the lightest one on the bottom and the darker ones on top, as these will be touched most.

When selling merchandise that will be used at various times of the day, provide several settings of illumination so customers can see what the color will look like when it is likely to be worn.

Here are some practical ideas from stores specializing in golf:

- ❖ Add a display coordinator with an extensive background in the retail fashion industry.
- ❖ To blur the line between soft goods and hard goods, incorporate clubs and bags with apparel displays and boutiques.
- ❖ Use antique props to create a pro shop atmosphere.
- ❖ The most worn piece of carpet on your shop floor reveals where most of the foot traffic goes. Place slow-moving items in that spot to see if sales increase because of the location.
- ❖ Everyone moves to the right. Place most impulse items to the right, inside the shop entrance.
- ❖ People buy items placed between 3 and 5 feet off the floor.
- ❖ Tell a story with merchandise by placing apparel, shoes, and equipment together in a space.
- ❖ Trade-ins are a way to discount without really offering a discount. Give the customer a dollar for their old glove if they buy a new one.
- ❖ Package a box of balls, a glove, and a hat together.
- ❖ Rotate stock. Built-in cabinets can be beautiful, but modular fixtures are more practical.
- ❖ Halogen lights are more efficient than standard light bulbs; they last longer, emit less heat, and are more cost-efficient. New colored halogen lights give a warm look.
- ❖ Appeal to all the senses. Use videotapes with banks of video monitors. Play audiotapes of, for example, the sound of a tennis ball popping off a racket.
- ❖ Use pellets with scents like leather or tobacco in men's clothing boutiques.
- ❖ Use lights to highlight high-ticket merchandise.
- ❖ Supply coloring books, crayons, and cookies for children so parents can shop more easily.
- ❖ Provide special services such as in-shop alterations, spike and grip replacement, club demos, shipping, gift wrapping, and gift certificates.[22]

OPERATIONS The importance of employees in increasing sales cannot be overesti-
mated. Resort retail staff in golf resorts estimate that a whopping 54 percent of their time is spent dealing with customers.[23] This completely over-
whelms time spent in giving lessons (13 percent) and dealing with
recordkeeping and product displays (10 percent). Research indicates that
any contact initiated by a store employee increases the likelihood that a
shopper will buy something. Shopper conversion rate—the percentage of
shoppers who actually buy—increases by half when there is a staff-
initiated contact and jumps by 100 percent when there is staff-initiated
contact and the use of the dressing room.[24] The dressing room, in fact,
may be the most important part of any apparel-selling store. Shoppers
want to experience merchandise before buying it. When shoppers are in a
dressing room, they are captive. Additionally, they have one thing on their
mind: the desire to buy something. Thus, it is important to make the
dressing room as conducive to buying as possible by ensuring that clothes
are displayed in their best possible light.

There should be plenty of large, high-quality mirrors. A little ante-
room outside the dressing rooms can be a good place for shoppers to
inspect the merchandise closely. Fresh flowers are a nice touch.

Customers hate to wait. The single most important factor in determining a shopper's opinion of the service he receives is waiting time.[25] When
people wait up to about a minute and a half, their sense of how much time
has passed is fairly accurate. Anything over this length distorts their
sense of time. If they wait two minutes, they say it has been three or four.
Waiting becomes a full-fledged activity of its own. Measures can be taken
to make waiting time seem less. Any interaction, human or otherwise,
makes a wait seem shorter. For example, the time a shopper spends waiting after an employee has initiated contact seems to go faster than time
spent waiting before that interaction takes place.[26] Simply acknowledging
that the shopper is waiting and offering some explanation for the delay
automatically relieves time anxiety.

The cash register/merchandise wrapping area is where customers are
separated from their money, which is a source of shopper anxiety. Most
retail stores do not make this zone exciting. Adding sound, light, and
color can do much to ease any anxiety felt in the financial transaction.

CUSTOMER Men shop differently than do women. Here are some of the differences:
SEGMENTS

How Men Shop
- ❖ Men always move faster through store aisles.
- ❖ Men spend less time looking. In one study reported by Underhill, 65
  percent of male shoppers who tried something on bought it, as

opposed to 25 percent of female shoppers. Men's dressing rooms should be clearly marked. If male shoppers have to search for dressing rooms, they may decide it is not worth it.

❖ Eighty-six percent of women look at price tags when they shop—only 72 percent of men do. Men are more easily upgraded to a more expensive item. It is almost as if they are so anxious to get out of the store that they will agree to anything.

❖ Conventional wisdom says, "Sell to the woman, close to the man." Men do not especially like the shopping experience, but they get a definite thrill from the experience of paying.

❖ Men hate to ask directions (just like when they drive!). They prefer to get information firsthand from written materials, instructional videos, or computer screens. Women, on the other hand, ask questions of employees.[27]

As noted earlier, how much customers buy is a direct result of how much time they spend in the store. When a woman is in a store with a man, she'll spend less time than when she is alone, with another woman, or with children.

How Women Shop

Compared to men, more women see shopping as a social activity.[28] They like to shop with friends. When two women shop together, they typically spend more time and money than women shopping alone. They also feel more comfortable being waited on by a woman.[29]

On the golf course, women need to dress conservatively for business while still maintaining an active look. Manufacturers are creating separates that women can wear on and off the course and get more value out of each piece. For the next few seasons, women's clothes will be characterized by:

❖ *Classic design*—Prep school, corporate, country club—the look is retro in feel but modern in design.

❖ *Brighter color*—Golfwear was dominated by earth tones coming into the 1990s. Some of the best new color pairings are the classics—navy and white, black and white, brights with neutrals, an overall neutral tone-on-tone.

❖ *High-tech fabrics*—Two fabrics dominate: microfiber and Tencel.

❖ *Texture*—The design is in the details. A subtle pattern may be woven into the fabric.

❖ *Pricing*—Price is still a sensitive issue in the golf market.[30]

What can a retail outlet do to take advantage of these characteristics? Here are some ideas:

- Customers can bring a friend to get a discount.
- Have a Women's Department label.
- Go narrow and deep with product selection.
- Stock specialty items such as gold earrings, necklaces, golf lapel pins, and mini golf balls for impulse sales and for holidays.
- Design a merchandising program around the store's spring fashion show. Describe the lines to be presented and list each date-of-purchase availability.
- Employ an apparel consultant to cultivate and build the shop's ladies' apparel business.
- Create exciting, well-organized, and visual displays.
- Offer seating areas just outside dressing rooms to allow for more relaxed try-ons and assessments.
- Have a café on the premises that allows customers to shop, then take a break without leaving sight of the selling floor. (Be sure that everything in the café is for sale.)[31]

Women are more demanding of the shopping environment than are men. For example, women do not like to examine merchandise displayed below waist level. Lowering previously elevated sets of clubs to waist level makes for easier access. Sales will increase because women can now see better and reach the merchandise.

If they can stand at the corner of a counter, where they can wrap themselves around the angle and nestle a bit, women are more likely to buy than if they have to stand just a few feet away along the main stretch of the counter. Nooks and crannies and cul-de-sacs are good for uninterrupted shopping. The narrower the quarters, the less time a woman will spend shopping. Almost two-thirds of women who buy something read at least one product package. Reading takes time; time requires space.[32]

Older Shoppers The graying of America has implications for retailers. Reading is more difficult for older shoppers. Type must be larger for them to read easily. As the cornea yellows with age, the difference between blue and green becomes harder to see. Yellow should be avoided, as everything looks a little yellow. Older people see a lot more black, white, and red and a lot less of other colors. The typical 50-year-old's retinas receive about one-quarter less light than the average 20-year-old's. Stores must be more brightly lit than they are now.

Children   If a store is set up to be unwelcoming to children, parents will get the message and stay away. Consider the needs of the child:

❖ Put merchandise where they can see it and reach it.
❖ Childproof the store the same way as a home.
❖ If the parent's sustained attention is required, someone must find a way to divert the attention of a restless child.
❖ Design a good area for children. Sight lines must allow parents to see their children at all times.[33]

Generation X   One segment of the golf market that might surprise some is Generation X. These young people are playing golf because so many of their role models—from Michael Jordan to Eddie Van Halen—are seen on the links. They are a "mix of anti-establishment rebels, country-club legacies, beginners, hackers and sandbaggers—low handicappers in baggy pants, t-shirts and goatees."[34] Although their look is logo-driven, they do not want to appear as if they have just walked off a golf course. They like the specialty-store environment if it is merchandised in an up-to-date manner.

PROFIT RATIOS   The two measures of sales analysis are productivity and merchandise.[35]

Sales Analysis   Productivity analysis measures sales relative to the space allocated to the goods. Retailers can measure the sales productivity of the entire shop, separate product categories, or individual items. Merchandise analysis, on the other hand, measures sales across departments or product categories without regard to floor space. It might, for example, compare product movement in golf shoes versus shirts.

Sales productivity starts with a measurement of the sales area used to sell goods. This is defined as the "open floor area that is devoted to the sale of goods, including all areas that are open to the customer."[36] The total sales area is then divided into the sales areas of each department. This yields the measure of sales per square foot. Comparing these data to those of other stores is useful when repeated over time. Various comparisons are possible:

❖ this month's sales to last month's
❖ this month's sales to the same month's last year
❖ sales on a rolling basis
❖ the most recent 12 months' sales to the 12 months prior to that[37]

Another useful figure is gross margin dollars per square foot. Gross margin is the difference between what was paid for the merchandise and its selling price.[38] High retail prices result in a higher sales volume per square foot. Lower-priced items may, however, cost less. Compare, for example, $50 in gross margin on a $200 retail price for one item and $55 in gross margin on a $100 item. If both items sell at the same rate and take up roughly the same space, the first item has higher sales per square foot, while the other yields higher gross margin dollars per square foot.

Another comparison involves share of space versus share of business. This measurement determines which items are and are not pulling their weight. The sales of one department are calculated as a percentage of total store sales and compared with the department's square footage as a percentage of the total store space. If a department has a significantly lower share of sales than share of space, it may be time to consider a space reallocation.

Price Zones   Price zones can also be analyzed. Each product category carried has several ranges of price points, each one of which is designed to appeal to a particular segment of a store's customers:

- ❖ *promotion zone*—low-end merchandise at low prices
- ❖ *volume zone*—middle price range
- ❖ *prestige zone*—high-status, high-end merchandise[39]

Many golf shops offer only one price zone in each product category. As such, selection becomes a crucial decision. The goal is to meet the needs of each customer who walks into the shop. The key is to match what the customer wants to spend with the price zones offered.

ECOLODGES

From the very beginning, I believed that ecotourism development was a pure art form, where the designer arranged all the indigenous cultural and natural assets into a guest experience.
—STANLEY SELENGUT
The Ecolodge Sourcebook

A specialized form of resort lodge is the ecolodge. An ecolodge or nature-based lodge is defined as a "nature-dependent tourist lodge that meets the philosophy and principles of ecotourism."[40]

TRADITIONAL   The table on the facing page illustrates some of the differences between
LODGES VERSUS   traditional lodges and ecolodges:
ECOLODGES

Traditional	Ecolodge
❖ Luxury	❖ Comfortable basic needs
❖ Generic style	❖ Unique character style
❖ Relaxation focus	❖ Activity/educational focus
❖ Facility-based activities	❖ Nature/recreation-based activities
❖ Enclave development	❖ Development integrated with local environment
❖ Group/consortium ownership common	❖ Individual ownership common
❖ Profit maximization based on high guest capacity, services, and prices	❖ Profit maximization based on strategic design, location, low capacity, services, and prices
❖ High investment	❖ Moderate/low investment
❖ Key attractions are facility and surroundings	❖ Key attractions are surroundings and facility
❖ Gourmet meals, service, and presentation	❖ Good/hearty meals and service, cultural influence
❖ Marketed within chain	❖ Marketed independently
❖ Guides and nature interpreters minor feature or nonexistent	❖ Guides and interpreters focus of operation

Ecolodges tend to be found in places such as Belize, Costa Rica, Ecuador, Peru, Brazil, Australia, Kenya, and South Africa. Ideally, they are designed using natural sustainable materials that are collected on the site. The objective is for ecolodges to generate their own energy from renewable sources and manage their own waste. Ecolodges blend in with the natural surroundings and build on and accentuate the local culture.

OPERATIONS In one survey of 28 ecolodges in nine countries, management indicated the key to success was being located in an area of outstanding natural beauty. Cultural attractions, while important, took second stage to nature. Most ecolodges feature a lodge and cottage facilities. A restaurant and bar are located in the lodge. In many cases, a patio is featured as a key attraction.

Cottages are private and designed so as to encourage air flow in order to reduce the need for electricity and cooling. Ecolodges are the equivalent of a one- or two-star urban hotel. Typically, they are small, with a capacity of around 24 guests. This provides for a 15-person group with a guide and a few places left over for independent travelers.

quick getaways 9.4

Ecotourism for the Industry

The Tourism Industry Association of Canada developed a code of ethics for the ecotourism industry:

- Commit to excellence in the quality of tourism and hospitality experiences provided to guests through a motivated and caring staff.
- Encourage an appreciation of, and respect for, our natural, cultural and aesthetic heritage among guests, staff, and stakeholders, and within our communities.
- Respect the values and aspirations of our host community.
- Strive to achieve tourism development in a manner that harmonizes economic objectives with the protection and enhancement of our natural, cultural, and aesthetic heritage.
- Be efficient in the use of all natural resources, manage waste in an environmentally responsible manner, and strive to eliminate or minimize pollution in all its forms.

Source: Tourism Industry Association of Canada, *Code of Ethics and Guidelines for Sustainable Tourism* (Ottawa, Ontario: Tourism Industry Association of Canada, n.d.).

Meals, often included in the package price, are homestyle and reflective of the local culture. The atmosphere is friendly and relaxed. Educational opportunities are often stressed, although, as one New Zealand operator noted, "We still make more money out of beer sales than we do out of guided walks."

TRENDS Operators tend to specialize in order to remain distinctive. Some ecolodge operators are improving their educational activities; others are emphasizing guest activities that relate to the natural environment. While ownership has traditionally been independent and small scale, corporate ownership is becoming more common. The P&O line is getting involved in Australia and Hilton in Kenya.

quick getaways 9.5

U.S. Virgin Islands National Park

After conservation-minded authorities running the U.S. Virgin Islands National Park on St. John objected to New York City developer Stanley Selengut's plans to build a resort on privately owned land inside the park's boundaries, Selengut turned instead to a more ecologically conscious approach. He scuttled his plans and put up a series of modest, wood-framed tent-cottages resting on simple platforms that barely disturbed the steep hillside on which they sat. Walkways connecting the cottages were raised so plants could grow underneath.

Visitors at Maho Bay Camps share communal toilets and cold-water showers, but pay just $90 a night. In 1993, Maho Bay's net income was close to $750,000 on $3 million in revenue.

Emboldened by his first foray into ecotourism, Selengut, in October 1993, opened Harmony, an environmentally correct resort that offers guests more traditional amenities. On the hill next to Maho Bay Camps, Harmony's four two-story villas are made almost entirely from recycled products. So far, Selengut has spent $600,000 on Harmony's construction.

Source: Suzanne Oliver, "Eco-Profitable," *Forbes* 153, no. 13 (20 June 1994): 110.

Question: Will ecolodges become increasingly popular development options? Justify your answer.

SUMMARY

This chapter concentrated on what makes condominiums, vacation ownership, and timeshare properties different from traditional hotels. In both design and operations, their significant differences are based on the arrival, stay, and departure patterns of the resort guest. Retail operations take on added significance for resort properties. Finally, the recent interest in ecolodges is expected to increase.

ENDNOTES

1. Arthur H. Simons and George Leposky, *AEI Resource Manual* (Washington, D.C.: American Resort Development Association, 1994), 10.
2. Ibid., 11.
3. Material for "Reservations and the Front Desk" was drawn from Robert A. Gentry, Pedro Manoki, and Jack Rush, *Resort Condominium and Vacation Ownership Management* (Lansing, Mich.: Educational Institute of the American Hotel and Motel Association, 1999), 49–64.
4. Material for "Housekeeping" was drawn from Gentry, Manoki, and Rush, *Resort Condominium Management*, 67–74.
5. Material for "Maintenance and Engineering" was drawn from Gentry, Manoki, and Rush, *Resort Condominium Management*, 88–103.
6. National Golf Foundation, *Operating and Financial Profiles of 18-hole Golf Facilities in the U.S.: Resort Facilities* (Jupiter, Fla.: National Golf Foundation, 1995), 5.
7. Adapted from National Ski Areas Association, *Economic Analysis of United States Ski Areas* (Englewood, Colo.: National Ski Areas Association, 1999), 34–35.
8. Paco Underhill, *Why We Buy: The Science of Shopping* (New York: Simon & Schuster, 1999), 184.
9. Material for "Layout and Design" was drawn from Underhill, *Why We Buy*, 37–80.
10. "New Consumer Spending Study Offers Multitude of Insights," *Golf Market Today* (May/June 1995): 1ff.
11. Steve Pike, "Competition Heating Up," *Golf Shop Operations* (May 1966): 35ff.
12. Eileen Rafferty Broderick, "A Very Fine Line: How to Strike the Balance Between Golfwear, Retail," *Golf Shop Operations* (March 1994).
13. Pike, "Competition Heating Up," 35ff.
14. "'95 Money Leaders," *Golf Pro* (May 1996): 21ff.
15. Steve Pike, "Getting the Message," *Golf Shop Operations* (May 1995): 27ff.
16. Underhill, *Why We Buy*, 62.
17. Ibid., 66.
18. Ibid., 70.
19. Ibid., 79.
20. Ibid., 84.
21. Ibid., 158.
22. National Golf Foundation, *The Retail Side of Golf: Trends and Techniques* (Jupiter, Fla.: National Golf Foundation), 53–68.
23. Pike, "Getting the Message," 27ff.
24. Underhill, *Why We Buy*, 159, 171.
25. Ibid., 189.
26. Ibid., 190.

27. Ibid., 98-111.
28. Ibid., 115.
29. Bob Seligman, "More Than an Afterthought," *Golf Product News* (October 1995): 16ff.
30. Eileen Rafferty Broderick, "Golfwear Goes Classic," *Golf World*, 29 September 1995, pp. 32-34.
31. Underhill, *Why We Buy*, 116.
32. Ibid., 118.
33. Ibid., 143-150.
34. Liz Lippincott, "Fishing for the New Breed," *Golf Pro* (July 1995): 24.
35. Michael L. Russell, "How Sales Analysis Can Help Maximize Retail Profitability," *Golf Market Today* (March/April 1993): 10-12.
36. Ibid.
37. Ibid.
38. Seligman, "More Than an Afterthought," pp. 16ff.
39. Ibid.
40. Material for "Ecolodges" was drawn from Donald E. Hawkins, Megan Epler Wood, and Sam Bittman (eds.), *The Ecolodge Sourcebook for Planners and Developers* (North Bennington, Vt.: Ecotourism Society, 1995), x-xii.

Chapter 10
RESORT ECONOMICS

INTRODUCTION

The variables involved in determining the break-even point for a resort are explored using a ski area as an exemplar. Financial statements are then analyzed for resorts in general and for ski areas, golf resorts, and destination resort marinas in particular.

ECONOMIC FEASIBILITY

The objective of an economic evaluation is to express development design concepts in financial terms to visualize the economic characteristics of the project, and to assess the probability of success.

—TED FARWELL
A Manual for Preparing Break-Even Analyses

CRITICAL VARIABLES   Four critical variables determine whether or not a resort will make a profit: capacity, the length of the season, the amount of capital investment, and the amount of revenue per visit.[1]

A ski area is used as an exemplar. However, the principles involved are true for any resort property.

Ski Area Capacity   While guidelines are given relative to ski area capacity, the number of variables that go into determining a range of figures is so great that a certain degree of subjectivity is unavoidable. It is quite common for a developer to identify the number of skiers required to break even and earn a specified return on investment and to make development and design decisions in order to achieve that financial result.

Capacity can be viewed in a number of ways. Physical and ecological capacity takes into account the physical and ecological limitations of the site. Social or normal capacity is where the majority of skiers do not consider the area overcrowded. Maximum capacity is when no more visitors can be served. The upper limit for safety can occur when a single element is at maximum use; for example, the amount of parking available limits the number of people who have access to the ski area. Comfortable carrying capacity is "the maximum number of participants who can utilize the facility at any one time without excessive crowding and without damaging the quality of the environment."[2]

Ski area capacity is, therefore, a measure of three factors: the capacity of the terrain, the uphill capacity, and the capacity of the supporting facilities.[3] Terrain capacity is affected by the steepness of the slope, the way the trail is designed, the amount and quality of the snow cover, the way the slopes are groomed, and the skill level of the skiers.[4] Skier skill level also affects the safety of the slope for all. Because more advanced skiers prefer fewer other skiers on the slopes, density decreases as slope, speed, and ability increase.

Uphill capacity is a measure of the number of vertical transport feet per hour needed. Skiers have a finite capacity for skiing per day. That capacity is based on their physical condition and their ability level. It might, for example, be assumed that beginners will ski for five hours a day and more advanced skiers for six hours a day. Thus, an area that targets advanced skiers will need more uphill capacity per hour than will one that targets beginners.

Finally, the capacity of the supporting facilities contributes to overall capacity. Facilities in a ski area base lodge comprise:

- ❖ food service
- ❖ rest rooms
- ❖ first aid
- ❖ ski school
- ❖ retail sales
- ❖ rental shop
- ❖ lockers
- ❖ ticket sales
- ❖ employee lockers
- ❖ bar/lounge
- ❖ nursery
- ❖ storage

Length of the Season For ski areas, the main determinants of the length of the season are weather and climate.[5] Ski areas measure season length in terms of skiing periods. One period is equivalent to seven hours. Thus, a resort that is open from 9:00 a.m. until 11:00 p.m. includes two skiing periods—one day and one night.

A growing number of ski areas now use machine snow in an attempt to lengthen the season. Ski area capacity multiplied by the length of the ski season is equal to capacity skier visits—the maximum number of skier visits the resort can handle.

❖ The economics of a short season. The Tran, Jackson Hole, Wyoming. [Source: Design Workshop, Inc.]

Capital Investment The third critical variable is the amount of capital investment needed to develop the ski area. The capital budget is highly specific to design and site. Here are the major cost elements that go into a ski resort:

- ❖ ski lifts
- ❖ ski slope and trail construction
- ❖ snow maintenance equipment
- ❖ snowmaking equipment
- ❖ day use lodge building
- ❖ maintenance center
- ❖ furniture and fixtures
- ❖ base area equipment
- ❖ parking
- ❖ power and slope lighting
- ❖ water and sewer
- ❖ site development

❖ planning

❖ financing

❖ land

❖ access roads[6]

Revenue per Skier Visit   The final variable is the amount of revenue generated from each skier visit. Determine this figure by totaling all revenue and dividing it by the number of skier visits. Revenue is generated from ski lift tickets and supporting services.

How well the resort does in maximizing these four variables ultimately determines its economic success.

ANALYZING FINANCIAL STATEMENTS

> *[A sound cost accounting system] . . . not only reveals our mistakes—it shows us who's doing a good job!*
> —BROR R. CARLSON
> *Managing for Profit*

INDUSTRY DIFFERENCES   The reader will note variations in the ways the financial information for ski areas, golf courses, and marinas is presented. Each industry has slightly different ways of presenting its financial information and deciding which ratios are important. Some financial problems are, however, common to all businesses. This section identifies the major potential problems and suggests appropriate causes and solutions.[7]

Low Solvency and/or Liquidity   Solvency and liquidity are measures of the business's ability to meet its short-term obligations. Problems with solvency are indicated by a low current ratio, while liquidity problems are identified with a low quick ratio. The causes and potential solutions are the same. Problems occur when current liabilities are too high and/or when short-term funds are used to fund long-term assets. The solution is to move some short-term liabilities to the long term or to sell and lease back some fixed assets.

High Debt to Equity   The relationship between debt and equity is a measure of how the business is financed. Businesses use the equity in the resort to secure outside debt, thereby leveraging the business. When the debt load is heavy, the business can grow in good economic times, but it is more difficult to repay the debt in an economic downturn. Net worth being too low or liabilities being too high causes a high debt-to-equity ratio. Capital can be added by

quick getaways 10.1

The Economics of Ecotourism

Setting tourism fees for ecotourism projects is done in four steps:

1. Choose the objective.
2. Estimate costs and revenue.
3. Set prices.
4. Monitor and adjust.

If the objective is cost recovery, ask if demand is great enough for revenues to cover costs. If it is, the price is set to generate revenue equal to costs. If not, ask if objectives are important enough to justify operating at a loss. If they are, fees can be set to maximize revenues subject to the constraints of the other objectives. Additional funding can then be sought based on benefits from other objectives. If no other worthy objectives exist, ecotourism opportunities should not be offered.

If the objective is profit maximization, determine if demand is *at least* great enough to cover costs. If the answer is *yes*, prices are set to generate the highest level of profits. If, on the other hand, the answer is *no*, the question of other objectives important enough to justify operating at a loss comes into play as before.

Finally, if other objectives exist, a determination is made as to whether revenue will at least cover costs. If it will, the goal becomes cost recovery or profit maximization. If not, and no other objectives are important enough to justify operating at a loss, the ecotourism opportunities are not offered. If other objectives do exist, fees are set to maximize revenues subject to the constraints of the other objectives.

Source: Kreg Lindberg and Donald E. Hawkins (eds.), *Ecotourism: A Guide for Planners and Managers* (North Bennington, Vt.: Ecotourism Society, 1993), 98.

selling stock, or company growth can be slowed and profits used to reduce liabilities instead of buying additional assets.

Low Operating Income Revenue less operating expenses equals operating income. Low operating income results from insufficient revenue and/or costs that are too high relative to the level of revenue. Low revenues can come from pricing the services at a level lower than the market is willing to pay or at a level that does not cover costs. The product mix may be wrong. Some departments produce a greater operating profit than others. Enhance operating income by pushing sales of the high-margin departments.

Because labor costs are such a major factor in running a department, increased costs are likely the result of low employee productivity—too many employees are scheduled for the amount of revenue being generated.

Low Revenue to Employee   The importance of controlling labor costs is noted above. The ratio of revenue to employee is a measure of how efficiently employees are scheduled relative to the volume of business being generated. When this ratio is too low, the number of employees must be reduced or revenue must be increased.

Low Pretax Profit Margin   Low profits are caused by an operating income that is too low to meet the level of overhead that must be paid. If the overhead cannot be reduced, the only other solution is to increase revenue to raise the operating income. This assumes, of course, that the level of operating expenses is appropriate for the level of sales.

Low Revenue to Assets   This ratio is a measure of how well management uses the assets under its control to generate revenues. A low ratio means that revenues are too low or assets are too high. Perhaps unused property can be sold or fixed assets can be sold and leased back. If not, attention must focus on increasing sales.

Low Return on Assets   A low return on assets means that net profits are too low and/or assets are too high. Net profits can be increased by some combination of increasing revenue and lowering costs. The strategies noted above for reducing assets might also be appropriate here.

Low Return on Investment   When the return on investment is low, the net profit is too low and/or the net worth is too high. Profit can be increased in ways noted above. Expanding the business using borrowed funds can reduce the relative net worth.

Low Accounts Receivable Turnover   This ratio is too high because accounts receivable is too high. The result can be a strain on cash flow. The solution is to reduce accounts receivable.

quick getaways 10.2

Analyzing Financial Statements for Country Clubs

Here, according to the Club Managers Association of America, are 1997 financial data about country clubs:

- food and beverage sales $3.66 billion
- number of club employees 268,109
- number of club members 2.03 million
- average country club food costs $332,489
- average country club beverage costs $ 86,570
- average country club hourly labor costs $403,052
- average country club food and beverage salaries $182,232
- average country club food revenue $626,599
- average country club revenue per cover by meal:
  - ❖ breakfast $ 5
  - ❖ lunch $ 7
  - ❖ formal dinner $20
  - ❖ informal dinner $13

Source: Ira Appel, "Getting into the Swing," *Restaurants USA* (June/July 1998) vol. 18: 35–38.

Question: How does the profitability of country clubs compare to that of other types of resorts?

SKI AREAS

The wise man understands equity; the small man understands only profits.

—CONFUCIUS
Analects

OPERATING CHARACTERISTICS

Recent years have seen a marked trend in the way ski area improvements are financed.[8] Increasingly, equity funds are available through the issuance of common stock from publicly held companies. Using this source of money, rather than debt, has meant that the net worth of ski areas has continued to grow. Money has increasingly been spent on product and quality upgrades—food and beverage, rental and retail, children's pro-

❖ Additional source of revenue.

grams, etc.—rather than on increasing the capacity of the resort. The effort has been to increase revenues from nonskiing activities by improving the overall ski experience for those who visit. As a result, for the first time ever, lift ticket revenues in the 1997–1998 season represented less than 50 percent of total revenues per skier visit.

To reduce dependence on Mother Nature, ski areas have increasingly turned to snowmaking equipment. From the years 1980 to 2000, the percentage of ski areas using snowmaking equipment has increased from less than 50 percent to 84 percent. At the same time, the percentage of ski areas offering night skiing has increased from 35 percent to 45 percent.[9] Both strategies are ways of increasing capacity. Less than 20 percent of skiable acreage nationally is covered by snowmaking equipment. However, the proportion varies regionally. Because total skiable acreage and reliance on natural snow is less in the Northeast, Southeast, and Midwest, ski areas in these regions use snowmaking more than in the Rocky Mountains and Pacific West, as shown in the following chart:

	Snowmaking		Night Skiing
Region	Percent of Skiable Acres Covered	Percent of Ski Areas Equipped	Percent of Ski Areas Offering
Southeast	96	100	89
Midwest	89	92	92
Northeast	81	100	44
Rocky Mountains	14	87	20
Pacific West	6	57	36[10]

As a rule, the largest resorts, as measured by vertical transport feet per hour (VTF/hour, the vertical rise of a lift multiplied by the lift manufacturer's rated skiers-per-hour capacity), offer the most acreage, skier capacity, beds in base area and within a 10-mile radius, and average annual visits.[11] However, the proportion of total terrain given over to snowmaking, the availability of night skiing, and the proportion of beginner terrain are inversely related to VTF/hour.

BALANCE SHEET Investigation of the balance sheet is useful in determining the ability of the industry to meet short- and long-term debt obligations. The balance sheet also indicates the way the resort is financed.

Net Working   Several ratios are of particular interest. Net working capital is defined as
Capital   current assets less current liabilities. A current asset is something the ski
area has or is owed that can be converted into cash within a year. A current
liability is something that is owed and that must be repaid within a year.
The difference is a measure of how much working capital is available for
unexpected expenditures. For the 1997–1998 season, resorts in the Northeast and Pacific West reported negative balances, while all other U.S.
regions reported surpluses. The larger resorts reported larger positive
balances. Balances ranged from plus $2 million to a negative $1.2 million,
with an average plus balance of slightly less than $200,000.

Current Ratio   The current ratio—current assets divided by current liabilities—is a measure of the resort's ability to meet short-term obligations. The ski industry
has a history of not being very liquid (current assets are greater than current liabilities). As such, current ratios are typically less than for other
capital-intensive industries. In 1997–1998, the current ratio was 1.05
overall. It was highest in the Southeast (1.52) and Rocky Mountains (1.28)
and lowest in the Pacific West (0.45).[12]

Debt Ratio   Resorts are financed through debt (liabilities) or owners' investment or
common stock (equity). Debt and equity ratios measure the extent to
which the business is leveraged. Lenders like to see significant equity in a
business. They view it as a measure of how committed the owners are to
the successful operation of the business. At the same time, a business
financed entirely through owner's equity is not utilizing outside financing
that might be available to allow the business to expand.

Percent liabilities, or debt ratio, is total debt divided by total assets. In
1997–1998, this ratio averaged 37 percent, down from 42 percent the previous year. It was highest in the Midwest (60 percent) and lowest in the
Pacific West (25 percent). The upside, percent equity, increased from 58
percent in 1996–1997 to 63 percent the following year. In recent years, the
ski resort industry has seen a number of mergers and acquisitions that
have resulted in money being raised through the sale of common stock.
This, in turn, has produced an increase in the percentage of assets
financed through equity.

INCOME   An income statement for a typical North American ski area is shown in
STATEMENT   Figure 10.1. The income statement indicates three major levels of analysis
and management responsibility.

REVENUE (PERCENT)	
Tickets	48
Lessons	9
Food and beverage	13
Ski equipment/clothing	6
Rental equipment	4
Accommodations/lodging	8
Real estate	6
Miscellaneous	6
TOTAL	**100**

EXPENDITURES (AS A PERCENTAGE OF TOTAL REVENUE)		
Direct Operating Costs		
Cost of goods	11	
Direct labor	23	
Other direct operating costs	15	
Payroll taxes	4	
Property operation	3	
TOTAL OPERATING COSTS	**56**	
Total Operating Income		**44**
Undistributed Expenses		
General and administration	8	
Marketing/advertising	6	
Insurance	2	
TOTAL UNDISTRIBUTED EXPENSES	**16**	
Gross Operating Profit		**28**
Occupation Costs		
Land use fees	1	
Property/other taxes	2	
Miscellaneous	1	
Depreciation	10	
Operating leases	1	
Interest	4	
TOTAL OCCUPATION COSTS	**19**	
Profit Before Taxes		**9**

❖ FIGURE 10.1 Income statement for North American ski areas. [Source: Adapted from National Ski Areas Association, *Economic Analysis of United States Ski Areas* (Englewood, Colo.: National Ski Areas Association, 1999), 34–35.]

Revenue	100 percent
less total direct operating expenses	(56)
totals total operating income	44
less undistributed expenses	(16)
totals gross operating profit	28
less occupation costs	(19)
totals profit before taxes	9

Direct expenses are those that can be attributed directly to an operating department. The cost of food and beverage is one example. Individual departmental managers can be held responsible for the operating results—revenue and expenditures—for their specific department. At the next level are undistributed expenses, such as marketing, which cannot be charged directly to one particular department. Their impact is felt by, and charged to, all operating departments.

Subtracting both direct and undistributed expenses from total revenue results in a gross operating profit. This is really management's bottom line in that a general manager (GM) has control over expenses above gross operating profit but has little or no influence over expenses below gross operating profit. These items, such as interest and depreciation, are usually determined by owners or at a level far above the GM.

Revenue   The income statement is an indication of the revenues, expenditures, and resultant profit or loss of the resort. As noted earlier, lift ticket revenue, as a percentage of total revenue, has been in decline in recent years and now represents less than half of all revenue generated. It remains, however, the largest source of revenue by far. Percentages vary from year to year, but a typical breakdown of sources of revenue looks like this:

Source of revenue	Percent of total revenue
Lift tickets	47
Food and beverage	13
Lessons	9
Accommodations and lodging	8
Real estate	6
Ski equipment and clothing	6
Rental equipment	4
Other	6[13]

These percentages vary by region. Lift tickets as a percentage of total revenue is greatest in the Pacific West and lowest in the Southeast, where food and beverage is of greater importance than the national average. Lessons account for a greater percentage of total revenue in the Rocky Mountains. The Midwest and Southeast cater to high proportions of new skiers—hence equipment rental plays a significant role for their ski areas. Interestingly, these two regions have relatively strong percentages in the area of accommodations and lodging revenues, with the Pacific West lagging behind all other areas. The Rocky Mountains led all others in real estate revenues as a percentage of total revenue.

In general, the larger areas get higher-than-average proportions of revenue from lessons, real estate sales, accommodations, and ski equipment and clothing, while the smaller areas have higher percentages from food and beverage, rental equipment, and accommodations and lodging.[14] The proportionate revenue from lessons is relatively high for both small and large areas and low for midsized resorts. Small areas specialize in introductory lessons, while the larger areas cater not only to beginning skiers but also have special clinics and private lessons for more experienced skiers.

Expenses   As with revenues, proportions vary from year to year. Here is a typical pattern of expenditures:

Expense category	Percent of total revenue
Direct labor*	23
Other direct	15
Cost of goods sold (F&B and retail)	11
Depreciation	10
General and administrative overhead	8
Marketing/advertising	6
Interest	4
Payroll taxes	4
Property operations	3

*Direct labor includes the major operating departments—lift department, ski school, food service, bar, retail store, rental shop, accommodations, real estate, sports department, summer slide.[15]

Profit before taxes for North American ski areas is just under 10 percent of total revenue.

Operations Management   Direct labor accounts for most of the costs in running a ski area. It is the largest single cost item for almost every operating department. The ski school, food and beverage, and accommodations/lodging account for over a third of the entire labor cost of running the operation. Lift operations and lift maintenance account for just under 40 percent of the direct labor cost for mountain operations and slightly less than 10 percent of the labor cost for the entire ski area. Cost of goods sold is approximately 29 percent of sales for food and beverage and 47 percent for retail stores.[16]

A contribution analysis for the major operating departments is shown in Table 10.1. The contribution margin is equal to revenue minus the direct variable costs associated with that revenue. The contribution margin ratio is the contribution margin in dollars divided by the revenue. For example, the contribution margin for the ski school is the revenue generated from lessons ($1,452,000 in 1997–1998) less the direct costs of operating the ski school ($865,999 in 1997–1998), or $587,000. The contribution margin ratio is the contribution margin ($587,000) divided by the revenue ($1,452,000), or 40.4 percent. It can be seen that the contribution margins vary from 64.1 percent from rental to 22.6 percent for retail stores. The contribution margin ratio is a measure of how much an additional dollar in revenue contributes to paying off the fixed costs of the operation. Under the cost structure outlined in the table, for every dollar generated in ski rentals, 64.1 cents is contributed to paying off the fixed costs of running the resort. In contrast, the retail stores only contribute

❖ TABLE 10.1 Departmental Contribution Analysis for North American Ski Areas

Item	Department						
	Tickets	Ski School	F/B	Retail	Rental	Lodging	Real Estate
Revenue	100%	100%	100%	100%	100%	100%	100%
Cost of goods	n.a.	n.a.	28.7	47	58	n.a.	60.6
Direct labor	18.5	43.9	29	16	18.2	40.9	2.9
Payroll benefits	2.4	7.5	4	2.3	2.3	7.3	0.7
Workers compensation	0.8	n.a.	n.a.	n.a.	n.a.	n.a.	n.a.
Other direct	10.3	8.2	12.9	12.1	6.9	23.6	9.9
Electrical power	4.4	n.a.	n.a.	n.a.	n.a.	n.a.	n.a.
Total*	36.4	59.6	74.5	77.4	85.4	71.8	74.3
Contribution margin	63.6	40.4	25.5	22.6	64.1	28.2	25.7

*Total may not be the sum of the percentages because of rounding.

Adapted from National Ski Areas Association, *Economic Analysis of United States Ski Areas* (Englewood, Colo.: National Ski Areas Association, 1999), 32, 44.

22.6 cents to fixed costs for every dollar generated. Other things being equal, it is more profitable for the ski area to push additional sales in departments with higher contribution margin ratios—here, rental, lift tickets, and ski school.

CRITICAL RATIOS   The ski industry has developed various critical ratios to help measure performance.[17] Viewed over a number of years, these ratios provide a moving picture of industry trends.

Debt to Cash Flow   Long-term debt divided by before-tax cash flow is a measure of the number of years required at existing levels of cash flow to retire long-term debt. Before-tax cash flow consists of the profit or loss before taxes plus depreciation, which is a noncash expense.

In 1997–1998, this ratio was 2.1 years. The relatively strong season resulted in increased skier visits, which, in turn, increased cash flow. Additionally, more areas are using equity rather than debt to finance expansion. The result of both these factors is a smaller ratio than in previous years. The improvement was most strongly felt in the Pacific West and, to a lesser extent, in the Rocky Mountains.

Operating Profit on GFA   Dividing the operating profit or loss by the gross fixed assets (GFA) allows for comparison of financially conservative areas that operate with little debt and those that are highly leveraged. Operating profit is defined as income before interest, taxes, depreciation, and operating lease expenses.

Profit, Before Tax, on Equity   This is a measure of the stockholder's or owner's return on investment. The standard measure of return on equity uses profits after taxes as the numerator. In the ski industry, many areas are part of larger corporations that consolidate the tax consequences of their ski area profits with those of the parent company. In addition, a number of areas carry forward loss balances to offset current profits. By assuming combined federal and state liability of 40 percent, the after-tax return can be determined by multiplying the before-tax figure by 60 percent.

In 1997–1998, while operating profit on GFA increased to 13.8 percent, profit before taxes on equity declined to 7.7 percent. The largest resorts showed the greatest increase in the former and the largest decrease in the latter over the previous year.

Capital Cost/ Capacity   The capital cost/capacity ratio is a relative measure of ski area attributes. It is calculated by dividing GFA by skier capacity.

quick getaways 10.3

Ski Areas: Managing the Economics

It takes a special kind of person to manage a ski area. The qualifications include:

- *Experience*—a minimum of six years in the business
- *Education*—a bachelor's degree in business or tourism/recreation
- *Communication skills*—to deal with the various publics of a ski area (employees, media, government agencies, etc.)
- *Leadership skills*—to conceptualize all parts of the ski area operation
- *Organizational skills*—to utilize available resources in the most efficient and effective ways

Source: Robert M. O'Halloran and Christopher Wong, "Ski Area Managers: A Profile," *Hospitality and Tourism Educator* 5, no. 3 (Fall 1993): 25–29.

Question: What additional qualifications are needed to effectively manage the finances in a ski area?

This ratio increases when investments in assets do not add to capacity. Examples include investments in restaurants, lodges, and rental shops. As noted elsewhere, recent years have seen an increase in investment in the overall ski experience rather than in the mountain per se. Thus, in 1997–1998, this ratio increased to $4349. The largest increase was noted in the Rocky Mountains, while the Midwest showed the greatest decrease over the previous year.

Total Revenue per Skier Visit

Total revenue per skier visit is the actual revenue generated by the ski area for each skier day. A skier day represents one skier visiting a ski area for all or part of a day. The ratio is determined by dividing total revenue from ski lift tickets and other ancillary operations by the number of skier visits.

In 1997–1998, the total revenue per skier visit increased to $47.87. While all regions experienced an increase over the previous year, the improvement was felt most strongly in the Southeast and was lowest in the Midwest.

Total Expenses
per Skier Visit
The actual expense for each skier day is calculated by dividing all expenses, including direct expenses, depreciation, leases, and interest, by the number of skier visits. The financial health of the ski area is linked to management's ability to budget expenses relative to forecasted revenues. Complicating the equation is the fact that ski areas are subject to factors, such as weather conditions, beyond the control of the resort. Constant monitoring of critical variables is essential to financial success. In 1997–1998, overall expenses increased to $47.99 from the previous season. The largest increase was felt in the Rocky Mountain region, while the Midwest showed the lowest average total expense per visit.

The key to profits is to increase revenue while reducing expenses or keeping them steady.

GOLF RESORTS

The only thing that matters is cash flow—not the cash flows they use today, but the old cash flows that laid out the source and application of funds—where it's coming from and where it's going and how much is left over. No company has ever gone bankrupt because it had a loss on its P&L.
—WILLIAM G. MCGOVERN
Chairman, MCI Communications Corp., *INC. Magazine*

OPERATING
CHARACTERISTICS
According to the National Golf Foundation (NGF), resort golf facilities are "operations located in a setting that usually includes other amenities (such as tennis, swimming, gym facilities, etc.) and are situated in conjunction with a hotel, motel, or other type of guest lodging."[18] Approximately 80 percent of resort golf facilities are daily fee operations.

For the purpose of their annual report, the NGF differentiates between the Frost Belt and the Sun Belt based on the length of the operating season.[19] The Sun Belt, which accounts for approximately 60 percent of all courses, covers the southern states in addition to the coastal regions of northern California, Oregon, and Washington. These courses are likely to be open year-round, while those in the Frost Belt, comprising about 40 percent of all courses and consisting of northern states in addition to the mountainous parts of southern states, usually shut down for a while during the winter.

Sun Belt courses have approximately 50 percent more rounds played than do Frost Belt courses. However, both regions indicate the same level of use—about 85 percent of capacity. Overall, one in eight rounds played were nine-hole rounds, slightly more in the Frost Belt and somewhat less in the Sun Belt. Just under 40 percent of all rounds were played on the weekend.

Playing fees in the Sun Belt tend to be higher than in the northern region. Though the size of the golf cart fleet is about the same in both regions, individual areas report different usage patterns. Over 40 percent of Sun Belt resorts require the use of a golf cart, about twice the rate for Frost Belt resorts. In fact, in the northern region, almost 40 percent of courses never require a golf cart. About three-quarters of all rounds played in the Frost Belt utilize golf carts, compared to over 90 percent in the Sun Belt. Frost Belt golfers prefer gas carts (78 percent), while Sun Belt golfers prefer electric carts (71 percent).

A majority of resorts report capital investment in the early 1990s. Anywhere from two-thirds to over 80 percent invested in clubhouse or maintenance buildings, golf course renovation, or maintenance equipment. A greater percentage of Frost Belt compared to Sun Belt resorts reported such investment.

In the Frost Belt, just under 60 percent of all courses irrigate using lakes and streams and 30 percent use wells. Over 233,000 gallons of water a day are used in the summer season, while over 83,000 are used in winter. In the Sun Belt, the figures for lakes and streams and wells are 44 percent and 40 percent respectively. The average course uses over 468,000 gallons per day during the summer season and over 168,000 during the winter season.

INCOME STATEMENT In 1994 (the last year for which data are available), U.S. golf resorts reported an average operating median (net operating income as a percentage of total revenues) of 28.9 percent.

Revenues The median revenues for U.S. golf resorts for 1994 are shown in Table 10.2. Most revenue comes from annual fees and green fees, almost twice as much as from the second most important source—golf cart rentals. Merchandise accounts for 13 percent of sales, while annual dues/passes and food and beverage each account for just over 10 percent of revenue.

❖ TABLE 10.2. U.S. Resort Golf Courses—Median Revenues by Category

Category	Revenue ($)	Percent
Green fees/Guest fees	500,000	41
Golf cart rentals	246,000	20
Total merchandise sales	159,000	13
Annual dues/passes	132,000	11
Food and beverage sales	130,000	11
Golf range	19,000	2
Other	30,000	3
Total*	**1,220,000**	101

*Does not total 100 percent because of rounding.

National Golf Foundation, *Operating and Financial Profiles of 18-hole Golf Facilities in the U.S.: Resort Facilities* (Jupiter, Fla.: National Golf Foundation, 1995), 5.

❖ TABLE 10.3 U.S. Resort Golf Courses—Median Expenses by Category

Category	Expense ($)	Percent
Maintenance payroll	197,000	23
Clubhouse payroll	144,000	17
Cost of merchandise sold	94,000	11
Cost of food and beverage	79,000	9
Lease expense/golf carts	71,000	8
General/Administration	57,000	7
Other	49,000	6
Property tax	41,000	5
Fertilizers/Chemicals	36,000	4
Utilities	32,000	4
Marketing	24,000	3
Facility insurance	19,000	2
Lease expense/equipment	11,000	1
Irrigation water	2,800	0.3
Total*	**856,800**	**100.3**

*Does not total 100 percent because of rounding.

National Golf Foundation, *Operating and Financial Profiles of 18-hole Golf Facilities in the U.S.: Resort Facilities* (Jupiter, Fla.: National Golf Foundation, 1995), 8.

The only noticeable difference between Sun Belt and Frost Belt resorts is that, in the former, golf cart rentals account for a greater percentage of total revenues. The top 5 percent of resorts by revenue differs in the distribution of revenues in two ways: golf cart rentals account for a smaller percentage of total revenues, and food and beverage accounts for a larger percentage.

Expenses Median expenses for resorts for 1994 are shown in Table 10.3. Payroll—maintenance and clubhouse—accounts for 40 percent of all costs. Labor costs appear to have a fixed component. They account for over half of all costs for courses in the bottom quarter for costs, 40 percent for the

quick getaways 10.4

Keeping Down Utility Costs at Golf Resorts

➤ Hire a firm that audits utilities. It will charge a percentage based on identified savings.

➤ Incorporate ceiling fans and portable fans.

➤ Use blinds and curtains for shading in the rooms.

➤ Keep the thermostat at a steady setting.

➤ Schedule regular maintenance on air conditioning systems.

➤ Put in gas water heaters.

➤ Set irrigation systems on timers for early-morning or late-evening waterings.

➤ In southern climates, install insulated doors and reflective heat barriers in attics.

➤ Install energy management thermostat systems that automatically adjust heat and air conditioning when the guest is out of the room.

Source: "How Do You Keep Your Utility Costs Down?" RCI Premier (January/February 2000): 18.

Question: What additional measures could be effective in reducing utility costs?

median, and 34 percent for resorts in the top 5 percent of costs. Cost of merchandise and cost of food and beverage are other major cost categories.

Resorts in the bottom 25 percent of costs have significantly less merchandise costs, an indication that they sell much less than other properties. Comparing Sun Belt and Frost Belt resorts, the former have much higher median costs in all areas except for maintenance payroll and lease expense for equipment. Most employees work in course maintenance, food and beverage, and the golf shop.[20]

DESTINATION RESORT MARINAS

I don't know any CEO who doesn't love numbers.
—JEFFREY SILVERMAN
CEO, Ply Gen Industries, Inc., *Nation's Business*

The International Marina Institute, in its annual benchmark study, defines a destination resort marina as "accessible both by land and water, [including] wet slips for visitors, hotel accommodations, restaurant facilities, swimming pool and other recreational amenities that create a resort atmosphere."[21]

OPERATING CHARACTERISTICS The occupancy rate for destination resorts is just under 80 percent. Forty percent of all slips are for boats in the 20-foot to 30-foot category. Craft in the 30-foot to 40-foot category make up an additional third of all slips. Only 6 percent of total berths are for boats longer than 60 feet. Spaces are rented monthly and range from $5.50 per linear foot for smaller slips to $9.31 for larger craft in uncovered slips.

BALANCE SHEET
Liquidity Current ratio, as noted above, is equal to current assets divided by current liabilities. For destination resorts, this ratio is 1.31, which is below the 2.0 generally accepted by the financial community.

Debt to Equity The debt-to-equity ratio compares the funds invested by creditors to those invested by owners. Lenders prefer this ratio to be less than 3.0. For destination resorts, it is a low 0.10. This indicates that, for every dollar of equity in the business, creditors are owed 10 cents. This is a very low ratio and indicates little use of outside financing.

Profit to Equity The net profit-to-equity ratio of 0.05 means that, for every dollar of equity owners have in the business, net profits are 5 cents. This measure of

❖ Improving
marina revenue.

return on investment indicates how the resort is situated for growth. It is generally accepted that net profit to owner's equity should be a minimum of 10 percent to provide for dividends and to fund future growth.

Return on Equity and Assets   The operating returns on equity and assets (operating income divided by equity or assets) are 12.3 percent and 12.7 percent respectively. The returns on equity and assets (pretax profits divided by equity or assets) are 4.7 percent and 4.3 percent respectively. The former means that every dollar invested by the owners in the business generates 4.7 cents in pretax profits. The latter is a measure of how well management uses the assets of the business to generate profits. When investors decide to put money into a business, they compare the rate of return they expect from the business to what they would achieve from another investment. The greater the risk involved, the greater the expected return. A return of 4.7 percent is low compared to the risk involved in operating a marina.

Sales to Assets   Total sales divided by total assets is a measure of sales generated from each dollar of assets. Resort marinas generate 58 cents in sales for every dollar invested in assets. A high ratio is a measure of how well assets are being utilized. A high ratio reduces total debt and produces better rates of return on owner's equity.

quick getaways 10.5

The Biggest Challenges Facing Resort Marinas

"What are the biggest challenges facing the marina industry?" When the International Marina Institute asked this question of marina operators, responses included:

- remaining profitable with increasing fixed expenses and mandated expenditures
- maintaining proper cash flows to meet operations while maintaining the required capital growth
- overhead costs—insurance, workers compensation, health insurance coverage
- increases in user fees
- continuing to improve and maintain the marina facilities
- service due to increased environmental costs
- escalating operational costs to satisfy both government and customer demands
- dredging to maintain facility

Source: International Marina Institute, *1998 Financial and Operational Benchmark Study for Marina Operators* (Nokomis, Fla.: International Marina Institute, 1998), 79–81.

Question: How do destination resort marina operators work to overcome the problems noted above?

Balance Sheet Management Resort marinas typically collect receivables (money owed to them) every 19 days, the same time it takes them to pay their suppliers. The former is a measure of how long the marina's cash is being used by its creditors, while the latter is a measure of how long the marina uses other people's money.

Inventory turns over every 62 days. This measure indicates how well inventory is being managed. The faster the inventory is turned over, the less money is tied up in short-term assets.

INCOME STATEMENT

The income statement for an average marina breaks down as follows:

Revenues	100 percent
less cost of goods sold	(20.3)
totals gross profit	79.7 (median 80.2)
less operating expenses	(51.4)
totals operating profit	28.3 (median 24.1)
less other expenses (depreciation and interest)	(13.1)
totals profit before tax	15.2 (median 6.4)
less taxes	(0.2)
totals net profit after tax	15.0 (median 6.4)

Revenues Three areas represent over half of all destination resort sales. Almost one-third of all revenue is derived from dockage fees. Sales of fuel and oil comprise an additional 10 percent of sales, while restaurants and concession sales account for slightly less than 9 percent of the total.

Expenses Labor expense is, by far, the largest operating expense. Together with employee benefits and taxes, it is almost 5 times as great as the next important cost category—utilities. Repairs and maintenance, rent and lease expenses, and insurance for business liability are also major expense categories.

Operations Management Various ratios are used to determine the operational efficiency of destination resort marinas. The ratios and 1997 figures follow:

average revenue per occupied slip	$ 2,202
average revenue per dry storage unit	$ 905
revenue per employee—high season	$ 95,791
revenue per employee—low season	$160,798
revenue per linear foot of wet moorage	$ 101

SUMMARY

Four critical variables determine whether or not a resort makes a profit: the capacity, the length of the season, the amount of capital investment, and the amount of revenue per visit. A relatively small number of ratios should be examined constantly for their potential to economically cripple a resort:

quick getaways 10.6

Determining the Economic Feasibility of Horse Parks

The Kentucky Horse Park hosts 60 equestrian events and 250 nonequine events a year. The construction was phased in over ten years. The land purchase of 1032 acres cost $3 million in 1972. Facilities constructed to date total $24 million. Annual operating costs total $5 million plus $500,000 of debt service. Annual revenue is $4 million. The Commonwealth of Kentucky subsidizes the Horse Park with over $1 million annually. It is estimated that the Horse Park generates $98.7 million in economic benefit each year.

The Horse Park of New Jersey is set up as a not-for-profit organization. The Horse Park leased the land from the federal Department of Agriculture for 25 years at $1 per year. The land is set within 5000 "green acres," of which it is required that 10 percent be in public recreational use. The horse park has been declared "agricultural," and a fund has been set up to promote horse recreation and racing. The fund receives a portion of horse racing receipts.

Stall rental, the primary source of revenue, is $25 a day, and rental of the facility is $1,000 per day.

The Virginia Horse Center was initiated as an economic development project within the local business community. The center is a not-for-profit entity for which the Commonwealth provides matching construction bonds. Total construction costs are $15 million, with annual operating costs of $2.4 million. The center is set on 60 acres and features ten event areas, including an indoor coliseum that seats 4200 and an outdoor grandstand that seats 2500. Six hundred permanent stalls are supplemented by 600 additional portable stalls and tents. Almost 100 events are scheduled a year.

Source: High Prairie Economic Benefit Analysis (Denver, Colo.: Design Workshop, 1999).

Question: How feasible is it to develop a horse park at a resort?

❖ low solvency and/or liquidity

❖ high debt to equity

❖ low operating income

❖ low revenue to employee

❖ low pretax profit margin

❖ low revenue to assets

❖ low return on assets

❖ low return on investment

❖ low accounts receivable turnover

Each type of resort prepares financial statements somewhat differently and considers some ratios more important than others. Resort managers must be aware of the financial ratios relevant to their business.

ENDNOTES

1. Ted Farwell, *A Manual for Preparing Break-Even Analyses* (Boulder, Colo.: Ted Farwell & Associates, 1993), 2.

2. Patrick L. Phillips, *Developing with Recreational Amenities: Golf, Tennis, Skiing, Marinas* (Washington, D.C.: Urban Land Institute, 1986), 126.

3. Farwell, *Preparing Break-Even Analyses*, 3.

4. Ibid.

5. Ibid., 5.

6. Ibid., 6.

7. International Marina Institute, *1998 Financial and Operational Benchmark Study for Marina Operators* (Nokomis, Fla.: International Marina Institute, 1998), A7.

8. National Ski Areas Association, *Economic Analysis of United States Ski Areas* (Englewood, Colo.: National Ski Areas Association, NSAA, 1999), 1.

9. Ibid., 9.

10. C.R. Goeldner, T.A. Buchman, G.S. Hayden, and C.E. DiPersio, *Economic Analysis of North American Ski Areas: 1976–93* (Boulder: Research Division, University of Colorado at Boulder, 1994), 7.

11. National Ski Areas Association, *Economic Analysis*, 7.

12. Ibid., 8.

13. Ibid., 20–21.

14. Ibid., 28.

15. Ibid., 29.

16. Ibid., 30.

17. Ibid., 32, 44, 45.

18. Ibid., 65–71.

19. National Golf Foundation, *Operating and Financial Profiles of 18-hole Golf Facilities in the U.S.: Resort Facilities* (Jupiter, Fla.: National Golf Foundation, 1995), iii.
20. Ibid., 8, 9.
21. Material for "Destination Resort Marinas" was drawn from International Marina Institute, *1998 Financial & Operational Benchmark Study for Marina Operators*, 5, 11, 14, 49–53, 64, 69.

Section 3
GUEST ACTIVITY PROGRAMMING

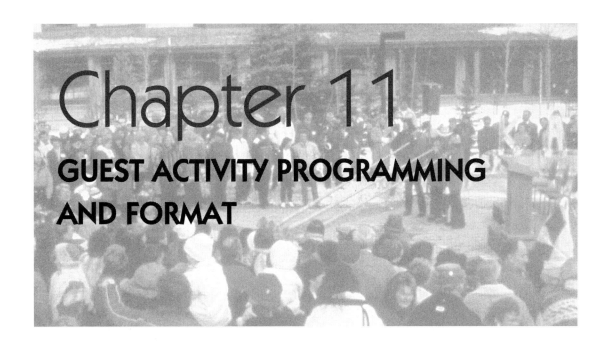

Chapter 11
GUEST ACTIVITY PROGRAMMING AND FORMAT

INTRODUCTION

Good programming does not just happen; it is carefully
planned for, thought about, and learned.
                                                —FARRELL AND LUNDEGREN
                          The Process of Recreation Programming: Theory and Technique

When guests are at a resort or on board ship for several days or weeks,
they expect the facility to cater to their need for something to do. At
resorts, this need is met by guest activity programs. What guests actually
do is called *recreation*. Recreation is "an activity that takes place during
one's free time, is enjoyable, freely chosen, and benefits the individual
emotionally, socially, physically, cognitively, and spiritually."[1] Note that
this definition contains a number of value-laden words. The activity
should be fun, it is something the guest chooses to do, and the guest
should receive some benefit from it. If these conditions are not adhered
to, the guests will not fully enjoy the activity and their stay will be less
enjoyable than it could be. For a guest to leave the resort or ship truly satisfied with the visit, it is imperative that the guest activity director take an
active role in planning activities to ensure that they provide the benefits
noted above. In this chapter, a model is suggested that will produce satisfied guests.

BENEFITS OF
GUEST ACTIVITY
PROGRAMS
The impact of a recreational or guest activity can extend far beyond the
immediate benefits.[2] Consider a couple hiking along a trail. They may
experience one or more of the following benefits:

- ❖ feeling good about getting exercise
- ❖ enjoyment of the sights and sounds of nature
- ❖ mental relaxation
- ❖ learning something about the natural environment
- ❖ feeling closer to their partner

Many of these initial benefits can extend into the long term for the
couple and even for society. Because they feel good about getting exercise,
the couple may commit to a program of exercise that improves their own
well-being while, in some way, lowering health care costs. Feeling relaxed
mentally might lead to increased performance and higher productivity
back on the job. Having learned something about the natural environment, they may return home with a greater stewardship ethic that will
result in greater care for the planet. Feeling closer to one's partner can

carry over beyond the vacation to the development of better problem solving within the relationship and a stabler family.

As noted above, to be satisfying, an activity must include:

❖ *Freedom*—Guests must be free to select the activities in which they want to participate.
❖ *Perceived competence*—Guests must be able to match their skill level to the activity such that they feel they can successfully participate.
❖ *Intrinsic motivation*—Truly satisfying activities are those that are chosen to satisfy an inner drive rather than to satisfy or impress others.
❖ *Locus of control*—Guests need to have some degree of control over the experience, be it in the selection of teammates or when or where the activity will take place.
❖ *Positive effect*—The result of a satisfying activity is that guests enjoy the experience after participating in it.[3]

APPROACH What are guest activity or recreation programs? "Recreation programs are purposeful interventions which are deliberately designed and constructed in order to produce certain behavioral outcomes."[4] The program is a means to the end—a satisfied and fulfilled guest.

The approach taken by guest activity directors and their staffs influences the design and management of the activities that are developed. The approach reflects the beliefs of the programmer and can encompass a continuum from the programmer as expert to the programmer as enabler.[5] At one end of the continuum, guest activity personnel see themselves as having specialized knowledge that enables them to determine what is best for the guest. At the other extreme is the idea that guests should participate in determining what is best for them—the guest activity director acts as a consultant to the guests to assist them in selecting activities. Somewhere in between is the marketing approach of offering people what they want.

Marketers are taught to take a guest-oriented approach to business. However, every business has to ask whether or not it is responsible for giving guests whatever they want, even if it is not in the best interest of the guest or society. Consider some of the programs offered at beach resorts during spring break. Many of these activities involve a great deal of alcohol and people in various stages of undress. They are undoubtedly popular. However, increasing numbers of people are asking whether or not the resort has an obligation to society that should be balanced against the satisfaction of guest wants. This concept of *social marketing* attempts to balance these ideas. This position moves the guest activity director farther along the continuum toward the idea of programmer as expert. These options are outlined below:

- ❖ *Programmer as expert*—The programmer knows what is best for the guest.
- ❖ *Social marketing*—The programmer attempts to balance the needs of the guest and those of society.
- ❖ *Marketing approach*—The programmer attempts to satisfy guests' needs.
- ❖ *Programmer as enabler*—The programmer acts as a consultant to guests in selecting activities.

quick getaways 11.1

Preparing for Spring Break

Here are some tips for preparing for spring break visitors:

- ✈ Inform spring breakers of the rules at check-in.
- ✈ Require a security deposit.
- ✈ Hire extra security.
- ✈ Have housekeepers give a daily report on all rooms and immediately report anything suspicious.
- ✈ Provide extra beach and pool chairs.
- ✈ Enforce house rules.

Source: "Don't Worry, Be Happy," *RCI Premier* (March/April 2000): 10.

Question: What are the advantages and disadvantages of targeting the spring break market?

MODEL Guest activity programming involves five steps:

1. Assess needs of guests.
2. Define objectives for the activities that will meet guest needs.
3. Perform cluster or activity analysis designed to meet the objectives.
4. Administer the activity.
5. Evaluate the experience with respect to its success in meeting guest needs.[6]

Evaluation of the activity might lead to a reassessment of any of the earlier steps. Development and operation of any program occurs within the context of, and is influenced by, external factors:

❖ *Historical influences*—the tradition and philosophy of the resort
❖ *Environmental influences*—time of the year, weather, etc.
❖ *Cultural influences*—ethnicity, age, and religion of the guests
❖ *Social influences*—fads, trends, news
❖ *Organizational influences*—values and mission of the company[7]

Finally, guests, staff, equipment, and facilities are brought together to deliver the guest experience. This model is illustrated in Figure 11.1 and serves as the basis for discussion in this chapter and the next.

❖ FIGURE 11.1
Guest activity programming model. [Adapted from Donald G. DeGraaf, Debra J. Jordan, and Kathy H. DeGraaf, *Programming for Parks, Recreation, and Leisure Services: A Servant Leadership Approach* (State College, Penna.: Venture Publishing, 1999), 52; and Patricia Farrell and Herberta M. Lundegren, *The Process of Recreation Programming: Theory and Technique*, 3rd ed. (State College, Penna.: Venture Publishing, 1991), 25.]

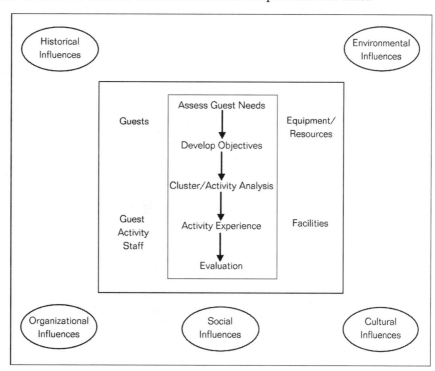

INFLUENCES

One way of getting an idea of our fellow-countrymen's miseries is to go and look at their pleasures.

—GEORGE ELIOT
As quoted in Felix Holt, *The Radical*

CULTURAL INFLUENCES

A basic premise of this chapter is that the activities people choose in their leisure time are adaptations to their sociocultural system. Obviously, attempting to categorize everyone in this way is risky. Two people of the same age and brought up in the same culture may very well prefer different recreational activities. However, by examining each factor separately, perhaps the reader will become more sensitive to influences on individual preferences and behavior.

The values of the culture determine which goals and behavior gain social approval or disapproval. For example, for many decades, a prevailing value in the United States was the so-called Protestant ethic. High value was placed on work relative to leisure, activity compared to idleness, and saving compared to spending. Activities were considered socially acceptable if they met these criteria. Time away from the job was intended to rejuvenate the individual so he could go back to work refreshed. Enjoyable activities could be justified if they prepared people for work or had a socially redeeming purpose. Thus, visiting museums or learning a new

❖ Everyone is different. Kananaskis Village, Alberta, Canada. [Source: Design Workshop, Inc.]

quick getaways 11.2

Top Ten Ways to Train for the Ski Season

10. Visit your local butcher and pay $30 to sit in the walk-in freezer for a half hour or so.
9. Afterwards, burn two $20 bills to heat up.
8. Soak your gloves in water. Store them in the freezer before you wear them.
7. If you wear glasses, smear a little glue on the lenses every morning.
6. Go to an ice rink. Walk across the ice for 40 minutes, wearing ski boots and carrying two pairs of skis, a bulky bag, and poles. Pretend you are looking for your car. Sporadically drop things and try to retrieve them without losing your grip on anything else.
5. Buy a new pair of gloves. Throw one of them away immediately.
4. Clip a lift ticket to the zipper of your jacket and ride a motorcycle fast enough to make the ticket lacerate your face.
3. Drive slowly for five hours—anywhere—as long as it's in a snowstorm and you're following an 18-wheeler.
2. Fill a blender with ice. Do not use the lid. Hit the pulse button and let the spray blast your face. Allow the ice to melt onto your clothes.
1. Dress up in as many clothes as you can. Now take them off again because you have to use the bathroom.

Source: Adapted from Clare Martin, "How to Train for the Ski Season," *Denver Post*, 12 December 1998, C2.

Question: What does this tongue-in-cheek list say about why people do and do not ski?

skill were acceptable; pursuing pleasure for its own sake was not. While many cultures and individuals still adhere to this concept, recent decades have seen growing acceptance of hedonism—the pursuit of pleasure for the sake of pleasure. Activities that were once taboo are now socially acceptable.

The United States places a relatively high value on the following:

- *Individualism*—The dominant culture places a great deal of emphasis on a high level of achievement motivation, which distinguishes it greatly from certain subcultures and cultures of other countries.
- *Precise reckoning of time*—Time is important to many because it is equated with money. Many activities are organized and run by the clock.
- *Future orientation*—Many people in the United States share an overall sense of optimism. The general feeling is that the future can and will be better than the past.
- *Work and achievement*—Hard work and hard play are valued. This stems from the ethic that idleness is evil. People place great value on the number of possessions they have and the necessity of being progressive, both materially and educationally.
- *Control over the natural environment*—Corporations and individuals continuously devise new technology and ideas that will be of benefit to their economic goals and to the goals of people striving to become knowledgeable and well educated.
- *Youthfulness*—Many people turn to youth activities and procedures for renewed inspiration.
- *Informality*—People are relatively unconcerned with the one "right" way of doing things. First names are used on first meetings.
- *Competition*—People achieve goals and become individualistic through intense competition.
- *Relative equality of the sexes*—Compared to many other cultures, the United States offers women the same opportunities as men.[8]

All of these characteristics influence the guest activities that are offered or selected by resort guests.

CULTURAL DIFFERENCES The cultures of different countries can vary greatly. In order to successfully develop programs suitable for international guests, one must be aware of these cultural differences.

One model for analyzing cultures has been suggested by Hofstede, who analyzed work-related values of over 50 countries. He found that the value patterns dominant in these countries varied along four main dimensions:

1. individualism-collectivism
2. masculinity-femininity
3. large-small power distance
4. strong-weak uncertainty avoidance[9]

Individualism–
Collectivism

On the first scale—individualism-collectivism—the issue is the closeness of the relationship between one person and other persons. At the individualistic end of the scale, individuals look after their own self-interests and those of their immediate family. At the collective end, the ties between individuals are tight. People are supposed to look after the interests of their in-group and have no opinions and beliefs other than those of their in-group. Broadly, wealthy countries are on the individualistic side, while poorer countries are on the collectivist side. We might speculate that people from countries that score high on individualism have different motives and behaviors than those from countries with high collectivist scores. High individualists might be more inclined to travel independently than in groups and to be motivated by the desire to improve themselves, for example.

Masculinity–
Femininity

The second dimension is masculinity-femininity—the division of roles between the sexes in society. At issue is the extent to which societies try to minimize or maximize the social sex role division. Masculine societies make a sharp division between what men and women "should" do. In these cases, men always take more assertive and dominant roles, while women take more service-oriented and caring roles. In masculine societies, importance is given to showing off, achieving something visible, and making money. In feminine societies, importance in placed on people relationships, the quality of life, and preservation of the environment. Masculine countries include Japan, Germany, Austria, Switzerland, some Latin countries, and most Anglo countries. On the feminine side are the Nordic countries. Placement on this scale has implications for appropriate marketing appeals. We expect major decisions, such as vacation plans, to be made by men in societies that score high on this scale, for example.

Power Distance

The third dimension is power distance—how society deals with inequalities among people. Some societies let inequalities grow over time into imbalances in power and wealth, while others try to play down inequalities as much as possible. Asian, African, and Latin American countries have large power index scores (indicating inequalities); France, Belgium, Spain, and Italy also score rather high. The Nordic and Anglo countries score low on this scale. We might expect messages of a more humanitarian and egalitarian type to appeal to cultures low on this scale.

Uncertainty
Avoidance

The last dimension is uncertainty avoidance—how societies deal with the fact that time runs only one way. We all have to live with the uncertainty of the future. Societies with weak uncertainty avoidance teach people to accept and live with this uncertainty. Their members take personal risks rather lightly, work less aggressively, and are relatively tolerant of behaviors and opinions different from their own. Members of other societies try to control the future through formal and informal rules to protect themselves from the uncertainties of human behavior. In societies like this, the word of experts is relied on much more heavily than in weak uncertainty avoidance societies. Latin countries score high on the uncertainty avoidance scale, while Asian and African countries, with the exception of Japan and Korea, score medium to low. Germany, Austria, and Switzerland score high, while the Nordic and Anglo countries score low. It might be expected that, in high-scoring countries, the role of opinion leaders (as experts) is stronger.

Eight clusters have been developed and are contained in Figure 11.2. While realizing the dangers of stereotyping (we run the risk of unfairly labeling all individuals with the characteristics and behaviors of a particular group), we present these profiles as a useful first step in determining the types of vacation behavior expected from people from these countries. This approach also suggests that countries in different clusters have cultures sufficiently distinctive to warrant targeted programming approaches.

TIME   Time—or, rather, the availability of time—acts as a major inhibiting factor to guest activity. The amount of available time and the form in which it is available is, in fact, a major shaper of the destinations that can be visited, the modes of travel that can be used, and the activities that can be engaged in at the destination or en route.

Schor suggests that, in the latter part of the last century, the amount of time Americans spend at their jobs has risen steadily.[10] According to her research, the average American enjoys only 16½ hours of leisure per week. The decline in the workweek ended abruptly in the late 1940s and since then, according to Schor, paid time off has actually been shrinking. Most recently, this is a result of the economic squeeze faced by many companies in the 1980s. Cost-cutting often reduced vacation time. Fearful of losing their jobs, many employees spent less time away from the workplace. Schor's figures indicate that in 1987, the average employed person spent 163 more hours per year on the job than in 1969.

In addition, many companies restructured their labor markets by firing long-term employees and hiring temporary workers. Because vacation time is based on the length of employment, one result was less time off with pay for many people. A third factor is the growth of the service

More Developed Latin	Less Developed Latin	More Developed Asian	Less Developed Asian
❖ high power distance ❖ high uncertainty avoidance ❖ high individualism ❖ medium masculinity Belgium France Argentina Brazil Spain	❖ high power distance ❖ high uncertainty avoidance ❖ low individualism ❖ range of masculinity Colombia Mexico Venezuela Chile Peru Portugal Yugoslavia	❖ medium power distance ❖ high uncertainty avoidance ❖ medium individualism ❖ high masculinity Japan	❖ high power distance ❖ low uncertainty avoidance ❖ low individualism ❖ medium masculinity Pakistan Taiwan Thailand Hong Kong India Philippines Singapore
Near Eastern	**Germanic**	**Anglo**	**Nordic**
❖ high power distance ❖ high uncertainty avoidance ❖ low individualism ❖ medium masculinity Greece Iran Turkey	❖ low power distance ❖ high uncertainty avoidance ❖ medium individualism ❖ high masculinity Austria Israel Germany Switzerland South Africa Italy	❖ low power distance ❖ low to medium uncertainty avoidance ❖ high individualism ❖ high masculinity Australia Canada Great Britain Ireland New Zealand United States	❖ low power distance ❖ low to medium uncertainty avoidance ❖ medium individualism ❖ low masculinity Denmark Finland Netherlands Norway Sweden

❖ FIGURE 11.2 Country clusters and their characteristics. [Source: Geert Hofstede, "The Cultural Perspective," in *People and Organizations Interacting* (New York: John Wiley & Sons, 1985).]

sector, where length of employment tends to be less than in the manufacturing industries.

Americans themselves seem to agree that they are working harder. A 1996 NBC/*Wall Street Journal* survey found that 59 percent of a random sample of Americans described themselves as busy, while 19 percent said life had become busy to the point of discomfort.[11] According to the Bureau of Labor Statistics, among men between the ages of 25 and 54, the percentage of those working more than 41 hours per week rose from 36 percent in 1976 to 43 percent in 1993. For the same years, among full-time working women of the same age, the percentage of those working more than 41 hours rose from 13 percent to 22 percent.

We can expect that the above distribution would change relative to changes in the family life cycle. This relationship is demonstrated in Figure 11.3. In the young-and-single phase, people are characterized by great physical capacity, disposable time, and few demands on their income. In the family phase, discretionary income and time decrease, and the physical capacity of the family is limited by that of its weakest member. The third phase is characterized by an excess of discretionary time and a decrease in physical capacity.

We can speculate on the impact this might have on vacation behavior. Young singles may have the time, money, and ability to participate in physically demanding activities. Family activities may be geared to those allowed by the youngest child. Older people may comprise a likely market during the off-season as well as for last-minute bargains.

Time and Activities Attempts have been made to show a relationship between the type of work and the type of leisure activities engaged in. Leisure has been seen as a compensation for work in that leisure activity is quite different from work activity. A passive job, for example, may result in active leisure-time activities. A second view is that the development of certain skills and lifestyles learned at work spills over into a demand for similar kinds of leisure-time activities. The problem, of course, is that any leisure-time behavior can be explained by reference to whichever theory is more appropriate to one's

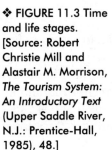

❖ FIGURE 11.3 Time and life stages. [Source: Robert Christie Mill and Alastair M. Morrison, *The Tourism System: An Introductory Text* (Upper Saddle River, N.J.: Prentice-Hall, 1985), 48.]

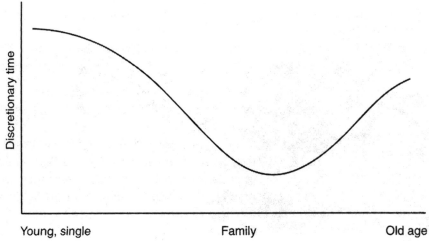

purpose. The link between type of work and leisure activities has not been demonstrated. In fact, several studies have demonstrated that no significant differences in leisure activity pertain between workers who do what they consider boring jobs and those who do more interesting and enjoyable jobs. It does seem clear, however, that the place of leisure in a person's life is becoming more important relative to that of work.

AGE The relationship between recreational activities and age has two components: the amount of leisure time available and the type and extent of activities undertaken at various age levels. The amount of leisure time available changes curvilinearly, with younger and older age groups having proportionately more leisure time.

Yet the amount of available time is, by itself, insufficient to explain age as a factor in leisure behavior. It is safe to conclude that the rates of participation in the overwhelming majority of leisure activities decline with age. Active recreational pursuits show a greater decline than do more passive forms of recreation. Preferred activities among the elderly are the relatively subdued ones such as visiting friends and relatives, sightseeing, fishing, and playing golf. Although the number of activities people participate in may drop on retirement, the amount of time they spend on each remaining activity, in terms of participation, often increases.

In summary, leisure time decreases with age until children leave the nest; then the amount of leisure time increases. This increase continues with retirement. Though participation in physical activities declines with age (together with a corresponding rise in participation in the gentler forms of recreation), interest levels in activities previously participated in remains high. Opportunities may exist for tapping these interests by developing nonparticipatory ways to express them. A skier, for example, may be unable to ski for reasons of age but may be interested in related activities, such as watching skiers or sharing experiences.

INCOME Many studies have attempted to determine the percentage of income spent on recreation as a whole. It appears that at the lower levels of income and education, approximately 2 percent of income is spent on recreation. As income increases, the proportion spent on recreation increases to between 5 and 6 percent for all education levels. The highest recreation expenditures, 7 percent, are reported by respondents who are heads of households, under 40 years of age, and without children. Other studies indicate a positive correlation between income and recreation expenditures. In fact, it appears that increases in income result in a pro-portionately greater increase in recreation expenditures.

As might be expected, higher-income tourists stay longer and spend more per day than do those with lower incomes. The type of recreational activities participated in differs based on income. Higher-income people tend to participate in activities such as reading, bridge, fencing, squash, and chess; middle-income people tend to engage in bowling, golf, and dancing. Lower-income families are identified with television viewing, dominoes, and Bingo. The implication is clear to companies who put together travel packages featuring specific activities aimed at particular market segments. A package, for example, aimed at a high-income seg-ment of the market might be built around a recreational activity in which people with high incomes tend to participate.

Research on the relationship between amount of participation in rec-reation and income has shown that participation in most recreational activities increases as income increases up to a point but declines slightly at incomes higher than this.

SEX Men and women exhibit more similarities than differences in terms of lei-sure participation rates. Overall, participation rates in leisure activities do not differ between men and women, although many women engage in slightly fewer activities than do men. As might be expected, nonworking women have slightly higher participation rates than do employed women, except for going out to dinner and either taking part in sports or watching sports. There is a clear difference between the sexes in terms of preferred activities. Women are more involved in cultural activities, and men lead in outdoor recreation and play and watching sports.

One study indicates that the traditional responsibilities of females relating to domestic work and child care have led to them viewing leisure activities in a way that are task- rather than time-oriented, social rather than physical, relational as opposed to self-interested. The study specifi-cally dealt with skiing and found that women placed more emphasis on the emotional and social benefits of skiing than on the physical benefits. Women, it was found, are more likely than men to ski if friends or family are involved. They view the activity as recreational rather than competitive.[12]

EDUCATION The strong correlation between education and income is well established. Independent of income, however, the level of education that an individual has tends to influence the type of leisure and travel pursuits he chooses.

The amount of education obtained most likely determines the nature of both work and leisure-time activities. By widening one's horizons of interest and enjoyment, education influences the type of activities undertaken. Education itself can serve as the primary reason for travel.

Researchers have found that participation in outdoor recreation tends to increase as the amount of education increases. Some evidence also suggests that more educated people prefer activities that require the development of interpretive and expressive skills, including attending plays, concerts, and art museums, playing tennis and golf, skiing, reading books, attending adult education classes, and undergoing wilderness experiences.

In summary, it appears that the more education people have, the broader their horizons and the more options they consider. Higher-educated travelers also tend to be more sophisticated in their tastes. They may not, however, be bigger spenders. A study of visitors to Hawaii found that those with less education spent more per day than those with more education. The authors suggested that the less educated visitor may equate having fun with spending money.

PHYSICAL ABILITY Under the Americans with Disabilities Act (ADA), it is illegal to discriminate on the basis of a person's disability. This means that resorts must not:

❖ Deny people with disabilities the opportunity to participate in a program that is available to those without disabilities.
❖ Use facilities and sites that exclude people with disabilities.[13]

Resorts cannot offer lower-quality services to people with disabilities and are required to make "reasonable accommodation" to allow them to participate fully in each activity.

LIFE STAGES Psychosocial theory indicates that "at each life stage, cultural aspirations, expectations, requirements, and opportunities are assumed to have an impact on individual development."[14] At each stage of an individual's life, certain issues become particularly important. Examples from two noted psychologists, Erik H. Erikson and M. Huberman, are shown in Figure 11.4. The point is that activity programmers need to take into account the issues that guests in different life stages are experiencing. Ways in which activity preferences are related to these issues are also suggested.[15]

SOCIAL INFLUENCES Within a general cultural pattern, movement is constant. Trends or fads influence which activities are hot and which are not. In *Generations at Work,* the authors argue that there are four distinct groups in the United

Life Stage	Issues	Activity Preferences
Infancy	Trust versus mistrust	Side-by-side play, not interaction Awareness of flaws, self-doubt Need for activity in which praise can be received
Early childhood	Autonomy versus doubt	Testing of independence High security needs and familiarity Movement of individualism to peer relationships
Play age	Initiative versus guilt	Hero worship Highly impressionable Willingness to seek risk and adventure Willing to work for external rewards
School age	Industry versus infinity	
Adolescence	Identity versus confusion	Seeking self-identity Testing boy–girl relationships Gender identification Group affiliation important
Young adulthood	Intimacy versus isolation	Independence from parents Need for belonging
Adulthood 18–30 30–40 40–50 50–60 60–70 70–80	Generalitivity versus stagnation Focusing oneself Collecting oneself Exerting and assuring Maintaining Disengagement decision Disengaging	High security needs Club orientation Committed to society More spectator leisure Volunteering as leisure
Old age	Integrity versus despair	Danger of boredom Clinging to the abstract Caution

❖ FIGURE 11.4 Life stages and important issues. [Source: Patricia Farrell and Herberta M. Lundegren, *The Process of Recreation Programming: Theory and Technique*, 3rd ed. (State College, Penna.: Venture Publishing, 1991), 31, 33–37.]

States, based on age, who have very different core values that influence their behavior. They define the Veterans, born between 1922 and 1943, as valuing dedication and sacrifice, hard work, conformity, law and order, respect for authority, patience, delayed reward, duty before pleasure, and adherence to rules and honor.[16]

❖ Taking care of the children, Aspen, Colorado. [Source: Design Workshop, Inc.]

Baby Boomers, defined as those born between 1943 and 1960, are optimistic and have a team orientation. They value personal gratification, health and wellness, personal growth, youth, work, and involvement.[17] Generation-Xers, born between 1960 and 1980, value diversity, thinking globally, balance, technoliteracy, fun, information, self-reliance, and pragmatism.[18] Finally, the Nexters, those born between 1980 and 2000, are optimistic and confident, and value civic duty, achievement, sociability, morality, street smarts, and diversity.[19]

A vacation plan aimed at any of these four groups would have to be adjusted to take the specific cultural values into account.

ORGANIZATION/ HISTORY/ ENVIRONMENT   While we have chosen to focus on cultural and social influences on guest attitudes and behavior, the values and mission of the company, the tradition and philosophy of the resort, together with such environmental influences as time of the year and the weather, play a part in type of guest activity program offered. For example, the Winter Park resort in Colorado is owned by the City and County of Denver. It was originally thought of as a mountain park for the use of the citizens. When, over 30 years ago, the idea of a ski program for people with physical disabilities was floated, the idea fit in well with the public-access history of the resort. These resort character factors are considered below in relation to program delivery.

GUESTS' NEEDS

Needs are viewed as motivators, or factors, that influence the drives people have in making decisions about involvement in leisure programs.
—DONALD DEGRAAF, DEBRA J. JORDAN, AND KATHY H. DEGRAAF
Programming for Parks, Recreation, and Leisure Services:
A Servant Leadership Approach

Activity programs could be much more meaningful to participants if the activity director knew what guests expected from the program. People participate in guest activities for a variety of reasons. They may wish to:

❖ Make friends.
❖ Belong to a group.
❖ Experience competition.
❖ Learn a new skill.
❖ Share a talent.
❖ Gain prestige.
❖ Get in shape.[20]

It might be argued that people pursue recreation for the same reason they pursue any goal—to satisfy needs and wants important to them. In so doing, they operate within, and are influenced by, the cultural and social environments in which they grew up and now find themselves.

NEEDS AND WANTS The key to understanding guest motivation is to see the activities they engage in as satisfiers of needs and wants. Guests do not participate in guest activity programs "just" to relax and have fun. They do so in the hope and belief that these activities will satisfy, either wholly or partially, needs and wants important to them. This view of guest motivation is critical. It is the difference between seeing a resort program as simply a hayride or a painting class and as a means for satisfying what is important to guests.

What are the needs that people seek to satisfy? Guest motivations can fit into Maslow's hierarchy of needs model. Maslow proposed the following listing of needs arranged in a hierarchy:

1. *Physical*—hunger, thirst, rest, activity
2. *Safety*—security, freedom from fear and anxiety
3. *Belonging and love*—affection, giving and receiving love
4. *Esteem*—self-esteem and the esteem of others
5. *Self-actualization*—personal self-fulfillment[21]

The hierarchy suggests that lower-level needs demand more immediate attention and satisfaction before a person turns to the satisfaction of higher-level needs. It might be better to think of the hierarchy as a series of nested triangles. This representation emphasizes that higher-level needs encompass all lower-level needs. It also illustrates the relative value size of each need better than a vertical list does.

It should be noted that Maslow's model has been criticized on the grounds that the original work was part of a clinical experiment rather than the foundation for a theory of motivation. Maslow himself expressed concerns about his own findings. Be that as it may, the fact is that the model does seem to explain why people behave the way they do.

Although Maslow's first listed need is physical, the other four are psychological. To the original list, Maslow added two intellectual words:

❖ *To know and understand*—acquiring knowledge
❖ *Aesthetics*—appreciation of beauty

The relationship between physical, psychological, and intellectual needs is unclear. It is thought that the intellectual needs exist independently of the others.

Physical Passive vacationers are seen as achieving tension relief by giving in or submitting to the surrounding environment. The result is their returning refreshed and renewed from their vacation. The overworked factory worker may relax by lying on a beach for two weeks. In contrast, the active vacationer achieves tension reduction through physical activity. The activity can also be seen as related to achievement and mastery of the environment and, as such, related to the need for self-esteem. Some people who have jobs that are not physically demanding compensate by engaging in physical activity when on vacation. This illustrates the point made earlier that, at any one time, one may be motivated to satisfy more than one need.

Safety   Traveling for reasons of health can be interpreted as a way of attempting to satisfy one's safety needs. By taking care of the body or mind, people protect themselves and help assure their longevity. Visits to spas can be seen in this light. Several references specifically link recreation and health, implying a relationship between the two.

Belonging and Love   The need for belonging and love relates to the desire for affection, for both giving and receiving love. The organized tour is often mentioned as a method of encouraging and satisfying this need for companionship and social interaction. Adolescents are motivated to experience this sense of belonging from a peer group.[22] When this is not available through organized activity, teenagers may turn to gang membership to receive it.

Esteem   Maslow's concept of the need for esteem breaks down into two components: self-esteem and the esteem of others. Self-esteem is embodied in the need to exhibit strength, achievement, mastery, competence, and independence. This may explain why people take whitewater rafting trips. The need for the esteem of others is manifest in concerns about reputation, prestige, status, and recognition. Travel can certainly boost the ego, both at the destination and on return. It may be that as people grow older, their status in society declines. Travel is one way to enhance that status.

Self-Actualization   Self-actualization can, in fact, be considered the end or goal of leisure. Leisure is freedom from the urgent demands of lower-level needs. Vacations offer an opportunity to reevaluate and discover more about the self, to act out one's self-image as a way of modifying or correcting it.

The need to know and understand can be viewed in light of the desire for knowledge. Many people travel to learn of other cultures. It is also true that contact with people of another culture offers an opportunity to discover one's own culture. This concept is also expressed as a motivation for education, wanderlust, and interest in foreign lands. The need for aesthetics is seen in those who travel for environmental reasons—to view the scenery.

Maslow proposed the idea of prepotency—that lower-level needs should be satisfied, at least to some extent, before the satisfaction of higher-level needs becomes a concern. Thus, while the goal of a recreation program should be self-actualization, if the lower-level needs of the guest remain unsatisfied, they will get in the way of programs aimed at satisfying higher-level needs.

quick getaways 11.3

College Campus Courses

Many resorts now offer classes previously taught on college campuses. Three examples are The Equinox, Disney Institute, and Hyatt Resort first-class hotels.

The eighteenth-century Equinox resort/spa in Manchester Village, Vermont, is home to the British School of Falconry. A 45-minute introductory course on handling birds of prey costs $120. A hunt at a nearby game preserve costs from $130 for a 90-minute walk to $398 for a full day hunt of rabbits, quail, and pheasants. The Equinox has also teamed up with Land Rover to provide courses on how to handle four-wheel-drive sport utility vehicles on icy roads or steep terrain.

Disney's theme vacations of "discovery and exploration" include classes on the inner workings of show business, self-defense, TV production, and outdoor photography. The typical course lasts three hours. This means that, theoretically, guests can take three courses a day. Demand is particularly high for culinary classes—Taste of the World, Healthy Cooking, Studio Baking—and animation classes—Computer Animation, Clay Animation, Disney Voices.

Hyatt Resorts recently launched several new enrichment programs. At its Hopi Indian Learning Center in Scottsdale, Arizona, it offers lectures on Hopi migration, burial grounds, and language.

The resort at Coral Gables, Florida, features a Hop on a Harley program. Licensed motorcycle drivers can rent a Harley for $699 a week. Novices can register for a 22-day training course at a nearby Motorcycle Safety Foundation. On graduation, guests are given a certificate that is redeemable for a license in most states.

Source: Faye Rice, "Hunting Down New Skills," *Fortune* 136, no. 5 (8 September 1997): 190.

Question: What are some additional examples of guest activity programs that combine fun and education?

❖ Climbing wall, Principality of Andorra. [Source: Design Workshop, Inc.]

Motivation   Motivation is an inner state that moves people toward a goal.[23] Motivation comes from within. Guest activity programmers cannot motivate guests to participate. They can, however, create an environment that makes it easier (or more difficult) for guest participation to occur.

Guests are better understood and better appealed to if they are recognized as people consuming products and services. Seeing them in this light results in a change of attitude on the part of the guest activity staff, who can then provide better products and services.

NEEDS ASSESSMENT

Through the use of needs assessments we can maintain customer loyalty while at the same time work to recruit new customers.
—DONALD DEGRAAF, DEBRA J. JORDAN, AND KATHY H. DEGRAAF
Programming for Parks, Recreation, and Leisure Services:
A Servant Leadership Approach

Needs assessment is "a systematic inquiry about needs, attitudes, behaviors, and patterns of both participants and non-participants."[24] Its purpose is to identify what is important to guests in order to better design and deliver guest activity programs that leave guests satisfied with the program and, consequently, the resort. Constraints should be noted. First, needs are infinite. The resort cannot totally satisfy the needs of every guest. Second, conflicts between different segments of the market are inevitable. Teens want different activities than seniors. On the slopes, there are differences between skiers and snowboarders. Satisfying each segment of the market without encroaching on the satisfaction of the others is a major task. Nevertheless, this task must be executed if the staff believes in the marketing or customer concept.

Several techniques can be used to conduct a needs assessment:

❖ Existing guests are asked what interests them or what activities they currently undertake. Information may be collected to create a demographic and usage profile for use in expanding the market segment, finding new segments, or forecasting future demand for existing and proposed services. The existing services can also be evaluated.

❖ People who do not use the programs and who do not take part in the activities might also be surveyed as to their reasons. This can provide useful information on how to improve the programs to make them more guest-friendly.

❖ National figures are available on trends in recreation. Noting which activities are growing in popularity can help staff identify likely future demand for specific programs.[25]

❖ Resort amenities can have primary and secondary uses. As an assist in thinking about secondary uses for facilities and areas, in addition to implementing the multiple-use concept, list all of the facilities and areas on the property and note the possible activities for which they could be used.[26] For example, the primary use of a golf course is to play golf. However, it could also be used for cross-country running and skiing, a jogging trail, sledding and tobogganing, orienteering, and bird-watching, to name only a few possibilities. This is, in essence, a product rather than a marketing approach to needs assessment. While not as useful as the other methods, it can be a useful complement.

quick getaways 11.4

Needs Assessment: RCI Members

Research by Simmons Market Research Bureau, Inc., found that Resort Condominiums International (RCI) members, while on vacation during 1997–2000, did the following:

❖ Dine out	90 percent
❖ Go sightseeing	85
❖ Shop	78
❖ Go to the beach	78
❖ Walk	70
❖ Attend a show, theater, or other entertainment	62
❖ Visit a museum	52
❖ Visit a theme park	52
❖ Visit a state park	52
❖ Gamble at a casino	44
❖ Hike	30
❖ Snorkel	30
❖ Golf	29

Source: "Simmons Says," *RCI Premier* (March/April 2000): 18.

Question: What implications does this information have for guest activity programming?

In this marketing model, needs assessment is the first step in providing services and programs to meet the stated and implied needs and wants of existing and future guests.

DEFINING GOALS AND OBJECTIVES

If one were to picture a staircase, objectives would be the
individual steps and the goal would be at the top of the stairs.
—DONALD DEGRAAF, DEBRA J. JORDAN, AND KATHY H. DEGRAAF
Programming for Parks, Recreation, and Leisure Services:
A Servant Leadership Approach

GOALS AND OBJECTIVES The goals and objectives of the guest activity programs nest within those set for the resort itself. Goals are broad, general, final outcomes. The overall goal of the resort might be to produce profits by satisfying guests. Within this framework, the guest activity goal might be to:

❖ Provide satisfying experiences for guests.
❖ Aid in skill development.
❖ Increase guests' health and well-being.
❖ Encourage social interaction among guests.[27]

Objectives are much more specific and short-term. The resort might set objectives relative to occupancy, rate, and percentage of guests who return. Again, within this framework, the guest activity director might set specific objectives in terms of the number of people who participate in activities, targets for guest satisfaction with programs, and so on.

Objectives should be set for the overall guest activity program as well as for every individual program and activity offered. Program objectives should be set before implementing an activity. A program has the guest perform or behave in a certain way, learn something, and/or receive instruction.[28] For the guest activity program to be meaningful (and, therefore, satisfying, to the guest), it is important that the programmer develop some idea of what the outcome of the program should be for guests and design activities (the next step in the process) to help ensure the objectives are met. Refusing to set objectives lessens the chance that guest needs, identified above, are met.

What is the expected outcome of the program? Should guests be able to ski, golf, play tennis better? Should they have a greater appreciation for the outdoors? Will they learn a new skill, make a new friend, or feel more relaxed?

Setting objectives involves certain assumptions: that the programmer is able to conceptualize what will happen during the activity; that the programmer is skilled in writing performance objectives; and that the program objectives are consistent with the objectives of participants in the activity.[29] The success of the program is reflected in the extent to which it realizes its objectives. Objectives, therefore, must be stated in specific terms and include some measurement to indicate whether or not the objective is met. This process is relatively sophisticated and holds the programmer accountable for the success of the program. The idea is to identify what the participants should think, feel, or do at the end of the program.

BLOOM'S TAXONOMY The classic reference in this area is *The Taxonomy of Educational Objectives* by B. S. Bloom. Objectives can be cognitive, affective, or psychomotor.[30]

Cognitive Cognitive objectives involve thinking, including remembering, reproducing something, or solving an intellectual task. The various levels of cognition are progressively more sophisticated:

- ❖ *Knowledge*—e.g., knowing the rules of a game
- ❖ *Comprehension*—e.g., demonstrating the ability to read music
- ❖ *Application*—e.g., applying what has been learned to a new situation
- ❖ *Analysis*—breaking down complex items into their components to show their relationship
- ❖ *Synthesis*—e.g., joining elements together to produce a play
- ❖ *Evaluation*—making value judgments to determine whether or not objectives have been met

Affective Affective objectives deal with feelings and emotions:

- ❖ *Receiving*—e.g., listening to a talk
- ❖ *Responding*—e.g., being enriched as part of a group listening to a singer
- ❖ *Valuing*—e.g., showing commitment by being a leader
- ❖ *Organizing*—e.g., bringing together values into an organized system; developing a personal philosophy of leisure
- ❖ *Characterizing*—e.g., demonstrating lifestyle behaviors consistent with a plan—for example, consistently engaging in recreational pursuits throughout the year

quick getaways 11.5

Defining Goals and Objectives: Lakota River Guides

The following information is taken directly from a brochure for Lakota River Guides.

NIGHT VISION RAFT AND 4 X 4 TOURS

The World's First Night Rafting and 4 × 4 Adventure
(excluding all military operations)

Picture yourself rafting down a beautiful river, or 4-wheeling across a remote mountain road. Seeing animals and experiencing nature in a way you have never felt before.

NOW PICTURE IT IN THE DARK OF NIGHT.

Lakota River Guides

The valley's most innovative adventure company has once again set the standards for exciting new trips. We invite you to experience the backcountry like you have always dreamed about under the dazzling Colorado night skies. Utilizing technology that has recently been declassified, we will provide you with the 3rd generation, ITT night vision goggles, as used by the military and movie industry.

Experience:

- the quiet of early evening
- the sweet sounds of riparian plants settling over the river
- the sensation of motion as you accelerate down Class II rapids
- the ease of identifying common constellations
- the wonder of being "out there"

The stars are especially stunning and we will bring star charts and teach you about common constellations!

Lakota River Guides wants to show you what you've been missing when the sun goes down.

Source: Brochure, Lakota River Guides, Vail, Colorado, 2000.

Question: Can you write goals and objectives that are appropriate for this activity?

Psychomotor   Psychomotor or behavioral skills deal with physical action:

- *Imitation*—e.g., imitating an action that has been demonstrated
- *Manipulation*—e.g., following instructions and performing an act with some understanding of it
- *Precision*—e.g., showing a high level of skill
- *Articulation*—e.g., showing consistency in a skill
- *Naturalization*—e.g., automatically responding to a stimulus

CLUSTER AND ACTIVITY ANALYSIS

If I had no duties, and no reference to futurity, I would spend my life in driving briskly in a post-chaise with a pretty woman.
—SAMUEL JOHNSON
As quoted in James Boswell, *Life of Samuel Johnson*, 1791

The next step in the process is to identify activities that can help guests meet the stated objectives. Two ways of doing this are activity analysis and cluster analysis.

ACTIVITY ANALYSIS   Activity analysis involves determining how each part of an activity can contribute to meeting goals and objectives. Each activity can be broken down according to the following criteria:

- behavioral domains—cognitive, affective, and psychomotor
- skill level, from low to high
- interaction patterns, from individual to group
- leadership required, from minimum to maximum
- equipment required, from none to required
- duration, from a set time through a natural end to continuous
- facilities required, from none to required
- participants, from one to any number
- age appropriateness[31]

The primary focus of a game of basketball, for example, is psychomotor activity at a high level—passing, dribbling, shooting. The secondary domain is cognitive, also at a high level—knowing the rules and various plays as well as some strategy. The tertiary domain is affective, at an average level—sportsmanship. A high degree of group interaction comes from the need to bond as a team to compete against another team. A certain amount of leadership is required. A basketball and court and hoops are needed. Any number from two to ten can play (ranging from one-on-one to five-on-five), at any age from five years up. The activity can last for a set time or until a set number of points are scored. Activity analysis can identify the activity that will best meet identified needs.

CLUSTER ANALYSIS Cluster analysis clusters activities that yield similar benefits. Each activity becomes a variable, the correlation between participation in two variables is computed, and the cluster is based on the correlation that results. Typically, the following criteria are used to determine clusters:

- ❖ degree of skill required
- ❖ level of activity
- ❖ nature of the group needed
- ❖ amount of risk or danger
- ❖ special facilities needed[32]

An example of a cluster model is shown in Figure 11.5. The implication is that people can be typed based on their choice of activity. The implications for the resort are obvious. From existing levels of participation, staff can identify which complementary activities might be popular.

Group A	Group B	Group C	Group D
Soccer	Rugby	Outdoor bowls	Ice skating
Tennis	Netball	Tenpin bowls	Roller skating
Golf	Athletics	Table tennis	Horse riding
Swimming	Basketball		Youth club
Fishing	Badminton		
Hobbies/Do-it-yourself	Fitness exercises		
Other activities	Cycling		
	Amateur dramatics/music		
Group E	**Group F**	**Group G**	**Group H**
Rowing	Hill walking	Picnicking	Visiting a cinema
Motorboat cruising	Rambling	Driving in the countryside	Visiting a theater or concert
Messing about in boats	Walking	Gardening	Dancing
		Dining out	
		Visiting a community or church center	
		Playing Bingo	

❖ FIGURE 11.5 Burton's eight cluster groups. [Source: Patricia Farrell and Herberta M. Lundegren, *The Process of Recreation Programming: Theory and Technique*, 3rd ed. (State College, Penna.: Venture Publishing, 1991), 88.]

quick getaways 11.6

Cluster/Activity Analysis: Floating Resorts

Today's cruise ships offer enough options to keep occupied attendees on board. Putting greens, swimming with sharks, aqua meditation, and, soon, even ice and in-line skating and rock climbing will be available to cruise ship passengers without ever having to leave the boat. The roster of exciting and exotic shipboard activities keeps expanding on the latest generation of cruise ships, with no end in sight. Life at sea has never been more active or entertaining as ships take on the role of floating resorts, many times just cruising to nowhere, with everyone perfectly happy.

Though most on-board activities are free, some, such as spa treatments, carry a fee. Until recently, spas were strictly for the enjoyment of those undergoing treatments, but now, cruisers can opt to pay a day fee and use the pool or other facilities outside the therapy rooms. For example, the Vista Spas on the new *Disney Magic* ship and the soon-to-be-launched *Disney Wonder* feature a tropical rainforest. After making the rounds of its thermal suites for a mild steam, a fog shower, or a tropical rain shower, spa-goers can lounge on heated ceramic couches beside a gently misting aromatherapy fountain.

Many cruise lines offer unique experiences, including Princess Cruises and Seabourn Cruise Lines. Princess Cruises is the only line where passengers can become certified scuba divers during a cruise, and Seabourn Cruise Lines' water sports marina comes equipped with a steel cage so passengers can swim in the ocean, even when the waters are shark infested.

Source: Joy Anderson, "Resorts Without Parks," *Incentive* 173, no. 6 (June 1999): 39–46.

***Question*: What guest activities can be developed that would be appropriate for the uniqueness of a cruise experience?**

If demand for tenpin bowling were great, for example, it would suggest that table tennis would also be a popular activity.

FORMAT Guest activity staff offer various activities in different formats. Program format is "the way in which an activity is organized and structured to the customer."[33] Guests select whichever format(s) they feel will allow them to satisfy important needs and wants (Figure 11.6). In determining which programs and activities to offer, it is useful to think of the various formats into which activities can fall.

Instruction Guests may participate in an activity for self-improvement—to learn a new skill or to develop or refine an existing one. Guests may want to achieve a specific performance goal. This format requires a high level of organization to satisfy the motivations of the participants. For best results, the guest activity staff should have specialized leadership skills. The program should be limited to a small number of participants who meet over a series of meeting times and dates. The program is characterized by heavy programmer control, responsiveness to many ability levels, and fees for participation.

Competition Some people participate to compete. The interest in competition may be intrinsic (competing against oneself, being the best one can be) or extrinsic (looking good in front of others, the adulation of the gallery). Competition is traditionally associated with sports, although board games, drama,

---

ACTIVITIES
are organized into various

FORMATS
Instructional   Competition   Social Activities   Trips
Drop-in Activities   Special Events   Spectator

which guests select to satisfy

NEEDS AND WANTS
important to them
Physical Safety   Belonging   Esteem   Self-Actualization

❖ FIGURE 11.6 Needs, wants, activities, and format.

and music, for example, offer opportunities for competition. Having an audience is important for the extrinsically motivated guest. (This opens opportunities for a category discussed below—the participant spectator.)

Tournaments are not regarded as appropriate at the preschool and early elementary school level. Little leadership is desired by the participants. Groups are usually formed by sex and stage in the life cycle. Decade age groupings are popular with adults.

Guests may also be grouped by skill level. It is important that people compete with others at a similar skill level and in the proper environment to ensure a fair contest. Competitions require limited equipment and strong administrator leadership skills. They are labor intensive, especially as a variety of competitions must be provided.

An alternative to competition among people at similar skill levels is the institution of some equalizing mechanism. For example, golfers with a greater degree of skill are often given a handicap to allow golfers of less skill a fairer shot at winning. In an intergenerational game of softball, the size of the bat and the ball could be changed for younger players.

Participants should feel safe on both physical and emotional levels when competing. They tend to feel more in control if they are given some say in setting rules and guidelines to maintain a degree of fairness.[34] Combining these concepts requires a balance between the skill level of the guest and the challenge present in the activity.[35] If the challenge exceeds the guest's skill level, he feels anxious. When the skill level exceeds the challenge inherent in the activity, he is bored. When skill level and challenge are matched, people can become totally engaged in the activity. At this point, the experience becomes satisfying to the guest.

Social Activities Some people take part in activities primarily for social reasons. They do this because they need people. Social activities need minimal programmer involvement once the activity is developed. Social programs should be open to all but carry some guidelines and rules and operate within the philosophy of the resort. Certain singles-only Club Med activities, for example, would not be appropriate in the family atmosphere of a Disney resort.

Trips Activities may be organized in the form of a day or overnight trip. This format is complicated in that it involves the movement of people around or away from the resort. Transportation must be arranged, increasing safety problems.

Drop-In Activities Some people prefer self-directed programs. These are the most difficult to define and manage. People sign up because they desire unstructured, unplanned, unsupervised activities. The young and the old, however, want more structure. The key concept is that self-directed programs need as much consideration as the others noted above. The following questions are appropriate:

❖ Is the facility free when people would use it for self-directed activity?
❖ Are the only unscheduled hours at times when no one is available to use the facility?
❖ What is the cost of opening earlier or closing later?[36]

Special Events   Resorts may organize special events, such as festivals, banquets, shows, and exhibitions, in which guests can participate. Special events tend to draw attention to the resort and, as such, can serve as excellent publicity that complements other marketing efforts. Because large special events incur problems of crowd control, parking, and sanitation, resorts may wish to partner with one or more additional organizations and use volunteer staff to supplement the paid staff.

Spectators   Most of the formats noted above offer opportunities for people who prefer to watch rather than to actively participate. They may look for playing tips as they ready themselves for participation, or their days of active participation may be over while their interest in the activity remains. Thus, every program should be planned with spectators in mind, bearing in mind that watching may be the only "participant option" for some. Spectators enhance the experience for active participants, especially those who are extrinsically motivated. Care needs to be taken from a liability viewpoint, as the resort assumes legal responsibility for people watching the event. The question of open versus designated seating needs to be addressed as a means of producing revenue for prime viewing spots.

This list of formats is now combined with the program areas aimed at specific life cycle groups to form the guest activity program of the resort—the subject of the next chapter.

SUMMARY

Guest activity programming requires a planned effort. Guest needs are assessed, objectives developed, and a cluster/activity analysis conducted. The actual activity then takes place and is evaluated. The guest activity director seeks to satisfy guest needs with a staff, facilities, equipment, and other resources against a backdrop of historical, environmental, organizational, social, and cultural influences.

quick getaways 11.7

Eco-Issues and Travel Planning

These results are based on a survey of 218 travelers conducted for
Conde Nast Traveler magazine.

➤ Have you ever had to change travel plans because of an environmental
problem at your chosen destination?

>   Yes: 25 percent   No: 75 percent

➤ Have you ever been adversely affected by the air quality at a destination?

>   Yes: 47 percent   No: 51 percent

➤ Have you ever decided not to go swimming because of water quality at
a vacation destination?

>   Yes: 55 percent   No: 45 percent

➤ Are you concerned about environmental conditions at your destination
when making travel plans?

>   Yes: 91 percent   No: 9 percent

Source: "Eco-Issues and Travel Planning," *Travel Weekly*, 21 November 1996, p. 15.

ENDNOTES

1. Donald G. DeGraaf, Debra J. Jordan, and Kathy H. DeGraaf, *Programming for Parks, Recreation, and Leisure Services: A Servant Leadership Approach* (State College, Penna.: Venture Publishing, 1999), 3.
2. Ibid., 7.
3. Ibid., 3.
4. Ibid., 5.
5. Ibid., 30.
6. Patricia Farrell and Herberta M. Lundegren, *The Process of Recreation Programming: Theory and Technique*, 3rd ed. (State College, Penna.: Venture Publishing, 1991), 25.

7. DeGraaf, Jordan, and DeGraaf, *Programming for Parks, Recreation, and Leisure Services*, 52.
8. Gary P. Ferraro, *The Cultural Dimension of International Business* (Englewood Cliffs, N.J.: Prentice-Hall, 1990), 94.
9. Geert Hofstede, "The Cultural Perspective," in *People and Organizations Interacting*, ed. Aat Brakel (New York: John Wiley & Sons, 1985), 102-104.
10. Juliet B. Schor, *The Overworked American: The Unexpected Decline of Leisure* (New York: Basic Books, 1991), 21.
11. "Just How Long Is the Work Week? Official Statistics Unclear," *Denver Post*, 8 September 1996, p. 8G.
12. Peter W. Williams and Christine Lattey, "Skiing Constraints for Women," *Journal of Travel Research* 33, no. 2 (Fall 1994): 21-25.
13. DeGraaf, Jordan, and DeGraaf, *Programming for Parks, Recreation, and Leisure Services*, 102-103.
14. Farrell and Lundegren, *Process of Recreation Programming*, 29.
15. Ibid., 133-137.
16. R. Zemke, C. Raines, and B. Fitzpatrick, *Generations at Work* (New York: ANACOM, 2000), 30.
17. Ibid., 68.
18. Ibid., 98.
19. Ibid., 132.
20. Farrell and Lundegren, *Process of Recreation Programming*, 14.
21. Abraham H. Maslow, "A Theory of Human Motivation," *Psychological Review* 50 (1943): 370-396.
22. DeGraaf, Jordan, and DeGraaf, *Programming for Parks, Recreation, and Leisure Services*, 49.
23. Farrell and Lundegren, *Process of Recreation Programming*, 40.
24. DeGraaf, Jordan, and DeGraaf, *Programming for Parks, Recreation, and Leisure Services*, 75.
25. Farrell and Lundegren, *Process of Recreation Programming*, 43.
26. Ibid., 19.
27. DeGraaf, Jordan, and DeGraaf, *Programming for Parks, Recreation, and Leisure Services*, 258.
28. Farrell and Lundegren, *Process of Recreation Programming*, 152.
29. Ibid., 7.
30. Ibid., 155-156.
31. Ibid., 84.
32. Ibid., 86.
33. DeGraaf, Jordan, and DeGraaf, *Programming for Parks, Recreation, and Leisure Services*, 122.
34. Ibid., 124.
35. Ibid., 47.
36. Farrell and Lundegren, *Process of Recreation Programming*, 114.

Chapter 12

PROGRAM MANAGEMENT AND EVALUATION

INTRODUCTION

Health and fitness is a social activity as well.
—ROBB PRICE
Marketing Manager, Guilford Spectrum

The job of the recreation programmer is to combine the guests' life stages, a variety of formats, and numerous program possibilities in order to design a guest activity program. The process for planning and evaluating programs is also discussed in this chapter.

PROGRAM AREAS

A recreation programmer cube is outlined in Figure 12.1. The cube suggests a comprehensive approach to guest activity programming by bringing together three areas—the life stages of the guests, the formats identified in Chapter 11, and the variety of program possibilities. A guest activity director matches the life stage of the guest with the format and the activity desired to develop a guest activity program. For example, a sidewalk craft fair might be set up to appeal to adults interested in crafts as spectators.

GUEST LIFE STAGES

Infancy

Infancy is when babies learn about themselves and their world. Babies grow as their senses are stimulated. Vision can be stimulated with mobiles in contrasting colors, mirrors to facilitate self-discovery and to have "another" person constantly around, and positioning babies so they can see others.

Hearing can be stimulated by repeating the sounds that babies make, playing heartbeat tapes or tapes of parents' voices, and playing music to soothe as well as stimulate. The sense of touch can be fostered by toys of different textures and by holding the baby when playing.[1]

Early Childhood

Toddlers are ready to explore their new world and examine the effect they can have on it.[2] Putting blocks in a shape sorter and taking them out, using toys that make a sound when touched or hit, pulling pull-toys, and playing in water are methods by which they do so.

Toddlers begin to develop physical abilities. They might do this by marching to music, kicking or throwing a ball, climbing in a play house, or running up a ramp. Once a bond is established with an adult, they begin to learn autonomy. Games such as peek-a-boo and hide-and-seek help this

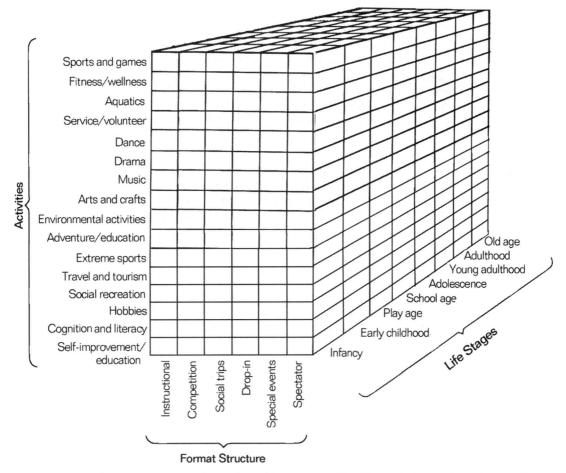

❖ FIGURE 12.1 The programmer's cube. [Adapted from Patricia Farrell and Herberta M. Lundegren, *The Process of Recreation Programming: Theory and Technique*, 3rd ed. (State College, Penna.: Venture Publishing, 1991), 172; and Donald G. DeGraaf, Debra J. Jordan, and Kathy H. DeGraaf, *Programming for Parks, Recreation, and Leisure Services: A Servant Leadership Approach* (State College, Penna.: Venture Publishing, 1999), 122–123.]

process. Finally, language is developed through reading stories, singing songs, and playing counting games.

Play Age   Preschoolers develop their abilities physically and cognitively. They work on completing small movements with fingers and hands. Playing follow the leader, jumping rope, playing catch and tag, and sliding down slides all help improve physical abilities. Detailed motor coordination is

❖ Playground,
Aspen, Colorado.
[Source: Design
Workshop, Inc.]

improved through coloring, arts and crafts, making necklaces, and play-ing with blocks and Play-Doh. Mental stimulation comes from playing Go Fish and storytelling. This is also the period in which children are unable to differentiate between fantasy and reality. So-called magical thinking is stimulated through activities such as dressing up, playing house, and building a tent.

School Age The primary tasks for school-age children are to increase their skills and knowledge while learning about the rules of and their role in society. Skills can be developed through advanced arts and crafts, sport clinics, making models, and playing musical instruments. Certain board games, such as Life, help participants learn about roles in society.

Adolescence During what are, for many, troubled adolescent years, individuals go through physical and cognitive changes. Important issues arise relative to body image, sexuality, independence, abstract thought, and identity formation.[3] Makeup and fashion shows and exercise programs are important tools for developing body image. Co-ed sports allow participants to explore issues of sexuality. Journal writing can help with the development of abstract thought, while field trips and cooking projects help develop independence.

Young Adulthood Young adults have issues related to social interaction, intimacy, and vocation choice. Social skills can be developed through special interest clubs, cooking classes, and co-ed sports. Playing versions of *The Dating Game* and *The Newlywed Game* allows guests to explore issues of intimacy. A "Dressing for Success" program can help prepare participants for work.

Adulthood Adults are primarily concerned with balancing productivity at work with family at home, and the individual's role in society. Programs to help at work might focus on time management. Scavenger hunts and camping trips turn the spotlight on the family. Volunteering and coaching are opportunities for people to give back to society.

Old Age As people approach old age, they attempt to come to terms with who they are, where they have been, and what they have (and have not) accomplished. Physical and mental faculties require stimulation, and social connections must be maintained, especially after a spouse dies. Older people desire to "bring it all together" and pass knowledge on to a younger generation. Walking, dancing, and exercise clubs help promote physical activity, while bridge clubs, pot luck events, and concerts assist with social connections. Current event lectures and card playing help maintain cognitive abilities. Classes on yoga and guest speakers on religious topics help with spiritual connections. Finally, journal writing, intergenerational programs, and video remembrances allow individuals to pass on accumulated knowledge to following generations.

FORMATS Chapter 11 outlined seven possible formats for activities:

- ❖ *Instruction*—to learn a new skill or to develop or refine an existing one
- ❖ *Competition*—either intrinsic (competing against oneself) or extrinsic (looking good in front of others)
- ❖ *Social activities*—because of the need to be with people
- ❖ *Trips*—either a day or an overnight trip
- ❖ *Drop-in activities*—for those who want self-directed programs
- ❖ *Special events*—such as festivals, banquets, shows, and exhibitions
- ❖ *Spectator*—for people seeking playing tips or for those whose active participation (but not their interest) is over

PROGRAM POSSIBILITIES It is important to offer programs that will appeal to guests. However, it is hard to differentiate between short-term fads and long-term trends. Several questions can be asked to help clarify the issue:

❖ Does the new development fit in with other basic lifestyle trends or changes in the consumer world? Increasing numbers of consumers are pressed for time. Activities that deliver value for the time invested are likely to remain popular.

❖ How varied, immediate, and important are the benefits associated with the new development? The more benefits gained in the short run by participating in the activity, the more likely it will become a trend.

❖ Can the product or service be personalized or modified to meet individual needs? Health and wellness can be expressed in many ways—through changes in diet, exercise, stress, and smoking status, for example. As a result consumers can customize how they want to improve their health. Thus, health and wellness will remain a trend.

❖ Is the product or service a trend in itself or the manifestation of a larger trend? The rise and fall in popularity of different ethnic restaurants is part of a broader trend toward spicier food.

❖ Has the new development been adopted by key consumers who drive change? Any development needs the support of baby boomers and working women to have a lasting effect in today's marketplace. However, the support in certain key segments must also be determined. In certain sports, acceptance by teens and young adults is critical to success.[4]

Sports and Games

Sports and games encompass field and team sports, individual and dual sports, recreational games, and fitness activities. While the tendency is to concentrate on competition, many people are increasingly emphasizing developing a lifetime sports orientation—that is, learning activities that they can participate in throughout their lives.

The National Sporting Goods Association (NSGA) surveys people currently taking part in various sports, asking how many anticipate increasing their participation. Sports showing high positive change in terms of future participation include:

❖ exercise walking (56 percent)
❖ fishing (50 percent)
❖ exercising with equipment (46 percent)
❖ bicycling (46 percent)
❖ camping (45 percent)[5]

Many activities require that tournaments be developed. Tournaments can be organized in one of several ways. They may be presented as an elimination tournament, a round robin, a challenge, or a scoring event. In an elimination tournament, opponents are determined by the resort staff, the winner moves on, and the loser drops out or is moved into a consolation activity. This form is appropriate when many people want to enter and limited time is available. If the ability of the players is known, the event is designed so that the two best players have a good chance of meeting in the final. This is known as *seeding*. Seeded tournaments place participants in brackets such that the two best seeds are placed in separate brackets. A tournament with eight players is illustrated in Figure 12.2. Players A through H are listed in terms of ability. A plays H and B plays G. In this scenario, there is a good chance that the two top seeds, A and B, will meet in the final. If the ability of the participants is not known, the draw should be a blind one.

If the number of participants is not equal to numbers of the power of two—2, 4, 8, 16, 32—then the next bracket number greater than the number of participants must be used. Byes are given to the better players in the first round. For example, if there are 12 players in a tournament, a bracket of 16 is set up in the first round. The four best players receive byes and play the four winners of players 5 through 12 in a second round of eight.

Some tournaments use flights to place participants of similar ability in the same bracket. A golf tournament may require all participants to play an 18-hole qualification round. The scores are tallied and the top eight players—those with the lowest scores—are placed into a championship flight. The next lowest eight are placed into the first flight, and so on until all participants are placed. This method allows for players of similar ability to compete against each other.

Tournaments may be organized for single or double elimination. In the former, a participant is eliminated once she loses a single game. In the latter, two losses are necessary for elimination. Consolation rounds may be arranged for players who lose in the first or subsequent rounds. The sting of defeat is lessened, and the accent is on playing as much as possible.

The round robin tournament allows every contestant to play every other player. Win-loss records are kept. The winner is the person with the best record. This format works when everyone wants to play everyone else, when time is not a problem, and when a limited number of entries—six to eight teams—is anticipated.

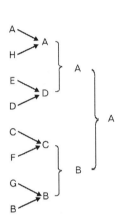

❖ FIGURE 12.2 Single elimination brackets. [Adapted from Patricia Farrell and Herberta M. Lundegren, *The Process of Recreation Programming: Theory and Technique*, 3rd ed. (State College, Penna.: Venture Publishing, 1991), 159.]

❖ Fly fishing, Colorado. [Source: Design Workshop, Inc.]

Challenge tournaments are scheduled by the competitors. Consequently, little structure is needed and special officials are not required. Facilities must be available for drop-in play and time cannot be a problem.

Events may be scored for the purpose of declaring winners in a variety of ways: objective scoring, as in a timed event; subjective scoring, as in a best costume contest; straight scoring events—for example, golf—where the competitors score themselves. Handicapping can be used to allow all competitors to start the competition evenly. In golf, for example, the handicap system attempts to put all golfers at par. A golfer who typically shoots par on a course is given a handicap of zero. One who shoots 77 on a par-72 course carries a handicap of five. Subtracting the par (72) from the actual score (77) makes the second golfer a par golfer like the first. When the two meet, the first golfer gives the second five strokes—making them, in theory, equal players for their round of golf. [6]

Fitness/Wellness Activities

Interest in fitness and wellness continues to increase. Guest interests include fitness activities, nutrition education, aerobic activities, and even weightlifting. According to the American Council on Exercise (ACE), the coming decade will see the following:

- ❖ Individualized exercise programs coached by a human or electronic personal trainer. Internet-based personal training sites will allow individuals to work directly with a personal trainer to design programs, track progress, and learn on line.
- ❖ A sharp increase in mindful exercises like tai chi and yoga. Yoga is popular, in part, because of its acceptance by such public figures as Madonna, Courtney Love, and Ricky Martin. Some brand-name clothing companies have come out with a trendy line of yoga outfits.
- ❖ An increase in exercise programs geared to older adults (the graying baby boomers). A prime example is yoga, which appeals to the need to do something about stiffening joints.
- ❖ Goal-oriented exercise training.
- ❖ Smart fitness machines designed to accept a computer disk or palm-size scanner containing a personalized exercise program.
- ❖ Adventure workouts that enhance body and spirit, such as rock climbing, hiking, and mountain biking.
- ❖ More people seeking fitness for health reasons instead of solely for appearance.
- ❖ Sport-specific personal training for such activities as golf and tennis. For example, people are doing the Salute to the Setting Sun yoga position to improve their golf game.
- ❖ Lifestyle exercises, incorporating fitness into everyday life.[7]

Many observers of leisure trends believe that exercise will become a way of life for increasing numbers of Americans and that this trend will become even more pronounced with each succeeding generation. Sports programs that build skills in soccer, softball, and basketball are aimed at kids who start playing at an earlier age. As children grow older, they need more diversified options, such as mountain biking and whitewater rafting, that are part of a high-adventure program.

Options exist to contract out a fitness program. Jazzercise is a successful example of this in the public sector. This dance–exercise program offers over 2000 classes weekly at 430 parks and recreation facilities across the United States. The operator pays either a percentage of the gross or an hourly rate for use of the facilities during a specific time.[8]

A special category of fitness and wellness involves rehabilitation programs for people with disabilities. While most rehabilitation programs focus on assisting participants in regaining physical strength and range of motion, sports programs seek to rehabilitate a person both physically and emotionally. When people with physical disabilities learn to ski, for example, it increases their self-confidence while gaining the respect of others.

A forerunner in the field of sports programs for people with disabilities is the National Sports Center for the Disabled at Winter Park, Colorado. Begun in 1970, it is the largest and best-known skiing program of its kind. Summer activities have been added over the years and include rafting on the Colorado River, hiking, backpacking, overnight camping, nature walks, chairlift rides, dance movement, adaptive swimming, rock climbing (for the visually impaired), and tennis. Teaching methods are adapted from the American Teaching System (ATS). The four fundamental skills taught are:

- *balancing movements*—required to keep the body in equilibrium when acted on by external forces.
- *rotary movements*—of the body as a whole, or parts of it. It is desirable to use the lower body for rotary movements.
- *edge control movements*—that affect the way the edges of the skis come into contact with the snow surface.
- *pressure control movements*—used to control the pressure the skis exert on the snow as they move.[9]

Maneuvers that are taught seek to provide building blocks for one or more of these skills.

It is possible to teach individuals with a variety of disabilities to ski. The three-track method is used for people who have one good leg and two arms. The adaptive equipment required consists of one ski and two outriggers. With the addition of a prosthesis, the method can also be used by a double amputee.

The four-track method uses four ski sources to maneuver down the slope. Two outriggers complement the two skis. This method is used for skiers with an aneurysm, cerebral palsy, spina bifida, muscular dystrophy, or multiple sclerosis. Reins or a bungee cord can be added to help control speed.

Monoboards or snowboards can be substituted for people who cannot risk independent leg action, such as those with severe hip problems or full leg braces. For people with severe disabilities, sit-skiing gives the experience of speed and motion. Students sit in a sled-type device controlled by the upper body and a short handheld pole. An able-bodied skier skis behind the sled holding an attached rope. The sit-ski is gradually being replaced with bi-skis. A sled consisting of a bucket that rests on two skis is substituted for the shell of the sit-ski. The equipment of the future for most paraplegics is the mono-ski, which allows students to ski in a three-track fashion. It is similar to the bi-ski except that it has one rather than two skis under the bucket.

Aquatics   An aquatic program can encompass swimming, water polo, scuba diving, lessons, pool parties, and water aerobics. Swimming is particularly attractive as a lifetime fitness activity. It offers numerous healthy benefits and few dangers. Water exercise is much less jarring on lower limbs than jogging. Some 70 million Americans claim to participate in swimming as a recreational activity.[10]

Service/Volunteer Activities   Many people find it rewarding to give to the community. They may volunteer to work with people with disabilities, as noted above, to coach, or to run social events. In recent years, volunteering has earned an increased prestige.[11]

Dance   The possibilities for dance programs are almost endless. They include:

❖ ballet
❖ children's rhythms
❖ contemporary/modern
❖ country/round
❖ folk
❖ popular/current
❖ precision movement skills
❖ show dance/modern jazz
❖ social dance/chorus line
❖ tap
❖ hip-hop

Dance programs also open up a wide variety of complementary activities such as choreography, costume, makeup, and directing.[12]

Drama   Drama allows participants to portray someone else or something else. Programs offer opportunities for performance, assistance, and watching. The scope of such programs is large and encompasses:

❖ creative dramatics
❖ creative writing
❖ film and videotape
❖ formal plays
❖ linguistic activities
❖ pantomime and clown activities
❖ puppetry/marionettes
❖ reenactments
❖ readings[13]

Music As with drama, music programs offer roles for performers, supporters, and spectators. Opportunities exist for classes in music appreciation, instrumental instruction, performances, and composition.

Arts and Crafts Art is thought of as creations that are appreciated as objects in and of themselves, while crafts are items that serve a functional purpose. Arts and crafts programs encompass:

❖ graphics
❖ painting
❖ photography
❖ printing
❖ sketching
❖ sculpture/welding

Arts and crafts has seen high growth for both participants and spectators. It can be a high-cost program that requires top leaders to be successful. The possibilities of art as therapy should not be overlooked.

Crafts are relatively simple to do, take little time, are inexpensive, and require minimal staff training.[14] However, they can become expensive when the activity is specialized into a single medium. Examples of activities are:

❖ ceramics
❖ jewelry
❖ leathercraft
❖ paper
❖ weaving
❖ woodworking

Crafts are subject to fads. Programmers must constantly be aware of changing tastes and adapt accordingly.

Environmental Activities: Typically, the goal of environmental activities is to learn about the interdependence of living organisms or to learn how to behave in the environment. Programs can include camping, environmental education, nature-oriented activities, outdoor living skills, conservation skills, and bird-watching.

Rapid growth in this area has meant that programs are increasingly taking on more complex issues, covering economic as well as technological aspects and their impact. Emphasis on biological characteristics and the environment as a resource base has increased.

Adventure Education: The popularity of rock climbing is due, in part, to a recent boom in indoor climbing walls. Although resorts are concerned about risk management, research indicates that climbing on a traverse wall produces fewer injuries than playing on the playground.[15]

quick getaways 12.1

Evaluating Activity Providers

Here are some questions travel agents can ask to evaluate suppliers before booking guests on a natural history tour:

- What level of experience and training do guides have?
- Are they educated in the natural sciences? trained in interpreting the environment for travelers?
- Are the guides truly bilingual?
- Are the guides local? Are they able to speak knowledgeably about both cultural and natural history?
- What kinds of vehicles are used, especially for wildlife viewing?
- If accommodations are in tented camps, what kinds of showers are provided? What kind of cots?
- How does the firm demonstrate its commitment to protecting the environment and benefiting local inhabitants?

Source: "Finding Clients Their Ideal Tour," Travel Weekly, 9 October 1997, supp., p. 15.

Adventure education, which encompasses backcountry travel, ropes courses, initiative activities, team building, and rock climbing, is concerned with two types of relationship: interpersonal and intrapersonal.[16] The former refers to how people get along in a group. Issues that are explored include communication, cooperation, trust, conflict resolution, problem solving, and leadership. Intrapersonal relationships deal with how an individual gets along with himself. The basic idea is that change can take place when individuals and groups are exposed to challenge, high adventure, and new growth experiences. Climbing activities help young people develop interpersonal skills (cooperation and communication), personal strengths (self-esteem and self-confidence), cognitive skills (decision making, problem solving), and physical abilities (fitness and motor skill development).

Adventure education programs aimed at children and teens can be offered in one or more of following ways:

❖ cooperative games and sports
❖ self-challenging activities
❖ resident camps[17]

When a sports unit is offered, the emphasis is on the team aspect of the activity. Students learn the skills involved in the game or sport, but team building is the primary objective.

During self-challenging activities, participants learn to compete against themselves rather than others. Examples include scaling an indoor climbing wall and outdoor rock climbing. For participants grades 4 through 6, an indoor wall has blocks of different sizes and types that are bolted to a wall at heights ranging from a few inches to 5 feet. The children climb the wall using a variety of hand- and footholds, never getting higher than the height of a balance beam. From this traverse wall, participants graduate to a vertical climbing wall that reaches to 20 feet. At the top, they can sign their names to demonstrate their mastery.

Another option is a five-day adventure camp. Camps tend to have central themes such as "Knights, Castles, and Dragons" and "Pirates, Rafts, and Treasures." In the former, participants get involved in building a real castle with drawbridge, walls, cardboard armor, shields, water balloon catapults, medieval feasts, and tournaments. In the latter, participants build a homemade raft out of 100 milk jugs and PVC pipe and float out of camp on the last day.[18]

Extreme Sports   According to American Sports Data, Inc., participation in extreme sports has increased dramatically in recent years. Snowboarding, as an example,

❖ Dog sledding.
[Source: Design
Workshop, Inc.]

has grown 113 percent in the past five years and now boasts 5.5 million participants. Mountain biking, skateboarding, and scuba diving are examples of other activities that have shown growth in recent years.[19]

Travel and Tourism Travel and tourism can range from trips, tours, and travelogues to adventure tourism and field trips. The range of adventure tourism possibilities is illustrated in Figure 12.3. Opportunities vary from soft to high adventure and involve low to high risk. Market segments can be targeted depending on the degree of risk the guest wants to undertake. Soft adventure activities involve the perception of risk and excitement without actual danger. Theme park rides or floats down the Grand Canyon on huge rafts fit this category. They are suitable for people with physical restrictions or who are just beginning to explore adventure possibilities.

Adventure activities offer more risk than soft adventure and include treks in the Himalayas and two- to six-person raft trips in the western United States. High-risk activities involve real risks, so participants may have to master specialized skills before being allowed to participate.

Developers of orbital tourism see space travel as a possibility by 2025.[20] Visitors would arrive at their Hilton (currently being designed) having traveled through space at 30 times the speed of jetliners. Arthur Frommer, the travel book publisher, already has issued *The Moon: A Guide*

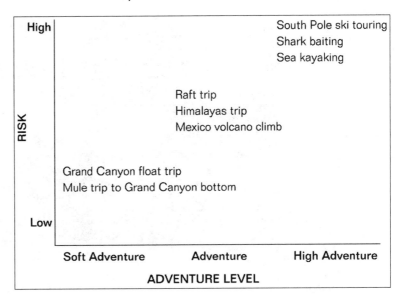

❖ FIGURE 12.3 Tour packages and levels of risk. [Source: Dale R. Christiansen, "Adventure Tourism," in John C. Miles and Simon Priest (eds.), *Adventure Education* (State College, Penna.: Venture Publishing, 1990), 436.]

for First-Time Visitors.[21] Civilians currently pay $15,000 for a weeklong program at Moscow's Star City Gagarin Cosmonaut Training Center to experience weightlessness during a parabolic flight, a spin in a giant centrifuge, and a scuba dive in a neutral buoyancy tank to simulate spacewalking.

Other forecasted opportunities include deep-sea safaris to 12,000 feet below the surface. At the moment, guests at the two-room Jules' Undersea Lodge in Key Largo, Florida, must dive 21 feet to enter. A Honolulu architectural firm is designing an 80-room underwater hotel and observatory, to be built at an as-yet undisclosed location.

Cybersafaris will satisfy those who hear the call of the wild but do not want to undergo the hassles involved in actually traveling to the location. As remote areas become tourist sites, rare animals become extinct, and isolated cultures are assimilated, demand may emerge for nostalgia tours to world capitals and former wildlife zones to recreate the days of gondolas, Galapagos turtles, rainforests, or reef life. History enthusiasts might time-travel through virtual trips to California's hippie days, Paris' Café Society of the 1930s, or the Roaring Twenties in Manhattan.

Social Recreation Social recreation includes activities that facilitate the social interaction process. Here are some examples:

❖ celebrations and festivals
❖ board games
❖ mixers

❖ mass participation games
❖ parties
❖ social interaction games
❖ table and electronic games[22]

Hobbies Typically, hobbies encompass:

❖ collecting
❖ creative work
❖ education
❖ gardening

As the baby boomers age, gardening is growing in popularity. Gardening is second only to walking as the most common form of physical exercise among adults, beating out jogging, running, aerobic exercise, riding a bicycle, swimming, tennis, bowling, and golf.[23] Gardening is popular for a number of reasons. About 46 percent of gardeners want to spend time outdoors, 39 percent find pleasure in aesthetic beauty, and 36 percent view the hobby as relaxation. It is most popular in small towns and rural areas in the West and Midwest. Anywhere from 36 percent to 43 percent of men and 21 percent to 30 percent of women participate in gardening, depending on age. The most popular activities are taking care of the lawn (47 percent of gardeners), growing flowers (39 percent), and growing vegetables (over 35 percent). Less than 10 percent of gardeners raise aquatic plants, fruit trees, ornamental gardens, or herbs. The trend is toward low-maintenance landscapes, local native plants, and wildlife gardens designed to attract birds and butterflies.

It is estimated that one in three people in both the United States and the United Kingdom collect something. Collecting is split evenly between men and women and cuts across all socioeconomic classes. Research in Israel concludes that people who collect strive for a sense of "closure, completion and perfection."[24] Others see it as a substitute for emotional support that was lacking in childhood. Collecting can be a way of coping with inner uncertainty.

Cognitive and Literary Activities This category includes:

❖ creative writing
❖ debating
❖ book clubs
❖ visiting museums

According to research by the NPD Group, Inc., fewer people are reading.[25] However, the older the age group, the more people in it read. People over 50 read an average of an hour a day, almost double the time of people in their 20s and below. As the baby boomer generation ages, the market for books may increase. Polls dating back to the 1920s show that reading declines with age. It remains to be seen whether or not this generation will break that pattern.

Another trend is the sprouting up of book clubs. Often, members get together for what some describe as equal parts of "gossip, books, dessert," but the inclination to arrange personal encounters with authors and concoct book-related field trips is growing.[26]

Self-Improvement/ Education
The number of adult learners participating in traditional college programs is increasing dramatically. Adult learners (those age 25 or older) make up 40 percent of undergraduate enrollment in U.S. colleges and universities. This percentage is expected to grow. Adults learn differently from younger students.[27] As people grow older, they move from having a dependent personality to being increasingly self-directed. In addition, they collect a growing body of experiences that they draw on as they learn. Their readiness to learn is heavily influenced by their social roles. Finally, their time perspective changes. Younger students are able to learn things while understanding that the knowledge may not be used until later in life. Adult learners want to apply their newfound knowledge immediately to solve problems facing them today.

Possible activities include:

❖ retreats
❖ conferences
❖ advocacy groups
❖ genealogy research
❖ stress management
❖ leisure education

PROGRAM PLANNING

On average, skiers ski for six hours and sleep for eight, which leaves them with ten free hours a day, every minute of which they fully intend to enjoy.
—JIM FELTON
Vail Resorts, Inc., *Urban Land*

Planning a guest activity program involves five steps:

1. leadership
2. budgeting
3. scheduling
4. facility availability
5. promoting the program[28]

LEADERSHIP Often described as the most important factor in determining the success of a program, selection of the appropriate leadership is certainly crucial. The process involves three important and sequential steps:

❖ job analysis
❖ job specifications
❖ recruitment of suitable candidates

First, the tasks involved in the job must be identified. This analysis identifies the job functions that must be carried out together with the skill level at which they need to be performed. This results in a job description for the position.

From the job description comes the knowledge, skills, and abilities necessary to perform the job. This is called a job specification and is the second step in the process. Finally, with job specification in hand, suitable candidates for the job can be recruited. It is important to consider both internal and external candidates, as both have advantages. Administrators are likely to be more familiar with the ability of an internal candidate compared to someone from the outside. No resume or interview can compensate for actually seeing a person in action. In addition, if the resort promotes from within, employees are likely to be more motivated than if the company regularly bypasses existing employees to hire from outside. On the other hand, external candidates can bring fresh ideas and a new approach to dealing with problems that an internal candidate may not have.[29]

Volunteers Depending on the size and type of program being developed, volunteers may be an integral part of the operation. Volunteers are "people who give service of their own free will with no obligation to act."

The consensus in the literature is that the success of a program relying on volunteers is based on the staff's ability to "keep volunteers motivated and to challenge them with meaningful assignment." What, exactly, motivates volunteers? Where people are doing something because they want to rather than because they have to, motivation tends to be intrinsic rather than extrinsic; the individual is motivated by reasons internal to herself rather than by external factors such as money or praise. People tend to be internally motivated by achievement, affiliation, or power.[30]

People motivated by achievement get a thrill from meeting standards, from the accomplishment of objectives. One of these objectives might be full-time employment. People may volunteer as part of a university internship requirement or strictly as a way of getting their foot in the door. The social interaction that comes from personal relationships is what motivates those who seek affiliation. Power motivation implies that satisfaction comes from encouraging others to perform. The task of the guest activity director is to correctly identify what motivates each volunteer and structure responsibilities for each person that will challenge them while allowing them to meet the needs they consider important.

Recruitment is best done one on one. However, an initial group meeting may be necessary to explain the program and its benefits to volunteers. People who are interested can be communicated with individually to determine motivation.

Volunteers should be treated with the same care as paid employees. They need to be oriented to the operation, trained in their responsibilities, motivated, and evaluated.

BUDGETING The process of setting a price for a guest activity program involves several steps.

1. Determine costs.
2. Set the proportion of costs to be covered.
3. Consider the appropriateness of differential pricing.
4. Set an initial price.[31]

Figure 12.4 is an example of a budget for a tennis program.

Program Cost A guest activity will incur two types of costs: indirect and direct. Indirect costs are those costs that cannot be directly associated with a particular program yet are incurred in operating the guest services program as a whole. For example, a director and staff are involved in running the entire operation; their salaries must be accounted for. Staff salaries must be paid and offices must be heated whether programs operate or not. Resorts have to decide how to allocate the indirect costs of running the guests activity department to the various programs that are offered. There are several possibilities:

Tennis Drill Clinic—Stroke of the Day

Revenue
    Lesson Fees*

370 hotel guests @ $25.00	$ 9,250	
246 members @ $12.00	$ 2,952	
154 individuals @ $40.00	$ 6,160	
	$ 18,362	

    Retail sales
        $500 per day $154,000

Total monthly revenue $172,362

Operating expenses
    Salaries

1 lead instructor	$20,000	
11 instructors @ $5,000	$55,000	
5 clubhouse staff @ $2,000	$10,000	
5 maintenance staff @ $1,500	$ 7,500	
	$ 92,500	
Facilities/utilities	$ 10,000	
Office/telephone	$ 5,000	
Maintenance	$ 5,000	
Advertising	$ 5,000	
Promotion	$ 10,000	
	$127,500	

Net income $ 44,862

❖ FIGURE 12.4
Program budget.

*12 hotel guests per day; 8 members per day; 5 individuals per day

- ❖ *Equal share*—Each program is assigned an equal share of the indirect costs involved in running the department.
- ❖ *Percentage of budget*—Each program is charged with a percentage of indirect expenses equal to its percentage of the overall department budget.
- ❖ *Time budget study*—Each program is charged for indirect expenses based on the amount of time spent on the program by the staff in developing and implementing it.
- ❖ *Space or measurement study*—Each program is charged for indirect costs based on its actual expenses.[32]

The objective is to determine the full cost of planning, operating, and evaluating a program. Indirect costs should be allocated equitably in a manner indicating how much of an indirect cost a program actually uses.

Direct costs, on the other hand, are specific expenses related to a single item. For example, a program on fly-fishing might include the costs of an instructor and promotional brochures. Direct costs may be fixed or variable. Fixed costs stay constant during a specified time—for example, the salary of an instructor. The cost may be fixed within a particular range. For example, if a standard is set of 16 guests per instructor, within the range of 1 to 16 guests, the instructor's salary is fixed. However, beyond 16 participants, another instructor must be hired. Thus, costs are fixed within a specific range.

Variable costs vary proportionately with volume. Suppose each guest who participates in an activity receives a souvenir of the occasion. The cost of providing the souvenirs is variable.

Pricing Objectives
A decision must be made as to which costs are to be covered. Resorts may decide that certain activities are free to guests, that programs cover only the variable costs of the program, that some of the overhead costs are covered, or that all costs, both direct and indirect, are covered. It is important to note that the indirect costs of running the guest activity department must be paid whether they are allocated to the various programs or not. Management may view the department as a necessary service to the guests in order to attract them to the resort. Seen in this way, the indirect costs involved in running the department can be viewed as a way of selling rooms, with programs being expected to cover only direct costs.

Differential Opportunities
Different prices may be set depending on:

❖ *Participants*—Children generally pay less than adults.
❖ *Product*—One price is charged for a group lesson and another for a private lesson.
❖ *Place*—People pay more for better seats at a concert.
❖ *Time*—Prices are lower during periods of low demand (off-season).
❖ *Quantity*—Season passes offer a discount because guests buy in bulk.
❖ *Incentives*—Prices are initially set low as an incentive to get guests to try a new activity.[33]

Initial Price
Development of a budget requires forecasting both revenue and costs associated with a specific program. A realistic rule of thumb for forecasting revenue is to assume that 80 percent of anticipated registrants will enroll in the program. Pricing can be based on cost, demand, or competition.

Cost-based pricing involves pricing the activity so that some or all of the costs are covered. Demand-based pricing sets prices according to what the market will bear. There are, for example, certain psychological aspects to pricing. Many people believe that price and quality are directly correlated—the higher the price, the better the quality. A program may be priced at a level that more than covers the costs involved as long as guests are willing to pay and believe that the value they receive is greater than the price they are asked to pay.

The costs involved in running a program set the floor for the price to be charged. The level of demand, what guests are willing to pay, sets the ceiling for how much is charged. The level of competition determines where, between the ceiling and the floor, the price is set.

SCHEDULING The key issue in scheduling is to offer programs that meet the time needs of resort guests. Three patterns are involved in scheduling activities. The first consideration is a seasonal one. Certain activities are season-specific. A full list of programs can be developed for each season, taking into account the constraints and appropriateness of each time of the year. A winter program, for example, would focus on activities involving snow— sleigh rides, ski lessons, etc.—while tapping trees for syrup and leaf tours would work in the fall.

A second aspect to scheduling involves a monthly or weekly focus. The time span must relate to the average length of stay. If most people stay for two weeks, for example, a varied 14-day schedule of activities must be developed so that the second week is not a repeat of the first.

Finally, resorts plan a daily time schedule. Depending on the pattern of activity of the guests, activities in several or all of the following time frames might be scheduled:

- ❖ morning
- ❖ early afternoon
- ❖ afternoon activity at lower level
- ❖ late afternoon
- ❖ early evening
- ❖ late evening

It is important, when scheduling activities, to consider when regular maintenance can be done. The best time for maintenance is when demand for participation in the program is low. For ski areas, for example, most maintenance takes place in the so-called mud season, after the ski season ends.[34]

FACILITY Facilities need to be convenient and accessible to the guest. They must be
AVAILABILITY attractive and safe places in which to undertake the activity. The safety
factor means being concerned about risk management.[35]

Risk management involves a proactive attempt to minimize the unde-
sirable risks inherent in any guest activity. Risks are "managed" in one of
four ways:

- ❖ *Elimination*—by, for example, not offering the program
- ❖ *Acceptance*—by continuing to offer the program
- ❖ *Transfer*—(through insurance) to another entity
- ❖ *Reduction*—by, for example, requiring participants to wear safety
  equipment[36]

Resorts have a duty to offer a safe environment to their guests because
a legal relationship exists between the resort and the guest. Staff are
expected to offer a standard of care that is reasonable to expect from a
trained professional. For a ruling of negligence, guests would have to
show that an injury was a direct result of an action or a lack of action by
the employee(s). Finally, there must be injury—physical, emotional, or
mental—to the guest, or damage to property.

❖ Pedestrian trails—
always available,
Pitkin County,
Colorado. [Source:
Design Workshop,
Inc.]

Creativity at Work: Sad Mr. Lion and His Lost Happy Song

Let's examine the difference creative programming can make in the delivery of a guest activity. As 50 children entered the activity area, they were greeted by volunteers dressed as a lion, Lorax a bird, Mother Nature a clown, Timothy Ugly and a princess. They were led into a pavilion by Mother Nature, who introduced them to Mr. Lion. She explained that he was sad because the wind had stolen the four lines of his happy song and hidden them all over the resort. Would the children help him find his song and make him happy again? To an enthusiastic *yes*, the children headed outside to look for clues.

Immediately outside, the children found a large birdlike creature who confessed he had the first line of the song. He would not give it up, however, until the children answered riddles and told him some jokes. In return, he taught them the first line of the song and led them to a playground where the Lorax was waiting. She gave them the second line of the song, but only after teaching them a complicated dance step. While dancing, they noticed Timothy Ugly off in a corner. He would not talk to any of the children because he thought them all prettier than he.

Mother Nature led them away and suggested that the children make the ugliest masks they could so Mr. Ugly would talk to them and help them find the third line of the song. The children worked for about 40 minutes making masks from materials that had been laid out. They crept up on Mr. Ugly to surprise him. Happy at what he saw, he gave up the third line of the song and led the children a short distance to a pretty princess, who took them on a search for the fourth line of the song. A great cheer went up when it was found under a nearby tree.

With great enthusiasm, the children rushed back to Mr. Lion and sang him the song several times. The happy lion led the children, still singing and dancing, back to the pavilion for cookies and lemonade.

Source: Adapted from *Parks & Recreation,* 9:6 (1974), National Recreation and Park Association.

Question: Can you develop a creative program using the guidelines included above?

The process of risk management involves scrutinizing every activity offered for anything that could possibly go wrong and developing procedures to prevent accidents from happening. All risks cannot, and should not, be completely eliminated. They should, however, be known, understood, manageable, and enhance or be an essential part of the activity.[37] Skiing is a good example. The risks are known to skiers and managed by the resort through trail marking and activity monitoring by the ski patrol.

PROMOTING THE PROGRAM Modern marketing calls for more than developing a good product, pricing it attractively, and making it available to target guests. Management communicates with customers—both existing and potential—through what is known as the promotional mix. The goal of promotion is behavior modification; marketers want to initiate or change the behavior of guests such that they participate in the guest activity offered by the resort. Specifically, promotion seeks to inform, persuade, and remind. The specific steps involved in developing and implementing a promotional effort were outlined in Chapter 8.

PROGRAM EVALUATION

[Program evaluation is a] process whereby, through systematically judging, assessing, and appraising the workings of a program, one gains information that indicates whether or not they are getting results or getting where they want to go . . . whether or not the program has value.
—PATRICIA FARRELL AND HERBERTA M. LUNDEGREN
The Process of Recreation Programming: Theory and Technique

EVALUATING PROGRAM EFFECTIVENESS The aims of program evaluation are twofold: to determine whether or not the program has value, and to determine whether or not the program objectives are being met. Thus, to evaluate the program, actual results must be measured against predetermined objectives. Quantitative and qualitative data are collected and compared to the preset objective. The process consists of five steps:

1. Prepare clear goal statements.
2. Determine what behaviors will indicate goal achievement.
3. Provide experiences that will lead to goal achievement.
4. Observe and assess behaviors.
5. Analyze results and change when necessary.[38]

quick getaways 12.3

Program Evaluation: National Sports Center for the Disabled

The following list of questions is used by the National Sports Center for the Disabled (NSCD) to evaluate their sailing program:

- Were the time of day and days of the week convenient for you?
- Was the length of the summer season agreeable to you?
- Did you feel that you were given enough information about what to bring for the trip?
- Please comment on the quality and appropriateness of the NSCD staff.
- Did you feel that the NSCD staff was prepared and cautious about safety issues?
- Were all directions and instructions made clear?
- Were the social aspects of the program appropriate for you?
- Did you reach your personal goals?
- Did the program costs fit into your budget?
- Was the reservation process easy and convenient for you?
- Do you plan to participate in the sailing program in the future?
- Do you have other comments or suggestions?

Source: Gigi Glass Dominguez, Operations Manager, National Sports Center for the Disabled, 2000.

Question: How would you evaluate this evaluation form in light of the material in the text?

APPROACHES TO EVALUATION

Programs can be evaluated in several ways—by the extent to which objectives are met, by the extent to which standards are met, and by the effect on guests.

Evaluation by Objectives

The importance of setting objectives was noted in Chapter 11. In this evaluation method, the appropriateness of the objectives is determined first—both the broad program objectives and the specific behavioral objectives for the guests. If the objectives are found appropriate, the program is successful if they are met. This process involves using various measurement techniques, which are examined later in this chapter.[39]

Evaluation by Standards

A standard is defined as "a degree or level of requirement, excellence, or attainment."[40] To the extent that a standard can be determined for an activity, the extent to which it is met can also be measured. While this method is easy to administer, it tends to measure things that can be counted rather than the impact of the activity on people.

Evaluation by Effects on Participants

The final method of evaluation is to measure the effectiveness of the program by looking at the impact on participants. Because the result of a guest activity program is related to guest satisfaction, this method seems more appropriate than the others described above. The nature of the effects of a guest activity on guests—and, therefore, the things that can be measured—can be:

- ❖ psychomotor (e.g., skill, strength, relief from stress)
- ❖ psychological (e.g., attitudes, need satisfaction)
- ❖ sociological (e.g., social behavior)
- ❖ educational (e.g., learning)

MEASURING INSTRUMENTS

A variety of instruments is available for measuring the success or otherwise of a program. Typically, tools are questionnaires, attitude scales, rating scales, observations, and checklists. Figure 12.5 shows an example of a rating scale. Whichever instrument is used must be reliable, valid, and objective.

Reliability means that the instrument must be dependable and consistent. It is reliable if similar results are obtained when the test is repeated under similar conditions. An instrument is valid if it measures what it is supposed to measure. Finally, it is objective if, for example, two people administering it produce the same results or come to the same conclusion.

	Excellent	Satisfactory	Needs to Improve
Equipment			
Quality of equipment	❑	❑	❑
Safety of equipment	❑	❑	❑
Quantity of equipment	❑	❑	❑
Provision of equipment	❑	❑	❑
Delivery			
Skill level of instructor	❑	❑	❑
Quality of instruction	❑	❑	❑
Concern for safety	❑	❑	❑
Class content	❑	❑	❑
Instructional progression	❑	❑	❑
Interpersonal relations	❑	❑	❑
Evaluation of students	❑	❑	❑

❖ FIGURE 12.5 Evaluation form. [Adapted from John C. Miles and Simon Priest, *Adventure Education* (State College, Penna.: Venture Publishing, 1990), 293.]

Questionnaires

Questionnaires require that individuals fill in information on a form or respond to an interviewer who then fills in the data. Development of a good questionnaire involves:

1. determining what information is needed
2. developing questions that will give the information desired
3. administering the instrument
4. analyzing the data

The first step is to determine what information is required. Is the objective to determine whether or not the guest enjoyed the program, learned anything new, or changed his attitudes? The objectives must be determined before the questions are formed.

The questions themselves can be closed, open, or scaled. Closed-format questions offer a fixed number or responses—e.g., Did you enjoy the program? [yes or no]. Answers are uniform and, therefore, more reliable. Responses, however, tend to be superficial, as guests cannot supply more information than is requested. On the other hand, open-ended questions offer respondents the opportunity to give more detailed, in-depth answers. The downside is that they take a long time to answer and an even longer time to analyze. The former means that guests may not fill out the questionnaire. The latter means that it is costly to analyze.

Observations An observation is a "planned, systematic procedure designed to note and record specific, selected occurrences." It may be a checklist or an anecdotal record. A checklist to evaluate the leader of a group might include the following:

> The leader of this program is:
>
> ____well organized
> ____well prepared
> ____motivating
> ____dull
> ____uninformed
> ____disorganized

To be considered valid, the observations must look for behaviors that are clearly defined. Because an observer is collecting the information, there is always the possibility that subjectivity creeps into the evaluation.

Attitude Scales Attitude scales measure the extent of feeling about particular items. Instead of asking "Did you enjoy the program?" guests might be asked to respond to the following:

> I enjoyed the program. (Circle one.)
> Strongly Agree   Agree   Undecided   Disagree   Strongly Disagree

EVALUATION OF In addition to evaluating programs, it is desirable to periodically evaluate
SPECIFIC AREAS the recreation areas and facilities for:

> ❖ adequacy
> ❖ use
> ❖ availability
> ❖ attractiveness
> ❖ appropriateness
> ❖ multiple uses
> ❖ accessibility

SUMMARY

A guest activity director matches the life stage of guests with the format and activity desired to develop a guest activity program. Guest life stages

Program Activities at the Broadmoor

The following activities are typical of those offered during the month of May at The Broadmoor in Colorado Springs, Colorado.

Daily

Hot-air balloon ride	6:00 a.m.–10:00 a.m.	$165.00
Jeep and horseback ride	8:15 a.m.–11:15 a.m.	$ 65.00
Bike down Gold Camp Road	1:00 p.m.–5:00 p.m.	$ 65.00
Twilight Jeep tour	6:00 p.m.–7:15 p.m.	$ 35.00
History tour (hotel)	3:00 p.m.	$ 5.00
Fitness Center	6:00 a.m.–8:00 p.m.	
Body sculpting	6:30 a.m.	
Tai chi	7:30 a.m.	
Yoga	8:00 a.m.	
Aqua Fit	9:00 a.m.	
Stretch	4:00 p.m.	
Box aerobics	5:00 p.m.	
Indoor pool	6:00 a.m.–9:00 p.m.	
Spa	8:00 a.m.–8:00 p.m.	
Aromatherapy massage	8:30 a.m.	
Movie theater	8:00 p.m.	

Tuesday

Whitewater rafting	12:00 p.m.–7:00 p.m.
Foothills Jeep tour	1:00 p.m.–4:00 p.m.

Wednesday

Fishing trip	7:00 a.m.–12:00 noon
City tour	1:00 p.m.–5:00 p.m.
History tour	3:00 p.m.–4:00 p.m.

Source: Brochure, Broadmoor, Colorado, 2000.

Question: Can you critically evaluate the activity offering presented above in light of the material in this chapter?

range from infancy to old age. Formats include instruction, competition, social activities, trips, drop-in activities, special events, and spectator. Programs range from sports and games to self-improvement and education. Program planning means putting leadership in place, budgeting, scheduling, checking on the availability of facilities, and promoting the program. Finally, programs must be continuously evaluated to ensure they are meeting the objectives of the resort.

ENDNOTES

1. Peggy Powers, *The Activity Gourmet* (State College, Penna.: Venture Publishing, 1991), 5-6.
2. Ibid., 6.
3. Ibid., 11.
4. Martin G. Letscher, "Sport Trends and Fads," *American Demographics* 19, no. 6 (June 1997): 53-57.
5. "Future Growth in Sports," *Journal of Physical Education, Recreation, and Dance* 70, no. 3 (1998), 4-6.
6. Patricia Farrell and Herberta M. Lundegren, *The Process of Recreation Programming: Theory and Technique*, 3rd ed. (State College, Penna.: Venture Publishing, 1991), 158-165.
7. Claire Martin, "Toughen Up Exercise Styles Being Reduced to Boot Camp," *Denver Post*, 2 January 2000, p. F4.
8. Carol Krucoff, "Fitness Trends for the Next Millennium," *Washington Post*, 4 January 2000, p. Z15.
9. Hal O'Leary, *Bold Tracks: Teaching Adaptive Skiing*, 3rd ed. (Boulder, Colo.: Johnson Books, 1994), 168.
10. Mel Goldstein and Dave Tanner, "Swimming for Lifetime Fitness," *Saturday Evening Post* 271, no. 4 (July 1999): 54.
11. Ginny Unold, "Inside Looking Out," *Parks and Recreation* (August 1999) vol. 40: 52-55.
12. Farrell and Lundegren, *Process of Recreation Programming*, 218.
13. Ibid., 184.
14. Ibid., 191.
15. Ibid., 179.
16. Martha A. Hyder, "Have Your Students Climbing the Walls: The Growth of Indoor Climbing," *Journal of Physical Education, Recreation, and Dance* 70, no. 9 (November 1999): 3233.
17. Simon Priest, "The Semantics of Adventure Education," in John C. Miles and Simon Priest (eds.), *Adventure Education* (State College, Penna.: Venture Publishing, 1990), 114.
18. Ibid., 376-378.

19. "Life on the Edge: Is Everyday Life Too Dull?" *Time* 154, no. 10 (6 September 1999): 28-29.

20. Judi Dash, "The New Millennium May Offer Travel Surprises Sooner Than You Think as Adventure Outfitters Embark on Future Treks," *Denver Post*, 2 January 2000, p. T1.

21. Frommer's *The Moon: A Guide for First-Time Visitors*, Wemer Kum/Ustenmacher (trans.) (New York: IDG Books Worldwide, 1998).

22. Farrell and Lundegren, *Process of Recreation Programming*, 212.

23. Jim Emerson, *Gardening*, Intertec Publishing Corporation, ISSN: 1046-4174, December 1999.

24. Laurence Zuckerman, "Why Hunt and Gather a Trove of Stuff?" *New York Times*, 22 January 2000, sec. B, p. 9.

25. Doreen Carvajal, "In Search of Readers, Publishers Consider Age," *New York Times*, 12 July 1999, sec. C, p. 1.

26. Jan Uebelherr, "Book Clubs Adding New Chapters," *Milwaukee Journal Sentinel*, 8 October 1999, p. 18.

27. Ian Patterson and Peggy Shane, "Adult Learning on the Increase," *Journal of Physical Education, Recreation, and Dance* 70, no. 5 (1998), 6.

28. Farrell and Lundegren, *Process of Recreation Programming*, 123.

29. Ibid., 125.

30. Ibid., 127.

31. Ibid., 133-134.

32. Donald G. DeGraaf, Debra J. Jordan, and Kathy H. DeGraaf, *Programming for Parks, Recreation, and Leisure Services: A Servant Leadership Approach* (State College, Penna.: Venture Publishing, 1999), 182-201.

33. Ibid., 190-192.

34. Farrell and Lundegren, *Process of Recreation Programming*, 141-149.

35. Ibid., 150.

36. DeGraaf, Jordan, and DeGraaf, *Programming for Parks, Recreation, and Leisure Services*, 134.

37. Ibid., 136.

38. Material for "Program Evaluation" was drawn from Farrell and Lundegren, *Process of Recreation Programming*, 233-262.

39. Ibid., 239.

40. Ibid., 242.

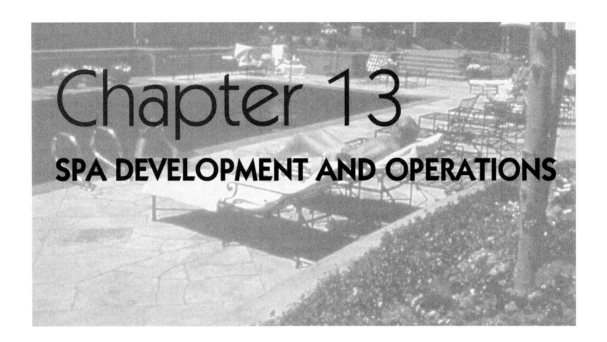

Chapter 13

SPA DEVELOPMENT AND OPERATIONS

INTRODUCTION

People are looking for other ways to take care of themselves through massage, exercise and education about how to live healthier lives.

—LAURA CRANDALL
Spa Director, Top Notch, Stowe Resort, Vermont

The market segments attracted to spas are outlined in this chapter, and criteria are given for the efficient layout of a spa operation. Treatments are noted and suggestions given for marketing the operation.[1]

DEVELOPMENT The original spa was a mineral hot springs place in Belgium in a village called Spau. "Taking the waters" became popular with the upper classes for reasons of health. Visits to spas included bathing and drinking the mineral waters in addition to mandatory social events. While European spas focus on cures and health, American operations concentrate on the promotion of a healthy lifestyle based on a combination of exercise,

❖ Spa development, Torquay, England.

weight loss, and pampering. In 1987, there were 156 spas in the United States. By 1997, the number had increased to 752.[2]

The following definitions are widely used:

❖ *Resort spa*—The resort spa is located on the property of a hotel, normally in a resort where other sports and activities are offered besides the spa program itself. Spa guests and hotel guests intermingle.
❖ *Amenity spa*—Similar to the resort spa, the amenity spa is added as an amenity to a hotel. The distinction is its unimportance as a profit center compared to the resort spa.
❖ *Destination spa*—The destination spa is hotel property targeted to the spa guest and program. Outside guests are not part of the program.

Benefits Having a spa at a resort seems to have economic advantages for the property. Resort general managers indicate that the spa enhances the following aspects of their business:

❖ room rate (57 percent)
❖ perceived value for money (70 percent)
❖ occupancy (73 percent)
❖ length of stay (43 percent)
❖ marketing advantage (97 percent)
❖ revenue per occupied room (83 percent)
❖ number of people per occupied room (27 percent)[3]

MARKET SEGMENTS People go to resort spas either because they feel stressed (47 percent of respondents) or because they want a small indulgence (42 percent of respondents).[4] Men overwhelmingly (70 percent of respondents) indicate stress as a reason for visiting a spa.[5] Sixty percent of resort spa-goers are baby boomers, while those aged 50 and older declined from 23 to 17 percent of the market between 1992 and 1997. This shortfall has been picked up by people under 30 years of age, whose market share increased from 13 to 17 percent over the same period. Over 80 percent indicated they would choose one resort over another because it had a spa.

More men are going to spas.[6] In 1987, 9 percent of spa visitors was male. Ten years later, one in four spa goers was male. In 1998, over one in three spa guests was a man.

quick getaways 13.1

Royal Hideaway Resort & Spa

Royal Hideaway Resort & Spa, the Caribbean and Mexico's finest luxury all-inclusive resort, brings the ultimate in service, amenities, and product to the incentive market. This new property opened in December 1998 in the popular resort area of Playa del Carmen, Mexico, just half an hour from Cancun International Airport. Royal Hideaway provides a luxury vacation for one prepaid price—a perfect choice for incentive travelers.

All groups are comfortably accommodated with a variety of meeting spaces for up to 140, beautifully appointed public areas, and the Supper Club, which features nightly entertainment. Full-service audiovisual equipment is available on request.

At Royal Hideaway, amenities are plentiful. The active guest can choose from water aerobics, kayaking, snorkeling, scuba classes, tennis, biking, and much more. The relaxed guest can sip a cocktail under a palm tree, enjoy a massage by the ocean, or challenge a friend to a game of oversized chess.

Royal Hideaway has just opened the Yucatan's only full-service spa, managed by Thalgo, Europe's leading spa company. The spa offers a range of treatments including thalassotherapy, a seawater-based treatment with sea-derived products; a fitness center with Cybex exercise equipment; an outdoor pool; a eucalyptus sauna/steam facility; and private changing rooms. Golf is also nearby at the championship Robert Von Hagge-designed course.

Source: "Royal Hideaway Resort & Spa (Playacar, Mexico)," *Incentive* Resorts Supplement, June 1999, 10.

Question: To what extent is this resort a true spa?

LAYOUT AND DESIGN

*Quality, durability and warranties vary greatly and must be
carefully evaluated.*

—ERICA MILLER
Day Spa Operations

EQUIPMENT A day spa targeted to the high-luxury market should occupy a minimum
of 4000 square feet. The following equipment is desirable:

- ❖ *facial equipment*—full complement of facial devices and a comfortable facial bed or chair for each room. The devices include a magni-
fying lamp, steamer, full machine with high-frequency brush and
vacuum/spray. Additional accessories include paraffin heaters,
depilatory wax heaters, wood lamps for analysis, electric masks,
mittens, booties, and blankets.
- ❖ *basic body treatment*—massage tables. Tables should be sturdy
and, for wet rooms, waterproof. Accessories include electric
bedwarmer pads and hydroculators for linen herbal wraps.
- ❖ *hydrotherapy*—hydrotherapy tub, steam shower or steam cabinet,
Scotch hose, Vichy shower, Swiss shower. The greater the number of
air and water jets, the better. A power draining system should be
included to speed turnover. A manual massage hose should also be
included. Surfaces must be nonstaining.

A Scotch hose needs a room 8 to 12 feet long and equipped with a
quick drain. Both the Vichy and Swiss showers benefit from water-
conserving heads and quick drains. The cost of constructing a wet room
can be as high as $150 per square foot.

The two main issues in a wet room are towels and hygiene. Two to ten
towels per visitor are necessary, depending on the treatment. Body treatments and hydrotherapy double or triple towel use. The tub and room
must be cleaned, disinfected, and dried between guests; this takes at least
15 minutes. In addition, wet employee uniforms must be changed. Tubs
without a power drain can take up to 30 minutes to drain, clean, and drain
again. Finally, products must be safe to go down the drain. Employee
responsibilities must be carefully thought out so guests are not kept waiting. Attention must be given to retail opportunities.

It is advisable to have separate check-in and check-out areas, if possible. Check-in areas can be noisy and rather hectic. A quiet, relaxed atmosphere makes retailing easier.

Luxury Market   The following day spa layout is appropriate for the luxury market. It consists of the following furniture, fixtures, and equipment:

Spa

   4 facial rooms
   4 massage rooms
   2 wax rooms
   1 Vichy shower with room hose, standard shower, glass block
      window, tiled walls and floor
   1 hydrotherapy room with room hose, standard shower, tiled walls
      and floor
   changing room with 6 half-lockers, hanging hooks, bench with
      hamper below
   1 Swiss shower with dry-off area
   1 small rest room
   seating for two with overhead skylight
   planters and display
   1 washer, 1 dryer, 1 water heater
   emergency exit
   mini-inner courtyard with 3 separate rooms

Hair

   8 hair stations
   3 shampoo stations
   2 hair dryers
   2 waiting rooms
   changing room with 6 half-lockers with bench and hamper below
   mixing room
   storage closet

Nails

   4 manicure stations
   2 pedicure rooms
   1 drying table
   1 waiting room
   storage closet
   display case

Public Areas

   check-in desk with computer terminal and 42-inch-high guest counter
   waiting room for 8 with phone for guest use
   check-out counter with computer terminal

quick getaways 13.2

Saddlebrook Resort

Just when you thought it couldn't get any group-friendlier, Saddlebrook Resort in Tampa, Florida, has added a 7000-square-foot European-style spa that offers special services to meeting groups. The new facility, which opened in the spring of 1997, has all of the usual features of a luxury spa: 12 treatment rooms offering tantalizing services like aromatherapy and shiatsu massage; four wet rooms; pedicure chair; hydromassage tub; aromatherapy soaking tub and couple's massage room; a Vichy shower room; whirlpools; and sauna and steam rooms.

With all this, one would expect meeting participants to have to wait in long lines behind leisure guests to use the spa. Not so! The resort works with meeting planners before an event to block out treatment times that are convenient for attendees. Planners can even book appointments for attendees or their spouses weeks ahead of a meeting, and Saddlebrook's staff includes an appointment reminder card for each guest in the registration packet.

Through its group activities department, Saddlebrook offers team building activities that can be customized to enhance the goals of meetings or conferences. Corporate challenges, team-building and sports events, as well as fitness classes, wellness seminars, and small group and spouse programs are among the choices offered to companies planning meetings on property.

The resort's facilities are more than large enough to accommodate such endeavors. For example, Saddlebrook's new Sports Village, within walking distance of the center of the resort, includes a 2½-acre activities field, a bocce ball court, a regulation-size basketball court, two grass volleyball courts, a 3000-square-foot open-air pavilion for fitness classes, a swimming pool, and a 3000-square-foot fitness center with state-of-the-art equipment.

Saddlebrook offers traditional recreational amenities as well: two 18-hole Arnold Palmer-designed championship golf courses and the Arnold Palmer Golf Academy. The resort also maintains 45 tennis courts and can arrange group lessons or tournaments through its Hopman Tennis Program.

Source: "Saddlebrook Resort: Tampa, Florida," *Successful Meetings,* New and Renovated Hotels Supplement, January 1999, 62.

Question: Compare this profile to the Royal Hideaway Resort & Spa. Which resort is better described as a spa? Defend your answer.

guest coat closet
makeup table for two
retail area with displays
rest room with handicap facilities
office
planters
courtyard with seating for eight, waterfall with pond

❖ Relaxing time,
Little Nell Hotel,
Aspen, Colorado.
[Source:Design
Workshop, Inc.]

Employee Area

1 washer
1 dryer
1 water heater
employee lockers and coat hooks
seating for nine
kitchen with dishwasher and refrigerator
employee rest room
employee entrance
cabinet for folding and storage

Purchase Criteria Concerns regarding the purchase of spa equipment are similar to those relative to the purchase of any other specialized equipment. Most equipment is delivered directly from the manufacturer. There are advantages to working with a full-service distributor who can either repair the equipment at once or provide replacements while repairs are being made.

Because equipment is both specialized and expensive, employees must be trained in its use. Who provides the training, and at what cost, is the subject of negotiation between spa management and the equipment manufacturer or distributor. Timely support and service from the distributor is crucial to ensure continuity of the spa operation.

Retail selling can be a lucrative profit center. Rather than discounting a special package, for example, the spa can offer a product as a gift. This "gift with purchase," or GWP, is common in the retail sector. It offers the advantage of getting the product into the hands of the guest. If the product does what it advertises it will do, additional retail sales may result.

TREATMENTS

Men used to think spas were only for women, but now they are looking to take advantage of the pampering and the stress-free environment. They are learning to take care of themselves.

—TANYA VASSELL
Spa Director, Elysium Spa at Cibony Ocho Rios, Jamaica

TREATMENT TYPES Spas typically offer three types of treatment: exfoliation, full-body treatment, and spot treatment.

quick getaways 13.3

Developing Spa Revenues

Here are some ways to develop spa revenues:

- *À la carte services*—Know which services are the most popular and the most profitable. Categorize and code services according to type (beauty, body, fitness, etc.).
- *Packages*—Identify how each package contributes to profitability.
- *Memberships*—Identify initiation fees and monthly dues.
- *Guests of members*—Identify what services they buy.
- *Gift certificates*—Show the breakdown by market segment and the amount spent per certificate.
- *Facility usage fee*—Consider that many resorts charge guests by the service used.
- *Retail*—Know which items what type of guests purchase and the average amount each guest spends.
- *Hotel rooms*—Allocate the room portion of a spa package to the spa budget.
- *Food and beverage*—Allocate the food portion of a spa package to the spa budget.

Source: Patrick Montenson and Judith Singer, "Turn Your Spa Into a Winner," *Cornell HRA Quarterly* (June 1992) vol. 33: 37–44.

Question: What are some additional ways to increase spa revenues?

Exfoliation   Exfoliation involves rubbing, polishing, or scrubbing the skin, or using enzymes on it, to remove dead skin and dirt. Removing dead cells allows the skin to more easily accept moisturizers and other skin treatments.

Exfoliation can be accomplished in several ways. A dry brush technique uses a loofah, brush, washcloth, or sponge to rub the dry skin away. A ten-minute exfoliation treatment is normally given prior to a body treatment and is not chargeable unless it is part of a 30-minute session involving a finishing lotion.

A salt glow is a popular destination spa treatment. It consists of rubbing special salt mixed with an oil or liquid soap on all or part of the body. It is chargeable when done on the full body and followed by a lotion application. When it is part of a spot treatment—for example, a spa pedicure—it is usually included in the price of that treatment.

A body polish uses salt or other abrasives in rubbing the body. It exfoliates and softens the skin at the same time. Treatments usually take 30 to 45 minutes for the entire body and 5 to 10 minutes for spot treatments. Enzymes and alpha-hydroxy acids (AHAs) can also be used to dissolve dead cells.

Treatment times determine appropriate booking times, which are important for the financial success of the operation. Treatments take 30 minutes when given alone or 5 to 10 minutes when given as part of an additional treatment. Cleanup and selling take an additional 5 to 10 minutes for a total booking time of 45 minutes. More time is needed for additional treatments.

Full-Body Treatment

Full-body treatments deal with and are intended to help the entire body. The face is usually excluded, as numerous procedures are intended for the face alone. Treatments are intended to condition the skin or for detoxification purposes. The former seeks to improve skin texture, color, and elasticity, while the latter seeks to help the body function better. This is achieved through stimulating circulation, which helps the body rid itself of wastes and toxins.

Full-body treatments include:

❖ *Full-body mud mask*—Mud is warmed, applied thickly, and the body wrapped in plastic or foil for 20 to 30 minutes. A full treatment takes 60 minutes. Fifteen minutes should be allowed between clients for cleanup and retail selling.

❖ *Herbal body wrap*—Linen or muslin sheets are heated and soaked in a machine in which herbal pouches or oils have been placed. The body is then covered with towels or rubber sheets, followed by the linen or muslin sheet. Additional sheets and blankets are laid over and the body allowed to rest for 20 minutes. Wet cloths need to be constantly placed on the guests' forehead. Due to the weight of the sheets, technicians can do no more than four to six wraps a day.

❖ *Paraffin body wrap*—Paraffin wraps generate heat that helps the body perspire, thereby allowing moisture and previously applied nutrients to be absorbed from the skin surface into the body. The paraffin may be used alone or in conjunction with mud or seaweed. Large strips of gauze, cut to fit the body, are dipped in the paraffin and molded to the body. The more layers (typically three to five) are applied, the greater the heat and the longer the effect. After wrapping the body in plastic or foil, it rests for 15 to 20 minutes.

❖ *Body massage*—These range from the basic Swedish massage to sports, deep tissue, Shiatsu, aromatherapy, and reflexology massages. They are booked for half an hour or a full hour.

❖ *Full-body facial*—Similar to a facial (hence, the seemingly self-contradictory name), this treatment involves cleaning, exfoliation, steam, massage, mask, and finishing lotion, and is booked for 60 to 90 minutes.

❖ *Body tanning/bronzing*—Exfoliation is followed by the application of a tanning emulsion.

Full-body treatments range from 30 minutes for a herbal wrap, body massage, or body tanning, to 1½ hours for a body facial. Most of the other treatments take 45 minutes. Wrap or mask waiting times take anywhere from 10 to 30 minutes, depending on the procedure. A body facial can be completely applied in 10 minutes, while a full-body seaweed or mud wrap takes 30 minutes. Wrap or mask waiting time is usually 20 to 30 minutes. Adding in 15 minutes for cleanup and selling pushes booking times anywhere from 45 minutes for a herbal wrap to 1¾ hours for a body facial.

Spot Treatment   Spot treatments work on a specific part of the body. They include spa manicures and pedicures; hand and foot treatments; scalp treatments; cellulite, antistress, and bust-firming treatments; back treatments; and facials. Adding exfoliation, oils, wraps, or massage qualifies the treatment as a spa treatment. Cellulite treatments involve exfoliation, application of a material that stimulates circulation, and massage followed by a mud or seaweed mask. Conditioning and moisturizing takes place after 20 minutes under wraps.

Most procedures take 30 minutes and wrap or mask time is 20 minutes. Adding 15 minutes for cleanup and selling pushes most booking times to 45 minutes. However, a spa facial can last 1½ hours.

WATER THERAPY   Hydrotherapy has become the term for treatments using water for professional purposes. Water has been used as a treatment for various diseases since the times of the ancient Greeks. Hippocrates himself used both fresh water and sea water for bathing and drinking as part of his treatment pro-

❖ Water treatment, Phoenician Resort, Phoenix, Arizona.

cedures. In England, Dr. Erasmus Darwin, father of Charles Darwin, utilized water to treat his own son, among others.

It is commonly believed that clean surface water contains great amounts of oxygen and nitrogen and little carbon dioxide. As such, it can be used to activate the body's own mechanisms. The therapeutic use of water extends to drinking it. Some people feel that, because of the saline content of water in the body, drinking small quantities of salt water is beneficial.

Water—either warm or cold—affects blood circulation to specific areas of the body. Warm or hot water dilates capillaries to improve the distribution of nutrients and oxygen to organs and tissues. Cool or cold water has the opposite effect of constricting capillaries, thus reducing swelling.

Warm to hot water:

❖ Has a strong anti-inflammatory and anti-infectious action.
❖ Relaxes the body.
❖ Increases blood flow.
❖ Eliminates toxins by inducing perspiration.
❖ Reduces pain and discomfort.
❖ Induces fatigue through muscle relaxation.
❖ Makes product penetration more effective by increasing circulation.

Cool to cold water, on the other hand:

❖ Is invigorating and stimulating, and adds tone.
❖ Helps reduce swelling through capillary contraction.
❖ Has a short-time tonic effect but a long-time depressing effect.
❖ Increases the body's resistance to disease.
❖ Can reduce pain.
❖ Stimulates the maintenance of skin elasticity.
❖ Can reduce allergic reaction tendencies.
❖ Can relieve headaches.
❖ Improves the absorption of applied substances by stimulating nerve endings, which results in improved circulation.

Because the human body is relatively dense in water, resistance or friction is greater than on land. As a result, exercising in water can accomplish more than the same effort made on land. Here are some forms of water therapy:

❖ *Hydrotherapy* refers to the use of water for well-being.
❖ *Balneotherapy* uses baths for beauty and therapeutic purposes.
❖ *Thalassotherapy* refers to the use of seaweed or seawater for beauty and therapeutic reasons. Seawater is close to blood plasma in composition. The mineral salts in seawater help skin cells take in more oxygen and draw toxins out of the body.
❖ *Herbal baths* use natural herbs or essences in baths for therapeutic purposes.
❖ *Aromatherapy baths* utilize oils for the same purpose as herbal baths.
❖ *Whirlpool baths* use water or air jets to give a bubbling effect. One type of whirlpool bath is the Jacuzzi, introduced in 1968 by Roy Jacuzzi and manufactured by the company that bears his name.

Hydrotherapy tubs have between 30 and 150 jets that can be operated at different pressures for therapeutic underwater massages. They are designed to be used by one person at a time.

For best hydrotherapy results:

❖ Clients should wait 30 minutes to an hour after eating and 15 to 20 minutes after vigorous exercise and should not have recently consumed any alcohol.

❖ Clients should use the rest room and have a warm shower prior to the session. The shower warms and relaxes muscles, which helps reduce tension.

❖ Treatment is more effective if the client is in the nude.

❖ After treatment, clients should be given water or juice, preferably orange juice, to replace lost potassium.

❖ During treatment, a cool, not cold, cloth can be applied to the head. Cool, not cold, water can be offered as well.

❖ Clients should never be left alone during treatment lest they fall asleep or faint.

The Tub   The tub itself should drain quickly. Temperatures range from 50° to 70°F for a cold bath to 98° to 105°F for a hot bath. Anything over 105°F causes the blood pressure to fall dramatically and consequent heart stress. Water and air flow in the tub increases water temperature.

Treatments usually start at 15 minutes and work up to 30 minutes maximum. Rest times between sessions should equal the time in the tub. A 30-minute session in the tub should be followed by 30 minutes of rest before commencing another tub treatment. Typically, however, a slimming or anticellulite hydrotherapy program involves treatment two to three times a week. A typical 30-minute treatment consists of 10 minutes of water jets working from the feet to the back of the neck, 10 minutes of underwater massage or additives, and 10 minutes of relaxation with gentle bubbling.

Underwater massage is accomplished by way of a hose, which is kept underwater and through which air is forced. Movements begin at the feet and work toward the heart.

TYPES OF WATER TREATMENTS   Three types of tub treatment are typical:

❖ *plain water baths*, which involve no additives but may include underwater massage

❖ *thalassotherapy baths*, which add seaweed, seawater, sea salts, or sea mud
❖ *aromatherapy* or *herbal baths*, which add herbs or oils

Most baths are based on relaxation, stimulation, and invigoration. The following oils are recognized for each of these:

❖ *relaxing*—lavender, chamomile
❖ *stimulating*—rosemary, thyme, pine
❖ *contouring*—pine, thyme, juniper

Alternating warm and cold baths is a recognized form of therapy. Warm baths relax; cold baths stimulate. More time should be spent in warm water than in cold. For example, five minutes of warm water followed by one minute of very cold water is recommended.

Showers   A variety of shower treatments exist:

❖ *Warm-ups and rinses*—initial shower, shampoo, and rinse for cleansing purposes.
❖ *Cold shower*—taken after a warm shower for the purpose of invigorating the body.
❖ *Rinsing*—one-minute showers between treatment steps.
❖ *Swiss shower*—surrounds the guest with 8 to 16 streams of water that can be concentrated to specific body areas from the upper torso to the thighs. This mild form of water pressure therapy uses alternating warm and cold water.
❖ *Vichy shower*—used in a wet room that is tiled floor to ceiling. Several showerheads direct water to guests as they lie on a bed or table. Hot and cold water pulse alternately. This shower is usually used after a salt, mud, or seaweed treatment in the same room.
❖ *Steam room, shower, or cabinet*—causes the body to perspire, helping eliminate toxins, stimulate circulation, and increase respiration. Should be followed by a cool shower or product application.
❖ *Scotch hose or shower*—a strong stream of water targeted at specific areas of the body to increase circulation and break up fat deposits. The guest stands at a wall, holding onto handles, while a technician shoots water from a device like a fire hose from a distance of 8 to 10 feet.

Products that are available for sale in the spa can be placed in the shower. As guests use the products, they can see, smell, and feel for themselves their benefits.

Massage   Massage offers a number of benefits to guests. It causes an increase in blood circulation that helps improve nutritional exchanges and eliminate wastes and toxins. Soreness and discomfort in the muscles is relieved. Massage has a sedative effect on the nervous system. Stress is reduced as the body relaxes. Skin texture and softness is improved. Finally, it just feels good!

Effleurage Massage. The classic Swedish effleurage massage consists of a gentle touch and a soft stroke that is directed toward the heart. Typically, the massage begins on the front of the guest, then proceeds to the back. Movements go from the foot to the thigh of one leg, then are repeated on the other foot and leg. Attention is then given to the arms, moving from the hand to the upper arm on one side, then the other. The head is then massaged down to the chest and the movements repeated on the guest's back.

Special care should be taken when having masseurs/masseuses perform massages on guests of the opposite sex. Because of potential liability, the resort may wish to offer only same-sex massages or have someone of the same sex as the guest in the room during the massage.

Aromatherapy. *Aromatherapy* refers to the "therapeutic use of aromatic essences from plants in treatment for beauty and well-being." These essences can come from flowers, stems, leaves, roots, bark, or an entire plant and are extracted by various means to produce a pure, aromatic essence. It takes, for example, 60,000 petals to produce an ounce of Bulgarian rose oil.

Oils affect the body in two ways: physiologically and psychologically. Physiologically, oils enter the body by infusion (through a room diffuser), by bathing with compresses, and through massage of the skin. Essential oils easily penetrate the skin and, as a result, are used as curatives in holistic medicine. They affect various bodily systems as follows:

❖ *Skin*—Dissolve dead surface cells, increase cell turnover, stimulate metabolism, improve texture.
❖ *Glands*—Soothe and tone.
❖ *Muscles*—Relieve fatigue, reduce soreness, improve elasticity.
❖ *Blood and lymph*—Facilitate smooth flow, increase waste elimination.

The psychological impact of aromatherapy comes from the sense of smell being controlled by the olfactory system, which has the capacity to produce an immediate effect on the nervous system. Any stimulation affects the limbic system, which is the part of the brain that controls emotions and personality. Essences may also play a part in producing neurochemicals like endorphins and enkephalins, which act as the body's painkillers and relaxants.

It is normal for oils to be diluted with a carrier oil, usually vegetable based. Oils are chosen depending on the characteristics of the skin. For example, dry skin might benefit from sweet almond, olive, or palm kernel oil. Oily skin, on the other hand, utilizes grapeseed, hazelnut, or sunflower oil. The degree of dilution depends on the application method. For massage purposes, the ratio is 25 drops of the essential oil to 2 ounces of the carrier oil, while a bath uses 10 to 30 drops of the essence on its own or 10 drops per tablespoon carrier oil when used as a combination. Infusions require 7 to 10 drops per quart of water. Compresses need 2 to 3 drops per 6 inches of wet gauze or linen squares. Guests should be advised to stay out of the sun, saunas, and baths for five hours after treatment. Alcohol should not be consumed but lots of water should be in the ensuing 24 hours.

CLIENT PREPARATION

While some guests may be familiar with spa techniques, it is likely that many will be unaware of basic spa practices. One area that is particularly sensitive is the need to undress prior to treatments. The vast majority of spa treatments involve the technician seeing only that part of the body being immediately worked on. However, guests may not be aware of this and will probably need reassurance. As noted earlier, this issue is particularly important when the employee and guest are of the opposite sex.

First-time visitors to the spa should fill out a form indicating basic demographic information together with a brief medical history, what products are presently being used on the body and face, and a section on lifestyle habits. A technical analysis is appropriate in the following areas:

- ❖ skin type
- ❖ skin conditions
- ❖ nails: type and conditions
- ❖ massage: areas of stress; types of massage; result
- ❖ skin texture/color

Finally, a history should be kept for each guest indicating the procedures and equipment used and body work done.

ROOM SETUP: WET ROOMS

The two basic setups are wet and dry rooms. Wet rooms are built so that they can get wet without damaging the room. Most are tile all the way to

Spa Treatments in Turkey, Poland, and France

Turkey

The real Turkish steam bath, known as the *hamam,* is a wonderful treat. According to observers, the hamam experience offers "a wonderful relaxation of muscles, mind, and spirit." Visitors are shown to a cubicle where they undress and wrap themselves in a cloth. Then they enter a room where they sit and sweat while occasionally pouring water over themselves from individual basins.

An attendant pours warm water over guests, scrubs them with a coarse brush, lathers them with suds, shampoos their hair, and rinses out the soap. Guests are then given a massage before being escorted to the cold room, covered in towels, and offered tea, coffee, or a cold drink.

Poland

Although they are not as luxurious as spas in the United States, facilities in Poland tend to sell out six months in advance. Typically, they attract Europeans pleased to pay $25 to $45 a day for most treatments and three meals. Approximately 1000 guests visit from the United States each year.

Most health spas specialize in ailments such as respiratory or back problems. Programs begin with an evaluation by a staff doctor, who prescribes treatments. Most guests stay for three weeks, although ten-day options are available. The 40-plus health spas in Poland are found alongside natural springs on the Baltic Sea, in the Sudrey Mountains of the southwest, and in the Carpathian Mountains in the southeast.

France

The accent in French spas is on beauty and rejuvenation rather than on exercise and aerobics, as is the case in the United States. The most famous resort in which to "take the waters" is Evian-les-Bains. Set on a lake in eastern France, the resort has been attracting guests to *thermalisme* (water cures) since the nineteenth century. The Sofitel Thalassa Hotel at the resort offers seawater therapy, which cleanses the body of impurities. The body is then "restored" through the absorption of marine minerals. In addition, a full-service spa offers algae baths, marine showers, spray treatments, mud baths, and facial and hair treatments.

Sources: "Hamam: A True Turkish Delight," *Travel Weekly,* 6 May 1999, p. E8; Linda Humphrey, "Nation's Health Facilities Typically Offer Bargains," *Travel Weekly,* 6 May 1999, p. E11.

Question: How do spa treatments in Turkey, Poland, and France compare?

the ceiling and have floor drains. Floors are sloped to allow fast drainage. Ceilings are also made of waterproof materials. Rooms are typically 9 by 12 feet (10 by 14 if a Scotch hose is included) and have both a shower for guest use and a hand-held hose for easy cleaning of the room. Indirect waterproof lighting and a dimmer switch for ambience complete the package.

The following treatments are best administered in a wet room:

❖ hydrotherapy tub treatments
❖ Vichy and other shower treatments
❖ Scotch hose treatments
❖ salt glows, mud masks, and seaweed wraps

Rooms should be cleaned, sanitized, and dried between guests. Because seaweed and mud can stain tiles, rooms must be cleaned immediately after use.

ROOM SETUP: DRY ROOMS Dry rooms tend to be 8 by 10 feet and, typically, untiled. As a result, they are quieter and more relaxing. A sink in the room is useful for preparing treatment bowls. A shower should be available nearby. Dry rooms are best used for massages. Wiring the room for music and installing dimmers on the lights permit variation of the ambience.

The overall experience demands sheets and towels that are clean and fresh. The same is true for bottles of massage oil. Taupes, beiges, and grays are the best colors for a mixed clientele, and the lighting is best subdued. Employee uniforms must be clean, dry, and fresh. Several uniform changes may be required daily. A wall clock helps the employee keep track of time, while soft music adds significantly to the experience.

COMBINATIONS Treatments can be combined with hydrotherapy and massage. Sample combinations include:

❖ massage, facial, manicure, pedicure
❖ hydrotherapy tub treatment, full-body seaweed mask
❖ salt glow tub, Vichy shower, full-body mud treatment
❖ deep cleansing facial, antistress body massage, spa pedicure
❖ aromatherapy body massage, facial, mud body wrap, spa manicure and pedicure, scalp treatment, hairstyle, makeup
❖ for men: anti-aging facial treatment, muscle-relaxing massage, aromatherapy scalp treatment, cleansing manicure and pedicure

MARKETING

The spa menu should be thought of just like a restaurant menu when it comes to marketing.

—ERICA MILLER
Day Spa Techniques

Combining treatments under a specific name can make them more marketable. For example, the Spa at Camelback Inn in Scottsdale, Arizona, features the Adobe Clay Purification Treatment inspired by the ancient healing rituals of Native Americans and involving a total body exfoliation, a clay application, an aromatherapy cleansing and application, and a sauna session. The Golfer's Massage at the Sonoran Spa, also in Scottsdale, concentrates on muscle groups in the neck, shoulders, lower back, and hamstrings, while the Hot Rocks Massage uses heated river stones to work away stress.

Instead of simply listing the treatments and the prices, descriptive words can be used to paint a picture and promote the treatment. For example:

Body Massage $55.00
A full hour of relaxing massage, designed to relieve stress and tension according to your body's own condition.

Salt Glow Rub $55.00
Special salts from the Dead Sea are mixed with moisturizing and conditioning lotions to slough off dead cells and hydrate while leaving your body feeling smooth and sleek. You'll enjoy the comfortable Vichy shower rinse along with this treatment.

Additional services that can be marketed are food and activities that focus on the mind. The Hyatt Regency Gainey Ranch in Scottsdale, Arizona, offers Cuisine Naturelle, nutritious gourmet food with moderate calories, and the Waterfall juice bar. The Phoenician Resort in Scottsdale has a Meditation Atrium where guests learn meditation techniques in one-on-one and small group sessions.

SUMMARY

People go to spas because they are stressed or because they want a small indulgence. A full-service spa contains a full complement of facial devices

quick getaways 13.5

Marketing a European Spa

In many ways, the spa philosophy is different in Europe than in the United States. According to Edith Nussbaumer, marketing director of the Grand Hotel Quellenhof Health, Spa & Golf Resort in Bad Ragaz, Switzerland, the spa's philosophy is to enjoy nature and oneself. She regards the atmosphere in American spas as too regimented.

At Grand Hotel Quellenhof, the accent is on freedom of choice. Rather than focus on low-fat foods, for example, a typical lunch might consist of a salad of rabbit filet with warm mushrooms followed by scallops with Pernod, spinach, and asparagus accompanied by a 1997 Riesling and ending with vanilla ice cream and berries. The focus is on healthy living through enjoying food and outdoor activities rather than "boot-camp-style exercise and denying oneself good-tasting meals." Fresh salads, fruits, and vegetables are emphasized, local wines are featured, and the spa offers its own brand of bottled Alpine water.

The five-star property pumps 98-degree water about 3 miles from the Tamina Gorge into the resort's indoor and outdoor pools. The latter offers a number of stations, each with its own water massage jets. The indoor spa offers a 7000-square-foot water landscape, a Roman thermal bathing "temple," a 56-foot swimming pool, saunas, steam baths, hot tubs, and frigid plunge pools. Aromatherapy steam-bath booths accommodate two people. Guests press buttons to release the scent desired—hayseed, chamomile, pine, or mint. Daily classes range from "active awakening," with exercises for people with varicose veins, to qi gong, a combination of meditation, breathing, and slow body movements.

Source: Cathy Carroll, "Swiss Spa Favors 'Freedom of Choice,'" *Travel Weekly*, 6 May 1999, pp. E6–E7.

Question: What is a suitable marketing slogan for a European spa?

and a comfortable facial bed or chair for each room, massage table for full-body treatment, and a range of hydrotherapy treatment options. Treatments themselves consist of exfoliation, full-body treatments, and spot treatments conducted in wet and dry rooms following strict guidelines to ensure a safe and enjoyable experience for guests.

ENDNOTES

1. This chapter draws heavily from two books by Erica Miller: *Day Spa Techniques* (Albany, N.Y.: Milady Publishing, 1996), and *Day Spa Operations* (Albany, N.Y.: Milady Publishing, 1996). Readers interested in finding out more about this subject are referred to these excellent publications.
2. "The Medium Is the Massage," *Fast Company* (May 1999) vol. 37: 247–258.
3. Judy Singer, "Studies Show Resort Spas Find Their Stride," *Hotel and Motel Management*, 14 June 1999, p. 10.
4. Ibid.
5. Kimberly Scholz, "More Men to Be Found at Spas," *Travel Weekly*, 5 April 1999, p. 16.
6. Ibid.

Chapter 14
THE FUTURE OF RESORTS

Note: The associates of Design Workshop, Inc., contributed this chapter. Design Workshop is a landscape architecture, land planning, urban design, and tourism planning firm. Founded in 1969, its mission is to create places that successfully bring people together with the land. The designers' experience ranges from master plans for counties, new communities, urban centers, and resorts to detailed design for public parks, residences, and amenities throughout the United States and the world.

INTRODUCTION

The future of resorts will be shaped by many interrelated factors: economics of a mature resort industry, expectations of travelers, shifts in society, and technology's far-reaching influence.

In this chapter, the factors shaping the resorts of tomorrow are noted and guidelines given on how to create the total resort experience that will be demanded by resort guests. Trends in resort development are forecasted and their impact on resort communities suggested.

❖ Proposed new village, Sunday River, Maine. [Source: Design Workshop, Inc.]

PAST, PRESENT, FUTURE Fifty years ago, the modern resort industry, still in its infancy, provided an experience very different than today. Travel to remote resort regions via train, automobile, and the still-novel airplane provided as much of the exotic allure as the grandeur of the resort hotel lobbies and restaurants. Resort activities focused on soaks in mineral springs, golf, skiing, and socializing. The few, generally upper-class guests were pampered by exceptional service, which was a trademark of the era.

Today, travelers spend less time considering how the resort will be reached, regardless of the location, and more time deciding on the type and number of activities they are able to fit into a few days snatched from a busy work schedule. Travelers have high expectations of the overall experience and return to those resorts able to meet their increasingly high standards.

THE SHAPING OF TOMORROW'S RESORTS

The high price of entrance into today's mature resort indus-
try, combined with seemingly limitless day-to-day operational
costs, has led to very few new, large-scale resorts being built.

ECONOMICS OF A MATURE RESORT INDUSTRY The arena within which contemporary resorts operate reflects a highly competitive environment. A few key players in the industry own many of the established resorts. Meadowbrook Golf Group, one of the nation's leading golf management companies, now owns KSL Fairway Golf, owners of Grand Traverse Resort in Michigan, La Quinta Resort in La Quinta, California, and the Claremont Resort Spa in Berkeley, California. Major ski resort operators such as Vail Resorts, American Ski Company, Intrawest, and Booth Creek Holdings combined own a significantly large portion of the world's ski resorts. The few remaining independent resorts are forced to compete against these conglomerates' powerful network of advertising strength and capital resources.

The textbook shake-out period experienced by mature industries results in corresponding operational adjustments for the future. Independent resorts need to prove they offer a unique experience not available at large corporate-owned resorts. Conversely, the resorts owned by large corporations need to prove they are capable of individual treatment as well as mass marketing.

TIME VALUE OF LEISURE As time replaces money as the currency of the new century, resorts must consider how their location and systems interact with the time value of their guests. Guests are seeking shorter vacation stays at resorts offering numerous amenities and excellent but transparent service. Leisure is now built around long weekend getaways, and consumers expect a maximum return on their vacation minutes. Market research by the Travel and Tourism Research Association suggests that an annual vacation experience consists of two shorter vacations (two 5-day trips instead of one 10-day trip). This contrasts drastically with what the industry used to rely on. Telluride's vice president of sales and marketing states, "We used to be known as a Saturday-to-Saturday-type destination. But the consumers told us they wanted three- or four-day packages, so we designed them."[1] This quick response to guest vacation expectations reflects the mode of tomorrow's successful resorts.

Packaging will be the key to providing guests with the optimum mix of activities within their limited amount of time. Guests will arrive with little or no understanding of the types of activities available for them to enjoy. They will need to have the opportunities presented and priced according to an appropriate value system. They will need to perceive that the value of the activities is greater than the price, or their expectations will not be met.

DEMOGRAPHIC AND LIFESTYLE SHIFTS IN SOCIETY

Aging Vacationer

Changing demographics will have a significant impact on future resort amenities and programs. Currently, there are more older (over 60) Americans than ever before. Six thousand people are retiring every day. By 2006, the first of the baby boomers will start turning 60, and for the succeeding 15 or 20 years, the retiree group will grow. This shift will have a tremendous impact on both the ski and the golf industry. Baby boomers will become the foundation of the golf industry. It is anticipated that, due to increased free time and disposable income, frequency will grow at nearly twice the rate of participation.

The aging baby boomers are healthier and more active than any previous generation. In their 40s and 50s, they think of themselves as in their mid-30s. They must be accommodated based on their actual age but marketed to based on their perceived age. The meaning of *middle-aged* has changed considerably over the last several decades, and the generation of baby boomers raised on the glory of a youth culture is still in denial and a state of arrested adolescence.

With new destinations and cushier, more innovative wilderness trips, no one is left out of the action. Adventure travel is growing up and slowing down. According to the Travel Industry Association of America, one-half of U.S. adults, or 98 million people, have taken an adventure vacation in the past five years.[2] This includes 31 million adults who participated in

quick getaways 14.1

Leisure Pattern Shifts

Shifts in travel and leisure patterns are influencing the redevelopment plan of resorts. People are:

- escaping briefly but frequently
- mixing business with pleasure
- living healthy
- traveling with family
- engaging in education, enrichment, and entertainment
- sensitive to the environment
- seeking diversity

Source: Robert J. Gorman, "Repositioning Paradise," *Urban Land* (August 1998) vol. 57: 30–35.

Question: **What implications do these market trends have for the resort of the future?**

hard adventure activities like whitewater rafting, scuba diving, and mountain biking. Though expeditions that push the endurance envelope remain plentiful, the new century brings a burst of active vacations that are amiably inclusive.

More Work, Less Travel — Americans are working more than ever before—at least that is what they say. Studies conducted by Harvard University, however, reveal that Americans today have an average of 40 hours of leisure a week—five hours more than their counterparts in the 1960s.[3] Work may seem longer now because of longer commutes, intensified pace and anxiety levels, and increasing duties both at work and at home. Travel planning must now be scheduled around both spouses' work schedules. The sense of time compression is a driving force in vacation decisions. With perceived fewer hours to relax and recreate, vacationers will increasingly cram more activity in the hours they have set aside as nonworking time.

Resorts and technology however, will provide an oasis for the seemingly longer workweeks. With the dramatic increase in telecommuting, videoconferencing, and portable wired offices, business travel will grow more discretionary. Workers have more options available at their work location, whether it be a resort or the home patio. Providing temporary offices by the pool, in the ski lodge, or near the greens will allow vacationing workers to extend their stay while staying in touch with the demands at work.

Whites in the Minority By the year 2010, people who are white will be in the minority in the United States.[4] The next generation of resorts must identify opportunities to attract all ethnicities. The importance of diversification to the tourism industry has recently been emphasized. The African American Travel and Tourism Association was founded in 1991 at the annual Multicultural Travel and Trade Show to help identify opportunities for African American-focused tourism. The National Brotherhood of Skiers now has 72 clubs nationwide. In 1991, the United States Tennis Association (USTA) formed a Minority Participation Committee to encourage full minority participation through an extensive outreach program. Several tourism trade publications have named Latin Americans "undiscovered tourists."

CREATING THE TOTAL RESORT EXPERIENCE

Successful resorts of the future will understand the fantasy of the resort experience and the interplay of natural environment, history, regional culture, architecture, art, food, housekeeping, recreation, leisure, romance, and group and family experiences.

SUCCESSFUL ELEMENTS
Participation The resort experience requires active participation by the guest. Management must plan for and encourage guest involvement in the resort. Only thus can visitor expectations be met.[5]

Fantasy The relationship between historical elements and interpretive fantasy will increasingly become an important element to integrate into the overall experience. Mimicking history is not genuine; history is created. The

❖ Proposed village, Winter Park, Colorado. [Source: Design Workshop, Inc.]

future resorts will offer the best natural environment around and will provide a wrapper to the overall resort experience.

Exceptional grand resorts such as the Greenbrier in West Virginia, the Boulders in Arizona, and San Moritz in Switzerland understand the interplay of their location and the fantasy of resorts. Spa treatments, the best entrée and wine selections, and service that anticipates their needs all leave guests with the feeling that every minute and dollar spent was worth the visit; their memories reinforce their initial destination decision.

Total Experience Successful resorts will combine the physical environment (both natural and built) with superior operations to satisfy guests and their desire to have a happy, pleasant, and fulfilling vacation. Table 14.1 summarizes the physical, spiritual, and operational elements that, when integrated, create the total resort experience.

Sense of People want to experience things with meaning. This often involves his-
Authenticity toric references. Authenticity is a key requirement underlying many of the issues facing resort communities. An authentic place is what many people are seeking when they select a vacation destination. People go to resorts to

❖ TABLE 14.1 The Total Resort Experience

Physical	Spiritual	Operational
Great entry and arrival	Self-discovery	Integration of anticipation arrival departure reservations dreaming
Icons	Introspection	
Gathering places	Self-actualization	
Great retail	Challenge	
Art and culture of the region	Accomplishment	
Postcard images	Learning	Arrival/Transport
Discovery	Personal growth	Lodging
Natural environment	Respect	Meals
Memorable architecture	Humility	Entertainment
Central places	Happiness/Joy	Guest service
Trails/walks	Safe haven	Hosting
Great and diverse activities	Fun	Convenience
Sense of place	Intimacy	
Walkability		

Source: Design Workshop, *Shoeshoe Resort Market Research and Analysis*, 1996.

re-create something missing from their lives. Connections to the natural and historic environment via the use of building materials found in the region, such as rock and timber, have traditionally provided an experience.

The Greenbrier Resort in West Virginia is a five-star, five-diamond, tradition-rich resort. The 6500-acre property has stately architecture, abundant scenic beauty, and rich history. Activities include golf, fly-fishing, skeet- and trapshooting, jogging, hiking, aerobics, bowling, indoor and outdoor swimming, horseback riding, and the services of a world-renowned spa and mineral baths. The Greenbrier's plan for the future is constant renovation and remodeling. Their success is in providing a consistent experience, year after year, since the beginning of the twentieth century.

Community Connection Successful resorts integrate employees and neighbors with the guests' experience. One of the pleasures of being on a cruise ship is residing with the crew and getting to know the workings of the ship. Resorts will become living, changing places as this trend accelerates.

Because resorts are located in attractive places where people want to live, the industry will need to consistently maintain a focus on community development. In this effort, civic facilities, animated public spaces, real neighborhoods, and alternate modes of transportation play a stronger role than ever before.

The challenge is that there remains a struggle for the heart and soul of most resort communities as they try to assimilate the ideas and values of the new residents and simultaneously cope with changing tourism economies. The consensus of the last several decades about the value of the tourism business is under siege by many new residents not tied to the tourism economy. The challenge for resorts will be to address community concerns so that tourists are still made to feel welcome.

High-Quality, Seamless Experiences

According to the consulting firm Arthur Andersen's 1998 publication *Hospitality 2000*, the hospitality industry has traditionally focused much of its attention on the assets it best understands: real property and the capital that finances it.[6] What will distinguish the successful resorts of the future is the ability to effectively manage intangible capital—human, information, and customer relationships. Resorts of tomorrow will utilize technology and high service standards to anticipate their guests' needs and preferences. From communicating with the potential destination to planning the vacation, arriving at the resort, and throughout the visit, vacationers will remain loyal to those resorts that provide a hassle-free, seamless experience through high-quality, premeditated service delivery.

High-quality service is the ability to anticipate guests' needs. The competitive advantage tomorrow's successful resorts will embrace is managing these service standards and, thus, acquiring guest loyalty via technology. Travel, accommodations, activities, and amenities will be provided either as a planned vacation decision or on arrival. A package may be planned by the resort staff prior to arrival, as in an all-inclusive resort, or after the guest's arrival by concierge staff, or online by the guest. The important element is that guest activities are personalized and customized with minimal effort required of the time-poor vacationer.

Convenience aside, value-conscious vacationers and their growing preferences for active vacations have boosted the popularity of all-inclusive vacations, which typically include accommodations, meals, recreational activities, airport transfers, service, and gratuity charges on one bill. Furthermore, the popularity of the Internet has made it possible to custom package to almost limitless extents.

Of importance to the resort operator is that, in addition to finding favor in the marketplace and the ability to extend the vacation stay, predetermined vacation activities are generally easier to operate. The various profit centers know their peak periods in advance and can schedule accordingly. They can forecast revenue and expenses with greater accuracy. So far, the all-inclusive concept has failed to gain a foothold in the U.S. mainland but remains popular in areas such as the Caribbean, where Club Med has been in the all-inclusive resort business for many years. Concierge services and online booking have increasingly been integrated into a wide variety of resorts and will continue to be implemented as a response to each guest's need for individualized services and amenities.

Unlimited Menu of Activities

The resort of the twenty-first century will have numerous amenities and offer something for everyone, especially opportunities to do things that guests cannot or would not do at home. Memories that generate repeat visitors are typically related to activities.

Jack Wolfe, a developer in Vail, Colorado, notes that the ski industry's evolution is like Disney's.

> The ski resorts today are about where Disney was 30 years ago. Ski areas are turning into winter resorts at which one activity you participate in is skiing, much like the concept of a theme park evolving into a ten-day vacation of which three days is spent at the theme park. The goal was driven by the attempt to offset the downtime, smooth out the trough. The key is how to market and how to be flexible to the consumer. The vacation market is a very fragmented business with highly defined target markets.[7]

Even avid skiers want to participate in activities other than skiing. During a six-day visit, three to four days are spent alpine skiing and two or three days spent cross-country skiing, visiting the health club or spa, shopping, ice skating, tubing, snowmobiling, etc. Vail reports that 20 percent of visitors to the valley in the winter do not ski in a single day.

Intrawest is developing Adventure Centers at Vail, Breckenridge, Copper Mountain, and Aspen in Colorado to address the issue of activities other than skiing. Modeled after the highly successful Whistler Mountain in Canada, the 10,000-square-foot Vail center will be the first Intrawest project completed in the United States.[8] The center combines retail with Intrawest's ability to promote mountain play. An Intrawest spokeswomen says guests will be able to come into the adventure center in the morning, rent a pair of shaped skis, switch a few hours later to a snowboard, and finish the afternoon on cross-country skis or snowshoes.

Leisure Time
Doubles as Self-
Improvement
Time

Many people are very goal oriented and often want to improve themselves on vacation. They want to get better at something rather than just relax. People want to reinvent themselves, so achievement vacations that combine pleasure and reward make for a trend worth watching.

Owners of the Aspen Club and Spa in Aspen, Colorado, spent 15 months and $8 million to transform the former tennis club into a one-stop health club. Its approach addresses both body and mind, inside and outside, and physical and spiritual aspects of health. The Club's latest push is to bring in corporate groups for the Eco-Adventure, an outdoor team-building experience that is essentially an Outward Bound for executives. The spa hired Trident as the firm to conduct these adventures. To maintain a high level of adventure expertise, Trident's instructors are former U.S. Army Green Berets or U.S. Navy SEALs. The firm's teaching philosophy accommodates the challenges in the corporate world, according to a Trident spokesperson:

> People in the corporate world face the challenge of always being asked to do more with less, and we use that metaphor in our programs. We get people to work together on survival problems under difficult conditions against deadlines and on very little sleep. People cry, not because they've been broken down like hostages, but because they've successfully gone through a very life-affirming event.[9]

Experience the
Newest Trends

Visitors are looking for unique experiences. Activities that offer snob appeal are expected, and resorts of the new century will constantly upgrade their packages with the newest trends in all resort experiences. The latest spa treatments and therapy rooms will be as varied as the type of equipment that brings guests down the mountain. C. J. Julin, sales and marketing director for Copper Mountain's resort development projects, stated, "We're no longer in the ski industry, we're in the mountain entertainment industry. It's more than just going up and making a couple of turns."[10]

**UTILIZING
TECHNOLOGY**

Guest Service

The most successful companies of the new century will be distinguished by the effective management of people, information, and customer relationships. Today's industry leaders are therefore challenged to develop the tools that will measure, manage, and influence these intangible assets as they contribute increasingly to the value of business enterprises.

For example, guest comment cards, relied on by many in the industry for customer feedback, offer extraordinarily ineffective results. Electronic surveys on check-out are much more efficient in translating guest com-

quick getaways 14.2

Adapting to Changing Market Preferences

Here are some ideas on how to take advantage of changing market preferences:

- *Take inventory*—Understand your market today and identify who will comprise it five to ten years from now. Identify who you want your market to be.
- *Understand your resources*—Categorize the assets and constraints of the facility.
- *Understand your competitors*—Where are they? Who is having most success? Why?
- *Define the framework*—Review the basics of your development. Identify the weak links. Look at infrastructure, internal circulation patterns, servicing, open space, ability to expand.
- *Catalog opportunities*—Can adjacent sites be leveraged? What about links between learning and leisure?
- *Find misused or underused space.*
- *Rethink in new directions*—Consider urban spa getaways, suburban retreats and wilderness lodges, big boutiques.

Source: Robert J. Gorman, "Repositioning Paradise," *Urban Land* (August 1998) vol. 57: 30–35.

Question: Select a resort and analyze it with respect to the above list. What are some new directions for the resort?

ments into a database and turning them into effective management tools within a much shorter time frame. Online booking, guest information data banks, and activity booking capabilities in the guestrooms are among the basic amenities resorts are now implementing to improve guest service.

The End of Remoteness Changes in information services have led to the end of remoteness because most places are now electronically accessible. This vastly broadens the opportunity to disperse and visit for extended periods in rural areas and resort settings. Resort developers are providing computer access to guests in varied settings outside of the guestroom.

More than extending the vacation, videophones, teleconferencing, and virtual reality will reduce the need for today's typical business travel. The vacation property that helps guests avoid the inconvenience, disruption, and additional expense of trips to the office while the family vacations will win over guests with a more leisurely vacation experience than a resort where technology is outdated can offer. Arthur Clark, a trends analyst, goes a step further to state that "in 30 years, all travel will be discretionary."[11] If only half of this is true, it infers a fundamental shift away from business travel toward leisure travel, and the impact on resorts will be tremendous.

Artificial Environments

Another use of technology to overcome remoteness is its ability to create artificial resorts in nearly any environment. According to Economics Research Associates (ERA), public and private reaction to the negative effects of resorts built in environmentally sensitive areas will lead to new leisure products being created in artificial but more durable settings. The Centerparc's Tropical Paradise resorts represent the first stage of artificial resort evolution, but others will follow. Kajima has developed an artificial ski hill near Tokyo Disneyland. Simulation and virtual reality experiences being developed within urban entertainment centers will revolutionize the design of resorts, attractions, and retail, education, and interpretive facilities.

Online Booking

Technological innovation through Internet and electronic commerce solutions is one way in which the resort business is changing rapidly. By becoming the primary platform for linking systems and data within the operation as well as linking customers, suppliers, and other stakeholders, the Internet will affect every facet of how the industry does business. Rapidly expanding uses will include paperless electronic transactions processing, online guest services, electronic information publishing, in-room entertainment, and training for employees.[12]

Aspen is expanding visitors' ability to engage in "ski-commerce." The 1999–2000 ski season allowed online purchases of lift tickets, ski lessons, and rental equipment all at once. The company is also creating an online concierge service in conjunction with American Express for guests who purchase lift tickets in advance. According to Aspen's online marketing manager, "our number-one goal is to make it easy for our guests to find information and plan their vacation online."

TRENDS IN RESORT DEVELOPMENT

What the visitors are seeking is what they have come to expect.

The following key trends in resort development set the arena in which both successful resorts and their surrounding communities will work.

COMMUNITY EXPANSION AND LIMITATIONS
Resorts around the nation are continuing to expand rapidly. Construction of employee housing as well as new high-speed ski lifts and new ski runs are common projects at most ski resort communities today. Mountain and base area expansion plans are underway at Jackson Hole and Grand Targhee, Wyoming; Stratton and Sugarbush, Vermont; Sunday River, Maine; The Canyons, Utah; and Mammoth Mountain, California.

In contrast, many resorts are limiting residential growth. Whistler and Canmore in Canada recently capped residential growth, while communi-

❖ Proposed new resort, Scottsdale, Arizona.

ties such as Aspen, Colorado, have restricted growth for 25 years. The results are a limited supply of properties and inflated home prices. This can be seen by Aspen's average home price of $2.5 million.

EMPLOYEE HOUSING PROGRAMS Due to the high housing prices in resort communities, many resorts are currently working on developing and managing employee housing projects. These projects make it affordable for employees to live and work in the community, spurring economic growth. Without affordable housing, the resort workforce will continue to diminish.

UPGRADING EXISTING HOTELS The increase in lodging prices in resort communities has encouraged current lodging facilities to upgrade their premises. Sun Valley, Idaho, feels that in order for the vacationer to receive value for money, hotels and lodges must be as luxurious as possible. Without renovating accommodations, hotel properties are having a difficult time remaining competitive with the new individually owned products being offered through property management operations at most resorts. This decline can be seen in Colorado at Keystone's Lakeside Village and at numerous hotel properties in Vail. Most resorts have plans for renovation to help entice guests who are now staying at newer properties.

GREATER VARIETY OF WINTER ACTIVITIES/ RECREATION Stagnant skier visits have led to a surge in alternative activities. Snowshoeing, tubing, ice skating, snowmobiling, mountain tours, and hiking are increasing in popularity nationwide. When these activities are offered together at a resort, a winter theme park can be created. Various members of a family or group of friends have more alternatives from which to choose.

VERTICAL INTEGRATION With finite revenue and profits made from ski operations, resort owners are getting into lodging, retail, restaurants, golf, and real estate development businesses. Furthermore, ski companies like Mammoth Mountain in California and Aspen Ski Company in Colorado are intelligently packaging these commodities into one travel experience for the visitor's convenience. The wide range of business activities has allowed resort owners to expand their current customer base and earn more profits with little new skier visitation growth and, in some cases, a decrease in skier visits.

POPULARITY OF BASE VILLAGES Although the number of skiers hitting the slopes is stagnant, shopping, dining, lodging, and real estate are profitable industries for resorts. Nonskiers are coming to the towns and spending their money on gifts, food, and lodging. A survey conducted in 1998 by the Travel Industry Association of America (TIA) identified shopping as the number-one activity of travelers. This trend has fueled base village construction and retail expansion at many resort areas.

Base villages provide guests with great dining and shopping and new options for accommodation and real estate purchases in addition to providing developers with profitable revenue streams. Prices for new base area real estate often begin at $350 per square foot and frequently climb past $1200.

MORE DESTINATION SUMMER TOURISM

Resorts are increasingly becoming destination locations for visitors rather than places to stop for the night. Marketing efforts and budgets are focusing on the summer traveler. A once-small market consisting of mostly families and drive-through visitors on their way to other destinations, summer tourism has become a big market with large amounts of room for growth. Communities such as Telluride, Colorado, have weekly festivals during the summer. In addition to these festivals, activities such as golfing, rafting, hiking, mountain biking, fishing, and camping are marketed. The push for summer tourism in resort communities has made resorts an alternative destination to national parks and other more traditional summer resort destinations.

ATTRACTING THE BUSINESS SECTOR

The nature of the resort business is seasonality. When spring arrived, traditional ski resorts of the past simply survived the summer and its lack of sustainable revenue base. Tomorrow's successful resorts will expand and stabilize their revenue stream by reaching into nonpeak seasons for expanded business opportunities. One of the more popular methods is catering to the lucrative business market by offering conference and meeting facilities. The capacity to host conferences makes the resort less weather-dependent, given the harsh realities of a bad snow season.

The business travel market is responding favorably to the resorts that have added meeting and conference facilities to their array of guest services. With limited vacation opportunities outside the demanding work culture, many business organizations and individuals are taking advantage of resort meeting spaces that allow the integration of business with more relaxing opportunities. Successes at popular resorts with conference centers in Keystone and Snowmass, Colorado, inspired Mammoth Mountain and the Big Mountain, Montana, to add such facilities to their base areas. In fact, the Keystone Center's popularity promoted an $11.5 million expansion that will double the 50,000-square-foot facility.

IMPLICATIONS FOR RESORT COMMUNITIES

The total resort experience integrates the physical, natural, and built environment, feeds the spirit, and leaves the visitor craving to do it again.

A NEARLY UNLIMITED MENU OF ACTIVITIES

Tomorrow's leisure travelers will increasingly prefer activity-based vacations that typically include sporting activities to traditional relax-by-the-pool vacations. Visitors will look for unusual and multiple activities in one trip; there will be more fracturing. Visitors are looking for something to tell their friends about. As a result, resorts will be places to try out the latest and greatest. Activities such as snowmobiling and spa activities such as herbal wraps and detoxifying treatments are gaining in popularity.

SEAMLESS EXPERIENCE

Vacationers will expect a seamless experience—all activities, lodging, eating, and purchases on one bill, with all options easily accessed through the Internet. Accordingly, vacation packaging at all price levels will continue to gain in popularity. Visitors will have the option of having an adventure or spending their trip without hard decisions, problems, or trauma. *Easy, friendly,* and *convenient* are the operative words in the future.

ULTIMATE CUSTOMER SERVICE

Visitor expectations of incredible customer service will become increasingly more important. Many resorts already offer personal assistants—staff dedicated to assisting with luggage, booking activities, running errands, and taking care of visitors' problems. A future challenge is created because the foundation of the tourism industry is hospitality, yet one of the most pervasive problems faced by resorts is retaining employees with great service skills, and many establishments are unwilling or unable to provide the training necessary.

PERCEIVED VALUE FOR THE VACATION DOLLAR

Regardless of the location, image, or reputation of the resort, it must provide a perceived value to the visitor. Meeting or exceeding the guest's expectations is the goal when attempting to construct value, but the future will prove that these expectations are a moving target. Whether vacationing on a budget or spending at will, visitors will expect to get a bargain for the money they spent. Value for their money and a variety of things to do are the most critical factors in tourists' destination decisions.

WOMEN WILL MAKE THE VACATION DECISION

Women today are increasingly making vacation decisions, and this trend will continue. The 1996–1997 National Skier/Boarder Opinion Survey showed that 72 percent of women at ski resorts were there with their children, up from 61.7 percent three years earlier.[13]

KIDS CAN DO THEIR OWN THING The future of the modern resort is predicated on satisfying the entire family. Highly organized and integrated children's programs will be important. Parents want to bring their family on vacation, but they don't want to do "kid's stuff" all day (and vice versa).

VISITORS WILL EXPECT ENVIRONMENTAL RESPONSIBILITY Virtually all ski areas today understand that their future depends on their wise response to issues of environmental protection and impact mitigation. People want to vacation in beautiful places, and the natural environment is the resort's most potent attraction. Visitors will expect that the environment is not being destroyed in the name of tourism development.

ETHNIC MARKETS WILL BECOME A BIGGER FOCUS By the year 2010, whites will be in the minority in the United States. The next generation of resorts must identify opportunities to attract all ethnic, racial, and cultural groups. The TIA conducted a survey in 1996 of travel habits and patterns of the three largest minority groups. Results revealed that these virtually untapped markets are characterized by a desire to travel and a willingness to spend discretionary dollars on vacations.[14]

LIVING IN THE FANTASY OF THE RESORT EXPERIENCE Successful resorts will understand the fantasy of the resort experience and the interplay of the natural environment, history, regional culture, architecture, art, food, recreation, leisure, housekeeping, romance, and group and family memories. People go to resorts to fill a void in their lives.

EXPECTING THE TOTAL RESORT EXPERIENCE The total resort will present a great entry and arrival experience, recognizable icons, gathering places, attractive retail, distinctive art and culture, memorable architecture, and diverse activities, and will enable visitors to experience the natural environment. Visitors' expectations of their vacation experience will continue to rise.[15]

SUMMARY

The resort of tomorrow will be shaped by the changing economics of a mature industry, new perceptions of the time value of leisure, and changing demographic and lifestyle shifts throughout society. Creating the total resort experience will mean successfully blending a variety of elements. Resorts will expand within the limits of the community. Employee housing will become an even more pressing problem. Existing hotels will need to be upgraded and a wider range of recreational activities will be added to

quick getaways 14.3

Environmental Issues Affecting Future Resort Operations

The following action areas for travel and tourism industries are reviewed in Agenda 21, the environmental action plan adopted by 182 nations at the Rio Earth Summit in 1992:

- waste minimization
- energy conservation
- management of freshwater resources
- wastewater management
- hazardous substances
- transport
- land-use planning and management
- involving staff, customers, and communities in environmental issues
- designing for sustainability
- developing partnerships

Source: "Strategy for Survival: Agenda 21 for the Travel and Tourism Industry," *WTO News,* n.d.

the development. Base villages will become more popular. Vertical integration will increase. Summer destinations will rise in importance as more resorts target the business sector. Each of these changes will have profound implications for resort communities.

ENDNOTES

1. Erika Gonzalez, "Skier Visits Plunge," *Rocky Mountain News,* 15 June 1999, p. 1B.

2. Travel Industry Association of America, *Travel Trends* (Washington, D.C.: Travel Industry Association of America, 1998), 14.

3. Design Workshop, *Shoeshoe Resort Market Research and Analysis*, 1998 (internal consultant's report).

4. Ibid.

5. John Naisbitt, "The Globalization of the World's Largest Industry," in *The Hospitality and Leisure Architecture of Wimberly, Allison, Tong, and Goo* (Gloucester, Mass.: Rockport Publishers, 1997), 102–115.

6. Roger Cline, "Hospitality 2000—The People: A Report on the Second Global Survey of the Hospitality Industry's Leadership" (New York: Arthur Andersen, 1998), 22.

7. Personal contact, 1999.

8. Matthew Skinner, "Copper Mountain Requests Up-Zoning for Downtown," *Summit County Journal*, 2 July 1999, 1.

9. Sebastian Sinisi, "Spa Pushes Limits," *Denver Post*, 14 June 1999, p. 11.

10. Personal contact, 1999.

11. Clive Jones, *The New Tourism and Leisure Environment* (San Francisco, Calif.: Economics Research Associates, 1998).

12. Francis Nardozza, Partner, National Hospitality Industry Director, KPMG.

13. *Transworld SNOWboarding Business/National Ski Areas Association 1997–98 Ski Resort Snowboarding Survey,* prepared for the National Ski Areas Association by RRC Associates, Boulder, Colo., 1998.

14. Travel Industry Association, "Profiling Ethnic Travelers," *Travel Weekly,* 22 August 1996, 13.

15. Design Workshop, *Shoeshoe Resort Market Research and Analysis*, 1996.

Index